Latin America's Global Border System

Latin America's Global Border System: An Introduction is the opening volume in the first collection of academic works devoted exclusively to borders and illegal markets in Latin America.

This volume features expert discussions on border issues of Argentina, Brazil, Bolivia, Ecuador, Guatemala, Italy, Mexico, and Peru, as well as studies on illegal markets, cities, and gender as a first step to understanding the intricacies of the global border system of illegal markets and Latin America's role in it. The book constitutes a rich source of information on the geographic, economic, demographic, and social characteristics of the most important Latin American border regions, and their relation to global illegal markets, while also offering deep insights into the ways illegal markets are organized in each country and how they connect across borders to create the global border system.

This book will not only be a valuable resource for academics and students of international relations, security studies, border studies, and contemporary Latin America, but will also prove relevant to national and international policy-makers devoted to foreign policy, security, and development.

Beatriz Zepeda is a research professor at the Center for International Studies at El Colegio de México, Mexico. She holds a PhD in Ethnicity and Nationalism and an MSc in International Relations from the London School of Economics and Political Science. From 2012 to 2014 she was director of FLACSO-Guatemala. She has lectured on International Relations at universities in England, Ecuador, Guatemala, and Mexico. Her research focuses on the Mexico-Guatemala border, illegal markets, nationalism, migration, and foreign policy.

Fernando Carrión Mena is Emeritus Professor at FLACSO-Ecuador. He has dedicated his life to the study of urbanization process, cultural heritage, violence, security, and drug trafficking. He was director of planning for the Municipality of Quito (1988–1992), general coordinator of RED CIUDADES for Latin America (1990–1993), director of

FLACSO-Ecuador (1995–2004), and councillor of Quito Metropolitan District (2005–2009). Fernando has founded eight thematic journals, and has published over 250 academic articles, 64 books (as editor or author) and 12 book collections (as coordinator). In 2015, he was recognized by ESGLOBAL as one of the 50 most influential intellectuals of Latin America.

Francisco Enríquez Bermeo, Department of Political Studies, FLACSO-Ecuador. Francisco holds a degree in Economics from Universidad Central del Ecuador and a Master's degree in Local Development from Universidad Complutense de Madrid. From 2015 to 2017, he coordinated the research project "Exploring the political economy of violence in Latin America's borders." Francisco is currently the Executive Secretary of the Latin American and Caribbean Organization of Border Cities (OLACCIF), a position he has held since 2016.

Borders and Illegal Markets in Latin America
Beatriz Zepeda (Series Editor, English Language Edition)
El Colegio de México

This series explores the strategic role that borders and borderlands play in the articulation of illegal markets to the south of the Río Bravo. Focusing on a variety of topics such as gender, contraband, migrant smuggling, drug trafficking, arms trafficking, and human trafficking, and many more, the series sheds light on the particularities of illegal markets and the enabling role borders play therein, while providing – when taken as a whole – a more general and complete picture of how borders across Latin America are linked in ways that facilitate global illegal flows.

Latin America's Global Border System
An Introduction
Beatriz Zepeda, Fernando Carrión Mena, and Francisco Enríquez Bermeo (Eds.)

Gender and Embodied Geographies in Latin American Borders
María Amelia Viteri with Iréri Ceja and Cristina Yépez Arroyo

Latin America's Global Border System
An Introduction

Edited by Beatriz Zepeda,
Fernando Carrión Mena, and
Francisco Enríquez Bermeo

NEW YORK AND LONDON

First published 2022
by Routledge
605 Third Avenue, New York, NY 10158

and by Routledge
4 Park Square, Milton Park, Abingdon, Oxon, OX14 4RN

Routledge is an imprint of the Taylor & Francis Group, an informa business

© 2022 Taylor & Francis

The right of Beatriz Zepeda, Fernando Carrión Mena, and Francisco Enríquez Bermeo to be identified as the authors of the editorial material, and of the authors for their individual chapters, has been asserted in accordance with sections 77 and 78 of the Copyright, Designs and Patents Act 1988.

Translation team: Lía Galván Lisker, Francisca Reyes and Daniela Salinas

All rights reserved. No part of this book may be reprinted or reproduced or utilised in any form or by any electronic, mechanical, or other means, now known or hereafter invented, including photocopying and recording, or in any information storage or retrieval system, without permission in writing from the publishers.

Trademark notice: Product or corporate names may be trademarks or registered trademarks, and are used only for identification and explanation without intent to infringe.

Library of Congress Cataloging-in-Publication Data
A catalog record for this title has been requested

ISBN: 978-1-032-06881-7 (hbk)
ISBN: 978-1-032-06884-8 (pbk)
ISBN: 978-1-003-20429-9 (ebk)

DOI: 10.4324/9781003204299

Typeset in Times NR MT Pro
by KnowledgeWorks Global Ltd.

To Jennifer Silva

In memoriam

Contents

List of Figures	xi
List of Maps	xii
List of Tables	xiii
Contributors	xiv
Preface to the English Edition of the Series	xviii
Preface	xx
Acknowledgments	xxii

Introduction: The Permanent Construction of Borders in Latin America — 1

FERNANDO CARRIÓN MENA AND FRANCISCO ENRÍQUEZ BERMEO

PART 1
BORDER SUBSYSTEMS — 13

Part 1.1: Producing Countries

1 The Global Border System and Illegal Markets in Peru: Notes for a Research Agenda — 16

MANUEL DAMMERT GUARDIA AND VIKTOR BENSÚS

2 Bolivia: The Tensions, Challenges, and Prospects of the Border Subsystem — 39

JOSÉ BLANES JIMÉNEZ

Part 1.2: Platform-Type Countries

3 Ecuador's Global Border Subsystem: From "Island of Peace" to International Crime Platform — 64

FERNANDO CARRIÓN MENA AND FRANCISCO ENRÍQUEZ BERMEO

x *Contents*

4 Borders, Crime, and State Responses in Argentina 89
GUSTAVO GONZÁLEZ, WALDEMAR CLAUS, LUCIANA GHIBERTO,
AND PABLO SPEKULJAK

Part 1.3: Strategic Countries

5 Guatemala's Border System: A First Approach 118
BEATRIZ ZEPEDA

**6 Mexico's Cross-Border Subsystem: Cocaine Trafficking
and Violence on the Northern Border** 144
CÉSAR FUENTES FLORES AND SERGIO PEÑA MEDINA

Part 1.4: Multifunctional Countries

**7 Projecting Borders across the Atlantic: The Case of Italy
from a Latin American Perspective** 172
FEDERICO ALAGNA

**8 Brazil and Its Borders: History and Limits of a
Sovereign State** 195
LETÍCIA NÚÑEZ ALMEIDA, AGNES FÉLIX, RAFAEL
MASSON, NATHAN BUENO, AND JENNIFER SILVA

PART 2
THEMATIC AXES 221

**9 Illegal Markets: A New Institutional Architecture and
Its Territorial Expression in Latin America** 223
FERNANDO CARRIÓN MENA

**10 Cross-Border Urban Complexes: The Urban Morphology
of a Global Structure** 250
FERNANDO CARRIÓN MENA AND VÍCTOR LLUGSHA GUIJARRO

**11 A Gender Perspective in the Study of Latin American
Border Systems** 266
MARÍA AMELIA VITERI AND IRÉRI CEJA

Index 290

Figures

2.1	Bolivia: Imports by Bordering Country in USD during 2013	47
6.1	Coca Leaf Production by Country (2003–2012)	157
6.2	Cocaine Seizures by Country in Central America (1995–2012)	158
10.1	Binuclear City: Tulcán and Ipiales	256
10.2	Triple Frontier: Ciudad del Este, Foz do Iguaçu, and Puerto de Iguazú	257
10.3	Ciudad Juárez-El Paso Metropolitan City	258
10.4	Manaus, Leticia, Iquitos, and Sucumbíos Border	259
11.1	Femicide/Feminicide National Legislation by Country, Including Year	274

Maps

1.1	Peru: Population Variation in Border Districts (1993–2007)	23
2.1	Bolivia: Municipalities and Border Crossings	52
3.1	Ecuador: Cocaine Processing Locations (2014)	79
4.1	Duos and Trios of Cross-Border Cities in Southern South America	95
5.1	The Borders of Guatemala	128
6.1	Binational Pairs on the US-Mexico Border	153
6.2	Formal and Informal Border Crossings on Mexico's Northern and Southern Borders	154
7.1	Italy and its Borders	174
7.2	The Schengen Area	176
8.1	Brazil's Border Strip Municipalities (2000)	197

Tables

1.1	Typology of border situations	20
1.2	Peru: Population variation rate by bordering country	23
1.3	Peru: Urban-rural distribution by bordering country	24
1.4	Characterization of contraband in Peru	30
1.5	Peru: Homicide rate by department 2011–2013	32
3.1	Ecuador: Homicide rate per 100,000 inhabitants by province (2010–2013)	80
8.1	Brazil: States and neighboring countries	198
9.1	Illegal markets in relation to GDP and population	231
11.1	Latin America: Number of femicides/feminicides	274
11.2	Latin America: Rate of femicides/feminicides per 100,000 women	275

Contributors

Federico Algana, University of Bologna, Italy, is a researcher of EU and Italian migration policies. He holds a PhD from the Radboud University of Nijmegen and the University of Bologna and currently collaborates with universities, research centers, and non-profit organizations. He has been active in social and political movements for several years and served as Deputy-Mayor for Culture and Public Education of the City of Messina, Sicily.

Viktor Bensús, PhD candidate in Sociology, City University of New York. Viktor holds an MA in City Planning from the University of California Berkeley and has worked as an instructor and researcher at the Pontifical Catholic University of Peru. Viktor is broadly interested in the relationship between the social production of space and urban politics. He has published academic papers and book chapters on public spaces, metropolitan governance, citizen participation, intermediate cities, and national borders.

José Blanes Jiménez is the founder and current research coordinator of Centro Boliviano de Estudios Multidisciplinarios (CEBEM), in La Paz, Bolivia. He holds an MSc in Sociology from Pontificia Universidad Católica del Perú and has been a lecturer at several Latin American and Spanish Universities. His research interests include population, development, border systems, and illegal markets.

Nathan Bueno was a researcher at Laboratório de Estudos e Pesquisas Internacionais e de Fronteiras (LEPIF), Brazil until 2018.

Fernando Carrión Mena, Emeritus Professor at FLACSO-Ecuador, has dedicated his life to the study of urbanization process, cultural heritage, violence, security, and drug trafficking. He has founded eight thematic journals, and has published over 250 academic articles, 64 books (as editor or author) and 12 book collections (as coordinator). In 2015, he was recognized by ESGLOBAL as one of the 50 most influential intellectuals of Latin America.

Contributors xv

Iréri Ceja is a PhD candidate in Social Anthropology at the National Museum, Federal University of Rio de Janeiro, Brazil. She is co-author of the books *Corpografías: género y fronteras en América Latina* (FLACSO 2017) and *Ah, usted viene por la visa Mercosur: integración, migración y refugio en Ecuador* (2017). Her research focuses on migration and forced displacement.

Waldemar Claus is an assistant professor in Sociology and Criminology at Universidad Nacional del Litoral, Argentina. He has published amply on prison sociology and illegal markets in border areas.

Manuel Dammert-Guardia is director of the undergraduate program in Sociology at the Department of Social Science of the Pontifical Catholic University of Peru. He holds a PhD in Sociology from El Colegio de México and a Master's degree in Anthropology from FLACSO-Ecuador. His research interests include urban inequalities, borders, violence, and stratification.

Francisco Enríquez Bermeo, Department of Political Studies, FLACSO-Ecuador. Francisco holds a degree in Economics from Universidad Central del Ecuador and a Master's degree in Local Development from Universidad Complutense de Madrid. From 2015 to 2017, he coordinated the research project "Exploring the political economy of violence in Latin America's borders." Francisco is currently the Executive Secretary of the Latin American and Caribbean Organization of Border Cities (OLACCIF), a position he has held since 2016.

Agnes Félix Gonçalves is a researcher at Laboratório de Estudos e Pesquisas Internacionais e de Fronteiras (LEPIF), Brazil. She holds a Master's degree in Social Sciences from Universidade Estadual de Londrina.

César Fuentes Flores is an associate professor at El Colegio de la Frontera Norte in Ciudad Juárez, Mexico. He holds a PhD in Urban and Regional Planning from the University of Southern California. His research focuses on cross-border urban planning, urban structure, urban segregation, and border security. He has authored two books and co-edited seven others on urban and border issues.

Luciana Ghiberto is director of the Public Security Observatory of the Province of Santa Fe and assistant professor of Sociology at Universidad Nacional del Litoral (UNL), Argentina. She is a PhD candidate in Social Studies at UNL and has published on police culture and its intersection with education, gender, and youth.

Gustavo Javier González is a professor in Sociology at Universidad Nacional del Litoral, Argentina. A lawyer by training, he holds a PhD

xvi *Contributors*

in Political Science from Universidad Nacional de Rosario, and has published on police reform, police work, security policy, and illegal markets in border areas. He is currently the Secretary of Criminal Policy and Human Rights of the Public Prosecutor's Office of the Province of Santa Fe.

Víctor Llugsha Guijarro is a professor and researcher at Universidad Técnica Equinoccial, Ecuador. He holds an MA in City Government from FLACSO-Ecuador and an MA in Innovation in Tourism Management from the University of Barcelona. He is the author of several works on tourism in cities, border cities, cross-border urban complexes, and citizen security.

Rafael Masson is a researcher at Laboratório de Estudos e Pesquisas Internacionais e de Fronteiras (LEPIF), Brazil. He holds degrees in Strategic Communication and International Relations.

Letícia Núñez Almeida is the research coordinator at Laboratório de Estudos e Pesquisas Internacionais e de Fronteiras (LEPIF), Brazil. She holds a PhD in Sociology from Universidade de São Paulo, and is a lecturer at Centro de Estudios sobre Políticas Educativas, at Universidad de la República del Uruguay.

Sergio Peña Medina is a professor and researcher at El Colegio de la Frontera Norte, Ciudad Juárez, Mexico. He holds a PhD in Urban and Regional Planning from Florida State University. His research agenda focuses on studying urban planning in Mexico, cross-border planning, governance and cooperation processes between the United States and Mexico. He is the co-editor-in-chief of the *Journal of Borderlands Studies*.

Jennifer Silva was a researcher and translator at Laboratório de Estudos e Pesquisas Internacionais e de Fronteiras (LEPIF), Brazil, until her untimely death in June 2021.

Pablo José Spekuljak is a lawyer and an MA candidate in Criminology at Universidad Nacional del Litoral, Argentina. He is the current Pro-Secretary of the Complex Crimes Prosecutor's Office – Regional Prosecutor's Office N° 1 – of Santa Fe Province, Argentina.

Maria Amelia Viteri is a research professor at the Department of Anthropology at Universidad San Francisco de Quito, Ecuador, and a research associate at the Department of Anthropology at University of Maryland, College Park. She is the author of *Desbordes: Translating Racial, Ethnic, Sexual and Gender Identities across the Americas* (2014), also published in Spanish (2020).

Contributors xvii

Beatriz Zepeda is a research professor at the Centre for International Studies at El Colegio de México, Mexico. She holds a PhD in Ethnicity and Nationalism and an MSc in International Relations from the London School of Economics and Political Science. From 2012 to 2014 she was director of FLACSO-Guatemala. Her research focuses on the Mexico-Guatemala border, illegal markets, nationalism, migration, and foreign policy.

Preface to the English Edition of the Series

Four years have gone by since *El sistema fronterizo global en América Latina: un estado del arte*, the first volume of this series, was launched in Ecuador. Since then, the collection grew to include studies on the borders of eight Latin American countries and four themes that are central to understanding how borders in this region are interconnected and contribute to structuring global illegal markets.

As the first collection of academic works devoted exclusively to borders in Latin America, the series constitutes a valuable source of information on the geographic, economic, demographic, and social characteristics of the most important Latin American border regions and their relation to global illegal markets. Moreover, the analyses on illegal flows (drugs, contraband, arms, migrant smuggling, and human trafficking) that the country studies put forward, and which the thematic volumes go into in greater depth, offer a unique and comprehensive view of the ways in which illegal markets are organized in each country and how they connect across borders to create the global border system.

Thanks to Routledge's interest, it is now possible to make this series available to an English-speaking audience and share with the readers the findings of an international team of more than 40 researchers from ten countries, who worked on this project over a period of three years.

While with the release of this collection we close a cycle, research on borders and illicit markets is more warranted than ever. Borders continue to gain importance not only in Latin America, but worldwide, and illegal flows evolve, almost by the day, creating new cross-border dynamics and global connections. We hope that this collection of works will contribute to illuminate the intricate relationship between the two of them not only in Latin America, but also on a global scale.

Finally, a note of thanks is due. In bringing these works to an English-speaking readership, no other person was more important than our editor, Natalja Mortensen. Natalja's permanent support since the publication of this series was but a proposal was essential to the completion

Preface to the English Edition of the Series xix

of this work and the greatest encouragement we could possibly get. For this we are deeply grateful.

Beatriz Zepeda
Series Editor (English language edition)

Preface

The research project "Exploring the Political Economy of Violence in Latin American Border Systems: Towards a Comprehensive Understanding" was developed under the coordination of Facultad Latinoamericana de Ciencias Sociales (FLACSO)-Ecuador and was made possible thanks to the support of the International Development Research Centre (IDRC), Canada. The project was carried out within a very far-reaching international institutional framework, with the participation of El Colegio de la Frontera Norte, Mexico, FLACSO-Guatemala, Fundación Paz y Reconciliación, Colombia, FLACSO-Ecuador, the Catholic University of Peru, Centro Boliviano de Estudios Multidisciplinarios, Laboratório de Estudos e Pesquisas Internacionais e de Fronteiras, Brazil, Universidad del Litoral, Argentina and Universidad San Francisco de Quito, Ecuador.

The study aimed at understanding the structure and characteristics of the global border system in Latin America, based on illegal economies and related crimes. In other words, it sought to elucidate how the cross-border relationship in Latin America is constituted on the basis of the actors (global crime network) and the "space of places" that structure the circuits, routes and nodes of illegality.

The research was conducted under a collaborative arrangement of social production of knowledge, conceived from a perspective that attempted to go beyond case studies, in order to build a comprehensive vision of the borders in the region. It was further premised on the understanding that borders acquire a systemic condition of global reach, i.e., that the borders between countries are integrated over and above the territories of adjoining states.

With this objective in mind, two convergent methodological approaches were adopted: that of national border realities understood as subsystems (eight countries) and that of the themes conceived as cross-cutting (four themes). At the same time, the starting point was a conception of the boundary as a line that demarcates the territory of adjacent states – therefore, agreed between them – while the border is a region constructed from the confluence of inter-state relations, which are born where neighboring states end or begin. This is why it can be said that boundaries

Preface xxi

are relatively immutable, while borders are social constructs that are in permanent change, for they reflect the dynamics of each state, and, nowadays, of the global economy as well.

This book marks the beginning of the second phase of the FRONTeras Collection,[1] consisting of a total of 12 volumes. The collection seeks to approach border studies in eight countries of the region (Argentina, Bolivia, Brazil, Colombia, Ecuador, Guatemala, Mexico, and Peru), as well as on four cross-cutting themes considered key to understanding the border system (illegal markets, gender, border cities, and comparative criminal legislation). Each one of the volumes constitutes a monographic study in its own right, while the reading of all the volumes of the collection offers the added value of providing a general panorama of the global border system in Latin America.

The name of the FRONTeras Collection comes from the plural of the Spanish word "frontera" (border). We conceive of it as a compound term between "front," which alludes to what lies ahead and "eras," which refers to different historical periods marked by transcendental events. In other words, we think of it as a way to look positively at the eras ahead in the areas of integration – and not of walls – between states.

<table>
<tr><td>Fernando Carrión Mena</td><td>Markus Gottsbacher</td></tr>
<tr><td>Project Coordinator</td><td>Senior Program Officer</td></tr>
<tr><td>FLACSO-Ecuador</td><td>Inclusive Economies</td></tr>
<tr><td></td><td>IDRC-Canada</td></tr>
</table>

Note

1. The first phase encompasses seven titles that can be consulted at FLACSO Andes: http://www.flacsoandes.edu.ec/

Acknowledgments

Bringing a project such as the publication of this book to fruition requires the effort and support of countless people and institutions. Here, I would like to express my gratitude to all of them.

First and foremost, I would like to thank the authors of the chapters that make up this volume for their committed and rigorous work. If this book has any merit, it is thanks to those who, from their areas of expertise, ventured into researching and seriously discussing the still little explored topic of Latin America's global border system.

The texts included here were refereed through a double-blind process. I thank the two scholars who reviewed the manuscript for their pertinent observations and suggestions and hope that this work, that so much benefitted from their comments, has done justice to their generous reading.

Without the invaluable support of Dr. Virgilio Reyes, Marcel Arévalo, Hugo de León, and Claudia Barrientos at FLACSO-Guatemala; Lina Magalhaes, Juan Pablo Pinto, María José Rodríguez, and Gabriela Ruiz at FLACSO-Ecuador; Dr. José Ignacio Chapela, Yosu Rodríguez Aldabe, and Gabriela Quiroz-Cázares at CentroGeo, Mexico, and Markus Gottsbacher at the International Development Research Center (IDRC), Canada, the publication of the Spanish edition of the book in 2017 would have been impossible. *Gracias una vez más.*

Four years later, I am delighted to be able to thank all the people who contributed to making the English edition a reality. My deepest gratitude goes to Natalja Mortensen, Senior Editor at Routledge. Had it not been for Natalja's unfailing support and faith in this project, this book might have never seen the light. Thanks also to Charlie Baker at Routledge for his immediate answers and enormous patience, especially as the deadline approached.

Getting the work ready for publication in English required a gigantic collective effort. I am forever grateful to Adriana Castañeda and Diana Robalo Rey for their research assistance, to Lía Galván Lisker, Francisca

Acknowledgments xxiii

Reyes, and Daniela Salinas for their invaluable support with the translation, and to Erika León for the beautiful maps.

Finally, I wish to thank El Colegio de México, its president, Dr. Silvia Giorguli, as well as Dr. Jean-François Proud'homme, Director of the Center for International Studies, for providing the stimulating and supportive environment that made it possible to embark on this project and bring it to a successful conclusion.

This book is dedicated to Jennifer Silva, young and promising researcher, dear colleague, and co-author of the chapter on Brazil, who, after battling Covid, left us in June 2021. May this book honor her memory and bear witness to our immense appreciation across borders.

Beatriz Zepeda
Mexico City, September 2021

Introduction

The Permanent Construction of Borders in Latin America

Fernando Carrión Mena and
Francisco Enríquez Bermeo

In November 2014, the project "Exploring the Political Economy of Violence in Latin American Border Systems: Towards a Comprehensive Understanding" was formally launched. Its first activity was an international seminar entitled "The Global Border System in Latin America: Illegal Markets and Violence." At this event, researchers dedicated to studying the border subsystems of nine countries, Argentina, Bolivia, Brazil, Colombia, Ecuador, Guatemala, Italy, Mexico, and Peru, as well as those investigating four cross-cutting themes, gender, border cities, illegal markets, and criminal justice, presented states of the art on their respective topics.

This book compiles the papers presented at the seminar, further enhanced by the discussions that took place at the event, as well as by the comments and suggestions of two anonymous referees.[1] All the contributions were expressly requested from each of the research team coordinators and follow a common structure, in line with the objectives of the project. This implies the existence of a general logic of the book as a whole, which also makes it possible to compare and aggregate the individual chapters.

In this sense, this work fulfills a double purpose: to be an input to the research project and, at the same time, one of the project's final products. The text thus becomes a raw material for general research, since it seeks to situate the problem, delimit its space, and understand what has been studied so far, while also being an autonomous academic work that helps to understand the borders, their dynamics, and connections with illegal markets from the perspective of the advances in the interpretation of the subject matter in the region. It is also a collective research work that discusses the state of the art on the borders of Latin American countries and helps us appraise how much we have learned about cross-border relations.

It must be said that one of the major challenges this project has faced is the lack of reliable and rigorous information. Obtaining hard and comparable data on border security has been a complicated task, due, among other reasons, to the fact that indicators and variables are not

DOI: 10.4324/9781003204299-1

2 *Fernando Carrión Mena and Francisco Enríquez Bermeo*

internationally standardized and that information on the topic is generally built under nationalistic signs and is, therefore, difficult to access. In a similar vein, reliable information on illegal markets and violence in border regions is hard to come by, not least because of the clandestine nature of these activities.

As much as a constraint, this situation is a motivation to continue researching the borders of Latin America and their relations with illegal markets. As the project progresses, we hope to be able to produce solid and comparable data that will aid our understanding of borders in our region and their pivotal role in the articulation of global illegal flows.

The Borders

In the 1990s, it seemed that national borders in Latin America would disappear because of two interrelated phenomena: state reform, embodied in state deregulation (privatization), the opening of world markets (free trade), and decentralization (localization) and globalization based on interdependence, technology, and communication. However, 30 years later, we do not observe the demise of borders, but rather, their major structural transformation. Borders have changed and have acquired an unparalleled strategic condition within the new world model of capitalist accumulation.

Border regions – peripheral and marginal – became visible as they began to gain certain autonomy. This autonomy stems from growing regional economies, decentralization processes that empower both local communities and intermediate governments, the important process of urbanization, the presence of violence, and the questioning of national centers of power.

Yet, the transformation of borders has been scarcely studied and, when it has been researched, especially in recent years, methodological nationalism has been privileged as a vantage point (Schiller and Salazar 2013, 185). This view approaches the border from the standpoint of the nation-state and neglects the specular reading (Besserer and Oliver 2014) that supposes looking at inter-border relations by way of a mirror. In addition, from an international perspective that looks beyond the simple adjacency of states, in the context of globalization, a new cross-border expression can be found that takes the shape of a system on a supra-territorial (global) scale, with the gravitational weight of illegal markets (global crime network). In other words, once again, borders change historically in a double condition: in their reality as containers of political and social geography, as well as in the very concept that defines them.

The publication of Frederick Jackson Turner's *The Significance of the Frontier in American History*, in 1893, marks the birth of the academic interest in borders in the American continent. Since then, academic production has proliferated, both in terms of topics and regions. Nonetheless, to our knowledge, in the English-speaking world, only the work edited by Jaskoski et al. (2015) has addressed the issue of borders in Latin America from geopolitical, security, and economic perspectives, an approach that is compatible with the interests pursued in this book. As regards border studies in Latin America, they have become increasingly important in the last three decades, attracting researchers from different disciplines, holding diverse points of view and heterogeneous conceptions.[2]

Borders are constantly changing. This trend has been accentuated in recent years with the shift from a binational logic, built on complementary asymmetries, to that of a global border system within the framework of illegal economies. Although each border embodies a particular reality, it cannot be denied that borders are strongly interconnected and have a common explanatory framework. However, there are no border investigations aimed at identifying the connections between borders, or – with the probable exception of Kassab and Rosen (2019) – between illegal economic circuits in Latin America. For this reason, scholarship has failed to understand the new functions of borders in the international context, while policy-makers continue justifying particularly rigid policies and institutions, despite crime's extreme adaptability and flexibility.

The Path Followed

The process of transformation of borders in Latin America presents four explicit moments. These moments, as will now become apparent, evidence the historical condition of borders, as well as the evolution of thinking about them:

1) Boundary: in the process of formation of nation-states, the definition of sovereignty is a fundamental element, which goes hand in hand with the demarcation of the space over which states exercise their supreme authority. The setting of boundaries is, thus, the basic component of the configuration of the nation-state, since it is boundaries that define the particular territory on which a population settles and exercises sovereignty through the government it gives itself. In Latin America, the establishment of boundaries was key in the formation of post-colonial states and has had a long trajectory, which began in the early nineteenth century, with the processes of independence. This moment appears to be coming to an end now, even though there are still territories in dispute on the continent, fundamentally due to three situations: inaccuracies in the delimitation inherited from the colony, the economic benefits around certain territories where there is, for example, oil, and the interests of access to certain strategic areas.

2) Border: with the demarcation of state territories, areas of interstate confluence are constituted in the confines of the states, which acquire the status of borders. These are adjacent areas on both sides of the line, which take on a particular political, economic, and social connotation,

4 *Fernando Carrión Mena and Francisco Enríquez Bermeo*

as they are simultaneously distant from the national political center and close to the neighboring country. In other words, they are spaces united by the very element that separates them: the boundary. Thus, while the border corresponds to a centrifugal force (outwardly oriented), boundaries correspond to a centripetal force (inwardly oriented) and give cohesion to the state (Hartshorne 1950). Furthermore, borders are, to some extent, a spatial continuum that goes beyond national boundaries due to multiple illegal networks, kinship ties, and the development of new communication technologies (Bottino Bernardi 2009).

3) Inter-border relations: with the import-substitution and inward development model, promoted since the 1950s by the Economic Commission for Latin America and the Caribbean (ECLAC), borders (be they zones or regions) began to take on a gravitational position, thanks to the weight of the macroeconomic policies promoted by each of the national states (protectionism). From that moment on, the border logic of complementary asymmetry (Carrión 2013), i.e., the functional integration of inter-state differences, came into play, based, for instance, on smuggling, which operates as a communicating vessel, so that one side of the border is linked to the other.

4) Cross-border relations: currently, border regions hold a strategic position within the global model of capital accumulation, which goes beyond inter-state spatial continuity. Today, borders are true world trade centers that attract major capital, masses of population, violence, and illegal activities. That is why border regions have begun to play a national and international role above the one that the centers of power assigned to them as marginal regions or peripheral spaces. Nowadays, borders demand greater attention, not only because of their new structural functions, but also because of the problems they accumulate, and because of their great potential.

For instance, understanding the border between Mexico and the United States requires knowing the links with the land, sea, and air borders of Central America and the Andean area (circuits, routes, and nodes), through the actors that sustain the illegal flows (global crime networks). In contrast, grasping what happens on Colombia's borders implies relating the sequence of borders (routes) that must be crossed in order to transport cocaine from Colombia to Australia, China, Europe, the United States, or Brazil. In reality, each of the inter-border regions is shaped as a platform for integration and multiple interactions (in the manner of a hub or router) to structure the global border system.

The union of borders in the form of a system makes it possible to innovate public policy design within the framework of the dynamics of international integration and decentralization at the national level. In addition, it presents an opportunity to public policy-makers, who must respond to the fact that, while crime is constantly innovating (permanently adapting), institutions are not doing so. Laws and policies themselves are tremendously rigid. For this reason, border research must identify the connections between borders in order to understand the

Introduction 5

economic circuits – legal and illegal – on which they are based. This is even more relevant if we consider that new economic circuits generated by illegal markets render borders an exceptional space for criminal integration.

While this process has been insufficiently studied, progress has been made recently, as new analytical inputs appear that consider that it is not possible to understand one side of the border without understanding the relationship with the other side; that is to say, without pondering the constitutive inter-border link. However, this is still not enough, because today there are at least three indissoluble dimensions that interconnect borders: the nature of the system (integration), the global condition (deterritorialization), and the gravitational weight of the illegal markets (global crime network), which make cross-border logic the dominant one. This modality corresponds to a different phase from that of the inter-border logic because the connection of one border with another one does not depend on spatial contiguity, but rather passes through border discontinuity.

This *problématique* has given rise to a space for reflection in which certain disciplines and approaches have prevailed. Among these, military visions (national security), historical visions (historical precedents), legal visions (international law), geographical visions (natural borders), diplomatic visions (international relations), economic visions (tariffs, customs, macroeconomics), demographic visions (migrations, urbanization), strengthening of local governments (decentralization), and violence visions (citizen security) should be highlighted. There is, in fact, an important bibliography on these topics, to which this work seeks to contribute.[3]

The Structure of the Book

The logic of distribution of the chapters comprised in the book is related to the methodological proposal of the research project, which combines two concurrent entries, a territorial one and a thematic one. These two entries make up the two parts into which this work is divided.

The first part of the book groups the texts stemming from the territorial interest of the study. It therefore encompasses the works on the countries that constitute the cases included in the project. These countries were selected according to the role each one plays in the international division of labor within illegal markets, mainly drug trafficking.

Producing Countries

Peru and Bolivia, together with Colombia, are the countries that, according to UNODC, have the highest levels of cocaine production in the world and, therefore, demand and import – both legally and illegally – a set of supplies (chemical precursors) and weapons from distant locations. They are also the places from where the greatest amounts of narcotics are

6 *Fernando Carrión Mena and Francisco Enríquez Bermeo*

exported to the largest and most distant markets of the planet through a variety of routes, circuits, and nodes.

In the chapter "The Global Border System and Illegal Markets in Peru: Notes for a Research Agenda," Manuel Dammert and Viktor Bensús address the issue of Peru's borders with reference to social, demographic, and economic indicators. Their account portrays a reality in which border populations are clearly at a disadvantage compared to the population in other regions of the country. It also sheds light on the significant socio-spatial impacts that the new population flows have had on Peruvian border areas. As regards illegal markets, the authors discuss the role that Peru has acquired as one of the largest producers of coca leaf in the world. In this context, they stress that, in the case of drug trafficking, Peru's borders are not only places of passage, but are also deeply impacted by illegal trafficking, since the latter's operation generates logics of location and reorganization of the border areas themselves.

In the chapter "Bolivia: The Tensions, Challenges, and Prospects of the Border Subsystem," José Blanes highlights the numerous transformations that Bolivia's borders have undergone since independence, resulting in significant territorial losses for that country. With claims against Chile for access to the sea still unresolved, Bolivia has inserted itself into the global economy in a context of institutional weakness, with important consequences for the state, society, and the economy. According to Blanes, informal cross-border trade is the axis that articulates "the new border subsystem with which Bolivia has incorporated itself into the global system" and is complemented by migration flows (formal and informal) to Brazil and Argentina, which for decades have structured the border routes. Informality is thus a central element in the configuration of Bolivia's border system. Far from being an exclusive feature of Bolivia, it is, as will be seen throughout this book, a common factor of the borders of the entire region.

Platform-Type Countries

Ecuador and Argentina are platform-type countries. Such countries are strategic within the inter-border system since they have become key spaces for the integration of global illegal markets for narcotics, arms, and contraband. While Ecuador is located between Colombia and Peru, the two countries with the highest coca leaf production in the world, Argentina opens the route to Australia and the rest of Oceania, where cocaine prices are the highest.

In the chapter "Ecuador's Global Border Subsystem: From 'Island of Peace' to International Crime Platform," Fernando Carrión Mena and Francisco Enríquez Bermeo describe the historical problems in the defense of territorial sovereignty that Ecuador had to face until the signing of the peace agreement with Peru in 1998. The authors further

Introduction 7

analyze violence rates by province and note that the highest are found on the border with Colombia, as a result of the action of criminal groups dedicated to drug trafficking and related crimes. Regarding border security policies, this chapter argues that Ecuador's policies are similar to those of the United States and Colombia, as expressed in Plan Colombia, and that local policies either do not exist or are very weak.

Gustavo González, Luciana Ghiberto, and Pablo Spekuljak present the case of Argentina in the chapter "Borders, Crime, and State Responses in Argentina." They argue that in Argentina the study of borders has come hand in hand with the discussion on the process of formation of the nation-state and the expansion of state power over the territory, thereby imbricating the notions of "external border" and "internal border." Moreover, the interest that the borders themselves have aroused in Argentina has varied over time, according to a pattern that the authors characterize as "pendular." Sometimes at the center of the public debate, other times, marginalized from the attention of the government, academia, and the media, Argentina's borders have been thought of in different ways, depending on the moment. In the field of public policy, during the last decades, these variations in the way borders have been conceived have led to the emergence of various strategies for the differentiated control, use, and regulation of border territories which, far from being imposed at any given time, end up coexisting with previous logics, thus generating what the authors term "different forms of coupling."

Strategic Countries

Guatemala and Mexico are obligatory places for the land transit of drugs between South and North America. According to López (2020), 90% of the cocaine seized in the United States transits Guatemala, while UNODC (2021, 24) estimates that 80% of the cocaine found on the United States market in 2019 had, in fact, passed through Mexico. These two countries have thus become strategic places for the action of illegal groups and display high violence rates, as well as the presence of criminal groups, *maras* (street gangs), and drug cartels. In addition, both Mexico and Guatemala suffer from widespread penetration of illegal groups in national and local politics.

In the chapter, "Guatemala's Border System: A First Approach," Beatriz Zepeda looks at the historical configuration of Guatemala's borders and highlights the role played by expanding transnational capital in the delimitation of Guatemala's territory during the second half of the nineteenth century. In reviewing the situation of the borders of Guatemala in more recent times, the author further points out that, in the face of the internal armed conflict that devastated Guatemala between 1960 and 1996, the borders acquired strategic importance, as their control became a central element of counterinsurgency efforts. Especially

8   *Fernando Carrión Mena and Francisco Enríquez Bermeo*

in the north and northeast of the country, the military dominance of borders, customs, and crossing points led to the emergence of activities (smuggling, drug trafficking) and illegal actors linked to the state, which, once the conflict ended, became operational in transnational criminal networks and activities. This contrasts with the dynamics in the south-western border, where traditional cross-border relations characterized by their fluidity and informality have become facilitating factors for different kinds of illegal flows.

"Mexico's Cross-Border Subsystem: Cocaine Trafficking and Violence on the Northern Border" is the title of César Fuentes and Sergio Peña's contribution. In this chapter, the authors present the case of Mexico as a paradigmatic example of border transformation in the era of globalization. Focusing on the drug – particularly the cocaine – market, Fuentes and Peña argue that, as a result of globalization, a phenomenon they conceive as "a spatial reconfiguration of capitalism to guarantee [...] accumulation," borders have become strategic points for flows, both legal and illegal, and therefore – they argue – their control is critical. In the case of Mexico's northern border, the gateway to the US market, control over the border territories has been disputed by increasingly strong criminal groups with impressive firepower. This would largely explain the wave of violence that, with different concentration points, hit the north of Mexico in the last two decades. Furthermore, the authors note the enormous attraction that the presence of the United States exerts on the population south of the Río Bravo and the effect it has on Mexican border cities, which, by taking in people who are unable to cross the border to the north, end up growing uncontrollably.

Multifunctional Countries: Transit and Consumption

The case of Italy, a country outside of Latin America, is included in this book to illustrate the global logic of the border system. In turn, the case of Brazil, which borders almost every other country in South America and is the second largest cocaine consuming country in the world and the first for crack, allows us to look at the whole cycle of production, circulation, and consumption of drugs, as well as at the opening of new routes to Europe and Africa.

In the chapter "Projecting Borders across the Atlantic: The Case of Italy from a Latin American Perspective," Federico Alagna discusses Italy's border system and emphasizes the strong connection between Italy and Latin America by virtue of the links that have existed for decades between Italian mafias and the main criminal organizations in South America. The case of Italy, as the author explains, also highlights the malleability of the concept of "border," since, within the framework of the European Union (EU) and particularly the Schengen area, the EU's internal borders and, therefore, Italy's borders with its EU-member

Introduction   9

neighbors have disappeared. In this context, says Alagna, "Italy's only real border is the maritime border on the Mediterranean, which is also the EU's southern border." As in the case of the other southern European countries that form the external border of the European Union, for Italy this condition has meant dealing with extra-regional migration, one of the main contemporary challenges for the EU.

Because of Brazil's enormous size and multiple borders, the border situation in this country is perhaps one of the most complex in Latin America. With an area of more than 8.5 million square kilometers, Brazil is not only the largest country in Latin America, but also the one that borders all the South American states, except Chile and Ecuador. In the chapter "Brazil and its Borders: History and Limits of a Sovereign State," Letícia Núñez Almeida, Agnes Félix, Rafael Masson, Nathan Bueno, and Jennifer Silva trace the process of demarcation of Brazil's boundaries. Over two centuries, this process has included multiple negotiations, first with colonial powers, and later, with neighboring countries, as well as international arbitration resources and warlike conflicts that ended in modifications of South America's political map. In a subsequent reflection on Brazil's contemporary borders, the authors discuss the negative coverage that the borders of southern Brazil – particularly the triple frontier between Argentina, Brazil, and Paraguay – have received in the media in recent years and draw attention to the stigmatizing effect that this has had, not only on this, but also on all of Brazil's borders.

In contrast to the first part of the book, which follows a territorial logic, the second part takes a sector approach and focuses on three issues that are essential to understanding the constitution of the global border system: illegal markets, which build the most complex cross-border relations; border cities, the nodes structuring cross-border regions; and gender, a variable that has been insufficiently studied with regard to borders and the violence associated with them.

In the chapter "Illegal Markets: A New Institutional Architecture and its Territorial Expression in Latin America," Fernando Carrión Mena addresses the new criminal architecture, the expansion of illegal economies, and the territories where they are anchored. Carrión Mena further problematizes the relationship between violence, borders, and illegal markets, as well as the differences between legal, informal, and illegal economies. The author argues that borders are platforms for the illegal economy and portrays them as dispersed spaces that meet strategic conditions within the global structure. Pointing out the new criminal modalities based on outsourcing, franchising, and holding, Carrión Mena stresses the shift that has taken place from isolated criminal organizations to the global networks that use to their advantage the complementary asymmetries created by the existence of borders.

In their contribution "Cross-Border Urban Complexes: The Urban Morphology of the Global Structure," Fernando Carrión Mena and

10   *Fernando Carrión Mena and Francisco Enríquez Bermeo*

Víctor Llugsha highlight the steady increase in Latin America's urbanization rate in the last 30 years, as well as the fact that this growth of the cities in Latin America has been uneven and has been accompanied by a deepening inequality. The potential of cities as development and growth hubs is, nonetheless, present, and, according to the authors, it is particularly evident in border cities. After offering the bases for a classification of Latin America's border cities, the authors emphasize that the development of the great potential for integration of these cities requires adequate planning and public policies that take into account local populations and problems, while understanding the international nature of the phenomena they seek to address.

In the final chapter of the book, "A Gender Perspective in the Study of Latin American Border Systems," María Amelia Viteri and Iréri Ceja highlight the ways in which gender structures operate to enable and justify certain types of violence, along with illegal markets, in the localized context of borders. Based on their understanding of gender, not as something given and immutable, but as "a series of processes from which it is defined and produced," the authors argue that patriarchalism and the various structures of social differentiation turn women's bodies into territories of vulnerability. This vulnerability is particularly evident at the borders, since the control over territories and bodies, associated with border protection, is intimately linked with violence. Viteri and Ceja argue that gender-based violence is naturalized at the borders, as well as in the context of illegal markets, something that becomes particularly evident in the vulnerability of migrant women transiting along transnational routes and of those women who, for various reasons, participate in drug trafficking.

***

The collection of papers presented in this volume offers a panoramic view of the borders of Argentina, Bolivia, Brazil, Ecuador, Guatemala, Italy, Mexico, and Peru, as well as the way in which the border question has been addressed in the national contexts of each of these countries. At the same time, the three chapters dedicated to cross-cutting themes address debates that, while concerning all borders of the world, help to delineate the complexity of the global border system in Latin America.

Notwithstanding, in all of the cases, they are exploratory works that offer an initial mapping of an object of study that is still in the process of definition; namely, the relationship between borders in Latin America and illegal markets in the era of globalization. Therefore, rather than providing explanations, the contributions contained here raise numerous questions and prefigure a pending research agenda. If this book motivates other researchers to investigate this topic in search of answers, it will have achieved its goal.

Introduction 11

Notes

1. For reasons beyond our control, in this English edition we have been unable to include the translations of the works on Colombia's border system and on criminal justice. The chapters on Guatemala and Italy are not translations of the works published in Spanish but have been written originally for this book.
2. Since all the contributions to this book devote a section to reviewing the literature on the borders of specific countries, or of Latin American borders and their intersection with particular issues, the discussion of these works is best left to the individual chapters.
3. The project includes the creation of a bibliography specialized in border studies that will be disseminated virtually by FLACSO Andes: http://www.flacsoandes.edu.ec/

References

Besserer, Federico and Daniela Oliver. 2014. "Etnografía especular y contiendas culturales." In *Ensamblando la ciudad transnacional. Etnografía especular de los espacios trans- nacionales urbanos*, edited by Federico Besserer and Daniela Oliver, 267–276. Mexico City: Universidad Autónoma Metropolitana-Iztapalapa, Colección Estudios Transnacionales.

Bottino Bernardi, María del Rosario. 2009. "Sobre límites y fronteras." *Estudios Históricos*, 1, 1–18.

Carrión, Fernando. 2013. *Asimetrías en la frontera Ecuador-Colombia: entre la complementariedad y el sistema*. Quito: FLACSO-IDRC.

Hartshorne, Richard. 1950. "The Functional Approach in Political Geography." *Annals of the Association of American Geographers*, 40 (2), 95–130.

Jaskoski, Maiah, Arturo Sotomayor and Harold A. Trinkunas (Eds.). 2015. *American Crossings. Border Politics in the Western Hemisphere*. Baltimore: Johns Hopkins University Press.

Kassab, Hanna Samir and Jonathan D. Rosen. 2019. *Illicit Markets, Organized Crime and Global Security*. USA: Palgrave-Macmillan.

López, Julie. 2020. "La pandemia ralentizó la producción (y tráfico de cocaína)". *Plaza Pública*. December 10. Accessed on 14 January, 2021, https://www.plazapublica.com.gt/content/la-pandemia-ralentizo-la-produccion-y-trafico-de-cocaina

Schiller Glick, Nina and Noel Salazar. 2013. "Regimes of Mobility across the Globe." *Journal of Ethnic and Racial Studies*, 39 (2), 183–200.

Turner, Frederick Jackson. 1893/2008. *The Significance of the Frontier in America History*. London: Penguin Books.

UNODC (United Nations Office on Drugs and Crime). 2021. *World Drug Report 2021*. June 2021. Accessed on 22 March 2021, https://www.unodc.org/res/wdr2021/field/WDR21_Booklet_4.pdf#%5B%7B%22num%22%3A76%2C%22gen%22%3A0%7D%2C%7B%22name%22%3A%22FitR%22%7D%2C-290%2C-3%2C998%2C711%5D

PART 1
BORDER SUBSYSTEMS

PART 1.1
PRODUCING COUNTRIES

1 The Global Border System and Illegal Markets in Peru

Notes for a Research Agenda

Manuel Dammert Guardia and Viktor Bensús

This chapter discusses the characteristics of the Peruvian border system and their links to different illegal markets in order to establish a research agenda on this intricate relationship.[1] Specifically, this work addresses the way in which borders – as a system and a space for the exchange of people, goods, and services, as well as for the location of activities and socio-territorial anchoring – relate to illegal dynamics, such as drug trafficking and smuggling. In doing so, the chapter aims to take stock of the existing discussion about the Peruvian border system and propose some lines for future discussion.

The document is organized as follows: The first part presents a state of the art regarding three topics that have been central to the debate on borders – sovereignty and territorial demarcation, urban and territorial dynamics in border areas, and legal, informal, and illegal economic dynamics in border zones. In all three cases, an effort is made to highlight the links and flows established in border systems. The second part identifies the main socio-economic characteristics of Peruvian districts in border areas and then describes the dynamics of migration flows in those districts. The third part provides an initial approach to the characteristics of the Peruvian border system by focusing on the dynamics of three illegal markets: contraband, drug trafficking, and related crimes. Finally, on the basis of the reviewed information, the chapter presents some preliminary remarks for a future research agenda.

State of the Art

The following is a brief review of the existing literature on Peruvian borders. It is organized along the three lines of inquiry discussed above.

Sovereignty and Territorial Demarcation

The delimitation of Peru's territory has been investigated mainly from a historical perspective by focusing on conflicts and diplomatic treaties. Thus, a central theme has been the interest in reconstructing the

DOI: 10.4324/9781003204299-4

The Global Border System and Illegal Markets   17

historical changes in the demarcation of national boundaries (Angulo 1927; Porras Barrenechea 1926; Cano 1925; Pons 1962; among others). Another group of works has focused on border conflicts and has highlighted the importance of the War of the Pacific (Peru-Chile), in the late nineteenth century, as well as the set of negotiations and subsequent treaties, which marked the climate of border relations with Chile (Calderón Cousiño 1919; Bocchio Rejas 1978; Calderón 2000), until The Hague resolution of 2014 regarding the maritime conflict (although that did not mean the end of the border disputes). A second conflict of great relevance in the literature has been the dispute with Ecuador throughout the twentieth century, especially the 1941 conflict and its resumption in 1991. Hocquenghem (2009) and Hocquenghem and Durt (2002) address this issue and focus on the developments that took place after the signing of the Peace Accords and the Brasilia Act in 1998, and in particular, the cooperation agreements based on the elaboration of a binational plan for the joint management of border areas.

In parallel to studies on territorial and boundary conflicts, a considerable corpus of academic work focuses on multilateral management. This literature seeks to problematize the notion of borders and to present borders as socio-spatial systems involving portions of the territory of more than one state. For instance, the work of the International Organization for Migration (IOM) suggests a series of guidelines to plan state intervention in border areas: (i) the coexistence of different jurisdictions in the community, on both national and international levels; (ii) the characteristics of cross-border human mobility; (iii) particular socio-economic and cultural realities; (iv) the geographical environment; and (v) border security (OIM 2012).

Approaches such as those of IOM are linked to much of the current Peruvian legislation such as Law No. 29778, Framework Law for Border Development and Integration (Ley marco para el desarrollo e integración fronteriza), and its by-laws approved by Supreme Decree No. 017-2013-RE. These regulations stipulate the national territorial organization in which the border dynamics are articulated: area, zone, region, and macro-region. They also provide guidelines for cross-border coordination based on the Border Integration Zones (BIZs). The proposal of BIZs is one of the most frequently discussed elements of border management in the current literature. The definition of the BIZs has as its antecedent the Andean Pact on borders signed within the framework of the Quito Protocol of 1987 and is the product of binational coordination initiatives and experiences, as well as of the impetus of the Andean Community (CAN) (Ramírez 2009). Peru has had BIZs with Ecuador since 2000, with Colombia since 2002, with Bolivia since 2001, and with Brazil since 2009. The first three were established within the framework of CAN Decision 501, while the BIZ with Brazil was based on a bilateral agreement (MRE 2012).

18 *Manuel Dammert G. and Viktor Bensús*

The relevance and applicability of these proposals are discussed by authors such as Grisales (2005) and Meza (2005), who find great potential in them, on the basis of the history of commercial exchange, in the case of the triple border Peru-Colombia-Brazil, and cultural exchange, in the case of the Peruvian-Bolivian border. Nonetheless, challenges associated with the illegal economies that emerge in these territories are also identified, especially for judicial coordination and the effectiveness of control (Grisales 2005), as well as the pollution and depredation of natural resources (Chiarella 2005). The absence of formal delimitation of a BIZ between Peru and Chile is, in turn, characterized as striking (Bernal 1986).[2]

In the last 15 years, part of the Peruvian academic production that addresses the issue of border integration has emphasized road construction projects associated with the Initiative for the Integration of Regional Infrastructure in South America (IIRSA). The emphasis on opportunities for territorial planning and development posed by the construction of infrastructure associated with IIRSA is the starting point for Chiarella (2011) and Castillo (2011), who characterize binational border processes as disorderly and marked by high socioeconomic inequality. In other words, despite intense trade in border areas such as Aguas Verdes-Huaquillas on the Peruvian-Ecuadorian border, social inequality and the lack of basic services persist (mainly on the Peruvian side), a situation that requires coordination for sustainable development (Castillo 2011).

Border integration plans or binational cooperation projects are not a recent issue. Bolognesi-Drosdoff (1986) reports on a series of border-cooperation initiatives throughout South America during the 1980s. In the case of Peru, the beginnings of coordination for the joint exploitation of natural resources between Ecuador and Peru and the use of the Puyango-Tumbes river basins stand out. In addition, there were cases of Peruvian-Bolivian intersectoral coordination that included creating a binational company and a proposal for the design of border integration plans (Bolognesi-Drosdoff 1986, 17). Grisales (2005) indicates that in the 1990s Colombia and Peru began to establish agreements to characterize and harmonize the Amazonian ecological-economic zone. However, it was the Binational Development Plan for the Peru-Ecuador Border Region that brought a portfolio of specific projects framed within a limited period of time.

The plan, originally designed to be developed during the period 2000–2009, was extended until 2013 and focused on social and productive infrastructure projects, as well as the promotion of private investment (Hocquenghem 2009; Hocquenghem and Durt 2002; MRE 2006). Although it was designed for the development of the population in the areas of intervention, Hocquenghem and Durt (2002) argue that its bias toward infrastructure projects and private investment meant that cultural diversity was neglected (especially in the Amazon region) and led to the exacerbation of problems linked to the presence of mining activity in the area.

Another set of proposals for border management can be identified. For example, Novoa (1993) emphasizes the management of binational basins between Peru and Bolivia as an alternative for ecodevelopment and border integration, which has been implemented for years in the Puyango-Tumbes rivers. Another proposal is that of Chiarella (2005), who maintains that the best development strategy for the Iñapari-Assis-Bolpebra conurbation, on the triple border of Peru, Brazil, and Bolivia, is the integrated management of urban services, infrastructure, and equipment through its operation as an "international city."

Gradually, the focus has shifted from a perspective of boundary delimitation to one concerned with border management, problematizing and broadening the definition of the border as a demarcation line. Despite the critical nature of much of the literature, many tasks remain pending, such as evaluating the application of these management and planning tools, their effect on the mitigation of crime and socio-economic inequalities, and the access to good quality basic services. Likewise, it is necessary to broaden the degree of coordination between the different actors involved in integrated border management. On this point, Hocquenghem's work (2009) particularly stimulates reflection on the scope of such plans and projects. Finally, it is essential to move beyond specific cases and advance a comparative view of border management as a system where different actors and institutions participate.

Territorial Dynamics and the Occupation of Space

A second topic present in the literature relates to territorial dynamics. These dynamics involve different analytical dimensions, such as those centered on population density, demographic characteristics, or on the predominant occupation types of the territory (i.e., urban and rural), and the relations between one side of the border and the other. A classification proposal (Table 1.1) has been drawn up by the Latin American and Caribbean Economic System (SELA).

From this classification, it becomes apparent that border areas differ from the rest of the territory in the degree of consolidation of population centers and the intensity of trade flows (SELA 2011). Examples thereof are the processes of state-driven colonization of uninhabited or sparsely inhabited territories that began in the twentieth century as a strategy for occupying and claiming the national territory. Such is the case of the basins that link Peru and Bolivia, which received significant Andean and – to a lesser extent – Brazilian immigration (Novoa 1993).

According to Aramburú (1980), from the 1960s onwards, migration to the jungle rim (*ceja de selva*) intensified, producing negative ecological

20 *Manuel Dammert G. and Viktor Bensús*

Table 1.1 Typology of border situations

By population and socio-economic dynamics	By degree of interrelation	By geographic scale
Isolated indigenous populations	Absent border	Local
Indigenous population with different degrees of articulation	Embryonic border	Zonal
Peasant communities with precarious agricultural resources	Border under construction	Regional
Peasant communities with access to agricultural resources	Consolidated border	
New human settlements		
Urban centers with local functions		
Intermediate urban centers		
Regional metropolis		

Source: SELA (2011)

effects and demanding changes in the colonists' traditional organization. In reference to contemporary processes in areas of major urban consolidation, Berganza and Purizaga (2011) argue that there has been a progressive increase in internal migration to border areas in northern Peru. These processes have transformed the type and scope of the occupation of border territories on both sides of the international boundary and generated situations of border consolidation, i.e., portions of the territory of different states operating as a single urban system.

Two types of approaches to urban border dynamics can be identified: one focused on the flows of people and trade and the other focused on the spatial effects of these flows, something that Dilla and Cedano (2005) call "urban intermediation." The first group observes the conurbation of border cities and focuses on the migration flows that make it possible to speak of these conurbations as a system (Bijsterbosch 2007; Chiarella 2005). Along the same lines, Berganza and Cerna (2011) establish a typology of migration on the Chilean-Peruvian border, which may be daily, weekly, or permanent, depending on the activity in question. The second group discusses, in turn, the territorial effects of border cities. Chiarella (2005) analyzes different cases of trinational border systems in jungle areas, which share an accelerated urbanization process, mainly linked to the intensification of illegal economic activities. This has led to disorderly growth, whose greatest risk is housing deficit, informal occupation, and depredation of natural resources.

Economic Characteristics of Borders

A third area of discussion identified throughout the literature concerns the economic characteristics of these spaces, mainly in terms of trade and the coexistence of formal, informal, and illegal markets. To understand the relationship that is established between the different zones that make up the border, Chavarría et al. (2012), following Ullman (1956), propose the use of the concepts of complementarity and comparative advantages, for both formal and informal markets. Complementarity and comparative advantages have served to promote formal, informal, and illegal economic relations within which actors tend to operate without difficulty. In other words, the formal-informal-illegal differentiation does not always exist for the actors involved in these activities that often complement each other (Giménez Béliveau 2011). Hence, the same person may spend part of his or her time working in the formal market and another part participating in informal or illegal activities.

Some works dealing with the subject of Peruvian border areas illustrate how these exchanges take place. For example, in the case of the border zone between Peru and Chile, Berganza and Cerna (2011), Bijsterbosch (2007), González Miranda (2006), and Podestá (2005) emphasize the attraction of Chilean cities for jobs (domestic work, trade, mining, and other activities associated with the intensity of economic activities in the free zone of Arica and for which Peruvian labor is extremely affordable). Although many businesses that generate jobs are formal, the condition of Peruvian workers is not.

In turn, Chavarría et al. (2012) address the issue of contraband between Peru, Chile, and Bolivia, and explain that price differences, as well as the opportunities generated by the Tacna duty-free zone, have allowed the development of trade flows, especially illegal ones, through Puno. Novoa (1993) and Valcuende del Río (2008), on the other hand, focus on the Amazon border areas and identify the importance of logging and other illegal commercial activities.

The borders with Colombia and Brazil are addressed in the work of Grisales (2005), which emphasizes commerce that has been especially fluid since the end of the Colombian-Peruvian war and is based on the trade of precious woods such as mahogany and cedar. Finally, the Peruvian-Ecuadorian border is studied by Berganza and Purizaga (2011), who identify different economic specializations between the border areas. Thus, Tumbes bases its wealth especially in transport, communications, and services, Piura in manufacturing, Lambayeque in trade, and Cajamarca in the primary sector. In addition, contraband is also important in the northern border because of the price differences between Ecuador and Peru, especially due to the Ecuadorian government's subsidy of fuel, which has motivated its import to the main cities of the Peruvian northern coast. This fuel is sold on the streets and highways, and those who buy it range from private users to motorcycle taxi drivers and associated transporters.

In sum, most of the work addressing the relations of complementarity and competition between the territories that make up the different Peruvian border areas has focused on the illegal economy and labor

22　*Manuel Dammert G. and Viktor Bensús*

flows. In this sense, formal and everyday dynamics have taken a back seat, despite being the ones that account for the larger part of the territorial dynamics in border areas.

Characterization of the Border System

Global border systems are the broadest manifestation of border dynamics, which, as OIM (2012) points out, can be found at different scales: border areas, zones, and regions. The following are the main socio-economic and demographic characteristics of border districts, understood as border areas.[3] Next, population flows are analyzed by reviewing data on regular and irregular migration, as a first approach to the dynamics of the global border system.

Socio-Economic and Demographic Data

Based on available official data,[4] demographic and social indicators are presented for the border districts (i.e., any district located at the border of the national territory). For the intercensal periods 1981–1993[5] and 1993–2007, the resident population in the border districts grew on average by 0.29% and 0.23%, respectively (Map 1.1). In many cases, the population growth is higher than the average growth at the provincial level, which may suggest a higher growth than in the rest of the nearby districts.

If the districts are grouped according to the country that they share a border with (Table 1.2), there is an increase in population in all cases during the intercensal period 1981–1993. However, during the following intercensal period (1993–2007), this growth was only maintained for the borders with Ecuador, Colombia, and Bolivia.

Regarding the distribution of the population in rural and urban areas (Table 1.3), there was an increase of four percentage points with respect to the total population registered (46% in 1993 and 51% in 2007) for the intercensal period 1993–2007. However, this percentage remained below the national average, which grew by an average of 11 percentage points (65% in 1993 and 76% in 2007). When the districts are grouped by the country that they share a border with, it becomes apparent that the districts with the greatest average variation are those bordering Colombia and Bolivia. In addition, there is a slight decrease in the urban population on the border with Chile.

Regarding the educational level of the population of 15 years of age or older in border districts, we observe: (i) a reduction in the average of the population without education[6] (22.81% in 1981, 13.07% in 2007); (ii) a slight increase in the average between 1981 and 2007 (43.75%) and 1993 (45.51%) and a decrease in 2007 (36.40%) with respect to primary education; (iii) an increase in the population with secondary education

The Global Border System and Illegal Markets 23

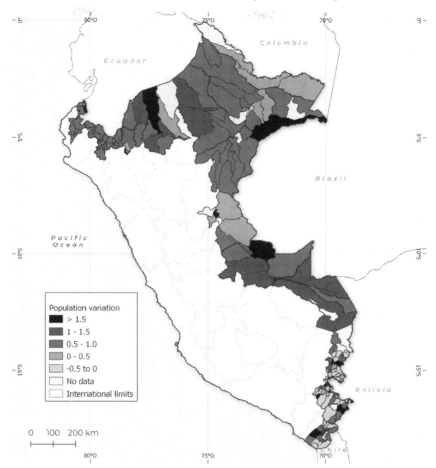

Map 1.1 Peru: Population Variation in Border Districts (1993–2007)
Source: INEI (1993, 2007)
Map by Erika León

Table 1.2 Peru: Population variation rate by bordering country

Bodering country	1981	1993	2007	Population variation rate (1981–1993)	Population variation rate (1993–2007)
Ecuador	174,770	224,511	308,759	0.28	0.38
Colombia	15,563	22,168	28,317	0.42	0.28
Brazil	123,019	197,470	169,362	0.61	−0.14
Bolivia	476,142	558,482	641,563	0.17	0.15
Chile	89,399	120,433	95,938	0.35	−0.2

Source: INEI (1993, 2007)

24   *Manuel Dammert G. and Viktor Bensús*

Table 1.3 Peru: Urban-rural distribution by bordering country

	Urban		Rural	
Bordering country	1993	2007	1993	2007
Ecuador	22.75%	27.65%	76.96%	72.35%
Colombia	26.51%	39.74%	73.40%	60.26%
Brazil	77.03%	80.19%	22.97%	19.81%
Bolivia	35.75%	49.23%	63.71%	50.77%
Chile	93.31%	92.30%	6.68%	7.70%

Source: INEI (1993, 2007)

(12.54% in 1981, 25.01% in 1993, and 37.71% in 2007) and access to university education[7] (1.31% in 1981, 2.81% in 1993, and 5.43% in 2007).

The illiterate population decreased from 28.75% in 1981 to 22.05% in 1993 and to 8.64% in 2007. Comparing the national percentages of illiteracy, we can see that although the levels are higher than the national average in 1981 (18.01% at the national level) and 1993 (12.12% at the national level), by 2007 this percentage began to approach the national average of 7.1% for that year. This trend continues when looking at the data by type of border.

As regards the population of the border districts that reported having a language other than Spanish as their mother tongue,[8] it is observed that, although this decreased in the last intercensal period, its variation was not very large in the average of the border districts (45.67% in 1993 and 43.40% in 2007). The population with a native language other than Spanish is concentrated in the border with Bolivia (67.42% of the border population in 1993 and 63.32% in 2007) and, in a lower percentage, in the border with Brazil (24.89% of the border population in 1993 and 27.90% in 2007). This situation highlights the existence of native communities located in the border areas.

Regarding the Economically Active Population (EAP) and the Economically Active Occupied Population (EAOP) of the border districts, the following can be pointed out: the average EAP among the border districts suffered a sharp drop in the first intercensal period, from 58.45% in 1981 to 28.92% in 1993. This figure rebounded in the intercensal period between 1993 and 2007, when it reached an average of 37.64% of the total population in the border districts.

In relation to inadequate housing,[9] it is possible to observe a decrease in the three intercensal periods from an average of 73.47% (1981)[10] to 65.56% (1993), reaching 46.41% (2007). When we disaggregate this indicator in the districts, differentiating them by bordering country, we notice a series of particularities. First, the most significant decrease is found in the borders with Bolivia and Chile (2007); second, we observe a reduced percentage of inadequate housing in the borders with Colombia

The Global Border System and Illegal Markets 25

and Brazil, in both cases well below the national averages of their respective years. Finally, it is noteworthy that the average of inadequate housing for the border districts on the border with Ecuador in 2007 is still above the national average for that same year.

The same trend is observed in the averages of the inadequately serviced housing[11] indicator for the border districts. This decreased from 89.93% in the 1981 census to 67.78% in 1993 and finally reached 47.52% in 2007. However, when the indicator is broken down by bordering country, once again, we observe a greater reduction in the southern border.

The low average achieved by the border districts in the 2012 Human Development Index (0.32) compared to the national average (0.5058) is also worth mentioning. Likewise, the average monetary poverty[12] (56.0%) doubles the national average (23.0%). Finally, we can see that the average malnutrition rate[13] (27.20%) is almost ten percentage points higher than the national average (17.5%).

Regular and Irregular Migration

Migration flows are a recurring theme in border studies. Aggregate data on entries to and exits from the national territory have increased steadily over the past two decades from 781,341 entries and 821,649 exits in 1994 to 6,772,749 entries and 6,916,151 exits in 2014. These figures are explained by different phenomena, such as the expansion of tourism at a global level, the establishment of Peru as a tourist destination and the country's economic and political stabilization, among other factors.

Beyond characterizing each area, it is interesting to establish the links between the forms of regular migration and those of an irregular nature. Two cases may allow us to account for this relationship and the way in which migration routes are established. First, there are the cases of regular and irregular migration routes of Haitian nationals. Between 2010 and 2012, the National Migration Authority recorded 9,678 entries and 7,118 departures of Haitian citizens, the highest figures for the flow of Haitians in the last two decades. Out of the total number of Haitian entries, 54.2% came from Panama and 31.41% from Ecuador, while 58.3% left for Brazil and 20.37% for Panama. Despite this figure of regular migration, several researchers (Bernal Carrera 2014; Vásquez et al. 2014; Nieto, 2014) have pointed out the existence of irregular migration routes of Haitian citizens to Brazil. Vásquez et al. (2014) have identified that one of the main routes of irregular entry into Peru is through Huaquillas, on the northern border, to Lima and from there to Cusco or Arequipa, and then on to Puerto Maldonado, and across the border through Iñapari. Carlos Nieto (2014) arrived at similar results, adding that, in addition to Iñapari, Tabatinga, on the triple border of Peru, Brazil, and Colombia, is one of the most important exit points on the migration route of Haitian citizens.

A second example is the migration, in recent years, of Colombian citizens to Chile via Peru. According to Mejía (2012), since the 2008 financial crisis, important changes have taken place in emigration patterns from Colombia. Whereas the main destinations used to be Spain, the United States, or Canada, since the crisis they have shifted to countries like Chile, Italy, or Germany (Mejía 2012). Thus, according to figures from the National Migration Authority, the outflow of Colombian citizens to Chile through the border post of Santa Rosa in Tacna presents a significant increase, especially since 2007, and in 2010 it showed a peak growth of 48.5% over the previous year. However, the entry into the neighboring country is not easy, due to the strict immigration controls that have caused many migrants to remain in Tacna for some time, while they gather enough resources to attempt to cross the border again. This context gives rise to migrant smuggling organizations as well as human trafficking networks (Rivadeneyra 2014).

Works such as Berganza and Purizaga's (2011) have shown that for the case of Peru's northern border, border areas are not just passages for entry or transit to another country. Borderlands also attract national migration and, in cases such as that of Haitian immigrants, may become places of residence – temporary or permanent – for foreigners. In other words, the new dynamics associated with increased flows of people also have socio-spatial repercussions in border areas.

Borders and Illegal Markets

In addition to what has already been discussed, it is necessary to point out the role that borders play in the dynamics of the main illegal markets in the country, which is why drug trafficking and smuggling activities will now be analyzed. It is also interesting to attempt a first reading on the incidence of crime in the border departments.[14] From the information reviewed, it can be stated that illegal markets (in a broad sense) are linked to border areas in at least four ways: (i) in terms of the configuration of circuits, routes, and crossings typical of the illegal market; (ii) as socio-spatial configurations, in which the particularities of the border areas acquire importance as a space for the reproduction and development of activities linked to illegal markets; (iii) as spaces that modify the conditions of vulnerability of the victims, insofar as they incorporate migration as a new axis of reproduction of vulnerability; and (iv) as giving visibility to institutional and organizational arrangements of the border subsystem, which do not depend solely on national or local particularities. Needless to say, each of these dimensions requires a deeper analysis than we can provide in this text. Nevertheless, some relevant clues are offered to guide the discussion on the relationship between borders and illegal markets.

Drug Trafficking

Drug trafficking is the main illegal market on a global scale. What is the role of borders in the processes and dynamics of drug production, distribution, and commercialization? The case of cocaine – that this section focuses on – serves to illustrate this situation. Here, we argue that borders are not only places of passage, but that drug trafficking operates by generating logics of location and reorganization of these areas. In other words, the export of cocaine requires the articulation of actors and places through which the drug is transported and even some of the stages of production that establish cross-border networks or systems.

The first stage of the production and distribution process is linked not only to the cultivation of coca leaves but also to the mobilization of the necessary inputs for their processing. However, the discussion on drug production and trafficking in Peru tends to focus on the issue of coca cultivation and cocaine trafficking, which was accentuated in 2012, when the United Nations Office on Drugs and Crime (UNODC) noted that Peru became, for the first time since records are available, the world's largest producer of coca leaf (UNODC 2013). Out of the total number of hectares under coca cultivation, about 90% is linked to drug trafficking and the remaining 10% is channeled to traditional consumption. This dynamic has not implied a progressive increase in cultivation, which would suggest that eradication figures and the success of alternative crop programs progress differently in Peru than in the world's second largest producer, Colombia. Additionally, changes in terms of productivity of the coca leaf crop (fewer hectares, but higher production) should be taken into account.

The largest coca leaf production is concentrated in the area of the Valley of the Rivers Apurimac, Ene and Mantaro (VRAEM), which includes territory of the departments of Junín, Huancavelica, Cusco, Ayacucho, and Apurimac. Crops in the VRAEM have come to occupy nearly 20,000 hectares, and in recent years, they represent about 30% of cultivated areas nationwide. The valleys of Alto Huallaga and La Convención-Lares are a different case, and their relative importance has decreased. The valleys that have experienced absolute and relative growth are Marañón-Putumayo-Amazonas, Inambari-Tambopata, and Palcazú-Pichis-Pachitea.

Since the early 1980s, the Peruvian state's anti-drug policy has focused on eradicating areas of cultivation with the support of USAID. In the case of coca leaf plantations, the number of hectares eradicated in the 2001–2013 period varied between 9,000 and just over 14,000 in 2012. The departments where the most important coca leaf eradication actions took place were Huánuco, San Martín, and Ucayali, of which the latter is the only one with border districts.[15]

28   *Manuel Dammert G. and Viktor Bensús*

When looking at the places where the main seizures were made, the presence of Lima and Callao stands out, as it is in those departments that the total amount in kilograms of drugs seized reached the first or second highest figure. The drug whose seizure in Lima and Callao was the highest was cocaine hydrochloride, which amounted to 12,000 kilograms in the last year for which data is available (2012), representing about 60% of the total amount of hydrochloride seized in the country. The department of Lima is neither a coca leaf production area nor a land border, so we assume that most of the seizures took place at ports and at the international airport. Consequently, in order to understand the Peruvian border system in relation to drug trafficking, it is of utmost importance to keep in mind that much of its cross-border interconnection takes place by maritime and aerial means.

Another important example of the relevance of air travel as a cross-border connection for drug trade is the valley of the Palcazú-Pichis-Pachitea rivers, between the departments of Huánuco and Pasco. This valley is the most important point of departure by air from the borders, due to its geographical conditions that allow for the existence of an infrastructure in accordance with this mode of transport. These valleys have experienced the highest increase rates in the area occupied by coca in the last five years. The coca paste, which is transported from the Palcazú-Pichis-Pachitea area, is both locally produced and from the VRAEM.

Over the years, coca paste seizures have largely occurred in the department of Ayacucho, followed by different districts. It is noteworthy that, although the amounts seized vary from year to year, as well as the departments in which they take place, large seizures have consistently been made in departments such as Piura, Lambayeque, Arequipa, and Puno. While the first two are on the northern coast of the country, suggesting that coca paste was seized on its way to the northern border or was intended for removal by sea (Piura has major seaports), the other two are departments on the route to the south. The case of Puno is particular, since it supports the most important flows of smuggled goods in the country (see section on contraband). This border dynamic also accommodates the outflow of drugs through Bolivia and is a route to Brazil.

This brief review of the drug production situation and the state's response allows us to identify some relevant points for the analysis of the Peruvian border system. First, Peru stands out for its high production of coca leaf and cocaine products, which are exported mainly to Europe and Asia, as well as to South American countries, such as Bolivia and Brazil. To a lesser extent, production also caters for the domestic market. Interviews with experts identified that the demand for coca paste in Brazil has been increasing in recent years. This has meant establishing routes linking the VRAEM production area, the country's main productive valley, with the southern border area (Puno-Bolivia) and, later, with Brazil as a final destination. Another land route that appears to be

The Global Border System and Illegal Markets   29

important is to the north, toward Ecuador. However, if we limit ourselves to seizure figures, Lima and Callao – as well as other coastal cities – show the importance of sea and air routes for the cross-border interconnection of drug trafficking. Nonetheless, it should not be forgotten that seizures are an indicator of the effectiveness of state control and not necessarily of the characteristics of the distribution routes. Finally, an important aerial means of exporting cocaine are the small airplanes that leave from strategic zones in eastern Peru, of which the Inambari-Tambopata valley represents a paradigmatic case due to its geographical conditions and the persistence of this means of transport for drugs.

Contraband in Peru

In border areas, economic exchanges are particularly relevant, as they articulate different economies (formal, informal, and illegal) based on comparative advantages and complementarity. This situation becomes more complex in the case of smuggling, since the limits of formal, informal, and illegal dynamics cannot be clearly identified. Moreover, there is a major limitation in terms of reliable indicators on this phenomenon. However, it is possible to point out some characteristics of interest for the purposes of this research project on the Peruvian border system.

First, according to article 1 of Law 28008 – Customs Offences Act – smuggling involves both the exit and irregular entry – bypassing the customs administration – of a product into the territories of different countries. The institution in charge of leading the fight against contraband in Peru is the Superintendence of Tax Administration (SUNAT), as stipulated by Law No. 27595 on the creation of the commission for the fight against contraband and customs income fraud of 2001. This commission consists of state institutions, as well as representatives of civil society and business associations. One of its functions is to draw up the national strategic plan to combat contraband and customs income fraud; however, it is SUNAT – through its customs division – that is responsible for monitoring the control of goods, persons, and means. SUNAT's work is carried out both through border control posts at strategic land border points, and at airports and maritime ports.

There is scarce reliable information on contraband. In this context, the studies carried out by SUNAT, which present a description of smuggling by areas, routes, and products sold, are worth mentioning. Based on SUNAT's classification and data obtained from news sources, Table 1.4 provides the following information: (i) differences in terms of products; for example, the southern zone is characterized by the passage of vehicles and artifacts of different kinds, while in the east, illegal logging and mining imply the existence of flows of wood and gold, especially through waterways; (ii) in the northern zone a wide variety of products is illegally traded, but the most relevant case is that of fuel

30 *Manuel Dammert G. and Viktor Bensús*

Table 1.4 Characterization of contraband in Peru

Zone	Main localities	Mode	Main products
North	Tumbes, La Tina, Paita, Salaverry, Chimbote	Land, maritime	Medicines, bedding, clothing, insecticides, fishmeal, cigarettes, footwear, fuel
Lima	Callao, Lima	Maritime, air	Cigars, fuel, computer parts, medicines, gadgets, clothing, used clothing
East	Iquitos, Tarapoto, Pucallpa, Puerto Maldonado	Land, river	Engines and parts, cigars, videotapes, gold, medicine, sugar, illegal logging
South	Puno, Cusco, Arequipa, Ilo, Tacna, Mollendo, Pisco	Land, river	Used clothing, vehicles, clothing, artifacts, cigarettes, footwear, food

Source: SUNAT and newspaper articles

smuggling from Ecuador because of the quantities, the scope – it reaches the city of Chiclayo – and the mode in which the fuel is transported; namely, *culebras* (snakes) – a method that involves transportation in cargo-truck convoys (Prado 2012).

An increase in contraband estimates can also be observed. The highest values are found in Puno, Tacna, and the Northern Zone, respectively. For the two cases that represent the highest figures (both add up to 73% of the total estimated contraband), there is a significant difference. While in the case of the Peruvian-Chilean border, the tariff benefits of the duty-free zone of Iquique have generated comparative advantages that encourage the entry of products that are later resold in Peruvian territory, in the case of the Peruvian-Bolivian border, it is the trade dynamics that activate economic and contraband flows, as well as the topographical characteristics of the Altiplano that facilitate the transport of products by road (Chavarría et al. 2012).

According to SUNAT calculations, the southern border presents the highest incidence of contraband. However, the smuggled good that accounts for the highest figures throughout the country is fuel. Gasoline enters mainly through the northern border, given the comparative advantages provided by the subsidized price of fuels in Ecuador (Prado 2012). According to Prado, middlemen gather the fuel in barrels or plastic bags in border areas and then cross the border in wheelbarrows or in *culebras,* evading border controls.

In addition to differences in product types and volumes, it is possible to distinguish between different modes of transport. Vela (2010) identifies the following: (i) *hormiga* (ant) (small-scale smuggling by camouflaging products in luggage or in the body); (ii) *caleta* (cove) (hiding products in individual vehicles); (iii) *culebra* (snake) (products are transported in a convoy of cargo trucks); (iv) *pampeo* (using alternative routes, often dirt

The Global Border System and Illegal Markets 31

roads, to cross the border); (v) *chacales* (jackals) (hiring customs officials to ensure border crossing; and (vi) *carrusel* (carousel) (repeatedly forging documents to pass border controls). These modes do not operate exclusively but overlap according to the type of goods being transported, their volume, the presence of state control, among other aspects. Moreover, these modalities usually complement each other. In fact, the *carrusel*, *pampeo*, and *culebra* modes are often used to cross the border, whereas the *hormiga* and *caleta* methods tend to be used for distribution within the country.

Regarding the routes, the following should be stressed: to the north, important arrival points are Tumbes and Chiclayo; to the south, the cities of Tacna and Arequipa, as well as the port of Ilo, are important final route points; finally, to the east, the presence of Iquitos stands out on the routes. While it may appear obvious, it is worth noting that most of the routes supply major cities, thus pointing to the demand for these products in larger markets. On these routes, border cities play an important role as nodes for the storage, marketing, and distribution of smuggled goods. These routes also provide a first hint as to how far the influence of the border systems extends. The global scale is commonly associated with the formal import of goods or services; yet these smuggling routes show us global-scale dynamics that occur through localized illegal and informal dynamics.

Smuggling takes on different mechanisms depending on the border area on which it is based: economic complementarity has led to more intense smuggling of fuel from the north; clothing and auto parts from the south; from the east, trafficking of wood from illegal logging or gold from illegal artisanal mining. These exchanges delineate routes, and those commercial routes and people networks get involved in some way or another at different stages in the process.

Incidence of Border Crime

As a final point of analysis, we present information on crime. This analysis requires some qualifications regarding the sources of information. First, the information provided by the various state bodies (police, judiciary, prosecution service, etc.) is unreliable and in many cases contradictory between one institution and another regarding the same crime. Second, it is important to point out that the data produced by these institutions do not register real crime rates, but only show the capacity of the state to collect judicial complaints and register legal proceedings. Thus, there is a significant dark figure in the register of victimization (those cases in which no complaint was presented). This is the case of the figures on which this section is based; namely, the complaints registered by the Peruvian National Police (PNP). Finally, PNP information is found at the departmental level. This means that there is no information by district

32 Manuel Dammert G. and Viktor Bensús

Table 1.5 Peru: Homicide rate by department 2011–2013

Quartile 4		Quartile 3		Quartile 2		Quartile 1	
Tumbes	17.27	Cajamarca	6.22	Cusco	5.41	Ayacucho	3.81
Madre de Dios	15.91	Tacna	6.18	Ica	5.36	Junín	3.61
La Libertad	14.54	Piura	6.16	Lima	5.3	Puno	3.2
Callao	12.05	Arequipa	5.88	Lambayeque	4.85	Apurimac	2.81
San Martin	11.26	Huánuco	5.5	Ucayali	4.38	Moquegua	2.3
Ancash	8.45			Pasco	4.14	Loreto	1.96
Amazonas	7.89					Huancavelica	1.94

Source: Data provided by PNP

or border city, with the exception of the data on homicides between 2011 and 2013, which were also registered by the INEI for the country's main cities. Table 1.5 presents the available information on homicides (2015), grouping the departments by quartiles.[16]

Based on 2015 homicide data, we can make some initial remarks. First, the departments of Q4 exceed the national average in all the years observed, and except for San Martín, which has been reducing its rate, and Amazonas, which has had variable behavior, the other departments have seen their homicide rates increase. Second, the departments in the highest quartile account for more than 50% of the homicides in the observed period. Q2 and Q1 group together the departments that are below the national average. In Q2, only the departments of Lima, Pasco, and Ica have seen a continuous increase in their rates. While Q1 comprises the departments with the lowest homicide rates, which, in many cases have nonetheless regularly increased over the three years observed, the department of Ayacucho stands out as being in constant growth. Finally, the Q3 data are extremely scattered, and since the observation period is noticeably short, no trends can be identified.

The border departments of Tumbes, Madre de Dios, Piura, Puno, and Loreto suffered consecutive increases in the three years observed. Tumbes, which is also the department with the highest rate in the country, saw an extraordinary increase in the homicide rate between 2011 and 2012 (from 4.89 to 21.03). Likewise, Madre de Dios not only shows high rates of homicides but also a rise. While no other border department shows a high rate that has also been increasing, it is important to note that most of the departments have suffered increases in the years observed. A longer period of observation is needed to determine whether these figures represent trends toward increased violence in border areas.

There are other recurring crimes in the border departments, to which a brief reference will be made despite the problems already mentioned regarding data reliability. Among the most frequently reported crimes within this group of departments are injuries, theft, and robbery. However, some departments stand out for exceeding national reporting rates. The case of Tumbes is a good example, since in 2012 it registered rates of theft (651.98) and robbery (428.96) that are four and even five times higher than those of the neighboring departments. Thefts in Tacna (297.65) and, especially, in Madre de Dios (499.06) also surpassed the national average in 2012.

Except for Puno, the rate of complaints of violence against sexual freedom[17] has been high in all the departments observed. In fact, in most of them an upward trend in the figures is identified. Yet, as explained at the beginning of this section, this may be due to the improved police capacity to record the occurrence of crimes, rather than to a significant increase in them. However, there is a disturbing reality in the country, which seems to have a particularly strong presence in border areas; namely, the high incidence of rape or sexual violence, whose main victims are women. For example, in 2012, Madre de Dios (53.28), Piura (75.24), Tacna (47.43), and Tumbes (51.26) exceeded the national rate (29.17) of reports of this crime.

It is commonly assumed that activities such as drug trafficking, mining, illegal logging, and other phenomena associated with violence in global border systems involve related crimes that increase violence in border areas. While this first review does not allow for the establishment of such links, it does identify the presence of high rates of violence in some departments linked to border systems, especially Tumbes and Madre de Dios, whose homicide rates are the highest at the national level. Thus, homicides, robberies, injuries, and violence against sexual freedom are the most frequently reported crimes, and all of them entail a high degree of physical violence. This calls for further analysis of the links between illegal economies and the degree of violence in border areas.

Final Notes

Based on the previous discussion, it is now possible to suggest a series of analytical lines to guide further research on border systems and their relationship with illegal markets. First, the approach to the border understood as a territorial limit and a limit to state action must be overcome in order to give way to a view that manages to envisage the dimensions and characteristics of borders as a locally articulated global system with a specific socio-spatial configuration. It is necessary to generate cross-cutting information on border spaces and propose a relational view thereof. This article is a first descriptive effort toward this goal.

Second, there are several limitations to the information available to address borders as a system. For one thing, academic and institutional research is not abundant, which means that there are limited sources of information and debate. For another thing, information on crimes associated with global border systems has two restrictions: (i) most of it is provided at the departmental level, this prevents having specific information for the local level, and (ii) the information on crimes provided by

34 *Manuel Dammert G. and Viktor Bensús*

the different institutions of the Peruvian state is not completely reliable. It is often the case that for the same crime there are different figures, and moreover, these are based on official reports, which conceal a dark figure for victimization. Finally, it should be noted that there is a lack of information on the economic dynamics in border areas and their importance as nodes and points of passage relevant to the national economy.

Third, a fundamental question requires further attention: what is the particularity of border areas? This question involves two issues. On the one hand, identifying and discussing the specificities on demographic, social, and economic terms. On the other hand, problematizing the possibility of speaking of "border violence" as a type of dynamic linked to particular kinds of criminality and violence. There are several indicators that allow us to raise this hypothesis (existence of border violence). However, the task of differentiating the characteristics and effects of the routes and dynamics of illegal markets and their link to the border is still pending.

Fourth, the information reviewed makes it possible to refine the question posed at the beginning of this chapter. Borders require analysis at different scales that allows for both the observation of structural and cross-cutting characteristics, and an account of their heterogeneity. Therefore, analyzing aggregate information requires accepting the limitations of this type of task. Furthermore, as proposed in one of the objectives of the general project that this chapter is part of, it is necessary to advance in the study of borders from a perspective that is not centered on the territory of the state. Approaching a border space only from the characteristics of a single state is a partial effort insofar as no information is provided on the set of interrelations with the existing dynamics "on the other side." Addressing border dynamics from a national perspective generates a series of analytical drawbacks and obstacles, given that, by its very definition, the border involves a relationship of more than one national territorial space.

Finally, it is necessary to assume that borders have a complementary (not a unidirectional) relationship with the characteristics of each illegal market. In other words, the characteristics adopted by the border system have a double link to these illegal markets, with the existing infrastructure and the role of state actors. Ultimately, the relationships that exist between illegal markets remain to be established. It would be wrong to assume that they operate in isolation; on the contrary, there is a set of dynamics that cross them, making the borders and the border system privileged research sites.

Notes

1. This document is a product of the International Project on Borders and Illegal Markets led by IDRC and FLACSO-Ecuador, which involves studies in eight countries. The case of Peru was researched by CISEPA-PUCP,

The Global Border System and Illegal Markets 35

and a team formed by Manuel Dammert Guardia, Viktor Bensús, Katherine Sarmiento, and Guillermo Prieto. The document was prepared as a first product; therefore, its reach is still limited.

2. To this date, no agreement has been signed to formalize the delimitation of the BIZ between the two countries.
3. In Peru, districts are political-administrative units of the sub-national government. Working with the district scale as a border-analysis scale has different limitations due among other things, to the heterogeneity of the districts' characteristics and because not all districts have the same relationship with the border. Nonetheless, we believe it is pertinent to make this first description in order to elucidate some of the border's main characteristics.
4. National Population and Housing Censuses of 1981, 1993, and 2007, National Institute of Statistics and Informatics (INEI).
5. The data presented here, especially for the intercensal period of 1981 and 1993, has the limitation that during this period, the subnational political delimitation was modified, a reason that made it impossible to find data for 14 border districts present in the 1993 subnational demarcation.
6. In the case of the population without education, it was not possible to corroborate the data, since the INEI uses two different data, one in the REDATAM and the other in its statistical tables.
7. In the case of university education, the distinction between completed and unfinished university education was ignored, and both categories were combined into one.
8. In the case of the native language, it was not possible to calculate the indicator for 1981, since it was not stated in the same way as in the questionnaires of the following two population and housing censuses.
9. "Inadequate housing" is defined as housing that has mat walls and/or a dirt floor.
10. In the case of the inadequate housing indicator, the impossibility of calculating the indicator for the 1981 census is added, since this information is not available in the electronic database of the Instituto Nacional de Estadística e Informática (INEI) (National Institute of Statistics and TICs).
11. 1993 census: this consists of households whose water supply is by truck/tanker; river, ditch, spring or other; or whose toilet facilities are in the "over ditch/channel" or "no toilet facilities" categories. For the 2007 census, it is composed of households whose water supply is by truck/tanker, river, ditch, spring or other; or whose toilet facilities are composed of the categories "river, ditch or canal" or "no toilet facilities."
12. Source: InfoMIDIS. Poverty at the departmental level: ENAHO 2013-INEI. At the provincial and district level: INEI 2009 estimates.
13. Source: InfoMIDIS. Chronic Childhood Malnutrition (WHO standard) at Departmental level: DHS 2012-2013-INEI. At the provincial and district level: INEI 2009 estimates.
14. The departments are an intermediate political-administrative division of the Peruvian state; they have a governor and are key elements in the decentralization process, as they are responsible for managing education, health, and other services in their territory.
15. Information taken from the Policía Nacional del Perú (PNP) yearbooks.
16. The use of the arithmetic mean was chosen, as this was a ratio between the number of observations (years) and the values (rates), which allowed a standardization for the classification into groups of departments, in addition to providing a further level of analysis by allowing comparison with the national arithmetic mean and the cumulative percentage.

36 *Manuel Dammert G. and Viktor Bensús*

17. These include rape, acts of indecency and the crime of seduction. The latter refers to the use of deception to attack the sexual freedom, mainly of adolescents and children.

References

Angulo, Juan. 1927. *Historia de los límites del Perú*. Lima: Imprenta de la Intendencia General de Guerra.

Aramburú, Carlos. 1980. "Las migraciones a las zonas de colonización de la Selva Peruana: Perspectivas y avances." Paper presented at FLACSO-INANDEP, Buenos Aires.

Berganza, Isabel and Mauricio Cerna. 2011. *Dinámicas migratorias en la frontera Perú-Chile: Arica, Tacna e Iquique*. Lima: UARM.

Berganza, Isabel and Judith Purizaga. 2011. *Migración y desarrollo. Diagnóstico de las migraciones en la zona norte de Perú. Regiones de Tumbes, Piura, Cajamarca y Lambayeque*. Lima: UARM.

Bernal, Raúl. 1986. "Alternativas para una integración fronteriza entre Arica, Tacna y Oruro." *Integración Latinoamericana* 11 (118), 57–64.

Bernal Carrera, Gabriela. 2014. "¿Por qué migrar? Algunos apuntes sobre las viejas y nuevas heridas de Haití". In *La migración haitiana hacia Brasil: características, oportunidades y desafíos*, edited by OIM 33-50. Cuadernos Migratorios 6. Buenos Aires: Organización Internacional para las Migraciones-Oficina Regional para América del Sur.

Bijsterbosch, Erik. 2007. "Peruvian cross border commuters in the Chilean-Peruvian border region." Master's dissertation. Nijmegen: Radboud University.

Bocchio Rejas, Luis. 1978. *Los tacneños y el corredor para Bolivia*. Lima: Editorial Minerva.

Bolognesi-Drosdoff, María Cecilia. 1986. "Análisis y clasificación tipológica de casos de integración fronteriza." *Integración Latinoamericana* 11 (118), 13–30.

Calderón, Félix. 2000. *El tratado de 1929. La otra historia*. Lima: Fondo Editorial del Congreso del Perú.

Calderón Cousiño, Adolfo. 1919. *Breve historia diplomática de las relaciones chileno-peruanas 1819–1879*. Santiago: Empresa ZigZag.

Cano, Washington. 1925. *Historia de los límites del Perú: dedicada a los alumnos de institución media*. Arequipa: Quiroz Perea Typography.

Castillo, Rodolfo. 2011. "Apoyo a la integración urbana y regional de la zona fronteriza del Eje Vial N° 1 Piura-Guayaquil: una aproximación desde la perspectiva binacional y sostenible." *Espacio y Desarrollo* 23, 31–46.

Chavarría, Cindy, Carlos Casquero, and Dionel Martínez. 2012. "Contrabando: importancia en la región trinacional frente a la estructura espacial." *Espacio y Desarrollo* 24, 75–88.

Chiarella, Roberto. 2005. "¿Conurbación o ciudad internacional? Gestión urbana e impactos en el territorio Iñapari-Assis Brasil-Bolpebra." *Espacio y Desarrollo* 17, 69–88.

——— 2011. "Redes y territorio: La iniciativa IIRSA en foco." *Espacio y Desarrollo*, 23, 5–29.

Dilla, Haroldo and Sobeida Cedano. 2005. "De problemas y oportunidades: intermediación urbana fronteriza en República Dominicana." *Revista Mexicana de Sociología*, 67, 1, 99–129.

The Global Border System and Illegal Markets 37

Giménez Béliveau, Verónica. 2011. "La triple frontera y sus representaciones. Políticos y funcionarios piensan la frontera." *Frontera Norte* 23 (46), 7–34.

González Miranda, Sergio. 2006. "Densidad, integración y conflicto en la triple frontera." In *La integración y el desarrollo social fronterizo 1*. Bogotá: Convenio Andrés Bello.

Grisales, Germán. 2005. "Amerita la frontera de Colombia, Perú y Brasil una zona de integración trinacional?" *Aldea Mundo*, 18, 54–61.

Hocquenghem, Anne Marie. 2009. "La región fronteriza peruano-ecuatoriana y el proceso de globalización." *Si Somos Americanos. Revista de Estudios Tranfronterizos* 9 (2), 101–116.

Hocquenghem, Anne Marie and Etienne Durt. 2002. "Integración y desarrollo de la región fronteriza peruano-ecuatoriana: entre el discurso y la realidad, una visión local." *Bulletin de l'Institut Français d'Études Andines* 31 (1), 39–99.

INEI. 1993. IX Censo de población y IV de vivienda.

—— 2007. X Censo de población y V de vivienda.

Mejía Ochoa, William. 2012. "Colombia y las migraciones internaionales. Evolución reciente y panorama actual a partir de las cifras." *Revista Internacional de Mobilidade Humana*, 39, 185–210.

Meza, Nilo. 2005. "Zonas de integración fronteriza (ZIF) Perú-Bolivia una experiencia a considerar." *Aldea Mundo*, 18, 36–43.

Ministerio de Relaciones Exteriores (MRE). 2006. *Plan Binacional de Desarrollo de la Región Fronteriza Perú-Ecuador*. Lima: MRE.

—— 2012. *Desarrollo e Integración Fronteriza*. Lima: MRE.

Nieto, Carlos. 2014. *Migración haitiana a Brasil. Redes migratorias y espacio social transnacional*. Buenos Aires: CLACSO.

Novoa, Zaniel. 1993. "La cuenca binacional de Madre de Dios: De la franja pionera a la integración fronteriza." *Espacio y Desarrollo*, 5, 117–157.

Oficina de las Naciones Unidas Contra la Droga y el Delito (UNODC). 2013. *Perú Monitoreo de Cultivos de Coca 2012*. Lima: UNODC.

Organización Internacional para las Migraciones. 2012. *Gestión Fronteriza Integral en la Subregión Andina Módulo 1 - Gestión fronteriza*. Lima: OIM.

Podestá, Juan. 2005. "Globalización y regiones fronterizas: notas a partir del análisis de la región de Tarapacá." *Revista de Ciencias Sociales*, 15, 4–24.

Pons, Gustavo. 1962. *Las fronteras del Perú (historia de los límites)*. Lima: Ediciones del Colegio San Julián.

Porras Barrenechea, Raúl. 1926. *Historia de los límites del Perú: texto dictado a los alumnos del Colegio Anglo-Peruano de Lima, conforme al programa oficial*. Lima: Libr. Francesa Científica: E. Rosay.

Prado, Francisco. 2012. "Los culebrones de la noche: estudio antropológico del comercio informal de combustible en Tumbes." *Ciencia y Desarrollo* 15 (2), 87–96.

Ramírez, Socorro. 2009. "Las Zonas de Integración Fronteriza de la Comunidad Andina. Comparación de sus alcances." *Estudios Políticos*, 32, 135–169.

Rivadeneyra, Dánae. 2014. "Esclavitud moderna en Madre de Dios" (Video). INFOS. http://utero.pe/2014/03/26/esta-es-la-mineria-informal-esclavitud-sexual-moderna-en-madre-de-dios/. Accessed on April 12, 2016.

Sistema Económico Latinoamericano y del Caribe (SELA). 2011. *La integración fronteriza en el marco del proceso de convergencia de América Latina y El Caribe*. Caracas: SELA.

38 *Manuel Dammert G. and Viktor Bensús*

Superintendencia Nacional de Migraciones. https://www.migraciones.gob.pe/

Ullman, Edward L. 1956. "The role of transportation and the bases for interactions." In *Man's role in changing the face of the Earth*, edited by William L. Thomas, 862–882. Chicago: University of Chicago Press.

Valcuende del Río, José María. 2008. "Fronteras y Límites: El caso de la Triple Frontera Brasil, Perú y Bolivia." *Ponto e Vírgula* 3 (1), 36–57.

Vásquez, Tania, Érika Busse, and Lorena Izaguirre. 2014. "La migración haitiana en Perú y su tránsito hacia Brasil." *La migración haitiana hacia Brasil: características, oportunidades y desafíos. Cuadernos Migratorios*, 6, 83–106.

Vela, Lindon. 2010. "El Contrabando y sus Rutas en América Latina y en el Perú, una visión desde el Norte del Perú, con énfasis en productos de Tabaco." http://web.ua.es/es/giecryal/documentos/contrabando-tabaco.pdf?noCache= 1354883302412. Accessed on November 14, 2014.

2 Bolivia

The Tensions, Challenges, and Prospects of the Border Subsystem

José Blanes Jiménez

As a landlocked country and exporter of raw materials, Bolivia has always depended on the fluidity of its borders with its neighbors. However, in recent decades, Bolivia's border areas have encountered new challenges as the country no longer depends solely on the trade flowing through them. Today, the country is deeply involved in a broad and complex new map of trade flows to and from distant borders. Internally, while these changes call for new policies for the affected border areas and their inhabitants, they also have a much wider impact on the living conditions of people in cities and rural areas, who are also being increasingly affected. The security of citizens is now endangered by new and quite different enemies than those that challenged national security in the past.

Bolivia's participation in global networks is ever more related to illegal markets, with severe consequences for the economy, the state, and the citizens' lives. The advance of the informal economy translates into institutional weaknesses, which affect many aspects of the country's life and result in increasing violence and deteriorating security. In their fight for territory, drug trafficking and contraband, which are vehicles of globalization, connect distant urban areas, with dire consequences for the lives of ordinary citizens.

This study is a preliminary attempt at addressing several of the dimensions that redefine the concept of borders in Bolivia today. First, the study highlights the key historical aspects of the constitution of Bolivia's border areas; second, it reviews the literature consulted on relevant issues for this approach to borders; third, the paper examines the most important national policies that affect border areas and elaborates on the particularities of each of such areas. Finally, the main scenarios that require future attention for the development and implementation of border policies are discussed.

The Evolution of Bolivia's Borders

The 6,834-kilometer-long border that connects Bolivia to its five neighbors and their respective economic and political regimes defines the

DOI: 10.4324/9781003204299-5

40 *José Blanes Jiménez*

conditions for local, regional, and global trade flows. The asymmetries of each stretch of the border present the country with different scenarios that define challenges for national and local policies.

Three processes illustrate the evolution of Bolivia's borders up to the present time: the first one (1825–1936), which is also the foundational one, took place from the declaration of independence to the Chaco War and is characterized by the dispute for natural resources on the border and the consolidation of the final boundaries with adjacent countries. A second process – which partly overlaps with the first one, from 1876 to 1970 – is the adaptation of borders and the structuring of land communication networks for the purposes of export and migration. The third one is still ongoing and overlaps with the second phase. It corresponds to the period from the late 1940s to the present day and is characterized by the transformation and adaptation of border operations in the context of globalization and the resulting increase in trade flows, the movement of persons and, above all, the growing operation of illegal markets.

Struggles for Territory and Natural Resources

On August 6, 1825, Bolivia, with a surface area twice as large as its current one, began a process of consolidation of its physical borders through successive disputes with her neighbors over forest and mineral resources. From the 2,363,769 square kilometers it held at independence, Bolivia lost 1,265,188 square kilometers; that is slightly more than half the original territory.

In the War of the Pacific, which originated with the Chilean expansion into Peru and Bolivia over the exploitation of saltpeter and guano, Bolivia lost 120,000 square kilometers and, following the signing of the Treaty of 1904, it also lost its access to the sea. After the Acre War, through the 1903 Treaty of Petrópolis, 490,430 square kilometers of territory rich in products such as rubber were ceded to Brazil. Treaties signed in 1880 and 1925 granted Argentina 170,758 square kilometers of the Central Chaco territory, while the 1902 and 1909 boundary agreements relinquished to Peru 250,000 square kilometers of a cinchona (quinine) and Brazil-nut producing area. During the Great Depression, after the Chaco War (1932–1935), also known as the "Oil War," Bolivia surrendered 234,000 square kilometers to Paraguay, securing, however, a territory that contains the richest gas deposits in the area (Klein 1982, 12–14; Mesa et al. 1988, 539–555).

Border Adaptation for the Export of Minerals from the West and Rubber from the East

Concurrently with the consolidation of its borders, in the last two decades of the nineteenth century, Bolivia developed new transport links aimed at connecting the country to ports on the Pacific coast for the export of minerals, as well as to ports on the Paraná River for the export of tropical products. These two independent overland networks that communicated Bolivia with the rest of the world were consolidated in the first decades of the twentieth century, but remained disconnected until the 1950s. This had an important influence on territorial development, as well as on the diversification of production during the 1940s (Gómez Zubieta 2006, 9–23).

A route along the Paraná River on the border between Bolivia and Brazil, for the extraction of rubber from the eastern Amazon, was initially projected toward Buenos Aires from the port complex of Puerto Suárez, Puerto Aguirre, and Puerto Quijarro, but in reality, the most viable route was consolidated overland by crossing the Chaco into Argentina. The river ports might have further developed had it not been for the expectations aroused by the signing of the treaty with Chile in 1904. Since then, they have lived in the hope of one day taking advantage of their position on the inter-oceanic corridor between the Atlantic port of Santos in Brazil and the Pacific ports of Chile and Peru.

During this period, the railway was the structuring engine for the west of the country and was organized to export minerals, the country's main export, to the Pacific through Chile and Peru. The railroads were, in fact, the main instrument of Bolivia's extractive economy and mono-export dependence. The same criterion was applied to the expansion of roads in the west, while communications with the eastern borders remained neglected and forgotten for several decades.

With no connection between them, the eastern and western networks separately structured border trade in the early twentieth century, giving rise to today's more diversified and complex system. In the 1940s, road communication was established between Cochabamba and Santa Cruz, linking both systems, then linking Beni, and a few years later, Pando. In 1972, the first paved road connecting the cities of Cochabamba and Santa Cruz was built, thus consolidating the country's so-called "central axis" (Blanes and Calderón 2003, 167–223). From then onward, despite Bolivia's being until recently one of the countries with the lowest rate of communications network densification in the region, border zones developed rapidly, connecting any point in the country with global trade, through Brazil, Paraguay, Argentina, Chile, and Peru.

The Global Border System and Illegal Markets

In the early 1970s, supported by the Latin American and Caribbean Institute for Economic and Social Planning (ILPES), Bolivia began to define development policies that are remembered as a commendable effort, embodied in a large number of documents, including the *Estrategia Socio-Económica del Desarrollo 1971–1991* (Socio-Economic Strategy for Development 1971–1991), drawn up by a group of young intellectuals who

42 *José Blanes Jiménez*

reflected on a possible path to import substitution (Bolivia 1977).[1] Due to their weakness, import substitution policies did not succeed in transforming the economic model, and Bolivia continues to be an exporter of raw materials. Agriculture and livestock farming have attained relative self-sufficiency and several agricultural products are exported from the east of the country. Meanwhile, in the west, where food production is peasant-based, there is a growing trend to import food for daily consumption from neighboring countries, according to the Bolivian Institute of Foreign Trade (IBCE). This represents "a step backwards" in the attainment of the food sovereignty ideal.

It was in this context of a highly extroverted economy, with growing dependence on industrialized products, that the main characteristics of the Bolivian border subsystem were configured. The flows that articulate the country with the region are in constant flux, defining the functions of the border points, which, in turn, are very sensitive to factors such as monetary policies, productivity differences, and legal aspects. As Carrión (2014) has pointed out, these are the main factors in the complementary asymmetries of borders.

In recent decades, commercial trade has contributed the most to the fluidity of borders, bringing together increasingly remote points in the interior of the country with the world markets of Europe, the United States, and Asia. Cross-border trade is the core of the new border subsystem through which Bolivia has joined the global system (Ferrufino 2015, 12–16).

Another important issue regarding the border system is migration flows from Bolivia to neighboring countries, particularly Brazil and Argentina, which combine temporary and permanent migration and have structured the border routes for decades (Hinojosa 2008, 5). Since the mid-twentieth century, Bolivian workers have settled in territories near the border areas, taking advantage of the benefits and opportunities offered by nearby zones, such as northern Argentina, as well as Buenos Aires itself. For the last 20 years, migration flows have, nonetheless, gone beyond the traditional destinations of Buenos Aires and Sao Paulo and have headed to Spain, Italy, and the United States, bringing with them Bolivian workers' expertise in construction and agriculture. The magnitude of this migration is such that the Bolivians of Sao Paulo and Buenos Aires together would add up to the equivalent of the population of Bolivia's main city.

Migration is becoming more global, while more artifacts of globalization emerge each day. Migrant smuggling and human trafficking blend in with them (Hinojosa 2008, 2–5). Border trade and migration are, then, two sectors that generate important changes in the character of borders which were once territorial outpost and have now become part of a large global system.

Due to their volume and characteristics, illegal markets are an engine for transformation that molds the functions of the physical borders in their adaptation to the global system. This has a significant impact on the country's economy, which finds itself challenged in a variety of areas by these changes in the ways that the borders function.

A Review of the Literature on the Bolivian Border System

Academic output largely reflects the changes in the configuration of Bolivia's borders with its five neighboring countries as already outlined above, as well as the most important features of the border trade through which Bolivia partakes in the global border system. Although it is uneven over time, this production incorporates various genres, notably diplomatic documents, novels, chronicles, and newspaper columns.

The review of this literature reveals a transition from the primacy of border sites that only link Bolivia and its neighbors, to a situation in which Bolivia inserts itself into globalization through the flows of goods and relationships that make up the complex Bolivian border system. The flows generated by both the illegal and informal markets, among which contraband and drug trafficking stand out, have gained a very prominent place in the literature of the last decades.

During the stage of territorial consolidation and definition of border sites, from independence until the end of the twentieth century, much of the work focused on the study of the limits with neighboring countries from a geopolitical and economic perspective. The texts on Bolivia's general history describe the circumstances under which the country's borders were consolidated, including wars, loss of territory, and active foreign policy. Thus, until the mid-twentieth century, these texts highlight the plunder by neighboring countries, followed by three decades of extractive activities, such as mining and rubber production, and interest in the Chaco War (1932–1935) (Klein 1982; Mesa et al. 1988; Vásquez 1990; Valencia Vega 2000; Felman Velarde 1967).

Since the mid-twentieth century, the construction of road infrastructure and the consolidation of railways have defined borders as the places where the extraction of raw materials connects to the foreign market. Nowadays, these places have become the main channels for the flows of globalization (Blanes et al. 2003; Villegas Nava 2013). The memory of territorial losses in the Chaco War, which is still powerful, has kept alive the concept of state security in the definition of border issues and the primacy of the nation-state as a central and almost exclusive actor in border discourse. Today, after more than 20 years of political and administrative decentralization, national policies still assign to the central government the role of guardian of resources against external predators (ADEMAF 2015).

44   *José Blanes Jiménez*

The catharsis that the Chaco War represented – which mobilized all social sectors, but particularly peasants and indigenous people – had a strong impact on the collective consciousness in the face of a country that was territorially, socially, and ethnically disjointed. The image of the borders acquired the sense of a critical scenario for the economy, politics, and culture, demanding transcendental changes that led to various stages of nationalism. Its first impact was the transition from the old liberal and conservative parties to the nationalist, indigenist, and revolutionary ones. A sort of social re-founding of the country was set in motion (Richard 2008), which led to a vast literary production, especially of novels, about the war and its consequences for the country. Some of these outstanding works are *Aluvión de fuego* (*Barrage of Fire*) (Cerruto 1935) and *El pozo* (*The Well*) (Céspedes 1936). An extensive systematization of this production can be found in Siles Salinas (1969).

The War of the Pacific and the subsequent treaties led to changing concepts of borders, resulting in today's relational one. While Bolivian demands for access to the sea revolve around physical territory, their content is more closely related to Castell's notion of points of flows (Carrión 2014; Castells 2001), in that they claim direct access to trade in the Pacific. Being landlocked is a great disadvantage in a globalized world, especially given the long distances involved and increasing volumes of trade. The prevalence of the claim to the sea in Bolivia's politics is due to the notion that the loss of maritime status is very important in the current scenario of global trade.

The literature produced over a century has fueled foreign policy proposals without precedent in the history of the republic and, above all, an imagery of Bolivia's relations with Chile and the rest of the world. *El libro del mar* (*The Book of the Sea*) (Estado Plurinacional de Bolivia 2014) summarizes more than 100 years of construction of socio-political imagery and is now a means of internal and external socialization about Bolivia and the sea. Leaving aside the challenge to the Treaty of 1904, concerned with geographical limits, Bolivia's demand before the International Court of Justice, which, for the first time, has brought together all former presidents, former foreign ministers, and political personalities, highlights the significance of globalization of trade flows. Bolivia is now resorting to the right to continue the dialogue with Chile, which has promised Bolivia a way out to the Pacific on no less than 48 occasions.

Despite the primacy of the sea as a topic, Bolivia's rich literature on relations with neighboring countries is not limited to the sea. The main focus of Bolivian foreign policy with Chile, Peru, Argentina, and Brazil is, in fact, the history of border delimitation (Abecia Baldivieso 1979; Fernández Saavedra 2013; Mercado Moreyra 1972; Ministerio de Relaciones Exteriores 2004; Vásquez 1990).

The issue of Bolivia's communication with the Atlantic by waterway is still very important today, as it seeks to address the projection of the country's eastern borders toward that ocean. The presence of Asian, particularly Chinese, interests in the continent renders the projected inter-oceanic corridor strategically important, opening up the possibility of exploiting the largest iron deposits in the region in Bolivia, as well as for the transport of soybeans from Bolivia and neighboring countries through the Pacific ports. The Initiative for the Integration of Regional Infrastructure in South America (IIRSA) and continental integration programs have produced a wide range of literature for national political debate, as have the integration proposals and programs put forth by international organizations (Carbone and Frutos 2014; Gómez García 1997; Villegas Nava 2013).

The border issue has also been approached in relation to the state's territorial policies. During the last 20 years, Bolivia's decentralized territorial management introduced new perspectives that implicitly touch on the border issue, insofar as administrative decentralization generated new relations between the central government and the municipalities and regions (Blanes 1989; FES-ILDIS 2004; Urenda 2007; Quiroga 2003). Because of the municipalization of the country, which began in 1994, almost half of Bolivia's territory is now composed of border municipalities and eight out of the nine departments have international borders. Despite this, there is not much literature on Bolivia's decentralized border areas (Campero 2012).

While border sites have constantly changed, as demanded by the dynamics of global trade, public policies have not continuously moved in the same direction. The last 20 years have seen setbacks regarding the decentralization law. Trapped by the return of centralism, border territories are now struggling to adapt border conditions to the advances of globalization (Galindo 2013).

The functioning of illegal markets has generated a series of scenarios such as large-scale contraband, drug trafficking, corruption, and the informalization of society. Critical panoramas have emerged in specific locations, as well as generational and gender issues (Campero 2012; Miranda 2016; Miranda and Agramont 2015). Studies on scenarios, however, can only provide a general overview of working hypotheses. Among the texts dedicated to critical violence scenarios are those that address drug trafficking and contraband, phenomena that emerge at the borders, some of which have begun to appear as hot spots (Courtis 2010; Miranda 2016). Works on the following topics stand out:

- Coca leaf production, eradication, and drug seizures, especially the annual monitoring reports by UNODC (2014) and CONALTID (2014a and 2014b)
- Corridors (PIE 2012); organized crime (Campero 2011 and 2014); contraband (CEPB 2009; Ferrufino 2015; Jemio 2013; Vidaurre Andrade 2005)

46 *José Blanes Jiménez*

- Customs evasion on imports (Bonilla 2014)
- The conditions of informality (Valencia and Alcides Casas 1998)
- The business of illicit gold production and export (Valencia 2015)

National Policies and Borders

The border conundrum points to major deficiencies in national policies, with difficulties for implementation due to the absence of adequate institutions in the local context. Bolivia currently requires attention in three areas of national policy, with correspondingly efficient mechanisms: contraband, drug trafficking, and money laundering. Due to their enormous complexity, changing character, and the fields of conflict they generate, these issues require national – albeit not necessarily centralist – policies, that respond to the problems of national development while having high levels of acceptance and legitimacy.

Border Economy and Illegal Markets

The structure, dimensions, and management of border economic flows produce an intricate local system, in which the legal interacts with both the illegal and the criminal; complex bureaucracies that in practice interact with corruption; abundant informal labor, and officials who are experts in international business. Customs activities, by definition temporary, specific, and transitory, evolve continuously and their managers have little interest in administrative institutionalization. Borders are a laboratory of informality, not only because of the way labor is organized, but also because the predominant type of business is based on the daily routine of using skills for evasion and exploitation of occasional advantages.

In border areas, especially in the three border posts between Bolivia and Argentina, a large sector of informal workers has emerged during the last decades and is possibly the most stable "institution" in those territories. These workers survive in the market under conditions of low reproduction of their labor force while evading public market regulations. This worker pool is a functional link in the chain of informality: shippers, *bagayeros* (smugglers), informants, contacts of key officials.

The economic growth cycle (2006–2013) had an important impact on the development of border areas, leading to the multiplication of clandestine border-crossing points. Imports rose from \$2.02 billion at the beginning of the century, to \$9.353 billion by the end of 2013, with an accumulated growth of 363% (2000–2013). The largest component corresponds to industrial supplies (\$2.735 billion as of December 2013), followed by motor vehicles for transporting personnel and agricultural machinery. Another group was composed of fuels (\$1.237 billion),

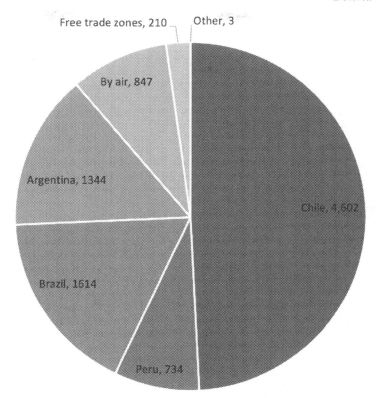

Figure 2.1 Bolivia: Imports by Bordering Country in USD during 2013
Source: INE, Ferrufino (2015)
Graph by the author

followed by food, beverages, consumer durables, appliances, and electronics. This growth in the external economy followed traditional routes and border specialization, strengthening, and deepening some of the differences (Ferrufino 2015, 14–16).

Figure 2.1 shows the hierarchy of border areas according to the value of legal imports. First, Chile's borders, through which goods of Chilean origin enter (12%), but mostly overseas products that are distributed from the Iquique Free Zone (Zofri). Brazil is the second origin, Argentina the third and finally Peru. These ports of entry and exit are fundamental to understanding Bolivia's insertion into the regional and global border system.

Contraband imports follow the same routes as legal imports and, according to estimates based on the analysis of bank financing, the goods in highest demand are those related to the real estate bubble, new and used cars, liquor, and electronic products. Import of these goods grew

48 *José Blanes Jiménez*

exponentially, from a total of $331 million in 2000 to $2.114 billion in 2013. Of the total for the period, $7.529 billion corresponded to Iquique's Free Zone, $1.029 billion to Chile, and $2.966 billion to Brazil. It is estimated that in 2013, 23% of all imports were smuggled and 70% entered through the Chilean border. In other words, the informal economy shares the legal routes and competes with legal trade by taking advantage of informality (Ferrufino 2015, 14–16). To these legal routes that pass-through control mechanisms, multiple border crossings without control, generally close to formal border posts, must be added.[2]

The export sector, especially the traditional one composed of minerals and gas, experienced a boom between 2005 and 2013, as did the eastern agro-industry, particularly the oilseed sector, and along with them, drug trafficking and illegal gold exports. Of the latter, only a small amount is recorded as national production (Valencia 2015, 33–39; Poveda et al. 2015a, 56–62; Poveda et al. 2015b, 65). The total export value increased from $1.042 billion in 1999 to $9.114 billion in 2011 and almost $11 billion in 2012. Hydrocarbons and minerals were the products that experienced the greatest growth (Fundación Milenio 2013).[3]

The GDP share of drug trafficking has declined over the last two decades, mainly due to the economy's growth. In the 1980s it reached over 50% of GDP (Blanes 1989, 135; 1990, 153). At the time, Bolivia was a small and undiversified economy. In recent years, the country's economic base has become larger but, although the percentage share of drug trafficking is lower, its real impact is greater.[4]

Coca leaf production has remained stable over the last decades, despite official reduction figures. Cocaine extraction has benefited from the technological revolution, as new solvents and release agents are now used, as well as simple devices such as blenders, washing machines, and microwave ovens. According to official figures, between 2010 and 2014, seizures of cocaine paste increased, and seizures of cocaine hydrochloride decreased, while the destruction of makeshift laboratories to produce both paste and hydrochloride increased.

Official figures state that drug trafficking contributes between $300 and $700 million to the economy, although, according to a former government minister, the real sum is around $2 billion.[5] This sum represents a large amount to be absorbed by the Bolivian economy, whether legally or illegally. Nevertheless, this volume does not signify such high handling costs as when it crosses US or European borders. It is easily handled locally by cartels, emissaries, and medium and small-capacity gangs. It is also easier to transit through Bolivia's borders because of their enormous institutional permeability and permissibility. Larger volumes of drugs do not tend to cross land borders; much of Bolivia's cocaine, along with Peru's, is transported by air.

The country's participation in the value chain of the coca-cocaine complex is enormous, if measured by its impact on the economy, although it is small in relation to the global drug-trafficking system. However, in relation to the border subsystem and the functioning of illegal markets, Bolivia is very important, not only because of the production volumes, or because it is a transit country, but also because of the high "efficiency" that institutional informality allows.

Institutional permeability, the development of low-level gangs for drug manufacturing, storage, transportation, etc., make Bolivia an important hub in the global border system. The widespread dominance of informal networks makes it easy to establish the operation of routes into Brazil and Argentina as important destinations, as well as departure routes to distant points in Europe and Asia. Bolivia has also achieved a reputation for the purity of its hydrochloride due to high quality control of Colombian chemicals.

Gold contraband is another illegal export sector that, alongside drug trafficking, reflects the importance of the illegal economy and its impacts on Bolivia's borders, as well as the routes through which Bolivia is incorporated into the flows to the United States (Ferrufino 2015, 18). The northern Bolivia-Peru border is where the main exchange and complementarity between the cocaine and gold businesses take place. The implications of these exports for the informal-illegal economy are easy to fathom, even though drug traffickers and gold smugglers are increasingly using air rather than land transport.

According to Castilla, a group of Bolivian airlines smuggled 35 tons of gold in bars of alleged illegal origin through Lima's Jorge Chávez Airport. The shipment was discovered when Peruvian agents, "used to detecting the clandestine entry of cocaine or millions of dollars in cash," focused on the trajectory of Bolivian airlines landing in Lima and noticed "dozens of gold bars in jute sacks and cardboard and plastic boxes" registered in the cargo reports of flights arriving from Bolivia's main airport (Castilla 2014).

Dirty money takes cocaine to Chile and brings *chutos* (illegally imported used cars) into Bolivia. Illegal exports are, in fact, closely related to illegal imports (García Mérida 2014). In 2012, illegal exports were estimated to be over $1.806 billion, including the important share of coca leaf and its derivatives, while contraband (imports) reached a value of $1.889 billion. For one thing, this shows the coherence between illegal exports, drug trafficking and contraband, which are closely related. For another thing, it suggests that a significant part of the foreign currency for imports would have been undeclared, something that is a clear indicator of money laundering.[6]

Another indicator of money laundering is the large amount of contraband-related money that enters the market, stimulates aggregate demand, and boosts both firms' and individuals' consumption by an amount that varies between 6% and 12% of GDP according to different estimates (Ferrufino 2015, 14–16). It is difficult to measure the impact of

50   *José Blanes Jiménez*

these three sectors of the illegal market on GDP, other than indirectly, by calculating their capacity to fuel economic activities. Currently, the economy is more diversified, so the room for laundering has increased. Among the main sectors fueled by this illegal money are contraband (EABOLIVIA 2016), real estate, banking, and others that could be estimated at an amount close to 6% of GDP (Campero 2014, 583).

> Most money laundering in Bolivia is related to public corruption, smuggling and drug trafficking. A weak regulatory framework facilitates the laundering of the proceeds of organized crime and drug trafficking, tax evasion and the legitimization of other illegally obtained profits.
>
> (GAFISUD)

The Prosecutor's Office has identified at least five areas in which sectors linked to drug trafficking in Bolivia partake in money laundering. Among them are the automobile industry, real estate purchases and sales, construction, investment in company shares, and the purchase of bonds (Larrea 2016). Money laundering is one of the most important stages of illegal markets, since the first step, or at least one of the most important ones is likely to be the relationship between the three main illegal trafficking activities and other illegal derivative circuits, such as corruption, purchase of protection services, migrant smuggling, and human trafficking. Smuggling activities are largely financed by black money (Ferrufino 2015, 24).

Violence and Informality

There are many forms of violence that are directly or indirectly linked to contraband, drug trafficking and other related illegal activities. Many of these forms of violence are present throughout the country and are perceived as an effect of the informality caused by drug trafficking and smuggling; however, some of them express themselves particularly harshly in border areas.

The forms of violence associated with border areas tend to be related to the control of territory required by the informal economy but are now more often found in remote locations, such as coca leaf and cocaine paste production zones. In these areas, local populations hamper police action to the extent of preventing the construction of barracks for drug-traffic control. For example, in El Chapare and northern La Paz, hot spots have emerged in which lynching is justified as an exercise of community justice, and it is no coincidence that a significant number of these cases occurs in coca-producing areas.

From 2005 to 2013, 13 men between the ages of 18 and 45 were burned to death in Cochabamba and statistics provided the United

Nations Verification Mission in Guatemala placed Bolivia in second place of the global ranking of executions by civilians, with 480 lynching incidents between 1996 and 2002. According to Navia, Ivirgarzama in the Cochabamba tropic is, in fact, "a sort of far west, a state within a state, where people take justice and security in their own hands" (Navia 2015).

The right to the city has been increasingly lost due to the rise in crime, insecurity, and mistrust in both police mechanisms and the justice system. A social imagery that relates all types of insecurity to drug trafficking and generalized crime has also arisen. Everything is attributed, directly or indirectly, to drug trafficking and the criminal economy. This is due to the existing evidence of organized violence in coca-producing areas and prisons, especially those of Palmasola in Santa Cruz and El Abra in Cochabamba. Press reports on street executions in the city of Santa Cruz, as well as kidnappings and lynchings of police officers in the north of La Paz and on the border with Chile abound.

> After waiting for almost two weeks, the families of the four policemen who were lynched by indigenous people from the north of the Andean department of Potosí were able to recover the bodies on Friday. The villagers handed over the bodies on condition that they would not be reported for the crimes.
>
> (BBC Mundo 2010)

Five Borders: Characteristics and Challenges

Starting in 1994, the Law of Popular Participation and subsequent changes to the Constitution, created decentralized territorial municipalities and departmental governments throughout the country. Like other public bodies, they were granted fiscal revenues regulated by law. Of all the local institutions, municipalities are worth highlighting, as they took on important duties in areas such as social infrastructure, communications, and local management issues, thus becoming actors at the subnational level and, consequently, in the borderlands.

The shaded areas on Map 2.1 show the border municipalities, whose joint surface is almost one-third of the country's territory. This proportion is not mirrored when considering population, since population density in these municipalities is low. Yet, from 2001 to 2012, the population of the 72 border municipalities increased from 818,703 to 971,000 inhabitants. These 152,453 people represent, however, a growth rate above the country's average urban population growth.

No border is the same as another. While all of Bolivia's borders are in a continuous process of change driven by illegal markets, these latter impact each border in a distinct manner.

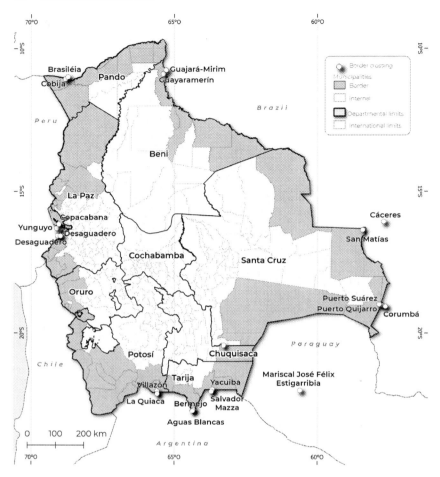

Map 2.1 Bolivia: Municipalities and Border Crossings
Map by Erika León

The Bolivia-Brazil Border

With an extension of 3,424 kilometers, the border with Brazil is the longest of the five. It has three main formal crossing points, in addition to many other informal points of entry that lack infrastructure and are generally known only to the inhabitants of the region. This extensive border encompasses different border zones and regions,[7] which are administered by three departmental governments and 20 municipalities.

The Bolivia-Brazil Amazon borderlands connect Bolivia with very important Brazilian urban areas and centers. Therefore, beyond centrally defined border programs such as the creation of councils and the like, there are opportunities for cooperation between cities and departmental/

state governments, depending on whether they are unpopulated areas or binational cities, areas with much activity and hot spots with high levels of illegal trafficking. For example, twin cities such as Cobija/Brasileaia, Guayamerín/Guajara-mirim and, to the south, Puerto Suárez and Puerto Quijarro/Corumbá, that are equipped with physical and administrative infrastructure, and have a long tradition of shared urban life, could facilitate spaces for collaboration. Recently built infrastructure, such as Puerto Evo to the north, also stands out.

> In late April 2007, the town of Montevideo – 200 kilometers from Cobija – was severely damaged by fire. One month later, its population founded the village anew under the name of Puerto Evo, a customs free zone and destination of the smuggling routes from the Chilean and Argentine borders.
>
> (Cortes Torrez 2008)

From a local standpoint, there is a broad potential for cross-border cooperation in areas such as habitability, citizen security and the creation of mechanisms for that purpose. Livestock, agro-industry, and forestry activities, as well as legal and illegal trade activities are fields in which there is daily cooperation. The issue of dams and reservoirs for electric power projects on the rivers of the north of the county has also elicited interest in the development of binational projects. In turn, drug trafficking and smuggling are important issues on this border, where several corridors have been built linking Colombia, Peru, Bolivia, and Brazil, on the one hand, and Peru, Bolivia, Argentina, and Paraguay, on the other hand.

Within the framework of these flows that Bolivia facilitates as a transit country to the five countries of the region, intergovernmental cooperation agreements have been signed over the last ten years, involving the military, police, and binational technical teams. This is a significant advance in the control of drug trafficking, since Brazil has not only become an important consumer of various forms of Bolivian cocaine, but also a transit country toward Europe. Drug-transporting aircrafts have more than 700 clandestine runways in this area and can therefore stop there on their way to Brazil and Paraguay (Ciudad del Este). Finally, the port complex of Puerto Suárez, Puerto Aguirre, and Puerto Quijarro could play an important role in river transport, related to the exploitation of the most important iron deposits in Latin America.

The Bolivia-Argentina Border

The traditional route to the sugar cane harvest of Northern Argentina and Buenos Aires can be found through this 773-kilometer border area.[8] Bolivian migrants and cross-border trade in food and beverages set the

54 *José Blanes Jiménez*

stepping-stones for the crossings that are now used for cocaine and coca leaf trafficking on this border. Large warehouses on either side of the border support the development of a significant border infrastructure for wholesale and retail trade, supported by an army of transporters and, above all, *bagayeros* (smugglers), who carry – in wheelbarrows and on their shoulders – goods that supply small-scale formal and informal trade in both nearby and distant cities of the country.

> In Pocitos (Argentina), activity is intense. There are more than a dozen currency exchange offices and several currency exchange street-stands per block. On both sides of the street and for several blocks there are stalls selling everything imaginable, from tools to shoes to food. In restaurants on the way, prices are in bolivianos and Argentine pesos, and any currency is accepted, which is not the case in Salvador Mazza.
>
> (James 2014)

Three border cities stand out: Yacuiba, in the department of Tarija, which is adjacent to the cities of San José de Pocitos and Professor Salvador Mazza; Bermejo, which is adjacent to Aguas Blancas; and in the department of Potosí, Villazón, which is connected to La Quiaca. The people on both sides of these twin cities share not only the economy but also their culture, with enormous possibilities for integration and border cooperation. A significant part of the drug trafficking to Buenos Aires and other Argentine cities takes place along this border, in addition to being a passage for Europe and Australia (Equipo Nizkor 2015). Contraband and much of the human trafficking and migrant smuggling toward Buenos Aires and other Argentine cities also flow through these border crossings (Hinojosa 2008, 18; Defensoría del Pueblo 2011, 22–23).

On both sides of the border, agro-industry and livestock farming are well developed and could serve as a basis for cross-border cooperation, thus facilitating the strengthening of the formal economy.

The Bolivia–Paraguay Border

Estranged after the 1930s Chaco War, Bolivia and Paraguay share a less dynamic border in comparison to the previously discussed ones. This is a result of poor land communication and, especially, the fact that the most important population centers are located far from the boundary. The 700-kilometer-long border stretches along the departments of Santa Cruz, Chuquisaca, and Tarija, in Bolivia, and those of Alto Paraguay and Boquerón in Paraguay. At two points it becomes a trinational border: Bolivia, Brazil, and Paraguay; and Bolivia, Argentina, and Paraguay across the Great Chaco alluvial region.[9] Without a pattern of territorial continuity, trade flows bear little relation to the small border populations and are directed toward the larger cities of Paraguay and Bolivia. The main trade is in food products and lumber, with a significant balance in favor of Paraguay. This border has few customs posts and is far from the main cities. This facilitates the contraband of drugs, cigarettes, cell phones, watches, shoes, clothing, computer equipment, and some agricultural and agro-industrial products (sausages, coffee, vegetables, among others), whose amounts could easily exceed official trade values (Romay 2010).

Currently, there are significant flows of both Peruvian and domestic cocaine from the Beni plains of Bolivia to Ciudad del Este, the trinational border between Brazil, Paraguay, and Argentina. The star product from Paraguay is marijuana, which is rated as the best in the world and of which Paraguay is the second largest producer globally (Borja 2013).

The Bolivia-Chile Border

On this 850-kilometer-long border, which is sparsely populated on the Chilean side, and stretches along a desert, four border posts control the goods coming from the free trade zones of northern Chile, Iquique, and Arica. People cross this border by bus, train, or air in order to reach the free zones of the North and the distant city of Santiago. The nearest Bolivian city for these trade flows is Oruro and the main border-crossings, Tambo Quemado, Pisiga, and Charaña, are the entry points for the largest flow of products from Asia (Japan and China), as well as from northern countries, especially the United States and Canada. It is a transit point on the way to farther destinations, such as Pando.[10]

Minerals and most soyabeans exports leave the country by rail and road for the Pacific ports of northern Chile. Imports comprise those from Chile and, most importantly, those from overseas, including used clothing and cars, especially used *chuto* cars from Asia. This is also a widely used crossing for the transfer of cocaine, hidden among cargo or in compartments of trucks, destined for Europe.

The Bolivia-Peru Border

Bolivia's second longest border is the one it shares with Peru (1,047 kilometers), along which are the two main border posts in the vast lake area (Yunguyo and Desaguadero). North of Lake Titicaca the terrain gives way to the mountainous and tropical zones, ultimately descending into the small trinational post of Bolpebra (Bolivia, Peru, and Brazil). This area, in which the lack of state controls facilitates cocaine and gold trafficking, displays high violence rates (Campero 2012, 12–15). Frequent violent deaths, including those of police and military personnel, are attributed to coca leaf producers. Moreover, this border is said to be the

56 *José Blanes Jiménez*

preferred place for the movement of guerrillas from the Revolutionary Armed Forces of Colombia (FARC) and Sendero Luminoso (Shining Path).[11]

In the Titicaca Lake area, the border is only a political demarcation, as there is ethnic and cultural continuity between the populations on both sides. Dozens of small islands are cultivated by Peruvian and Bolivian families alike, making this one of the most difficult borders to control, with numerous unrecognized crossings used mainly for smuggling contraband, drugs, and gold. The remote semi-tropical, unpopulated, and remote area also hosts innumerable informal border crossings along the rivers that separate Bolivia from Peru and is therefore commonly used as a route for cocaine and gold trafficking. In addition to the illegally mined gold in northern Bolivia, there is gold from Peru and Colombia, which is re-exported by air as Bolivian gold to Peru. Cocaine trafficking and smuggling of Bolivian fuel (gas and gasoline) into Peru feeds this business.[12] Peru's border with northern Bolivia is, thus, the most important land corridor for cocaine trafficking to Argentina and Brazil (Aliaga 2013).

Air and Water Borders

In recent years, Brazil, Argentina, and Paraguay's main concern on the issue of illegal flows has been the shifting and unpredictable air routes, along which enormous amounts of cocaine, firearms, and gold are transported between countries, avoiding the difficult and narrow land routes that do not necessarily adapt to the conditions of drug trafficking.

Small and modern aircrafts are versatile and can land on any road or on temporary clandestine runways. There have been official reports of stolen airplanes in the United States that operate between Bolivia and Peru, transporting drugs from Peru to Brazil and Paraguay and using the more than 70 clandestine runways in the Amazon department of Beni to refuel. This is evidenced by the frequent accidents and captures of small planes with cargoes of around 350 kilograms of cocaine that the press reports (Enlaces Bolivia 2013).

Finally, as already mentioned, air routes used to export Peruvian gold from Bolivia through Jorge Chávez Airport in Lima have been discovered. These illegal exports amount to nearly 35 tons per year. Until recently, gold was exported directly from Bolivia to the United States in the form of "amalgam and industrial waste." Nowadays, it is exported in the form of metallic gold ingots, clandestinely traveling the Peru-Bolivia-United States route, passing through Peruvian airports. Thus, Bolivia contributes to tax evasion in Peru. Other flights stop at the cities of Guayaramerín and Riberalta in the Northwest, and the Pantanal area (Puerto Suárez and Puerto Quijarro) and other smaller points (Castilla 2015).

Future Scenarios

National policies are still ineffective in confronting the new challenges in the administration of border areas, despite their crucial importance for the country's integration with global trade circuits. The country's links with the global system through illegal markets have reached historic highs, giving them the ability to exert control over legal markets in times of crisis.

There is still little awareness that in twenty-first century Bolivia, national security is threatened by criminal global forces, and no longer by armies from neighboring countries. The approach to the border issue must be different from that which prevailed in the stage of consolidation of territorial limits, in the country's founding period of wars with the neighbors. New forms of violence threaten citizen security, calling for new approaches based on development and binational cooperation programs that contribute to the institutional and social development in the border municipalities.

Borders, subjected to the impacts of illegal global flows, have contributed to the development of hot spots related to illicit and criminal activities, not only at the borders, but also in the main cities of the country. In some cases, territorial enclaves controlled by organized crime have been created, giving rise to strong distortions in the administration of order and justice and dangerously impacting other scenarios by making it legitimate to take justice "into people's own hands."

The great diversity of border situations is a challenge for the central administration, which must declare these territories a priority, if they are to facilitate Bolivia's insertion into the increasingly extensive and diversified global flows, thereby limiting the spread of insecurity. This will be the new form of national sovereignty.

After more than two decades of decentralization and municipalization policies, adequate institutions to deal with border issues are still missing. The border question requires the management of very specific areas, such as exchange policies at each border, and binational cooperation, to help solve problems such as violence and the insecurity of citizens. Yet, these municipalities do not generally have full competences over the police, education, and health policies.

Moreover, the new local urban systems, including medium-sized and small cities, as well as binational cities, that display complementary asymmetries and living conditions on both sides of the border, can be a significant starting point to promote cross-border cooperation tests that may foster better security conditions for citizens, as well as development in the borderlands.

Border issues are controlled and governed by large corporate interests. This leads to the weak implementation of policies that, on the one hand, show little progress in their modernization and, on the other hand, are

58　*José Blanes Jiménez*

increasingly penetrable by the large cartels that control global flows. This is the new threat to national sovereignty.

Corruption related to the increase in economic crime, such as drug trafficking and smuggling, is one of the main factors of erosion in state management and has serious repercussions. It also highlights the huge gap between national security policies and citizen security.

Bolivia has become increasingly attractive for global markets, particularly illegal ones. There is a voluminous informal army of workers on all borders which, combined with flexible and corrupt administrations, as well as the weakness of the judicial system, and the inefficiency and saturation of the prison systems, facilitates the activities of illegal markets and small-scale contraband. There are family clans that control wholesale businesses and contribute capital to the transport network. In this scenario, a porous economy flourishes with abundant cracks for the penetration of dirty money. This quick list of factors describes only one aspect of the "efficiency" of Bolivia's border subsystem in the global market.

Notes

1. Plan Decenal 1962–1971, Estrategia Socio-Económica del Desarrollo 1971–1991, Hugo Banzer Suárez's Plan Quinquenal (1976–1980), Hernán Siles Suazo's Plan de Desarrollo (1984–1987), Gonzalo Sánchez de Lozada's Plan de Todos, and Plan Nacional de Desarrollo (PND) 2006–2011.
2. One example is the Chile-Bolivia border: for the four official checkpoints, there are 117 clandestine ones for the passage of smuggled cars.
3. "In 1999, hydrocarbons represented 7.2%, minerals 38.1%, and non-traditional products 54.7%. In 2005 the composition changed to: hydrocarbons 50.3%, minerals 19%, and non-traditional products 30.7%. In 2012, hydrocarbons maintained the same share as in 2005, minerals increased, and non-traditional products dropped to 18.8%" (Fundación Milenio 2013).
4. In 1999, the GDP reached $5.5 billion and at the end of 2013 it exceeded $36 billion (INE).
5. Statements by Vice President Álvaro García Linera.
6. The "sources and uses of the balance of payments" method makes it possible to estimate foreign exchange income flows associated with undeclared exports; one can therefore link undeclared exports with unrecorded foreign exchange income that could physically enter through the borders (Ferrufino 2015, 20–21).
7. "Border situations according to their geographical scale, based on the territorial extension of each one of them, that recognize the subtypes of local scale (border area); zonal scale (border zone); and, regional scale (border region)" (SELA 2012, 21).
8. Fourteen municipalities in the departments of Tarija and Potosí (320,075 inhabitants according to the CNPV 2012) constitute an area of relative prosperity on both sides.
9. Bilateral trade between Bolivia and Paraguay grew between 1995 and 2008 from $6.3 million to $101.18 million, expanding trade 16 times since 1995.
10. From this border, used or stolen cars, kitchen appliances and electronics, among others, are directed to the free zones established in other cities throughout the country, including Pando, which is more than 1,300 kilometers away and from where smugglers attempt to bring the goods into

Brazil. This makes it possible to illustrate several of the national and international drug trafficking routes that transit through or originate in Bolivia, seeking to reach the Pacific Ocean.

11. In mid-October, 2014, in an ambush near the Peruvian border, coca farmers killed four uniformed personnel and left 14 wounded. The government said the ambush was organized by foreign, mainly Peruvian, drug traffickers to prevent the destruction of plantations (Farfán 2013).

12. As fuels are subsidized in Bolivia, they are sold at up to five times the Bolivian price. At the same, Bolivian fuel is an important material for the production of cocaine. In Bolivia, there are restrictions to the amount of fuel that can be purchased in the border strips up to 50 kilometers from the line.

References

Abecia Baldivieso, Valentín. 1979. *Las relaciones internacionales en la Historia de Bolivia*. Cochabamba: Los amigos del Libro.

ADEMAF (Agencia para el Desarrollo de las Macroregiones y Zonas Fronterizas). 2014. *Macroregiones y Fronteras* 1 (4).

———— 2015. *Memoria 2014*. La Paz, Bolivia.

Aliaga, Javier. 2013. "La ONU ve riesgo de violencia en Bolivia por paso de cocaína hacia Brasil." http://www.la-razón.com. Accessed 20 February 2016.

BBC Mundo. 2010. "Bolivia: devuelven cuerpos de policías linchados." Accessed 4 June 2010. http://www.bbc.com/mundo/america_latina/2010/06/100604_2054_bolivia_linchamiento_devuelven_cuerpos_lav.shtml

Blanes, José. 1989. "Cocaine Informal Sector Urban Areas." In *The Informal Economy, Studies in Advanced and Less Developed Countries*, edited by Alejandro Portes, Manuel Castells and Lauren A. Benton. Baltimore and London: The John Hopkins University Press.

———— 1990. "La cocaína, la informalidad y la economía urbana en La Paz, Bolivia." In *La Economía informal. Estudios en países avanzados y menos desarrollados*, edited by Alejandro Portes. Buenos Aires: Planeta.

———— 2003. "La descentralización en Bolivia. Avances y retos actuales." In *Procesos de Descentralización en la Comunidad Andina*, edited by Fernando Carrión, 177–220. Quito: FLACSO-Ecuador

Blanes, José and Fernando Calderón. 2003. *Formación y evolución del espacio nacional. Cuaderno de Futuro 18. Informe de Desarrollo Humano*. La Paz: Plural Editores.

Bolivia. 1977. *Estrategia socio-económica del desarrollo nacional 1971–1991*. La Paz: Ministerio de Planificación y Coordinación.

Bonilla, Claudio A. 2014. "Análisis de la evasión aduanera en las importaciones." *Report for the Subsecretaría de Hacienda*. 20 October 2014.

Borja, Flavia. 2013. "La marihuana desmitificada." Accessed 13 March 2016. http://www.abc.com.py/nacionales/la-marihuana-una-historia-desmitificada-622829.html

Campero, José Carlos. 2011. "El crimen organizado (vinculado al narcotráfico) en Bolivia." *Crimen organizado y gobernanza en la región andina: cooperar o fracasar*, edited by Catalina Niño, Memorias Quito, October 10 and 11.

———— 2012. "Estudio exploratorio sobre problemáticas de seguridad en ciudades frontera. Caso: Ciudad de Cobija." *Foro de Seguridad Regional, FES Bolivia, Policy Papers, 03*. La Paz.

60 *José Blanes Jiménez*

—— 2014. "Los retos para Bolivia ante un nuevo marco mundial de política de drogas." In *Bolivia, encrucijadas en el siglo XXI. Visiones e ideas para una agenda país.* La Paz: Plural Editores.

Carbone, Daniel and Mariano Frutos. 2014. *Corredores interoceánicos, análisis bibliográfico para su aplicación.* Argentina: Universidad Nacional del Sur.

Carrión, Fernando. 2014. "Explorando la economía política de la violencia en los sistemas fronterizos de América Latina: Hacia una comprensión integral." Unpublished paper.

Castells, Manuel. 2001. "Information Technology and Global Capitalism." In *On the Edge: Living with Global Capitalism,* edited by Will Hutton and Anthony Giddens, 52–74. London: Jonathan Cape.

Castilla C., Óscar. 2015. "Los vuelos secretos del oro ilegal." *Ojo Público.* http://ojo-público.com/mineria-ilegal-el-millonario-rastro-de-las-refinerias-suizas/

CEPB. 2009. *Comercio exterior ilegal en Bolivia. Estimaciones 2000–2008.* Confederación de Empresarios Privados de Bolivia.

Céspedes, Augusto. 1936. "El pozo". In *Sangre de mestizos.* Santiago: Ediciones Ercilla.

Cerruto, Oscar. 1935. *Aluvión de fuego.* Santiago: Ediciones Ercilla.

CONALTID. 2014a. *II Estudio nacional 2014 sobre prevalencia y características del consumo de drogas en hogares bolivianos de las nueve capitales de departamento, más la ciudad de El Alto.* La Paz: Consejo Nacional de Lucha Contra el Tráfico Ilícito de Drogas.

—— 2014b. "Informe institucional 2012–2014." La Paz: Consejo Nacional de Lucha Contra el Tráfico Ilícito de Drogas.

Cortes Torrez, J. J. 2008. "Puerto Evo. Una plaza cuestionada del comercio con Brasil." *Comercialización Agrícola.* Accessed 19 February 2016. http://comercializacionagricola.blogspot.com/

Courtis, Corina. 2010. *Migración y salud en zonas fronterizas: el Estado plurinacional de Bolivia y la Argentina.* Santiago: CELADE.

Defensoría del Pueblo. 2011. *Informe defensorial. Sobre la salida de niños, niñas, y adolescentes por fronteras de Villazón, Bermejo y Yacuiba.* La Paz.

EABOLIVIA. 2016. "Viceministra Ríos asegura que el contrabando sirve para lavar dinero ilícito." Accessed 20 February 2016. http://www.eabolivia/economia/

Enlaces Bolivia. 2013. "Bolivia estima que hay unas 70 pistas clandestinas de narcos en frontera con Perú." Accessed 27 November 2013. http://www.enlacesbolivia.com/sp/noticias_proc.asp?Seleccion=3732

Equipo Nizkor. 2015. "Según Achá las narcocisternas salían de Yacuiba." *Página Siete,* La Paz. Accessed 20 February 2016. http://www.derechos.orgq/nizkor/bolivia/doc/narcos44.html

Estado Plurinacional de Bolivia. 2014. *El libro del Mar.* Ministerio de Relaciones Exteriores de Bolivia Dirección Estratégica de Reivindicación Marítima-Diremar.

Farfán, Williams. 2013. "Diputado afirma que hubo emboscada a erradicadores." Accessed 31 October 2013. http://la-razon.com/index.php?_url=/seguridad_nacional/Diputado-afirma-emboscada-erradicadores_0_1934806546.html

Felman Velarde, José. 1967. *Memorándum sobre política exterior boliviana.* La Paz: Ed. Juventud.

Fernández Saavedra, Gustavo. 2013. *Memorando Bolivia-Brasil 2012.* La Paz: Plural Editores.

Ferrufino, Rubén. 2015. "La economía transfronteriza de Bolivia: aproximación a los flujos económicos ilegales." Conference prepared for the Centro Boliviano de Estudios Multidisciplinarios, CEBEM. Unpublished paper.

FES-ILDIS. 2004. *Municipalización. Diagnóstico de una década*. Volume 1 and 2. La Paz: Plural Editores.

Fundación Milenio. 2013. "Informe Nacional de Coyuntura." Coy 177. La Paz. Accessed 13 March 2016. http://www.fundación-milenio.org/Informe-Nacional-de-Coyuntura/coy-177-bolivia-y-el-boom-exportador.html

GAFISUD. "El lavado de dinero y delitos financieros en Bolivia." Accessed 5 May 2011. http://www.lostiempos.com/media_pdf/2011/11/05/307264_pdf.pdf

Galindo, Mario. 2013. *Construcción de agenda pública alternativa oxímoron: Las autonomías centralistas de Bolivia o de las autonomías a la heteronomía*. La Paz: CEBEM.

García Mérida, Wilson. 2014. "Llevan cocaína a Chile, traen autos 'chutos' y mercadería ilegal llegando hasta Pando." Accessed 17 September 2014. http://www.soldepando.com/

Gómez García, Vincent. 1997. *Corredores interoceánicos e integración en la economía mundial Bolivia ante los desafíos de la globalización económica, la competitividad internacional y el desarrollo humano sostenible*. La Paz: UDAPEX, ILDIS.

Gómez Zubieta, Luis Reynaldo. 2006. *Políticas de transporte ferroviario en Bolivia: 1860-1940*. La Paz: Bolset.

Hinojosa C., Alfonso. 2008. *La visibilización de las migraciones transnacionales en Bolivia*. 11, no. 25. La Paz: Tinkazos.

James, Daniel. 2014. "Se reactivará 'contrabando hormiga' en frontera boliviano-argentina." *Los Tiempos*. Accessed 27 October 2014. http://www.lostiempos.com

Jemio, Luis Carlos. 2013. *Comportamiento de las importaciones en Bolivia*. La Paz: Cámara Nacional de Comercio.

Klein, Herbert S. 1982. *Historia general de Bolivia*, La Paz: Editorial Juventud.

Larrea, Freddy. 2016. "Narcos lavan dinero en 5 rubros legales." *Los Tiempos*. Accessed 18 January 2016. http://www.lostiempos.com

Mercado Moreyra, Miguel. 1972. *Historia internacional de Bolivia*. La Paz. Don Bosco.

Mesa Gisbert, Carlos D., José de Mesa and Teresa Gisbert. 1988. *Historia de Bolivia*. La Paz: Editorial Gisbert.

Ministerio de Relaciones Exteriores. 2004. *Raíces de la doctrina internacional de Bolivia*. La Paz: MMRREE.

Miranda, Boris. 2016. "Etnografía de la vulnerabilidad: Escenarios críticos del narcotráfico en Bolivia." In *Seguridad regional en América Latina y el Caribe. Anuario 2015*, edited by Catalina Niño Guarnizo, 38–47. Bogotá: Friedrich Ebert Stiftung.

Miranda, Boris and Daniel Agramont eds. 2015. *El rostro de la (in)seguridad en Bolivia. Siete crónicas sobre circuitos delictivos*. La Paz: Friedrich Ebert Stiftung.

Navia, Roberto. 2015. "Tribus de la inquisición." *El deber*. Accessed 12 February 2016. http://eldeber.com.bo/bolivia/tribus-inquisicion.html.

PIE. 2012. "Corredores ilícitos entre Bolivia y Perú. ¿Rutas escondidas y extrañas?" *Puente Investigación y Enlace*. Cochabamba: Bolivia.

Poveda Ávila, Pablo, Neyer Nogales Vera and Ricardo Calla Ortega. 2015a. *El oro en Bolivia. Mercado, producción y medio ambiente*. La Paz: CEDLA.

62 *José Blanes Jiménez*

—— 2015b. *La economía del oro. Ensayos sobre la explotación en Sudamérica. Industrias extractivas series, 185.* La Paz: CEDLA.

Quiroga J., Antonio. 2003. "Descentralización. Reconfiguración territorial del Estado boliviano." *FES-ILDIS, La descentralización que se viene: propuestas para la (re)constitución del nivel estatal intermedio.* La Paz: Plural.

Richard, Nicolás (Ed.). 2008. *Mala guerra. Los indígenas en la guerra del Chaco (1932-1935).* Asunción/Paris: ServiLibro-Museo del Barro/CoLibris.

Romay Hochkofler, Marco Antonio. 2010. "Frontera y comercio entre Bolivia y Paraguay." *Bolpress.* Accessed 20 February 2016. http://www.bolpress.com/

SELA, Sistema Económico Latinoamericano y del Caribe. 2012. "La Integración Fronteriza en el Marco del Proceso de Convergencia de América Latina y El Caribe." Caracas: Secretaría Permanente del SELA.

Siles Salinas, Jorge. 1969. *La literatura boliviana de la Guerra del Chaco.* La Paz: Universidad Católica de San Pablo.

UNODC. 2015. *Estado Plurinacional de Bolivia. Monitoreo de cultivos de coca 2014.* La Paz.

Urenda, Carlos. 2007. *Autonomías departamentales. Un aporte a la Asamblea Constituyente boliviana.* Santa Cruz de la Sierra: La Hoguera.

Valencia Vega, Alipio. 2000. *Geopolítica en Bolivia.* La Paz: Juventud.

Valencia A., José Luis and Justo Alcides Casas. 1998. *Contrabando e Informalidad en la Economía Boliviana.* La Paz: FUNDEMOS.

Valencia, Lenin. 2015. *Las rutas del oro ilegal. Estudios de caso en cinco países. Programa de ciudadanía y asuntos socioambientales.* Lima: SPDA.

Vásquez, Humberto. 1990. *Para una historia de los límites entre Bolivia y Brasil.* La Paz: Juventud.

Vidaurre Andrade, Gonzalo M. 2005. *Impacto de la importación de ropa usada en Bolivia.* Santa Cruz de la Sierra: Instituto Boliviano de Comercio Exterior.

Villegas Nava, Pablo. 2013. *Geopolítica de las carreteras y el saqueo de los recursos naturales.* Cochabamba: CEDIB.

PART 1.2

PLATFORM-TYPE COUNTRIES

3 Ecuador's Global Border Subsystem

From "Island of Peace" to International Crime Platform

Fernando Carrión Mena and Francisco Enríquez Bermeo

Introduction

From its independence in 1830, until the end of the twentieth century, Ecuador faced continuous border conflicts with its neighbors, especially Peru. Because of this, the notion of "border" in Ecuador came to be strongly associated with the notion of national security. While most of the border conflicts were diplomatic in nature, in some cases, they did turn into military confrontations. These border conflicts were mainly caused by the absence of a precise demarcation between the neighboring countries; hence subsequent border policies tended to have an eminently military, diplomatic, and customs-oriented character. From that perspective, security threats came from the neighboring country, and it was necessary to watch over the latter, in order to exercise sovereignty and protect the national territory. This perception and dynamics of the borders were valid until the end of the twentieth century.

In 1998, Ecuador and Peru signed the Peace Accords that ended their territorial dispute, thus changing the notion of the border, as the conflict between the two countries had been limited to the demarcation of the *boundary*, the line separating the two states. After the Peace Accords, the border became a meeting space that integrated the border areas of the two countries in the form of a cross-border region. Therefore, we stress that the meaning of border has a historical character.[1]

Immediately after the signing of the Peace Accords and largely because of Plan Colombia, whose implementation began in 1999, Ecuador's border conflict shifted from its southern border with Peru to its northern border with Colombia. In this case, it was not a border or a territorial dispute with the neighboring country that caused the tension, but the overflow of Colombia's internal conflict and the balloon effect, product of the illegal economies that crossed to Ecuador. The land (586 kilometers) and maritime dividing line, that departs from the point that separates San Lorenzo and Mataje, up to 200 miles off the coast, structures a porous reality that enables the continuous – and mostly illegal – flows of

DOI: 10.4324/9781003204299-7

Ecuador's Global Border Subsystem 65

people, goods, and services. Such flows expand the cross-border region, generating multiple social, economic, and political relationships, in both contiguous and removed terrains.

While the conflict with Peru stemmed from the lack of a clear territorial demarcation, the conflict with Colombia was caused by the permeability of the borders to illegal markets and the overflow of violence from irregular forces into Ecuador. In the context of globalization, and in light of the solution of the boundary dispute with Peru, on the one hand, and the integration of Ecuador's territory to the underlying logic of Plan Colombia, on the other hand, borders tended to integrate. As a case in point, one could mention the flows of narcotics, which enter Ecuador through the Colombian and Peruvian borders (import) and leave Ecuador, through the Pacific Ocean to be transported to the United States along Central American routes, or through the Amazon Basin toward Brazil, from where they are then shipped to Africa and Europe (export). Other cases are the irregular trans-regional migration flows (especially from Asia) that, following the enactment of the 2008 Constitution and the recognition of the principle of universal citizenship, currently cross Ecuador *en route* to United States, as well as the firearms flows with different origins that seek to supply the actors of the Colombian armed conflict. In this vein, Ecuador has become a strategic location between the two countries with the highest cocaine production in the world (Colombia and Peru), between the countries of origin and destination of international migration, and between the countries of production and trafficking of firearms to the market generated by the Colombian conflict. All these factors contribute to Ecuador's evolving into a platform or hub for illegal markets, while structuring, at the same time, the Ecuadorian border subsystem. To reach this point, the Ecuadorian border subsystem had to undergo a process of change since the mid-twentieth century, in which at least two different moments can be identified.[2]

First Moment: Borders as Separation and Border Conflicts

The Ecuador-Peru Boundary Conflict (1941–1998)

A first moment in the process is associated with the period between the war with Peru (1941) and the signing of the Peace Accords in 1998. Works such as Pérez Concha (2008) and Tobar Donoso and Luna Tobar (1979), among others, are the expression of that period marked by the border conflict that led to a distancing between the two countries.

The most critical moment in these conflicting border relations occurred between 1941 and 1942, when the Peruvian army invaded the south of Ecuador and the latter was forced to sign the Rio de Janeiro Protocol, which imposed a territorial limit.[3] Subsequently, several Ecuadorian

66 *Fernando Carrión M. and Francisco Enríquez B.*

governments questioned the agreement, arguing that it was signed under duress, given that, at the time of signing, southern Ecuador was still under Peru's military occupation. For Ecuador, signing this agreement entailed losing a third of its total territory.[4]

The Rio Protocol established a boundary that was impossible to execute at certain points, as the characteristics of the territory did not coincide with those described in that document. This led to countless diplomatic and even armed conflicts between the two countries over a period of 60 years, the most serious of which took place in 1995, involving military action, a considerable number of troops, and casualties on both sides (Bonilla 1999).

Jorge Pérez Concha (2008) describes the border conflict with Peru as an expression of the lack of agreement between the parties to accurately establish the demarcation line: "The Rio de Janeiro Protocol cannot work there, nor can it be applied, because it refers to a non-existent geographical element and, therefore, there is no delimited line nor can there be a demarcated line, until the two parties, with the help of the Guarantors, agree on a borderline" (Pérez Concha 2008, 623).

Ecuador claimed as its territory the one that once corresponded to the colonial Real Audiencia of Quito that stretched to Brazil to the east. Moreover, since Quito was the place from where the Spanish expedition that led to the "discovery" of the Amazon River departed, Ecuador claimed direct access to that river as its right.

Subsequently, through other international treaties, Ecuador's territory was further reduced. Despite its claim on the Amazon River, it was only in the first half of the twentieth century that the Ecuadorian state began to build roads into the Amazon region. Peru, on the other hand, maintained a greater presence in the disputed area because of the navigation facilities that its rivers offered to access the Amazon.

The conflict between the two states was a dispute over territory, where the border was a national symbol that accounted for different and opposing identities, and where the security of one state implied the insecurity of the other, due to the contradictory and irreconcilable handling of interests.

It should be noted that in Ecuador there are countless writings on the boundary conflict with Peru, which seek to legitimize Ecuador's actions while questioning Peru's, and which leave aside the possibility of sharing common political objectives. During the conflict period (1941–1998), border policies were based on the notion of national security and their clearest expression was the occupation of space, the mobilization of troops and the professionalization of the army. Nonetheless, during this period some attempts can be identified to gradually modify the notions of border and national security and replace them with policies that sought to overcome the discourse of national security against the neighboring country.

Jorge Pérez Concha (2008) reports that in the 1960s, Fernando Belaúnde Terry, then president of Peru, proposed the construction of the Marginal Jungle Road, a project that was intended to link Colombia, Ecuador, Peru, and Bolivia by means of a road, whose purpose was to integrate the countries of South America and provide them with a direct exit to the Atlantic Ocean. This initiative sought to facilitate the colonization of the territory and expand agricultural production. The broader objective was to regionally integrate the countries with coasts on the Pacific and to connect the three major South American river systems: Amazon, Orinoco, and Rio de la Plata (Pérez Concha 2008, 439–440). However, the project proposed by Peru's president did not materialize.

It would not be until 1991, that the notion of the border changed, following a proposal by Rodrigo Borja, then president of Ecuador. Indeed, Borja suggested resorting to papal arbitration to resolve the conflict with Peru and issued an invitation to all South American presidents to declare the region a zone of peace. However, the proposal did not succeed, and the conflict escalated dramatically before a negotiated agreement could even be conceived. According to Francisco Carrión, the "starting point for a new, more constructive and self-confident attitude of the armed forces, Ecuadorian diplomacy, and society as a whole" was the military conflict in Alto Cenepa in 1995, a "focalized war, in which Peru was not able to impose itself by force, as had frequently been the case in the past, and, very much to the contrary, Ecuador achieved a significant victory" (Carrión Mena 2008, 36–37).

These events brought about two fundamental changes in the political behavior of the two countries, which made it possible, in the years following the War of Alto Cenepa, to initiate negotiations for a definitive peace process. The first change was Peru's recognition that there was indeed a border conflict caused by the impossibility of demarcating the line. This opened the door to a dialogue on the subject with Ecuador. The second important event was Ecuador's admission of the validity of the Rio de Janeiro Protocol of 1942.[5]

On October 26, 1998, at Itamaraty Palace in Brasilia, both countries signed a definitive Peace Accord that launched a transition phase toward a new definition of the border and border policies. With the signing of the Peace Accords, a period marked by good intentions of binational integration and fraternal relations began.

This was expressed by both countries' official delegations in October 2008, at a meeting whose purpose was to evaluate the joint achievements after ten years of peace. On that occasion, María Isabel Salvador, then Ecuadorian Foreign Minister, stated that in the ten years since the signing of the Peace Accords, $1.62 billion had been invested on the Ecuadorian side of the border, a figure which, according to the Foreign Minister, proved the political will and interest in promoting development in the border area which had previously suffered from the neglect of the

68 *Fernando Carrión M. and Francisco Enríquez B.*

state (quoted in Donoso 2009, 20). In turn, sociologist Manuel Chiriboga asserted that trade between the two countries had grown from $300 million in 1998 to nearly $2 billion in 2007, a favorable increase for Ecuador, since the trade balance with Peru tripled during the decade.

> In 2007, Ecuador exported $1.5 billion to Peru and imported $481 million, generating a positive balance of $1.023 billion [...]. Peru became Ecuador's second largest trading partner after the United States since 2001.
>
> (Chiriboga 2009, 76–77)

Claudia Donoso, who compiled the presentations at the meeting in commemoration of the ten years of peace between Ecuador and Peru, claims that:

> Peace brought about an atmosphere of trust, which fostered the movement of goods and people. Migration flows energized the economy of the inhabitants of the region. The topics on both countries' foreign policy agendas have moved away from the military and now focus on cultural exchange, trade, investment, and integration. We can therefore say that, a decade later, binational cooperation has been strengthened.
>
> (Donoso 2009, 30)

Yet, as Minister Salvador stated, beyond the governments' accomplishments "we must highlight the achievements of private traders and investors, which are nothing more than a reflection of the atmosphere of détente and cooperation established since 1998" (quoted in Donoso 2009, 23). This assertion highlights a process that not only has the states as its protagonists, but also civil society. With the signing of the Peace Accords, border dynamics between Ecuador and Peru shifted from a context of distance between the two states, to the conformation of an area of integration and complementarity, both in terms of legal and illegal activities.

The Ecuador-Colombia Cross-Border Conflict: 2000–2015

Parallel to this peace process, by the end of the twentieth century, the armed conflict in Colombia on Ecuador's northern border had acquired regional dimensions due to the presence of innumerable irregular military forces, which were not only linked to internal political conflicts, but also to the production and trafficking of drugs, mainly cocaine. During those years, in addition to the Revolutionary Armed Forces of Colombia (FARC) and paramilitary groups, large drug-trafficking cartels operated in Colombia, which supplied the continent and the world with cocaine.

By that time, Ecuador became a supply and rearguard zone for these irregular groups, as well as a transit zone for narcotics.

In this context, the interest of the United States, one of the guarantor countries of the Rio de Janeiro Protocol, in putting an end to old border conflicts between states in the region, as well as in containing the military conflict within Colombia, influenced the signing of the Peace Accords between Ecuador and Peru in 1998.[6]

After the signing of the Peace Accords with Peru, a period of exacerbation of the internal conflict, and of restructuring of drug trafficking linked to Plan Colombia began on the northern border with Colombia. On the military field, increasing contamination by the Colombian armed conflict toward Ecuador took place. This period was also marked both by the growing presence of displaced Colombian citizens in Ecuador, many of whom claimed refugee status, and the incursion and presence of irregular groups from Colombia in territory of Ecuador, which was not only used as a retreat and rearguard zone, but also as a theater of operations and a space for military confrontation between regular and irregular Colombian forces, as 2008 events in Angostura showed.[7]

In terms of contraband, Ecuador, along other countries, had been giving shape to regional markets that complement each other and operate through multinational criminal gangs. As regards drug trafficking, Ecuador, traditionally a transit country, had been complementing its activities with the production of cocaine and acting as a space for the operation and articulation of networks that have replaced the old drug cartels.

It was in this context that Ecuador and Colombia put into effect two parallel national programs, which conflicted with one another at the time: Plan Colombia[8] and Plan Ecuador. Regarding the validity of these plans, Roque Espinoza (2013) maintains that they reflected two different views on security in the region: while Plan Colombia was based on a notion of "democratic security," Plan Ecuador reflected what Espinoza calls "comprehensive security."

Plan Colombia was signed in 2001 by the governments of Colombia and the United States, with the aim to promote peace and economic development, increase security, and end the illegal drug trade in Colombia. From initially being oriented toward the war on drugs, Plan Colombia was gradually transformed into a plan to combat the irregular armed groups and mafias that used the drug business to finance Colombia's domestic war.

After the Plan came the so-called "democratic security," which was conceived through its very antithesis: a war aimed at "recovering both the territory and society, that had been appropriated by certain violent actors [...]. The idea was to put an end to the internal enemy that affected democracy and was associated with the three contemporary

70 *Fernando Carrión M. and Francisco Enríquez B.*

scourges of humanity: arms trafficking, drug trafficking, and terrorism" (Espinoza 2013, 32).

In turn, according to the Ecuadorian government, Plan Ecuador (Ministerio Coordinador 2007), was an integrated and multisector plan aimed at strengthening the presence of state institutions in the Ecuador-Colombia border area, in order to improve basic infrastructure, natural resources, and the living conditions of the border populations, including the indigenous peoples, as well as Colombian displaced persons and refugees escaping the armed conflict.

According to Espinoza (2013), Plan Ecuador was inspired by the concept of human security, promoted by United Nations Development Program (UNDP), and embodied in the notion of comprehensive security. In this sense, security is conceived as linked to social and economic development, "it is a political issue, [...] which implies the realization of citizenship in terms of freedom and the ability to mobilize citizens, within the perspective of building a just future" (Espinoza 2013, 32). Espinoza further points out that whereas Álvaro Uribe's government had bet on a war with Plan Colombia, Ecuadorian authorities had bet on a culture of peace.

Despite its good intentions, Plan Ecuador had no major achievements and was not positively evaluated by Rafael Correa's government. It was therefore cancelled in 2010, thus turning into a failed attempt at converting the northern border into a zone of peace and development. The success achieved by the Colombian government in significantly weakening the armed actors, mainly the FARC, and Plan Ecuador's failure led to

> [d]emocratic security, conceived as a radical policy of imposition of force (read: repression) throughout the Colombian territory, becoming dominant as a condition for democracy-building in the region, while the development proposal, in which peace and *buen vivir* (good living) are conditions for security, became increasingly diluted.
>
> (Espinoza 2013, 33)

Perhaps the most concerning aspect of this strategy is that democratic security implied the imposition of sovereignty in order to secure the territory and, along with it, society's belonging to the state. Hence, security became a matter for specialists in solving war and conflicts that trigger uncontrollable situations. Arms and drug traffickers, as well as smugglers, threaten internal and international security; this required the adoption of defense measures. In this context, "war [...] is essential if a society wants to move forward toward peace and, consequently, toward the constitution of a democratic society" (Espinoza 2013, 35). Thus, war, and not development or living a fulfilling life, became a condition for peace.

Given Plan Ecuador's failure in the region, the policy of democratic security prevailed over the policy of comprehensive security. This even caused a change in Ecuadorian border policy, that "gave origin to a rapprochement between the positions of the Colombian and Ecuadorian armies; [resulting in] a shared reading in practice on the issue of security between Colombia and Ecuador" (Espinoza 2013, 37–38).

In the discourse of democratic security, population and border societies were not important; instead, territory was. It was therefore fundamental to keep the territory free from internal and external threats, which is why it was deemed necessary to occupy it with the exponents and protagonists of sovereignty: the armed forces and the police. Hence, from this perspective, the true subject of sovereignty was not those who lived on the edges, but rather the territory, which is part of the legal-political reality of the state. The discourse on sovereignty further defined a permanent statute of exclusion of the border population in regard to both national society and the state (Espinoza 2013, 38–40). This was a moment led by the states and their policies, where, in the Ecuadorian case, the autonomous and decentralized governments did not participate; much less so the border populations and citizens in general, who were, rather, relegated to the role of spectators.

It is important to differentiate comprehensive security, promoted by Rafael Correa's government, and citizen security. The first notion has state action as the main and only protagonist and assumes that citizenship is a natural result of that action to improve basic infrastructure and the living conditions of border populations. The exercise of citizenship is limited to the guarantee of rights and does not imply taking the population into account as a fundamental actor. Citizen security, by contrast, emphasizes popular participation, institutions, and organizations, and, in general, the strengthening of the social structure as the fundamental factor for the sustainability of security (Sozzo 2008). Following this definition, the security of a society basically depends on the latter's social cohesion and its capacity for consultation between the various actors, on basic rules of coexistence that ensure respect, dignity, and justice between people and their institutions.

Second Moment: Borders as an Integrated System (2000–2015)

The second moment is marked by the transition from perceiving borders as limits, that is to say, as geographic lines that separate the physical spaces that characterize the states, to conceiving them as spaces that integrate regions and markets within a global logic. Beyond the limits between countries, the border often integrates territories that are not necessarily contiguous or adjoining.

72 *Fernando Carrión M. and Francisco Enríquez B.*

Since the 1980s and 1990s, globalization (interdependence, technology, communications) and state reform (trade liberalization, deregulation, structural adjustment), have significantly influenced this new dynamic, including that of the illegal markets, of which violence and crime are important components.

On the one hand, globalization made it easier for crime to rely on new technologies; on the other, deregulation led to the organization of crime on a global scale. The old binational contraband was replaced, in this new context, by transnational or global platforms for the trafficking of illegal goods and services that have redefined the notion of border and questioned the idea that threats to security are external phenomena. In Fernando Carrión and Víctor Llugsha's words:

> Crimes are neither external nor internal, because in reality they are part of inter-criminal systems, whose expressions go beyond national territories; hence, nowadays, a criminal act must be understood in its articulation with others that may even take place in distant territories.
>
> (Carrión and Llugsha 2013, 11)

With globalization, borders become important due to the economic and development asymmetries between the territories they divide; as such asymmetries generate competitive advantages between the parties, which are then profited from by groups dedicated to illegal trade. These groups include highly specialized gangs, as well as citizens and families who join these activities to improve their income.

For Fernando Carrión and Víctor Llugsha (2013), boundaries are state constructs, political expressions born in the centers of power located in the capital cities, while border regions and their populations are considered distant and marginal. In this framework, border policies prioritize the safeguarding of sovereignty and macroeconomic balances and neglect the improvement of the living conditions of borderland inhabitants. This produces an image in which borders appear as violent, and border populations as potential threats to security, because they are the social basis of illegality. Hence, two key issues must be stressed: on the one hand, border areas become meeting spaces for different national economies, constituting complementary asymmetries; on the other hand, "border cities face the dilemma caused by the differentiation between national security and citizen security" (Carrión and Llugsha 2013, 16).

The challenges to public security policy lie in how to articulate and complement national security with citizen security without affecting people's rights, while, at the same time, controlling and punishing those actors who violate territorial sovereignty and commit crimes affecting citizen rights. Similarly, transnational economic policies that reduce asymmetries or build spatial zones of economic integration must be promoted. For these reasons, local governments should be strengthened through decentralization, in such a way that they can promote local development processes and fulfill preventive functions, unlike the national government, whose role is to fulfill control functions.

The State of the Ecuadorian Border Subsystem

There are historical events that determine significant changes in the notion of the border, as the case of Ecuador shows. Until the end of the twentieth century, Ecuador was seen as an "island of peace," as a consequence of the fact that both Colombia and Peru had very serious internal conflicts.[9] In the case of Peru, armed groups such as Shining Path and the Tupac Amaru Revolutionary Movement (MRTA) were active, while in Colombia there was a larger plurality of armed groups, such as Quintín Lame, Movimiento 19 de abril (M-19), FARC, National Liberation Army (ELN), and People's Liberation Army (EPL). Interestingly, despite the critical nature of the conflicts in the two neighboring countries, prior to 2000, these conflicts did not contaminate Ecuador. They were internal conflicts that did not extend beyond their borders. However, from the last years of the twentieth century and fundamentally from the first years of the 2000s, three key events configured a new reality on Ecuador's borders.

The Border with Peru

The first event is related to the already mentioned signing of the Peace Accords between Ecuador and Peru in Brasilia in 1998, which managed to defuse the conflict that the two states historically maintained over the border demarcation. It was a typical border conflict between two states that disputed territorial sovereignty; a conflict that marked Ecuador in a significant way throughout its history, to the point of building a culture around it.

Indeed, for many years, young Ecuadorians attending public schools were taught a subject called "History of Limits," which gradually forged the culture of a "territorially deprived" country. Institutions such as the Foreign Ministry and the Armed Forces were directed at responding to the territorial conflict, as was their infrastructure. This culture had a significant weight in the training of the members of both the Armed Forces and the Ministry of Foreign Affairs.

Once the peace was signed in 1998, the imagery of Ecuadorian borders changed. Before the signing took place, the country's southern border was seen by the Ecuadorians as if it were exclusively with Peru, while the eastern border was thought to be with Brazil. Since the Itamaraty Agreement, another imagery, which reflected the reality of the border with Peru, both to the south and to the east, was constructed.

74 *Fernando Carrión M. and Francisco Enríquez B.*

As already mentioned, shortly after the signing of the Peace Accords with Peru, Plan Colombia began to be implemented, transferring the conflict to Ecuador's northern border. The Colombian conflict's spillover to Ecuador responded to two different logics that were the product of policy focalization. The first one was related to the so-called "balloon effect," which refers to the displacement of a problem toward other spaces, without losing the connection to the origin. In other words, there was an expansion of the fields of action of illegality. The second logic has to do with the so-called "flea" or "cockroach effect" – as it is known in Mexico – which refers to the fact that the phenomenon is suppressed in a certain place, yet it "leaps" to another, while losing the articulation with the origin. With Plan Colombia these two processes occurred in parallel, transferring the problem both to Colombia's borders and to other countries, including Ecuador.

The Border with Colombia

Since 2000, after the implementation of Plan Colombia, Ecuador became a strategic location for the actors involved in Colombia's internal conflict and for those linked to illegal economies. Ecuador, which until then had only been used as a location for storage and transit of narcotics, began to perform new functions within the narcotics value chain: its internal market has benefited from around 20% of the drugs that pass through the country (use), cocaine processing laboratories have been discovered (production) and money from these activities has been laundered, thanks to the dollarization of the economy, which took place in 2000. The country became, thus, a strategic place, a sort of a platform, hub, or router.

In Ecuador, the *modus operandi* of the actors linked to illegal activities has changed throughout time. Prior to Plan Colombia, the territory of Ecuador was used to store and transport narcotics abroad, without these actors' having a direct presence on it. However, because of the atomization of Colombian cartels and the ensuing formation of global networks, these groups' explicit presence is observed in the conformation of links between national, regional, and international cartels, and the increasingly strategic role Ecuador has assumed within the geopolitics of drug trafficking. For this reason, these articulations should be referred to as "networks" rather than as "groups," since the dynamics reflects a chain of different links in the business, that does not constitute a cohesive structure (Briscoe et al. 2014, 162).

As a result of these changes, different types of crimes related to this new logic have emerged in Ecuador, such as the so-called *chulco* (usury) which, based on traditional money-lending activities, has been increasingly used to launder money through illegal, unregulated loans with high interest rates, and with predominantly drug-trafficking money (pyramid scheme). This is an activity that also serves drug trafficking as a mechanism for subjecting the population to the *chulquero* or usurer. Other activities are *sicariato* (contract killing), kidnapping, and money laundering, which were previously insignificant in Ecuador, but started to gain relevance with the country's new role in international drug trafficking.

Because of Plan Colombia, the network of networks became explicitly organized as an articulated institutional complex of criminal organizations, in the form of outsourcing or even franchising within the holding company. Criminal gangs are organized by type of crime or "business activity:" there are gangs specializing in jewelry theft, others in car theft (sometimes whole or in parts), others in cellphones or computers theft. Each type of crime involves different organizations that are, nonetheless, linked by illegal marketing circuits.

The organization of illegal markets linked to drug trafficking is totally different from the one previously mentioned; it is broader and much more complex. It does not work with only one type of product, but with multiple products. It follows a general process, in which the sites of production, trafficking, and consumption of any kind of good vary according to the situation and adapt themselves as required.

Since the early days of Plan Colombia, cocaine-trafficking routes also began to determine the entire criminal structure. If previously it was production, i.e., the transformation of coca leaf and paste into cocaine, that structured the criminal organization, now it is transportation. That is why Colombian cartels such as Pablo Escobar's Medellín Cartel, the Rodríguez Orejuela brothers' Cali Cartel, and the Gonzalo Rodríguez Gacha and Carlos Lehder's cartels controlled all the phases of the process from production to large circulation and micro-trafficking. They directly introduced drugs and narcotics to the North American markets, entering through Florida. Today, after the implementation of Plan Colombia, that possibility has disappeared, and cartels attempt to enter the United States by land through the border with Mexico.

The actors who control the passage from Mexico to the United States now dominate the entire criminal structure, from the production phase, the transfer, commercialization, and, as a part thereof, micro-trafficking. The command of these criminal networks within the holding has also changed: Mexican transport cartels were preeminent until the great crisis of 2008, when the globalization of consumption took place, causing new cartels and mafias to gain weight in the drug-trafficking structure, albeit as a result of the control of the merchandise's final price. While a kilogram of cocaine is worth $2,000 in Colombia, on the Mexican border with the United States its value is $60,000; on the streets of New York, it reaches $120,000; and in Australia $250,000. Hence, the great accumulation of capital does not take place in the Latin American region, but outside, in the sites of consumption. Bruce Bagley (2012) states that, in 2012, 20% of the money generated by drug trafficking stayed in Latin

76 *Fernando Carrión M. and Francisco Enríquez B.*

America, while the remaining 80% went to the United States, as a direct consequence of drug price management.

Moreover, the monetary mass generated around drug trafficking makes it necessary to resort to a dark phase that does not exist in the case of traditional merchandise: money laundering, a new phenomenon that is not required by the commercialization of goods and services in the legal markets as they operate in a niche of their own.

Although marijuana is the most commonly used illegal drug in the world, for it is the cheapest and can be produced anywhere, it is not the mainstay of drug trafficking and related crimes. Rather, the axis for the criminal organizations is the trafficking of cocaine, a substance that can only be produced in the ecological niche of the Andean area; hence, the importance of that region in the trafficking of narcotics. In fact, the high price of cocaine, its high profitability, and the organization that it requires, make this product the one that commands the illegal markets. Other illegal activities such as trafficking of other drugs, arms trafficking, human trafficking, smuggling of stolen and counterfeit goods, illegal mining, etc., all revolve around cocaine trafficking.

The logic behind the concentration of coca production in the Andean area and the global diffusion of consumption made the circuits and routes gain a fundamental weight within the sector, to such an extent that their articulation required that of the different border regions in order to form a truly integrated system of global scope. Hence, from binational or trinational border relations of a contiguous nature, there was a transit to cross-border relations, structured between distant and discontinuous borders, but integrated into a system. Globalization and liberalization made the virtual state and not the geographic one an important factor. Globalization liquified borders, but it did not eliminate them; it redefined, enhanced, and, above all, articulated them.

The Dollarization of the Ecuadorian Economy

Another important factor in the constitution of the Ecuadorian border subsystem is dollarization, which was adopted in the first days of January 2000, as a consequence of a deep crisis in the financial system, mainly of the private banks settled in the coastal region. Dollarization sought to stop the rapid devaluation of the national currency, the sucre, in order to achieve macroeconomic stability and restore economic growth.

Once the economy was dollarized, Ecuador ceased to have an autonomous monetary policy, instruments to issue money and directly influence production, investment, consumption, and inflation. At the same time, the dollarization of the economy turned Ecuador into a country with notable possibilities for money laundering. In fact, this latter has grown significantly, thanks to both dollarization and remittances. What is interesting about the presence of organized crime in Ecuador is not only that it is growing, but also its strategy of adaptation and incursion into new economic sectors, as has recently been the case with mining (Briscoe et al. 2014, 162).

Even though the Ecuadorian economy is small, since it is dollarized and has limited working capital control and regulation mechanisms, it facilitates money laundering. There are estimates of the magnitude of the circulating money that is laundered in the country. According to Briscoe et al. (2010), 21 cases of money laundering, representing a value of more than $1.5 billion, were reported to the public prosecutor's office. A significant part was laundered "outside the financial system, through the illegal transportation of cash, and in the informal economy and the real construction sector [...]. The informal economy, in turn, has grown more robust, thanks to the influx of capital from illegal sources, mostly through the purchase of luxury goods [...]" (Briscoe et al. 2014, 168).

Violence and the Illegal Economy in the Border System

Plan Colombia provoked a global restructuring of drug trafficking and related crimes; it integrated the markets of Mexico and the Andean area, thus making it possible to conceive of a global border system in Latin America, of which Brazil and Argentina are also part. It should be stressed that Plan Colombia was not an exclusively Colombian plan. Rather, it involved two signatories: Colombia and the United States. Although Plan Colombia was meant to combat drug trafficking, it resulted, paradoxically, in its strengthening. In this sense, Plan Colombia has performed as a sort of "boomerang."

In Colombia, the most significant aspect of the implementation of the plan was the disappearance of both criminal gangs and the so-called "drug cartels," which were severely hit until they were completely dismantled, as happened to organizations such as Pablo Escobar's, the Rodríguez Gacha brothers', Carlos Lehder's, and Rodríguez Orejuela's. The disappearance of the large cartels led to a pluralization of criminal actors; in fact, the general drug-trafficking system operates nowadays with smaller organizations, in an outsourcing or franchise mode, thus increasing its productivity and efficiency. In other words, the criminal actors have multiplied and become more diverse; they are no longer just two or three, but a growing and more articulated set of cartels, operating under new forms, each with specific functions within the networks they belong to.

In this new structure, laboratories and cocaine processing were expelled from Colombia to Ecuador. This "balloon effect" was caused by economic factors. Previously, the chemical components for processing cocaine entered from Ecuador into Colombia, and once cocaine had been produced, it was sent back to Ecuador, from where it was distributed to international markets. This process was not justified, as it represented higher production costs. Therefore, the restructuring rationalized and

78 *Fernando Carrión M. and Francisco Enríquez B.*

optimized the cocaine production process and incorporated Ecuador into the international drug-trafficking circuit in a more prominent role.

Additionally, Ecuador is strategically located. It is close to the two main cocaine-producing countries of the world, Colombia and Peru, and near consumption centers, such as Brazil (the second largest consumer in the world) and the United States (the largest consumer). Ecuador is even connected to Asia, through the provinces of Esmeraldas and Galapagos, as well as through the port of Buenaventura in Colombia. In the new structure of international drug trafficking, Ecuador has greater proximity to production and consumption and has since become a strategic location for processing.[10] From a country of storage and transit, Ecuador became a country of drug-processing, use, and money-laundering, which led to the appearance of related crimes.

Regarding the location of drug laboratories, some processing areas can be identified. The first one is Esmeraldas, a border area with Colombia, where the presence of submersibles as a means of transporting drugs has been discovered. The coca leaf from Colombia enters Ecuador in this way to be processed. Thence cocaine is sent by submarine to the consumption centers.

Map 3.1 shows, in first place, the laboratories in the eastern provinces of Orellana and Sucumbíos, where the coca leaf from Colombia and Peru arrives, is processed, and then reexported to Brazil as cocaine. It also shows the laboratories located in the central highlands' region of Ecuador, which probably process cocaine for local use within the country, mainly in the larger urban centers such as Guayaquil, Quito, and Cuenca, among other cities. The second zone is the arch formed between Guayas and Manabí, where coca leaves and paste enter from Colombia and Peru; they are then processed in Ecuador and distributed to other points in the world through the Pacific Ocean.

Ecuador's borders are very vast; the longest of them is that with Peru (1,529 kilometers), which is three times longer than the border with Colombia. In addition, Peru and Colombia share borders with each other. Further east, toward the Amazon, is the triple border between Colombia (Leticia), Peru (Iquitos), and Brazil (Manaus), with which Ecuadorian cities such as Lago Agrio have a close relationship through the river system. Ecuador does not have a physical or territorial border with Brazil; however, it does have a border with said country because of this type of relationship (waterway). Finally, there is Ecuador's maritime border, where the reconstruction of the circuits will allow us to identify the continent's borders with the countries of Asia and Oceania.

An important element in the border dynamics is the presence of the state, or rather, the lack thereof. Perhaps because of the extension of its borders, Brazil is the country with the least state presence in border zones. Brazil is also the second major cocaine consumer in the continent and the first one in Latin America; therefore, it has a significant gravitational weight in all this process. The increase in consumption in

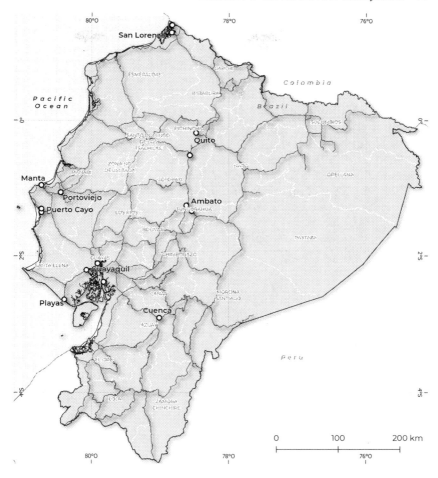

Map 3.1 Ecuador: Cocaine Processing Locations (2014)
Map by Erika León

Brazil was triggered by Plan Colombia, one of whose effects was market diversification. Currently, less cocaine is being sent to the United States, although it is still being produced on a large scale in the Andean region.

The Migration-Violence Border Dynamics in Ecuador

In 2013, the highest homicide rates per 100,000 inhabitants in Ecuador were found on the northern border, in Sucumbíos (40.36/100,000 inhabitants) and in Esmeraldas (28.23/100,000 inhabitants). The average rate in Ecuador in 2013 was 10.92/100,000 inhabitants, while in the previously mentioned provinces on the northern border it was three to four times higher. In contrast, in Carchi, the other province bordering Colombia, that same year the rate was even lower than the national

80 *Fernando Carrión M. and Francisco Enríquez B.*

average (5.66/100,000 inhabitants). This can be a result of state presence and its institutions, which include the military, in that province, as well as of the presence of civil society, with its social organizations and strong structure expressed in solid relationships between actors. All of these factors are important in reducing the violence derived from drug trafficking and related crimes. Despite not being a border province and being located at a considerable distance from the above-mentioned provinces, Los Ríos also displays high homicide rates (21.5/100,000 inhabitants). In turn, homicide rates on the border with Peru are strikingly low: Orellana (7.53/100,000 inhabitants), Napo (4.36/100,000 inhabitants), Morona (3.01/100,000 inhabitants), Zamora (7.79/100,000 inhabitants), and Loja (3.1/100,000 inhabitants). The only border province with Peru, to the south, with a rate higher than the national average is El Oro with 18.21/100,000 inhabitants.

The provincial data on homicides (Table 3.1) show that criminal logic varies strikingly throughout the territory. The highest rates are found in

Table 3.1 Ecuador: Homicide rate per 100,000 inhabitants by province (2010–2013)

Province	2010	2011	2012	2013
Azuay	5.54	4.91	5.08	5.63
Bolívar	6.78	3.1	4.6	6.58
Cañar	5.51	4.16	5.72	5.21
Carchi	9.9	9.23	4.57	5.66
Chimborazo	4.2	2.28	2.05	5.08
Cotopaxi	4.71	5.8	4.11	5.63
MD Guayaquil	23.57	19.72	13.69	13.33
MD Quito	11.9	9.43	9	7.81
El Oro	29.61	20.96	17.08	18.21
Esmeraldas	51.48	46.83	36.58	28.23
Guayas	19.5	17.96	17.22	10.82
Imbabura	5.8	8.33	8.92	5.09
Loja	4.92	4.65	5.22	3.1
Los Ríos	33.02	31.68	23.26	21.5
Manabí	19.64	19.77	15.91	10.97
Morona Santiago	7.83	10.16	11.73	3.01
Napo	9.35	7.31	4.46	4.36
Orellana	22.5	10.66	13.94	7.53
Pastaza	11.56	10.11	7.63	5.3
Pichincha	3.45	3.36	3.27	6.37
Santa Elena	8.8	5.21	3.29	3.21
Santo Domingo	31.63	26.98	16.7	16.62
Sucumbíos	44.13	36.01	29.86	40.36
Tungurahua	4.77	6.41	5.77	4.23
Zamora Chinchipe	–	3.07	2.99	7.79
NATIONAL	17.57	15.36	12.4	7.79

Source: Ministry of the Interior

the provinces of the coastal region (Esmeraldas, Manabí, Santa Elena, Guayas, and El Oro). Violence in the northern border is very different to that of the southern border.

Between 2010 and 2013, the provincial and national homicide rates fell, except in Pichincha and Zamora, provinces that have low, albeit rising, rates. It is noteworthy that in provinces such as Sucumbíos, after the decrease of the homicide and murder rate for two consecutive years (2011 and 2012), the rate would rise again in 2013 to levels slightly lower than those of 2010. The case of Esmeraldas reveals a different pattern: from a rate of more than 50/100,000 inhabitants in 2010, it was reduced by 2013 to a little more than half. Esmeraldas had until 2012 the highest homicide rate per 100,000 inhabitants in the country; despite its reduction, this rate is still higher than in the rest of the provinces and the national average.

Regarding the entry and exit of persons (migration balance), the most frequent points of entry and exit are the ports of Manta and Esmeraldas, reenacting the arch-shaped cocaine-trafficking route already discussed. These are the sites most of the people who migrate go to, thus confirming a kind of fatal attraction: the places where most people die from violent causes are also the places most people are drawn to. This is also the case in the province of Sucumbíos, which, as already mentioned, has the highest murder rate per 100,000 inhabitants, and also presents large migration flows. In contrast, in Santo Domingo de los Tsáchilas and in the Amazon, migration is high, but lower than in the aforementioned provinces, although mobility in this area is internal and a product of colonization processes.

In the case of Manabí, with the new century, new actors of violence emerged. Such is the case of the criminal gang Los Choneros, a group that gained notoriety at the local, provincial, and national level for the variety of its illicit activities (drug trafficking, bank robbery, kidnapping, extortion, contract killing, among others). Although this group originated in Chone, it later expanded to Santo Domingo de los Tsáchilas, Guayas, Los Ríos, and Pichincha. The origin of this group was micro-drug trafficking in their canton; however, as its activities expanded to other cantons, the group entered into conflict with Los Queseros, a gang from Manta also linked to drug trafficking. After annihilating the Manta gang, Los Choneros took advantage of Manta's port location and further expanded their practices until they became a criminal organization with several cells at the national level and connections with Colombian criminal actors (see Pinto Vaca 2015).

Functional Sites in the Ecuadorian Border Subsystem: Internal and External Circuits

The Attorney General Office estimates that every year between $3.5 and $4 billion from drug trafficking remain in Ecuador. This approximation

82 *Fernando Carrión M. and Francisco Enríquez B.*

gives an idea of the magnitude of illicit activities in the national economy. Hence the question: to what extent does dollarization, which has been in effect since 2000, run the risk of failing, if drug-trafficking activities are weakened? Narcotics mobilize approximately $600 billion a year worldwide, $120 billion of which remain in Latin America and $400 billion in the United States.

Institutional Changes

During Rafael Correa's administration (2007–2017), important institutional changes were implemented in the fight against drug trafficking. In particular, since the promulgation of the 2008 Constitution, important normative changes took place in the areas of citizen security and the integrality of rights. In 2014, the new Organic Code of Criminal Procedure was approved, which in many aspects, is more punitive than the previous one. Institutionally, the ministries of Justice, the Interior and the Coordinating Ministry of Security were created. Local governments, in turn, lost competencies in the area of security and a process of centralization of security policies took place. Significant changes also occurred in the use of technologies for internal security. The 911 system began to operate in 2012 with an investment of about $270 million. Currently the whole national territory is under 911. This represents a substantial advancement in the area of internal security.

As regards intelligence, the influence of the US Embassy was curtailed, and intelligence operations began to be carried out autonomously and without foreign interference. This yielded good results, especially in the fight against drug trafficking, as evidenced by the increase in the volume of drug seizures. Changes were also implemented in the administration of justice, mainly through the adoption of procedures that involve the use of new technologies. For instance, the Ministry of the Interior undertook a broad reform of the National Police, which included the increase in personnel, provision of weapons, vehicles, and infrastructure. The Ministry of Justice, in turn, overhauled the prison system, emphasizing the construction of infrastructure.

The amount of confiscated drugs by the police in Ecuador has consistently increased. During 2014, 55 tons of drugs were seized, which is the highest amount since 2009, when the police captured 68 tons. Data from the Ministry of Interior indicate that between 2007 and 2014 the police seized 320.82 tons of drugs. In 2014, 87% of the seized drugs corresponded to substances with international destination, while 13% were intended for domestic consumption. The United Nations Office on Drugs and Crime, in its 2014 report (UNODC, 2014b) states that Ecuador is the third country in the world with the most seizures of alkaloids; only behind Colombia and the United States. According to the US State Department (2014), Ecuador is an important transit point for cocaine trafficking; air, land, sea, and river routes are used in the country for that purpose. According to the same source, about 110 metric tons of cocaine are shipped from Ecuador each year and the police seize only half of the drug that is trafficked annually. As stated by UNODC: "in view of its strategic location, not only as a transit country but also for being situated between the two countries with the highest production of coca leaf, it is necessary to seek adequate and consensual mechanisms to foster joint efforts between Ecuador, Colombia, and Peru in combating illicit drug trafficking and organized crime" (UNODC 2014a, 7). Between 2009 and 2014, Ecuador captured nine planes associated with illegal drug trafficking. The US State Department asserts that criminal groups from Colombia, Nigeria, Russia, and China are active in Ecuador, as well as the Mexican cartels of Sinaloa, El Golfo, Los Zetas, and others.

Another interesting parameter of the border dynamics related to the illegal economy is the data on legal complaints by type of crime that were filed with the Attorney General Office between 2010 and 2014. In the case of drug trafficking, an upward trend can be observed at the national level. At the provincial level, the province with the highest number of reports in 2014 (January–August) was Guayas with 40.9% of the total, followed by Pichincha with 17.9% and, to a lesser extent, Manabí with 7.4%. It is interesting to note that in the reports of drug trafficking, the border provinces are salient.

The second most important type of report at the national level is that of crimes for illegal possession of weapons. Indicators show an upward trend until 2012 and, as of 2013, a downward tendency. By province, the highest frequency occurs in Guayas with 42.8%, Los Ríos with 11.8%, and Esmeraldas with 10%, the latter being the only border province.

Legal complaints of crimes for illegal trafficking of oil and its derivatives are important in Ecuador, since the price of fuel is subsidized by the government and is very competitive with the prices of fuels in neighboring countries. At the national level, this type of complaint shows an upward trend, with a significant decrease by 2013, and a recovery from 2014. The contraband or illegal trafficking of oil is mainly concentrated in the border provinces, particularly El Oro (border with Peru), which, from representing 2% of the total in 2010, was estimated to represent 68% by 2014. Other provinces where this illegal activity is significant are Sucumbíos, Esmeraldas, and Carchi, all of which are border provinces.

Reports of human trafficking at the national level consistently increased between 2010 and 2014; however, in 2014, they began to decrease. By province, in 2014, most of the reports concentrated in Pichincha with 25.9%, El Oro with 17.3%, Santo Domingo with 13.6% and, to a lesser extent, Guayas and Imbabura. Of the five provinces with the most complaints, only one, El Oro, is a border province.

Regarding the reports of migrant smuggling, at the national level there is an upward trend from 2012. By province, the highest concentration

84 *Fernando Carrión M. and Francisco Enríquez B.*

is in Cañar with 41.7%, followed closely by Azuay with 33.3%, none of which is a border province. At a lower level are the provinces of Guayas, Pichincha, and Chimborazo.

Reports of money laundering show a downward trend at the national level, with a significant concentration in the large urban centers of Quito and Guayaquil, which account for 78.6% of the reports. Less significant are the border provinces of El Oro and Carchi with 16.7% and 4.8%, respectively.

Final Considerations

The homicide rates in recent years and the reports presented to the Office of the Attorney General on various types of crimes have decreased in some cases, while in others they show an increase, remaining at high levels. These fluctuations show that, although state action has dealt important blows to criminal organizations, the latter have a great capacity of recovery that allows them to replace weakened and even liquidated structures with others that are more sophisticated and equipped with state-of-the-art technologies, including military ones. In view of this, states must allocate ever more resources for the containment and control of criminal groups.

The high recovery capacity of drug-trafficking groups is largely due to the high profitability of this type of crime, especially cocaine trafficking, from which such criminal groups obtain enormous resources that enable them to make the changes noted above. Such is the amount of resources coming from these activities that, in addition to what has been said, these organizations are able to bribe state officials and the state security forces and infiltrate their structures in order to reduce or neutralize their control and security actions. Hence, the fight against drug trafficking and related crimes develops a dynamic of a growing spiral where two apparatuses, one state-led, the other parastatal, each with its own strategies, confront each other. Plan Colombia was precisely a strategy to combat drug trafficking and related crimes, based on the notion of democratic security. Given the failure of Plan Ecuador and its notion of comprehensive security, Plan Colombia gradually acquired a binational (including Ecuador) and even regional dimension, as the strategies of several Central and South American countries have been woven together under the same logic.

As Roque Espinoza has pointed out, the problem with democratic security is that, from this perspective, border populations and societies are not important. What is important is the territory, which must be kept free of both internal and external threats through the control by the Armed Forces and the Police. Following this logic, the populations and societies of the border are not seen as independent social actors, but

Ecuador's Global Border Subsystem   85

as objects that must be subordinated to the strategy of combat or war against drug trafficking and related crimes. For the state's security apparatus, civil society is a potential collaborator, who might inform the state security forces about drug traffickers' behavior and activities. Instead, for the parastatal drug-trafficking apparatus, local populations can provide cover by concealing them, lowering their visibility, and preventing their public exposure, mainly before the state's security forces. Moreover, there have been cases where certain "cartels" have sought to build a local social base of support for drug trafficking, sustained by the provision and delivery of social benefits (the Medellín Cartel of Pablo Escobar in the 1980s, for example).

There have even been cases in which certain groups have promoted the military involvement of civil society in the conflict, through the formation of the so-called "self-defense" forces, which in the cases of Colombia and Mexico have been transformed into paramilitary forces to combat progressive political expression. In those two cases, civil society is not recognized, either by the state or by the drug trade, as a social actor with its own dynamics, its own interests, needs, and aspirations. This has led to the situation in which, in the confrontation between the state and parastatal apparatuses, civil society is only a spectator, in most cases, a victim of the confrontation, without voice or social agency.

Hence, public policies to combat drug trafficking and related crimes are predominantly of a police and military nature with little, if any, association with other areas of public policy, such as human development, peace, and public health. This also explains why issues such as the legalization of marijuana and other drug use, or the treatment of drug use as a public health problem, are barely discussed in Ecuador.

The project "Explorando la economía política de la violencia en los sistemas fronterizos de América Latina: hacia una comprensión integral" has the responsibility to contribute with information, analysis, training, and public policy proposals to help Ecuadorian civil society become an active and proactive social actor who will promote the understanding of drug trafficking and related crimes as a phenomenon that goes beyond the strictly military. Only an active participation of civil society in the fight against drug trafficking will make it possible to overcome the fluctuating results of the fight against this type of crime and turn it into a sustained process of containment of illicit activities.

Notes

1. It is essential to consider the methodological criterion of differentiation between *boundary*, as a demarcation line of territorial sovereignty, and *border*, as a space that is constituted and modified according to the behavior of each of the states.

86　*Fernando Carrión M. and Francisco Enríquez B.*

2. For some authors such as Jorge Pérez Concha (2008), Julio Tobar Donoso, and Alfredo Luna Tobar (1979), border conflicts with neighboring countries have their antecedents in the pre-Hispanic and colonial periods, and especially, with the founding of the republic. Despite this, the present article focuses on the twentieth and twenty-first centuries.
3. The Rio de Janeiro Protocol was signed on February 29, 1942, in the city that bears its name, with the participation of Argentina, Brazil, the United States, and Chile as guarantors.
4. Currently, Ecuador and Peru share a 1,420-kilometer-long border.
5. Between 1942 and 1998, Ecuador had ignored the validity of the Rio de Janeiro Protocol. In the same period, Peru refused to recognize the existence of any border conflict with Ecuador. These two attitudes hindered the dialogue for nearly 60 years.
6. During these years, through an agreement signed in 1998, Ecuador ceded to the US Air Force a military base located on the Pacific coast (Manta). This concession lasted for ten years (1999–2009) and was meant to support US drug interdiction efforts. President Correa did not renew the agreement with the United States after 2009 and the military base was again placed under Ecuador's control.
7. On March 1, 2008, the Colombian army bombed a FARC camp located in territory of Ecuador (Angostura). The attack killed Raúl Reyes, the FARC's second in command, and other 23 people, including guerrillas, four Mexican students and an Ecuadorian citizen. The Colombian military incursion was carried out without the authorization or knowledge of the Ecuadorian government and caused the severance of diplomatic relations between the two countries. See Montúfar (2008) and Lasso Amaya (2011).
8. According to José Steinsleger, "one of Plan Colombia's goals was to make Ecuador the most important strategic country in the Andean area. In order for this to happen, Washington had to put an end to the (in its opinion) 'anachronistic' and old border conflict with Peru in the Condor Mountain Range" (2002).
9. Before the end of the twentieth century, Adrián Bonilla announced the end of this vision when he stated that "[t]he multiple interconnections and hierarchies on which the international system is conformed make it impossible to think of a supposed Ecuadorian autarchy; the conception of Ecuador as an 'island of peace' is simply utopian." Cited in Bagley et al. (1991, 3).
10. Two aspects must be highlighted: Ecuador's borders with Peru and Colombia, and the "free mobility policy" that has produced many benefits in terms of human rights, especially with regard to the protection of refugees, but also poses significant security problems. "This has helped make Ecuador a strategic point for the transit of goods and people, including illegal drugs such as cocaine" (Rodríguez 2011, quoted in Briscoe et al. 2014, 168).

References

Bagley, Bruce, Adrián Bonilla and Alexei Páez. 1991. "Introduction". In *La economía política del narcotráfico: El caso ecuatoriano*, edited by Bruce Bagley, Adrián Bonilla and Alexei Paéz, 1–8. Quito: FLACSO-Ecuador-Miami University North-South Center.

Ecuador's Global Border Subsystem 87

Bagley, Bruce. 2012. *Drug Trafficking and Organized Crime in the Americas: Major Trends in the Twenty-First Century*. Washington: Woodrow Wilson Center Update on the Americas.

Bonilla, Adrián. 1999. "Fuerza, conflicto y negociación: Proceso político de la relación Ecuador y Perú." In *Ecuador-Perú: Horizontes de la negociación y el conflicto*, edited by Adrián Bonilla, 13–30. Quito: FLACSO-Ecuador, DESCO-Perú.

Briscoe, Ivan et al. (Eds.) 2014. *"Illicit Networks and Politics in Latin America."* Stockholm: International IDEA, NIMD, Clingendael.

Carrión, Fernando and Víctor Llugsha. 2013. "Introducción. La frontera: inseguridad por desencuentro de diferencias." In *Fronteras: rupturas y convergencias*, compiled by Fernando Carrión and Víctor Llugsha, 9–29. Quito: FLACSO-IDRC.

Carrión Mena, Francisco. 2008. *La paz por dentro. Ecuador-Perú: Testimonio de una negociación*. Quito: Dinediciones.

Chiriboga, Manuel. 2009. "El Acuerdo de Paz Ecuador-Perú: ¿hubo un rédito económico?" *In Ecuador-Perú: Evaluación de una década de paz y desarrollo*, compiled by Claudia Donoso, 71–92. Quito: FLACSO-CAF.

Donoso, Claudia. 2009. "Ecuador-Perú: Evaluación de una década de paz y desarrollo". In *Ecuador-Perú: Evaluación de una década de paz y desarrollo*, compiled by Claudia Donoso, 27–37. Quito: FLACSO-CAF.

Espinoza, Roque. 2013. "Discursos de seguridad." In *Fronteras: rupturas y convergencias*, compiled by Fernando Carrión and Víctor Llugsha, 31–42. Quito: FLACSO-IDRC.

Lasso Amaya, Carolina. 2011. "Impacto del conflicto armado en la frontera colombo-ecuatoriana y sus implicaciones en las relaciones diplomáticas a partir de la implementación del Plan Colombia hasta diciembre de 2009." Bogotá. http://repository.urosario.edu.co/hand- le/10336/1161

Ministerio Coordinador de la Seguridad Interna y Externa. 2007. "Plan Ecuador 1. Hacia la seguridad humana con paz y desarrollo." Quito. http://www.resdal. org/ultimos-documentos/plan- ecuador07.pdf

Montúfar, César F. 2008. "Aproximación a la crisis diplomática entre Ecuador y Colombia, a raíz de los sucesos de Angostura." In *De Angostura a las computadoras de Uribe: Prensa escrita y crisis de marzo*, coordinated by Fernando Checa Montúfar, 21–51. Quito: Abya-Yala.

Pérez Concha, Jorge. 2008. *Ensayo histórico-crítico de las relaciones diplomáticas del Ecuador con los Estados limítrofes*. Quito: Comisión Nacional Permanente de Conmemoraciones Cívicas.

Pinto Vaca, Juan Pablo. 2015. "Chonewood: etnografía, cine popular y asesinato por encargo en Chone." Masters dissertation, FLACSO Ecuador.

Sozzo, Máximo. 2008. *Inseguridad, prevención y policía*. Quito: FLACSO-Municipio Metropolitano de Quito.

Steinsleger, José. 2002. "Ecuador y el Plan Colombia." In *La Jornada*, June 5.

Tobar Donoso, Julio and Alfredo Luna Tobar. 1979. *Derecho Territorial Ecuatoriano*. Quito: Ministerio de Relaciones Exteriores.

United States Department of State. 2014. *Drug and Chemical Control*, Vol. I. Washington.

UNODC, Oficina de las Naciones Unidas contra la Droga y el Delito – Gobierno de la República del Ecuador. 2014a. *Indicadores de Cultivos Ilícitos en el Ecuador 2013*. Quito: UNODC.

88   *Fernando Carrión M. and Francisco Enríquez B.*

—— 2014b. *Informe Mundial sobre las drogas 2014. Resumen Ejecutivo.* New York: UNODC.

Statistical Data Sources

Delitoscopio de la Fiscalía General del Estado
Ministry of Interior

4 Borders, Crime, and State Responses in Argentina

Gustavo González, Waldemar Claus, Luciana Ghiberto, and Pablo Spekuljak

Introduction

This work aims to make progress in the construction of a baseline or "state of the art" that will allow us to approach analytically, in a second stage and with greater depth, the intersection between borders and crime in Argentina.[1] The two parts in which the content of this chapter is structured must therefore be interpreted and analyzed in the context of this general objective.

The first part of the text is divided into two sections. The first one roughly describes the process of construction and historical transformation of the borders in Argentina. The second section, which is more limited, aims to produce a socio-demographic anatomy of the most important border areas, based on a survey of geographical and statistical data.

The second part is structured to meet two purposes: (1) to identify the most relevant themes around which a specific field, defined indistinctly as "border studies" or "trans-border studies,"[2] has been generated within the local academic world, and (2) to recover the research produced in this field of study, addressing some of the emerging themes of the intersection between crime and borders in Argentina.

Exploring the Socio-Historical Anatomy: The Construction of Borders in Argentina

Pursuing the goal of historicizing the process of construction of inter-state borders in Argentina inevitably leads us to think about it and reconstruct it in relation to another long-lasting process; namely, the formation of the nation-state, and, more specifically, the delimitation of the territoriality, the identity, and the economic structure of the nation, all of which are dynamics where the central state operated as main definer and regulator (Halperin Donghi 1980; Oszlak 1983). In this sense, drawing from the works and proposals of local authors (Cacopardo 2007; Benedetti 2007; Kralich et al. 2012; Benedetti and Salizzi 2014) we believe

DOI: 10.4324/9781003204299-8

90 *Gustavo González et al.*

the intertwining of the above-mentioned processes can be reconstructed in three broad cycles:[3] *the cycle of diffuse visibilization, the cycle of accentuated visibilization, and the cycle of reconfigured visibilization.*

The starting point for these cycles emerged with the processes of fragmentation and reconfiguration of the Viceroyalty of the Río de la Plata, driven by the Latin American independence movements that occurred during the early nineteenth century. From then on, the "border issue" materialized for the incipient construction of the nation-state on two more or less differentiated levels: (a) "external" borders, in terms of territorial delimitation and differentiation from bordering countries, and (b) "internal" borders,[4] linked to the articulation of three "local" dynamics: the rugged political process of consolidation of the federal state, the structuring of the agro-productive profile of the national economic matrix, and the process of "endogenous colonization" marked by the so-called "Indian" or native peoples' question. Although it is necessary to recognize the articulation between the processes of construction of the "external borders" and the "internal borders," given the characteristics of the project in which the present text is inscribed, we will concentrate on a brief historicization of the first of the mentioned processes.

Cycle of Diffuse Visibility (1810–1860)

We locate this first cycle, which we have delimited and isolated analytically, from the beginning of the independence process, in the early nineteenth century, until the early 1860s (1810–1860). It is a period where a tendency prevailed that could be characterized as inertial, for although there were actions aimed at setting territorial boundaries, the latter did not occupy a central place among the concerns of the new Argentine State. On the contrary, a quick mapping of the governmental actions undertaken to fix the "external" borders shows a marked continuity with colonial demarcation policies (Kralich et al. 2012, 117–118; Benedetti and Salizzi 2014, 123–126).[5]

Cycle of the Accentuated Visibility (1860–1890)

From 1860 to 1980, the "border issue" became ostensibly visible at times; however, it also displayed pronounced fluctuations. In this cycle, two phases can be distinguished with some degree of differentiation: the first (1860–1970) is characterized by the fact that the problem of "external borders" was conveyed by the dynamics of delimitation of the "internal borders." In turn, the second phase (1970–1980) is characterized by the accentuated visibility of inter-state borders associated with geopolitical programs articulated through the doctrine of national security and the development of potential military conflicts with neighboring countries.

Once the central state had managed to symbolically materialize the territorial limits with the neighboring countries, be it by means of military conflicts or diplomatic legal instruments, it was faced with the dilemma of "controlling the vacuum" (Cacopardo 2007, 27). This refers to the need to undertake concrete actions tending to achieve the political, cultural, and economic homogenization of the extensive Argentine territory. Among the actions taken, we can highlight three vitally important corpus of regulations in this period: (a) Law No. 817 of 1876, which established a regime of public land distribution (known as the Avellaneda Law); (b) Law No. 947 of 1878, also called "Boundary Line against the Indians;" and (c) Law No. 1532 of 1882, which was aimed at the "organization of national territories." As a result of this normative scaffolding and the deployment of compulsive and violent plans for the domination and extermination of the indigenous peoples, the central state managed to extend the "internal borders."

These actions of "emptiness control" had a direct impact on the visibility and problematization of the "external borders," as the initiatives implemented by the central government highlighted the importance that these border territories had acquired for the Argentine State. Among those initiatives were (1) the division and organization of the territorial extension through the creation of two political-administrative units; namely (a) the provincial states (provinces), with political, administrative and financial autonomy; and (b) the so-called "national territories," which depended directly on the administration and control of the central government;[6] (2) the creation of national parks;[7] (3) the creation in 1938, by Law No. 12367, of the National Gendarmerie;[8] (4) the creation of the Argentine Naval Prefecture by Law No. 18398 of 1969;[9] (5) as a complement to the establishment of the two security forces (Gendarmerie and Naval Prefecture) mentioned above, the creation, in the 1940s, of the maritime border zones (1944), the National Security Zones Commission (1944) and the security zones (1946);[10] (6) In the 1960s, a series of specific policies that promoted integration with neighboring countries aimed at facilitating the extension and consolidation of regional economies began to be developed. This resulted in a series of projects, some of which materialized in the 1970s, focusing on the construction of bridges, river, rail, and land connections, as well as on the creation of bilateral or multilateral organizations for the regulation of "border areas" and navigable border rivers, mainly in the case of the Paraná and Uruguay rivers.

The second part of the cycle of accentuated visibility was more limited in terms of time and was the stage for the presence of active geopolitical programs stemming from mutual distrust among neighboring nations. This was a consequence of the plans deployed by military governments in the country, in the context of the Cold War, which determined that "border issues, territorial losses, control of strategic resources and internal security legislation" had a decisive impact on how inter-state borders

92　Gustavo González et al.

were thought of and governed (Kralich et al. 2012, 117). During this time, border spaces were conceived as rigid and closed. In other words, what prevailed was a rationality of "closed borders" (Sassone et al. 2001).

In global terms, we could say that this period was strongly marked by the consequences of the March 1976 coup d'état. The Military Junta established relations of an antagonistic tone with the neighboring countries, especially Chile, with whom Argentina was on the verge of war in late 1978 for the control of the Beagle Channel. The paroxysmal expression of this political tone was the war with Great Britain in 1982 for the possession of the Malvinas (Falkland) Islands (Cicalese 2009, 1).

The actions deployed during this phase were characterized by their aim to foster

> [...] those bordering territorial portions, which were sparsely populated due to isolation and scarce economic development. Thereby, the state sought to ensure control of the entire territory in order to consolidate security. However, these policies remained at the level of discourse and rhetoric, with a strong ideological content, but without practical support [...]; the economic and institutional resources applied to achieve the objective were of little relevance and the results were meagre.
>
> (Laurín 2003, 109)

Cycle of Reconfigured Visibility (1980–present)

This last cycle began to take shape in the mid-1980s, with the emergence, in these latitudes, of regional integration programs, which, while recognizing previous efforts, were characterized by

> [...] the energy destined to this action by governments of different institutional scales [...] who agreed on joint actions to promote political, social, and economic integration processes, modernizing existing infrastructure and carrying out specific actions to stimulate the integration and development of isolated subregions.
>
> (Kralich et al. 2012, 118)

These processes had a decisive impact on the visibility and relevance of the borders, since the latter were construed as necessary spaces through which a large part of the general process of binational integration would "transit." As Laurín (2003) states, it was then foreseeable that the immediate effect of regional integration actions (which in principle had a more comprehensive character) would be located only in the border subspace, mainly because of "the particularity of their condition as areas of application of special legal regimes and border policies that go beyond the exclusively economic. Because of their condition of borders and their

Borders, Crime, and State Responses 93

primary function, they have traditionally been the most sensitive spaces to the changes, both political and economic, operated at the national level" (Laurín 2003, 107).

This cycle is characterized by the dizzying and fragmented development of regional integration initiatives and political programs of various kinds, in which Argentina played a very active role. This involvement would generate diversified impacts in terms of border and cross-border integration, since, at least in the rhetoric, what prevailed was the idea of a country with "open borders" (Sassone et al. 2001). We have therefore considered it pertinent to mention only the most important or emblematic initiatives of this period: (1) In 1984, the presidents of Argentina and Brazil signed the Declaration of Foz do Iguazú (border city);[11] (2) in 1986, Argentina and Brazil signed the Act of Argentine-Brazilian Integration; (3) the implementation, since the early 1980s, of the so-called "border committees;" (4) in 1987, through Decree 1182/87, new territorial jurisdictions were defined for the regime of "border areas for development," which were to be distinguished from security areas; (5) in 1988, Law No. 23554 on National Defense was passed, which established that Argentine citizens would enjoy preference for the use of the territory of border areas; (6) in 1991, Law No. 23981 was passed, ratifying the Treaty of Asunción between Argentina, Brazil, Paraguay, and Uruguay, whereby the Southern Common Market (Mercosur) was put into operation;[12] (7) in 1994, Decree 887/94 was issued unifying the border areas for development (which, in turn, included the border areas) with the security areas that had been created in 1944. By 1994, 22 border areas had been established and delimited; (8) in 1999, Mercosur member- and associate countries decided to form the so-called "integrated control areas;"[13] (9) In 2004, Law No. 25871 on immigration was enacted, which entailed a shift in the conception of the migration question in Argentina, as it brought about an adjustment and adaptation of local migration policy to the international covenants and treaties on human rights in force since 1994; and (10) finally, in 2008 Argentina signed the Constitutive Treaty of the Union of South American Nations.

In short, this set of government initiatives designed or implemented is an indicator of the specificity and importance that inter-state borders now have within the new regional integration scheme. In this direction, drawing from Laurín, we believe that in this cycle, which is dominated by the local border question, "the change of spatial strategy is expressed in fundamental norms and is accompanied by the change in the notion of border that such process requires; such notion now conceives of borders as union and opening [...], thus abandoning the conception of border as something rigid to be developed and integrated only 'inwards'" (2003, 110).

These three broad cycles constitute, in some way, indicators of the pendular movement that the border question has displayed in Argentina. Insofar as this theme describes a non-linear trajectory, it is possible to

94 *Gustavo González et al.*

see how at certain moments the border question has been placed at the center of the political and social scene, only to transit, in other periods, to having a much lower or even null visibility.

Second, the ambivalent trajectory of the "border issue" in our local context finds a decisive explanatory factor in the contradictions derived from the various rationalities that have cyclically oriented the central state's programs for the border territories. As we have seen throughout this brief exercise of historical reconstruction, these rationalities and strategies have governed the borders in direct connection with the way they have been "thought," in the sense that they were either constructed as imaginary dividing lines of a rigid and closed nature, or were represented as open, malleable, and necessarily flexible spaces for the purposes of regional integration. Both rationalities "constructed" a differentiated use, control, and regulation of the border territory.[14]

Third and finally, it is possible to hypothesize that, although these governmental rationalities and strategies acquire a certain hegemony in different historical periods, there are, at the same time, forms of coupling and coexistence of these ways of "thinking" and "building" border spaces, which translate into the development of a multiplicity – in terms of complementarity, tension, and contradiction – of governmental plans and actions on border spaces.

General Socio-Demographic Characterization of the Current Border Areas in Argentina

We begin this section by making explicit a methodological decision regarding the analytical and geographical self-limitation of our approach. In principle, our geographical field of inquiry will focus on the northern and eastern borders, which include the international borders with Brazil, Paraguay, and Bolivia. The reasons for limiting our inquiry to these spaces are the following: (a) the considerable extension of the border zones and areas that the Argentine Republic possesses (9,376 kilometers). In this sense, we consider that it is impossible to tackle, in practice and rigorously, such a large geographical area and, (b) in view of the specificity of our research topic within the field of border studies and taking into account the available historical, political, economic, demographic, and social data, we consider that the problem of crime and violence has greater relevance and visibility on the northern and eastern borders, where the presence of factors and variables directly or indirectly linked to the object of research is noted, such as the existence of cross-border urban agglomerations, the development of dynamics associated with border asymmetries, the existence of mirror or twin cities, the presence of greater flows and mobility of people, goods, services, and financial assets, among others. By contrast, these variables have a low or no presence whatsoever in the remaining border areas. Map 4.1 depicts

Borders, Crime, and State Responses 95

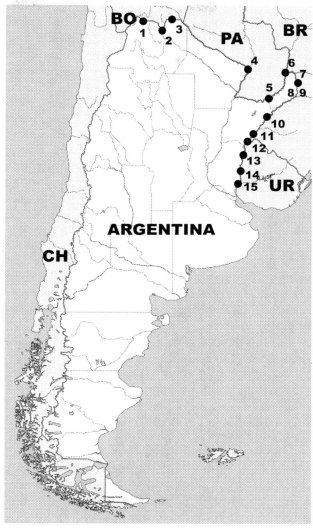

Map key

References:	8. Bernardo de Irigoyen - Barracao
1. La Quiaca - Villazón	9. Bernardo de Irigoyen - Dionísio Cerqueira
2. Aguas Blancas - Bermejo	10. Santo Tomé - Sao Borja
3. Prof. S. Mazza (Pocitos) - Yacuiba	11. Paso de los Libres - Uruguayana
4. Clorinda - Asunción	12. Monte Caseros - Bella Unión - Barra Quareim
5. Posadas - Encarnación	13. Concordia - Salto
6. Puerto Iguazú - Foz de Iguazú - Ciudad del Este	14. Colón - Paysandú
7. San Antonio - San Antonio Do Sudoeste	15. Gualeguaychú - Fray Bento

Map 4.1 Duos and Trios of Cross-Border Cities in Southern South America
Source: Kralich, Benedetti, and Salizzi (2012, 14)
Map by authors

96   *Gustavo González et al.*

the cross-border cities and shows how these are mainly grouped in the North and East of the country.

Below we will provide a basic and global description of the geographical characteristics of the border areas based on data and information provided by the Argentine Geographic Institute, which depends on the National Ministry of Defense.

First, we must bear in mind that Argentina borders Bolivia and Paraguay to the North, Chile and the South Atlantic Ocean to the South, Brazil, Uruguay, and the South Atlantic Ocean to the East, and Chile to the West. Second, as far as the length of the borders is concerned, the Argentine Republic has a border perimeter that, only in the American continental portion, stretches along approximately 15,000 kilometers. Of this total, 9,376 kilometers correspond to the limits with the five countries mentioned above and 5,117 kilometers to the river coast of the Río de la Plata and the Argentine Sea. If we break down the total perimeter by bordering countries, the distribution is as follows: Chile 5,308 kilometers, Paraguay 1,699 kilometers, Brazil 1,132 kilometers, Bolivia 742 kilometers, and Uruguay 495 kilometers. Finally, as for the length of the coasts, these are distributed as follows: Argentine Antarctica and Southern islands: 11,235 kilometers, Atlantic coast: 4,725 kilometers, and Río de la Plata: 392 kilometers.

In addition to this generic reference of geographical data, it is pertinent to present some more significant socio-economic indicators of the northern and eastern border areas, for they evidence the specificity of these spaces.[15] Among them we highlight the following:

a Resorting to the index of *Necesidades Básicas Insatisfechas* (unsatisfied basic needs – UBN) as an indicator of structural poverty, it can be stated that all provinces with border areas on the North and East register high levels of poverty. With the sole exception of Entre Ríos, all of them register levels of poverty that are at least 7 percentage points (ranging from 19.5% to 25.2%) above the national average of 12.5%.

b The activity rate in all provinces with border areas in the North and East is between 3.8 and 9.2 percentage points below the average activity rate for the country, which is 5.6%.

c Something similar occurs with the employment rate, which is 61.7% at the national level, while in these provinces it ranges from 53.6% in the province of Corrientes and 58.9% in Entre Rios. This latter province, which borders Uruguay, has lower levels of population with UBN, and higher rates of activity and employment than the rest of the provinces that share a border with Paraguay, Brazil, and Bolivia.

d If we disaggregate these indicators by department and consider those that are located along the northern and eastern borders, we can obtain interesting data. Regarding the percentages of the population with UBN, 27 out of the 40 border departments analyzed in

Borders, Crime, and State Responses 97

these provinces register higher percentages of population with some UBN indicator than their relative provincial average. This contrast becomes even more evident if we consider the percentage of population with UBN in the whole country, which is much lower than the percentages registered in these departments.

e In the case of the province of Formosa, five of the seven departments[16] that border Paraguay register higher percentages of population with UBN than the provincial average. Particularly, Bermejo and Ramón Lista, which are the poorest considering the other ones positioned at the border.

f The situation in the provinces of Jujuy and Salta is similar to the one previously discussed. In Jujuy, the three border departments register higher percentages of UBN than the provincial average; and in Salta, the same happens with the four-border departments.

g In the case of Misiones, it is not useful to make this distinction, since only two of its departments do not have a border. Particularly, the department of Iguazú, where the homonymous city forms the cross-border conurbation with Ciudad del Este in Paraguay and Foz de Iguazú in Brazil – a geographical point also known as Triple Frontier – registers 24.82% of population with UBN and occupies the second place in the province, 5.72 percentage points above the provincial average and 12.32 points above the average percentage of population with UBN of the country.

h In the province of Corrientes, the linkage of border departments with high levels of population with UBN becomes loser: only five out of eleven departments have a percentage of population with UBN higher than the average of their province.

i The province of Entre Ríos does not adapt to this regularity found in the rest of the provinces. The departments of this province that border Uruguay do not have higher levels of population with UBN than others, but these values exceed the average of the province, as well as their corresponding activity and employment rates, which in five out of six departments, stand above the average of the province.

j At the same time, it can be pointed out that the three departments that reach critical percentages of UBN in those provinces – exceeding 50 points – belong to border regions: Rivadavia (57.4%) in the province of Salta, and Bermejo (52.94%) and Ramón Lista (76.28%) in the province of Jujuy.

k About the 14 cross-border conurbations on the Argentine side of the border, it can be noted that they are generally small cities with populations of less than 85,000 inhabitants, except for Concordia (151,086 inhabitants) – in Entre Ríos – and Posadas (275,305 inhabitants) – in Misiones –. Likewise, they are municipalities – except for Colón and Gualeguaychú in Entre Ríos – with higher UBN levels than the total of the national average (12.5%).

98   *Gustavo González et al.*

l   In 2010, all the cities bordering Bolivia had high rates of UBN: La Quiaca (19.82%), Professor Salvador Mazza (32.50%), and Aguas Blancas (35.82%).

m   Within the Province of Misiones, the Puerto Iguazú conglomerate, has an average UBN of 24.5%, far exceeding the other cross-border conglomerates in the province (Posadas 13.76%, Bernardo de Irigoyen 15.99%, and San Antonio 19.89%).

Regarding security, official statistics in Argentina have unfortunately not been published since 2011 – when they became the responsibility of the Ministry of National Security – so there is only information regarding the border areas until 2009. In that year, intentional homicide rates – the type of crime with the lowest level of underreporting in this sort of statistical source and, therefore, a relatively reliable indicator (Sozzo 2008, 21–41) – in most of the provinces with border areas in the North and East were equal to or below the national average of 5.8 per 100,000 inhabitants. These rates were 4.4/100,000 in Corrientes, 4.7/100,000 in Salta, 5.9/100,000 in Misiones, and 6/100,000 in Entre Ríos. The relatively moderate exceptions were Jujuy with 6.8/100,000 and Formosa with 7.3/100,000.

In some of the jurisdictions, the rates of intentional homicides recorded in the last available year are substantially lower than those seen 30 years ago. Such is the case of Misiones (–54%) and Corrientes (–77%). In the case of Formosa, the difference is smaller (–13%), but in this province, the difference becomes more evident if the comparison is made with 1989 (–85%), a phenomenon that can also be observed in in Misiones (–63%) and, although not to the same extent, in Corrientes (–24%) as well. In contrast, in the northeastern provinces of Salta and Jujuy, there are currently higher levels of intentional homicide than 30 years ago (47% and 28% higher, respectively). In the case of Salta, the difference becomes clearer if compared to 1989 rates, when the level was extraordinarily low. But in the case of Jujuy, the relationship is reversed, with a 19% reduction in the last 20 years. Entre Ríos stands out, in an intermediate position, for its stability in the comparison over a long period, both with 1979 and 1989 figures. Finally, in all jurisdictions, except for Jujuy, there are lower rates of intentional homicide in the last available year than those recorded in 2002, at the height of the strongest economic, political, and social crisis experienced by the country since the beginning of the transition to democracy: –29% in Misiones, –41% in Corrientes, –39% in Formosa, –30% in Entre Ríos, –46% in Salta. Based on these data, it is therefore possible to state that the incidence of intentional homicides in the border areas is low, and in general terms, has even decreased in the last 30 years.

Beyond intentional homicides, official statistics – even when they exist – do not provide adequate information about certain illegal markets that are particularly developed in Argentina's border areas. For example, with respect to the trafficking of illegal drugs, these statistics only provide information about the number of alleged criminal acts linked to these illegal substances, without differentiating between the production and circulation of narcotics and, surely enough, they only account for this mass of cases when they are detected by the respective police institutions, masking a significant volume of non-reported cases that is very difficult to estimate. This consideration is valid for other illegal markets in the country's border areas – arms trafficking, smuggling, human trafficking. It is for this reason that the only way to approach these other forms of criminal activity in these geographical areas at present is by means of the incipient social research on the issue carried out in Argentina, to which this project intends to contribute.

Border studies: The Issue of Crime and State Responses to Crime in Argentina

In the mid-1990s, the theme of "borders" began to emerge and became consolidated as an area of study in the research agendas of some of the disciplines of the social sciences (mainly history, geography, anthropology, and sociology).[17] The new importance accorded to borders materialized in a vast academic production that fostered the consolidation of a field of study with a certain identity, but which, at the same time, proved to be very heterogeneous. This responds to the quantity and quality of the bibliographic production, to the diversity of topics surveyed and analyzed, as well as to the varied constitution and levels of consolidation of academic teams with or without thematic exclusivity on this renewed object of research.

While the increased academic interest in borders coincides, to some extent, with the cycle that we have called "reconfigured visibility," we should not entertain the distorted idea that we are facing an academic novelty. On the contrary, prior to the 1990s, a body of texts and research had been produced that addressed the issue of borders in the national context.[18] From 1995 onwards, we have witnessed, as already mentioned, the structuring of this heterogeneous field of academic studies on borders, where we can visualize a range of concerns, debates, and topics that have gained ever greater relevance.

First, we find works that pose debates of a general nature and try to clarify theoretical and methodological positions that coexist within the field of "border studies." Benedetti's work (2007), constitutes a substantial contribution in this sense, as it identifies three major trends in this knowledge-area:

> The first one takes interstate borders as its object. This work usually reconstructs the process of defining international boundaries during the period of state organization and consolidation in the Southern Cone, and the historical or contemporary changes in the

100 *Gustavo González et al.*

> dynamics of local societies in relation to the border [...]. The second trend focuses on the study of 'expansion frontiers', either between nation-states and indigenous societies, or between colonial states and indigenous societies [...] Some of these works propound the coincidence between one and another type of frontier [...]. Finally, in the third trend, a concept or metaphorical notion of border is generally used to analyze the processes of change in societies located in border areas.
>
> (Benedetti 2007, 5–6)

On this same level of discussion, we find the works that stem from the intersection between anthropology, historiography, and sociology. Such works pose, from a genealogical perspective, the debates around the construction of borders, the relevance of the use of polysemic concepts such as limits, boundaries, border, or trans-border areas, etc., among other important issues (Blanco et al. 1997; Losada, 2000; Karasik 2000; Gordillo and Leguizamón 2002; Ratto 2001; Gascón 2003; Benedetti and Laguado 2013).

Second, it is possible to reconstruct the aforementioned academic field, based on the disciplinary origin of the contributions and research that has nourished it. In this sense, three major tributary disciplines can be identified. On the one hand, anthropology, where ethnographic approaches and the problematization of the so-called "symbolic borders" have become more important (Grimson 2000 and 2003; Trinchero 2000; Jerez 2006; Caggiano 2007; Linares 2008; Giménez Béliveau and Montenegro 2006). On the other hand, political and economic geography, which have focused on the topics of interstate borders, expanding borders and the relevance of borders within the processes of globalization and regional integration (Blanco et al. 1997; Reboratti 1999; Laurín 1999 and 2003; Zusman 2000 and Escolar 2000; Sassone et al. 2001 and Sassone 2004; Benedetti 2007 and Benedetti and Salizzi, 2011a and 2011b; among others). Finally, history, which has generated significant contributions focused on the historicization and reconstruction of the dynamics of "external and internal" borders-construction, the historical trajectories of inter-ethnic relations and the shaping of border relations or societies, among other topics (Areces 1999; Hevilla 1999; Bandieri 2000 and 2001; Lacoste 2003; Cacopardo 2007).

Third, we can identify the thematic axes or problems addressed with a greater degree of specificity in this field of study, regardless of the disciplinary area of origin. On this basis, we can isolate groups of research according to the following criteria:

a) By geographical area or region: here we find works referring to the Triple Frontier (Grimson 2003; Rabossi 2008 and 2011; Giménez Béliveau and Montenegro 2006 and 2010; Montenegro 2013;

Borders, Crime, and State Responses 101

Renoldi 2013 and 2014); focused on the Argentina-Paraguay border (Grimson 2000; Gordillo and Leguizamón 2002; Renoldi 2005a and 2005b; Linares 2009 and 2010; Arellano 2012); on the Argentina-Bolivia border (Karasik 2000; Losada 2000; Benedetti and Salizzi 2011a and 2011b); on the Argentina-Chile border (Hevilla 1999; Escolar 2000; Gascón 2001; Bandieri 2001; Laurín 2003; Lacoste 2003) and on the Argentina-Uruguay border (Garavaglia and Merklen 2008; Ovalle and Burgueño 2009; and País Andrade 2010).

b) Studies on the dynamics of mobility in cross-border agglomerations and the development of logics of asymmetric relationships between border cities (Schiavoni 2005; Benedetti and Salizzi 2011 and 2014; Kralich et al. 2012).

c) Works focused on the processes of delimitation of interstate borders and on the transformations triggered by regional integration processes (Pérez Vicich 1993; Lavopa et al. 1997; Cisneros and Escudé 2000; Laurín 2003; Linares 2009).

d) Analytical contributions that deal with the transformation of migration policies in Argentina and their impact on the border system (De Marco and Sassone 1995; Sassone et al. 2001; Sassone 2004).

e) Research aimed at describing social, political, economic, and cultural conflicts in border clusters (Grimson 2000; Linares 2008; País Andrade 2010).

However, specifically with regard to research promoted from the social sciences, aimed at exploring some of the emerging issues at the intersection of crime, state responses and border spaces, there is a marked area of vacancy in the context of "border studies," since academic production is, to date, incipient and of differing rigor. Given the specificity of this background for the construction of our research, we will now group them around the topics they have tried to address.

Contraband

On this topic, we identified, first, a series of anthropological investigations developed by Brígida Renoldi (2014), which are based on ethnographic research in the Triple Frontier of Argentina, Paraguay, and Brazil. Acknowledging the vast range of the research produced by Renoldi, it is, nonetheless, possible to identify a common thread in her work; namely the effort to highlight the existence and extension of everyday social and institutional practices, in which customs agents and security forces allow the display of illegal activities, such as the unregistered transit of people and the entry of illegal merchandise through border areas. According to Renoldi, such activities feed and sustain the formation of labor markets and the trade of informal and illegal products in border cities.[19] In more general analytical terms, Renoldi observes that each state

102   *Gustavo González et al.*

establishes a malleable hierarchy of criteria to make a law functional at a given moment, making it possible for official, be they customs or police agents, to interpret the phenomena in a web of meanings given by the context, that can sometimes be far removed from what the law provides (Renoldi 2014).

Second, we can mention the work of Diana Arellano (2012), who seeks to describe and analyze the socio-economic relations of border cities such as Posadas (Argentina) and Encarnación (Paraguay). For, as the author states, "border citizens create, perfect and render more complex highly dynamic socio-economic practices, by describing and paying special attention to this capacity to create and recreate strategies that allow them to overcome obstacles in each situation and maximize economic opportunities in a framework of inter-legalities at the local level" (Arellano 2012, 1).

Third, we recover the work of Benedetti and Salizzi. Based on the analysis of the border between Argentina and Bolivia, these authors maintain that the border is an economic resource, to the extent that it enables the development of trade circuits that take advantage of exchange rate disparities and the different possibilities and dysfunctions created by state controls. Traders in these circuits possess a know-how about the transport of goods from the mountains, which goes back to the use of llamas and mules in caravans. Through that system, they achieve both the economic complementation of their communities and, in the long term, the accumulation of capital, product of the provision of some urban populations. This is an underground circulation, with great spatial fluidity and capacity to adapt to changes, with territorialities designed on a Southern Cone scale, superimposed on those of the nation-state (Benedetti and Salizzi 2011a, 167).

Finally, we refer the work of María Dolores Linares (2010), who maintains that one of the dominant modalities of cross-border dynamics is the daily commercial practice of the Paraguayan women, called *paseras*.[20] According to Linares, the commercial exchange of the *paseras* is linked to knowledge and practices that refer to a "subculture of the border," where the inhabitants "are linked in their daily lives to several national systems at once, speak several languages, do the math to handle several national currencies, always trying to get more out of the dynamics of the border" (Linares 2010, 337). The *paseras* can enter and leave Argentina as many times as they wish, thanks to the modality of *Tránsito Vecinal Fronterizo*, an agreement between the Mercosur member states, that allows the inhabitants of border cities to cross the border and remain in the neighboring country for a maximum of 72 hours.[21] Yet, entering the country with the purpose to pursue profit (i.e., working without permit) and introducing goods "for own consumption that are not from the country of origin" (AFIP 262/98) is illegal. This notwithstanding, *paseras* bring into Argentina cigarettes,

Borders, Crime, and State Responses 103

imported alcoholic beverages (prohibited by the customs code), and textiles, among other products.

Drug Trafficking

Despite the marked visibility of this topic both in the media and in the political debate, we find scant development from the social sciences regarding the incidence of drug trafficking in border areas in Argentina. Brígida Renoldi, one of the researchers we mentioned in the previous topic, has published amply on the representations that certain agents have about drug trafficking in the Triple Frontier (Renoldi 2005b, 2007, 2012, 2013, and 2014). In one of her studies on the perceptions of drug trafficking in Argentina, Renoldi points out that in the judicial or police spheres, the expressions *narcotráfico* (drug trafficking) and *"el narco"* are used to refer to the universe of the drug trade, with a background idea that associates the practices of such trade with organizations with political power or important businessmen. However, neither police action nor criminal investigations go beyond the flagrant cases that have been committed – that generally affect people involved as *mulas* (mules) (who transport the drugs in vehicles, backpacks, etc.) or *camellos* (camels) (who ingest drugs to transport them to their destination) – nor is there evidence that elements of this trade beyond the weakest links in the chain are found among these populations (Renoldi 2014, 13).

In general terms, the author argues that

> [...] Misiones Federal Justice intervenes in all cases of violation of the law on drugs that occur within the territorial limits of that province. Cases of *flagrante delicto* are usually for the transportation of marijuana (only seldom cocaine) within the country, and sometimes for contraband (border crossing). In other words, the Police, the National Gendarmerie and the judiciary intervene in a fragment of the drug trafficking network. [...]. The limitation is that federal investigations can only reach the border with Paraguay.
>
> (Renoldi 2005b, 174)

In parallel, we found four works that make their contributions from different perspectives. Jorge Depetris (2011) briefly describes the phenomenon of drug trafficking, both for the regional and the local contexts. He further reviews the role of the customs authority in relation to it and describes the historical changes that the models of control in the Argentine customs have undergone. In this vein, Depetris identifies a first period of "heavy hand" (1983–1991); a second one of "light hand" (1992–2001); and a third period characterized as "regulatory craft" (2002–2007). Depetris' work further describes the fundamental changes in this latter period due to drug trafficking: structural modifications in the organization of

104   *Gustavo González et al.*

customs, incorporation of technology, development of computer systems and databases of the Federal Administration of Public Revenues, non-informatic technologies, satellite tracking of transit and transfers, trained dogs, alliances and internal coordination within the customs structure, databases, and other sources of information. The author analyzes four cases where the customs authority managed to detect and seize cocaine for export, based on risk-management approaches, and emphasizing the role of regulatory agencies.

In the field of international relations, we find the work of Gastón H. Schulmeister (2009), who argues that Argentina has ceased to be just a place of transit of narcotics to become a destination for consumption, and even a location of incipient production of illegal drugs. Given the change in its condition, mainly due to its consolidation as a transit bridge, the new reality deserves an analysis of both its internal and external effects. Schulmeister argues that it is appropriate to note the modification suffered by Argentina as a transit country caused by exogenous factors – pressures exerted on Colombia and Mexico in the fight against drug trafficking – which, in turn, redefined the impact that Argentina has on the world's illicit drug market.

As stated by the 2009 report of the State Department's Bureau of International Narcotics and Law Enforcement Affairs, Argentina is a transit country for cocaine produced in the Andean region – from Bolivia, Peru, and Colombia – to Europe and, to a lesser extent, for Colombian heroin destined for the United States. This diagnose is consistent with information provided by multiple United Nations reports (Schulmeister 2009, 4).

In order to analyze the growing importance that Argentina has acquired as a transit country, Schulmeister warns that Spain – which along with Portugal is the major entry point into Europe – already records more cocaine seizures from Argentina – where no coca leaf is grown – than from Colombia, the world's largest coca leaf producer. Thus, Argentina is, according to this author, among the top ten cocaine exporting countries to Europe and among the top twenty countries of origin of cocaine and marijuana seizures in the world. Based on a report issued by the Secretariat of Planning for the Prevention of Drug Addiction and the Fight against Drug Trafficking (SEDRONAR), Schulmeister maintains that there are two main trafficking circuits to Argentina: cocaine from Bolivia and cannabis from Paraguay. As for cannabis, Argentina ranks third in terms of global seizures in South America, with 67 tons. "In turn, while cocaine, ecstasy and other designer drugs are exported from Argentina mainly to Europe, heroin, ephedrine or methamphetamines – highly demanded drugs in the U.S. – are transported from the port of Buenos Aires to Mexico, from where Mexican cartels orchestrate the traffic to its US neighbor" (Schulmeister 2009, 6).

In line with this trend, the ephedrine business elicited particular attention in Argentina during 2008, after its illegal trade to Mexico emerged as one of the main hypotheses behind a triple murder committed in General Rodríguez in August 2008. According to customs authority figures released by the press, during 2008 – until December 10 – 4,657 kilograms of ephedrine had been seized in Argentina, with the intention of being illegally traded.

A last piece of information that the author highlights regarding the geographical distribution of illicit drugs in general, is that cocaine is seized predominantly in the city of Buenos Aires, and in the provinces of Buenos Aires, Salta, and Jujuy, while marijuana – 80% from Paraguay – is mostly seized in Misiones and Corrientes. In turn, the diversion of chemical precursors occurs mostly in the city of Buenos Aires and in the homonymous province (Schulmeister 2009, 7).

Human Trafficking

Regarding the issue of human trafficking in border contexts, we note that the contributions of the social sciences in Argentina have been marginal to this topic. In addition, they have focused primarily on human trafficking for the purpose of sexual exploitation. The text by Georgina María Barvinsk (2014) which analyzes the Triple Frontier region must be highlighted. Barvinsk asserts that border populations are neglected by the central powers of the different countries, leading to the economic, cultural, and social impoverishment of such populations. This fosters the emergence of illegal economies in general, as well as the naturalization of criminal acts and the consequent participation of large segments of the population as victims, perpetrators, or accomplices. "[In this area] there is no presence of the state in its role as guarantor of the welfare of the population. Thus, this unprotected population begins to weave links with alternative sources of authority, represented by organized crime groups" (Barvinsk 2014, 10). The author further considers that the origin of the practices of non-consensual sexual exploitation, which are carried out in border areas, has a direct relationship with the conditions of socio-economic vulnerability (low educational level, structural unemployment, high rates of informal employment, etc.) that drive women, usually deceived by job offers (or by the conditions in which sex work will be carried out), toward the neighbor countries. In this way, recruiters use techniques of persuasion and deception to convince victims of the benefits of the alleged trip to the neighboring country, and of the benefits of the job offer they propose.

A different approach to the problem was taken by the International Organization for Migration in a 2008 report (OIM 2008), that provides

106 *Gustavo González et al.*

a global analysis of the phenomenon of human trafficking, its dynamics and modalities in Argentina, Chile, and Uruguay. The report briefly studies the case of the province of Misiones, explores a series of demographic indicators, and presents an extensive casuistry of recruitment and modes of operation. This work also notes the predominance of domestic trafficking over the international one in the case of Argentine victims (OIM 2008, 98). However, in line with other studies, the report notes that many women of Paraguayan nationality were detected as victims of trafficking, entering the country through the Encarnación-Posadas's route.

Another report, also carried out by IOM, within the framework of the Comprehensive Assistance Program for Victims of Human Trafficking in the Tri-Border Area between Argentina, Brazil, and Paraguay (OIM 2010) concludes that, in this area, prostitution or sexual exploitation of children, adolescents, and adult women is an everyday occurrence for the local population. Moreover, the report states that one of the major difficulties for its combat is the naturalization of this form of exploitation, as well as the lack of understanding about the historicity of the processes of inequality on which the various forms of sexual exploitation are based (and often also justified).

In regard to the trafficking of minors, María Cecilia Zsögön (2013) addresses the problem from the perspective of the characterization of the area as one marked by strong contrasts where, in the specific geographical border context, intense tourism and cultural activities coexist with inequality, misery and exclusion. For her part, Mónica Tarducci (2006) strongly criticizes the reports produced by various institutions, which point to exorbitant numbers without accurate data or from dubious sources, concluding that the phenomenon of child trafficking is not as serious in the Misiones area as it is often assumed (Tarducci 2006, 53–56). Also in relation to child trafficking, Benedetti and Salizzi (2011a) point out that the Immigration Pastoral of the Prelature of Humahuaca, detected that about 9,000 children from the poor rural areas of Potosí and its surroundings cross the border between Bolivia and Argentina every year, without leaving any record of their destination. According to the organization's research, Bolivian peasant families in extreme poverty hand over their children to people who offer work opportunities on the Argentine side. They claim that these displacements would take place on a daily basis, in conjunction with the development of semi-slave labor markets in rural areas of the country (Benedetti and Salizzi 2011a, 171).

The Instituto de Estudios Comparados en Ciencias Penales y Sociales (INECIP) in collaboration with the Fiscal Assistance Unit for the Investigation of Extortive Kidnapping and Human Trafficking of the Federal Prosecutor's Office, produced a series of reports on the issue. One of them looks at Argentinean and Paraguayan law in detail, and

Borders, Crime, and State Responses 107

then analyzes the various dynamics of human trafficking and its phases, including international trafficking, which – according to the report – has its axis in Paraguay as a place of recruitment of girls and Argentina as a place of destination and exploitation (INECIP 2013, 237). Furthermore, the report suggests that the networks observed in both countries do not indicate a broad territorial scope and states that it is not possible to identify clear links between the Paraguayan and Argentine networks, except for the presence of Paraguayan traffickers in sexual exploitation cases in Argentina (INECIP 2013, 241). In the same vein, in 2012 INECIP published another report where suggestive figures regarding international trafficking in Argentina emerge. Succinctly, the report states that 36% of women rescued – whose cases were prosecuted – were Paraguayan, and 51% Argentinean, against a contrasting 3% of other nationalities (INECIP 2012, 19).

From these studies it can be concluded that the question of human trafficking and borders in Argentina is concentrated mainly in the Northeast, where the most pressing problem is the recruitment of women from Paraguay in the border province of Misiones for the purpose of sexual exploitation, as well as the illegal transit (by means of forged documents and bribery) and/or the "legal" – albeit not consented – transit of women, through Paraguayan border crossings, to be sexually exploited throughout the Argentine territory. These activities further reveal the existence of a cross-border criminal circuit that involves precarious human trafficking networks.

State Responses to the Problem of Crime in Border Areas

The issue of state policies against crime on Argentina's borders has been addressed in a fragmented way by social studies. As we already saw when analyzing the main topics related to different forms of crime (drug trafficking, human trafficking, terrorism, etc.), academic works tangentially address the issue by making brief references to the state responses tested, both unilaterally by the national state in Argentina and through agreements and joint actions with bordering states.

This swift mapping of the field of border studies allows us to reaffirm the idea, and, at the same time, agree with some tributary researchers of this field, that this is an area of study that shows dynamism, heterogeneity, and diverse depths in the case of Argentina. At the same time, while it makes it possible to throw light on certain emerging processes and dynamics in border territories, it leaves in the dark other processes and dynamics that are also significant in such enclaves. Specifically, on the problems associated with criminality and violence, there is a clear area of vacancy in the context of "border studies," as academic production is incipient and of differing rigor.

Conclusion

To conclude, we would like to restate the most significant ideas that we have put forward in this process of building, in an exploratory key, a "state of the art," which may allow us to think in greater depth about the intersection between borders, crime and state reactions to crime in the Argentine context:

- It is necessary to recognize the impact of the various rationalities and strategies of border governance, in the sense that they act as a conditioners for the variety of processes of visibility, as well as the symbolic and material construction of borders.
- It is necessary to point out the sedimentation and coexistence of different rationalities and strategies for the use, control, and regulation of border areas.
- There is a marked entanglement of the historical processes of shaping the so-called "external borders" with the "internal borders."
- On the basis of specific socio-demographic indicators, it is possible to state certain specificities of Argentine border areas, which for the most part present conditions of greater social vulnerability – with respect to national averages. However, this is not necessarily connected with high levels of crime and violence, at least on the basis of the weak official information available.
- In recent years, a field of study has developed within the social sciences, focusing on the issue of borders, which is characterized by its dynamic and heterogeneous conformation.
- The research agendas in the field of "border studies" in Argentina, highlight some significant problems of border areas, while ignoring others, thus rendering them invisible.
- There is an incipient and limited development of social research related to the rigorous and reliable analysis of crime and violence in cross-border spaces; namely, smuggling, drug trafficking, human trafficking, arms trafficking, and money laundering. Very few cases offer rigorous empirical research and most of them depend on officially produced information – with the limits that this implies. Furthermore, there is a very strong area of vacancy with respect to state responses to crime.

Notes

1. This article is a first product of a series of research tasks of greater scope and depth included in the framework of the project "Exploring the political economy of violence in Latin American border systems: Towards a comprehensive understanding. Argentina's Global Border Subsystem" (IDRC – FLACSO – Ecuador – UNL).

2. Throughout the text we will use these terms interchangeably, although we recognize that there is an ongoing debate on the pertinence of using one form or another for this field of study.
3. The present exercise of historical reconstruction by appealing to the identification of "great cycles" does not imply ignoring two derivations that we consider important to explain. In the first place, it might entail over-simplifying historical and social processes by presenting them in terms of a logical and evolutionary sequence. Second, and directly linked to the first point, it could imply a lack of knowledge of the trajectories of social processes, which, far from being linear, are marked by breaks, folds, bifurcations, and concealment. However, we consider that, given the characteristics and objectives of this work, the recourse to periodization is useful for illustrative purposes.
4. This distinction comes from British political geographer Peter J. Taylor, who postulated that it is possible to differentiate between state actions that "look inward" (define a territorial limit of differentiation) and those that "look outward" (define a zone of contact with the "outside") (Taylor 1994, 144 and ff.).
5. In the case of the border with Bolivia, after this country's declaration of independence in 1825, tensions arose from territorial disputes that were finally settled with the 1889 Treaty of Limits, where both countries agreed to respect the boundaries that existed prior to independence. Regarding Brazil and Uruguay, there were a number of significant historical events. First, the recognition in 1828 by the United Provinces of Río de la Plata (current Argentine Republic) and the Empire of Brazil, through the signing of the so-called Preliminary Peace Convention, of the existence of the Eastern State (current Eastern Republic of Uruguay). This instrument not only implied the beginning of Uruguay's autonomy from Brazil and Argentina, but also put an end to the war with Brazil. Second, this delimitation with respect to Uruguay and, more generally, with respect to the border with Brazil, was enshrined in law with the Treaty of Peace, Friendship, Commerce and Navigation, concluded between the Argentine Confederation and the Brazilian Empire in 1856. As regards the territorial limits with Chile, these were established during this cycle by means of two instruments: the Treaty of Friendship and Alliance and the Treaty of Peace, Friendship, Trade and Navigation, signed in 1828 and 1856, respectively. Through these instruments, Argentina and Chile agreed to respect the limits that existed during the Spanish colonial period and to negotiate peacefully and through arbitration any possible border disputes. Finally, the case of the border with Paraguay is the only one that extended beyond the referenced time cycle. This process of delimitation was crossed by the so-called War of the Triple Alliance, a strategic military alliance between Argentina, Brazil, and Uruguay, to combat Paraguay, after this country declared war on Argentina in 1865. This war took place between 1865 and 1870 and culminated with the signature of the Treaty of Limits between Argentina and Paraguay in 1876. Although the belicose bidding ended in favor of the Triple Alliance, this did not translate into substantial modifications of the limits that existed before the armed conflict, at least as far as Argentina was concerned.
6. In the 1880s, the latter were geographically located in the south, north, and northeast of the country, in inter-state border areas, somehow demonstrating the importance that the central government gave to the "border issue," since it reserved for itself, and not for the provinces, the management and direct control of these territories.

110　*Gustavo González et al.*

7. These were put into operation in the 1930s and were preferably located "[...] on the international borders of the country [...] they were emblematic institutions in the process of consolidating the state's presence in international border areas" (Benedetti and Salizzi 2014, 127).
8. Security force in charge of border control.
9. From the period we are analyzing, this institution exercised more actively "the navigation police service and the security and judicial police service and partially the administrative jurisdiction of navigation" in maritime areas, ports and rivers bordering neighboring countries.
10. These political initiatives, aimed at organizing border security institutions and generating territorial areas with a special legal regime, emerged as state responses to certain tensions and problems in the border areas (Sassone 2004, 224).
11. In this declaration, the parties set out to start planning for economic cooperation between the two nations and "close the era of confrontation." In this way, a process of "open regionalism" was set in motion that had a significant impact on border areas (Sassone 2004, 232).
12. Although the treaty implies the relationship with only three of the five countries bordering Argentina (Brazil, Paraguay, and Uruguay), in the case of Bolivia and Chile, these have the status of associated states;" hence, the contemplated effects also have some degree of relevance for border relations with these two countries.
13. These are devices at land border crossings, where officials from different agencies (security, transport, customs, etc.) from neighboring countries carry out controls sequentially and, if possible, simultaneously, thus implying that the jurisdiction and competence of the agencies and officials from the neighboring country are considered to extend to the host country.
14. It is necessary to clarify that there are different analytical modalities used to reconstruct a sort of historical periodization of the process of construction of the inter-state borders for the case of the Argentine Republic (see Sassone et al. 2001 and Sassone 2004; Cacopardo, 2007; Kralich et al. 2012; Benedetti and Salizzi, 2014).
15. The following data have been produced by the Instituto Nacional de Estadísticas y Censo de la República Argentina, Dirección Nacional de Estadísticas Sociales y de Población. Special processing by the Dirección de Estadísticas Sectoriales con base en el Censo Nacional de Población, Hogares y Viviendas, 2010.
16. Departments are second-order administrative units.
17. According to Benedetti, "this set of studies shows an effort to work with different spatial and temporal scales, to confront the traditional geopolitical and nationalist view of borders; to make the concept of region more flexible, trying not to condition the regional delimitation by the existence of international limits; to carry out detailed ethnographic work which in many cases is complemented by the systematic analysis of archives and, finally, to carry out a historical analysis of the process of configuring border territories" (2007, 3).
18. More specifically, we refer to that group of researchers coming from the field of history and partly from geography, who were oriented to the study of the dynamics of the formation of the so-called "internal borders," which we have mentioned in the first part of the present work. In this direction we can highlight the works of Halperin Donghi (1980); Viñas (1982); Giberti (1970); Oszlak (1983); Clementi (1987); Rey Balmaceda (1977); among others.

Borders, Crime, and State Responses 111

19. According to the author, when it comes to the justifications put forward by state agents for this type of practice, reasons can be found such as "not considering them harmful," that they are "honest people" and "professions" that record the passage of several generations, or that they are practices that "allow for solutions to the problem of unemployment."
20. This is the name given to the women whose job it is to "pass" small quantities of goods across the border without paying taxes on a daily basis for sale, resale, or delivery. This activity generates different articulations that translate into family, friendship, and contractual relationships. It is a work naturalized as "traditional," even if it is illegal.
21. See: MERCOSUR/CMC/DEC. Resolution No. 14/00.

References

Areces, Nidia. 1999. "Regiones y fronteras. Apuntes desde la historia." *Andes. Antropología e historia*, 10, 19–33.

Arellano, Diana. 2012. "Dinámicas comerciales transfronterizas. Posadas-Encarnación." Paper presented at the V Simpósio Iberoamericano em Comércio Internacional, Desenvolvimento e Integraçao Regional, organized by RedCIDIR (Red Interuniversitaria de Internacionalización del Conocimiento, Orientada al Conocimiento, el Desarrollo y la Integración Regional) y FEMA (Facultades Integradas Machado De Assis), Santa Rosa, Rio Grande Do Sul, Brazil, November 7–9, 2012.

Bandieri, Susana. 2000. "Ampliando las fronteras: la ocupación de la Patagonia." In *El Progreso, la Modernización y sus Límites (1880–1916), Nueva Historia Argentina*, directed by Mirta Lobato, Volume five, 119–177. Buenos Aires: Sudamericana.

———— 2001. "Estado nacional, frontera y relaciones fronterizas en los Andes nor-patagónicos: continuidades y rupturas." In *Cruzando la cordillera… La frontera argentino-chilena como espacio social*, coordinated by Susana Bandieri, 345–374. Neuquén: Centro de Estudios de Historia Regional – CEHIR, Facultad de Humanidades, Universidad Nacional del Comahue.

Barvinsk, Georgina María. 2014. "La trata de mujeres con fines de explotación sexual En la región de la Triple Frontera." *Urvio, Revista Latinoamericana de Estudios de Seguridad*, 2014 (June) (14): 68–78.

Benedetti, Alejandro. 2007. "El debate sobre las fronteras en la Argentina." *Revista Estudios Socioterritoriales. Revista de Geografía* 6, 2005/2006, 11–36.

———— 2014. "Fronteras en la construcción del territorio argentino." *Cuadernos de Geografía. Revista Colombiana de Geografía*, 23 (2) (July–December), 121–138.

Benedetti, Alejandro and Esteban Salizzi. 2011a. "Llegar, pasar, regresar a la frontera. Aproximación al sistema de movilidad argentino-boliviano." *Revista Transporte y Territorio*, 4, 148–179.

———— 2011b. "Frontera y movilidad. Aproximaciones al caso argentino-boliviano." *Ideação*, 13 (1) (First Semester), 55–80.

———— 2014. "Fronteras en la construcción del territorio argentino." *Cuadernos de Geografía*, 23 (2), 121–138.

Benedetti, Alejandro and Íñigo Laguado. 2013. "El espacio fronterizo argentino-chileno: definición de categorías operativas y primera aproximación descriptiva." In *Fronteras, territorios, y montañas: la cordillera de Los Andes como*

112 *Gustavo González et al.*

espacio cultural, edited by Andrés Núñez, Federico Arenas and Rafael Sánchez, 451–483. Santiago de Chile: Instituto de Geografía, Universidad Católica de Chile.

Blanco, Jorge, Victoria Fernández Caso and Raquel Gurevich. 1997. "Integración y frontera: una revisión conceptual." 6° Encuentro de Geógrafos de América Latina. Instituto de Geografía, Facultad de Filosofía y Letras, Universidad Nacional de Buenos Aires, Buenos Aires.

Cacopardo, Fernando. 2007. "El estado en la definición territorial de la Argentina en el Siglo XIX." *Perspectivas Urbanas*, 8, 26–38.

Caggiano, Sergio. 2007. "Madres en la frontera: género, nación y los peligros de la reproducción." *Íconos. Revista de Ciencias Sociales*, 27, 93–106.

Cicalese, Guillermo. 2009. "Geografía, guerra y nacionalismo. La Sociedad Argentina de Estudios Geográficos (GAEA) en las encrucijadas patrióticas del gobierno militar 1976–1983." *Scripta Nova. Revista Electrónica de Geografía y Ciencias Sociales*, 13 (308). Accessed November 5, 2014. http://www.ub.es/geocrit/sn/sn-308.htm

Cisneros, Andrés and Carlos Escudé. 2000. *Historia general de las relaciones exteriores de la República Argentina*. Buenos Aires: CARI.

Clementi, Hebe. 1987. *La frontera en América*. Buenos Aires: Leviatán.

De Marco, Graciela and Susana Sassone. 1995. "Movilidad geográfica y migraciones en el Cono Sur: situación actual y posibles impactos de los proyectos de integración regional." *Signos Universitarios*, 28, 103–148.

Depetris, Jorge Augusto. 2011. "Deportes Extremos. Construyendo capacidades estatales en la lucha contra el Narcotráfico: Caso Aduana Argentina 2005–2010." *Cuadernos de la AFIP*, 17.

Escolar, Diego. 2000. "Identidades emergentes en la frontera argentino-chilena. Subjetividad y crisis de soberanía en la población andina de la provincia de San Juan." In *Fronteras, naciones e identidades. La periferia como centro*, edited by Alejandro Grimson, 256–277. Buenos Aires: Ciccus-La Crujía.

Garavaglia, Juan and Denis Merklen. 2008. "Los dos márgenes de un problema." *Revista Nuevo Mundo*. Accessed November 3, 2014. http://nuevomundo.revues.org/17383

Gascón, Margarita. 2001. "La transición de periferia a frontera: Mendoza en el siglo XVII." *Andes Antropología e historia*, 12.

——— 2003. "El debate teórico de la frontera: un comentario." *Revista de Estudios Trasandinos*, 8 and 9, 181–185.

Giberti, Horacio. 1970. *Historia económica de la ganadería argentina*. Buenos Aires: Solar-Hachette.

Giménez Béliveau, Verónica and Silvia Montenegro. 2006. *La Triple Frontera, Globalización y construcción social del espacio*. Buenos Aires: Miño y Dávila.

——— (Eds.). 2010. *La Triple Frontera. Dinámicas culturales y procesos transnacionales*. Buenos Aires: Espacio.

Gordillo, Gastón and Juan Leguizamón. 2002. *El río y la frontera. Movilizaciones aborígenes, obras y Mercosur en el Pilcomayo*. Buenos Aires: Biblos.

Grimson, Alejandro. 2000. *Fronteras, naciones e identidades. La periferia como centro*. Buenos Aires: Ciccus-La Crujía.

——— 2003. *La nación en sus límites. Contrabandista y exiliados en la frontera Argentina-Brasil*. Buenos Aires: Gedisa.

Halperin Donghi, Tulio. 1980. *Una nación para el desierto argentino*. Buenos Aires: CEAL.

Borders, Crime, and State Responses 113

Hevilla, María C. 1999. "San Juan (Argentina): el papel cambiante de una frontera." *Scripta Nova*, 45 (36). Accessed November 25, 2014. http://www.ub.edu/geocrit/sn-45-36.htm

Instituto de Estudios Comparados en Ciencias Penales y Sociales (INECIP) and Unidad Fiscal de Asistencia en Secuestros Extorsivos y Trata de Personas del Ministerio Público Fiscal (UFASE). 2012. *La trata sexual en Argentina: aproximaciones para un análisis de la dinámica del delito.* Edited as a part of "Abre Puertas. Contra la explotación sexual de niños, niñas y adolescentes." Buenos Aires: INECIP-UFASE.

——— 2013. *La trata sexual. Argentina y Paraguay en perspectiva comparada. Un análisis del marco normativo y la dinámica del delito.* Edited as a part of "Abre Puertas. Contra la explotación sexual de niños, niñas y adolescentes." Buenos Aires: INECIP.

Jerez, Omar. 2006. "Ciudad, identidad y fronteras." *Cuaderno Urbano*, 5, 7–34.

——— 2009. "Un puente en la zona transfronteriza: representaciones sociales, identidades y conflicto. El caso Posadas–Encarnación." *Estudios Fronterizos*, 10 (20), 47–77.

——— 2010. "Prácticas comerciales fronterizas de las mujeres paraguayas 'paseras' en la ciudad de Posadas, Argentina." *Contribuciones Científicas GAEA*, 22, 327–338.

Karasik, Gabriela. 2000. "Tras la genealogía del diablo. Discusiones sobre la nación y el estado en la frontera argentino-boliviana." In *Fronteras, Naciones e Identidades*, compiled by Alejandro Grimson, 152–184. Buenos Aires: CICCUS-La Crujía.

Kralich, Susana, Alejandro Benedetti and Esteban Salizzi. 2012. "Aglomeraciones transfronterizas y movilidad. Una aproximación desde casos sudamericanos." *Boletim Gaúcho de Geografia* 38, 111–136.

Lacoste, Pablo. 2003. *La imagen del otro en las relaciones de la Argentina y Chile (1534–2000).* Buenos Aires: Fondo de Cultura Económica.

Laurín, Alicia. 1999. "Ensayo metodológico para un estudio particular: Las transformaciones territoriales fronterizas del proceso de integración física." *Neuquén. Boletín Geográfico*, 21, 37–50.

——— 2003. "Las transformaciones territoriales fronterizas según la concepción ideológica de frontera (1991–1995)." *Boletín Geográfico*, 23, 105–120.

——— 2008. *Geografía Política de la integración regional.* Neuquén: Educo editorial. REUN-Red de editoriales de Universidades Nacionales.

Lavopa, Jorge et al. 1997. *El Mercosur explicado. Cuatro países y un mercado común. Unpublished paper.* Buenos Aires: Consejo Argentino para las Relaciones Internaciones y Fundación Konrad Adenauer.

Linares, María Dolores. 2008. "Las fronteras argentinas en el contexto de la integración regional: el caso Posadas-Encarnación." *Nuevo Mundo Mundos Nuevos.* Accessed 14 March 2016. http://www.nuevomundo.revues.org/document16372.html

——— 2009. "Un puente en la zona transfronteriza: representaciones sociales, identidades y conflicto. El caso Posadas-Encarnación." *Estudios Fronterizos.* Accessed 14 March 2016. http://www.scielo.org.mx/pdf/estfro/v10n20/v10n20a2.pdf

——— 2010. "Prácticas comerciales fronterizas de las mujeres paraguayas paseras en la ciudad de Posadas, Argentina." *Contribuciones Científicas GAEA*, 22, 327–338.

114   *Gustavo González et al.*

Losada, Flora. 2000. "Comunicación en la puna jujeña: de fronteras y representaciones." *Revista de Investigaciones Folclóricas*, 15, 25–34.

Mercosur. 2000. Resolución MERCOSUR/CMC/DEC. No. 14/00.

Montenegro, Silvia. 2013. "La Triple Frontera entre Argentina, Brasil y Paraguay." In *Fronteras: rupturas y convergencias,* compiled by Fernando Carrión and Victor Llugsha, Quito: FLACSO Ecuador and IDRC-CRI

Organización Internacional para las Migraciones (OIM). 2008. *Estudio exploratorio sobre la trata de personas con fines de explotación sexual en Argentina, Chile y Uruguay* (2008). Rosario: Edit. Serapis.

——— 2010. *Asistencia a víctimas de trata de personas. Experiencias en la triple frontera.* Buenos Aires: PROA Editores.

Oszlak, Oscar. 1983. *La formación del estado argentino. Orden, Progreso y Organización Nacional.* Buenos Aires: Ariel.

Ovalle, René and María Burgueño. 2009. "El Bajo Río Uruguay: territorio-frontera. Completo escenario de la producción agropecuaria sudamericana." *Estudios Históricos–CDHRP- Agosto*, No. 2. Accessed 6 November 2014. http://www.estudioshistoricos.org/edicion_2/boretto-burgueno.pdf

País Andrade, Marcela. 2010. "Identidades y conflictos en las ciudades de frontera." *Revista Avá*, 18,149–161.

Pérez Vicich, Nora. 1993. *Nosotros y los otros. Las fronteras del trabajo en el Mercosur.* Buenos Aires: Ediciones INCASUR.

——— 2003. "La movilidad de trabajadores en la agenda del Mercosur." *Studi Emigrazione*, 149, 45–66.

Rabossi, Fernando. 2008. *En las calles de Ciudad del Este: Una etnografía del comercio de frontera.* Asunción: Centro de Estudios Antropológicos de la Universidad Católica.

——— 2011. "Como pensamos a Tríplice Fronteira?" *A Tríplice Fronteira: espaços nacionais e dinâmicas locais.* Macagno, edited by Lorenzo Macagno, Silvia Montenegro, and Verónica Giménez Beliveau, 39–61. Curitiba: Editora UFPR

Ratto, Silvia. 2001. "El debate sobre la frontera a partir de Turner. La New Western History, los borderlands y el estudio de las fronteras en Latinoamérica." *Boletín del Instituto de Historia Argentina y Americana*, 24 (2), 105–141.

Reboratti, Carlos. 1999. "Frontera, regiones y población." *V Jornadas Argentinas de Estudios de la Población*, Universidad de Luján-AEPA, Luján.

Renoldi, Brígida. 2005a. "Somos los que encarnamos la sociedad: Jueces federales y narcotráfico en la frontera Argentina-Paraguay." *Intersecciones antropológicas*, 6, 167–186.

——— 2005b. "Las pruebas del delito. Investigación y procesamiento del tráfico de drogas en la frontera Posadas-Encarnación (Argentina)." *Avá. Revista de Antropología*, 6, 90–105.

——— 2007. "El Olfato. Destrezas, experiencias y situaciones en un ambiente de controles de fronteras." *Anuario de Estudios en Antropología Social 2006*, 11–127.

——— 2012. "Otro dolor para América Latina. La política de guerra a las drogas y sus consecuencias." *Revista de Salud Pública*, 16 (3), 33–41.

——— 2013. "Fronteras que caminan: relaciones de movilidad en un límite trinacional." *Revista Transporte y Territorio*, 9, 123–140.

——— 2014. "Conceptos que hacen el estado: crimen organizado y prácticas policiales en la Triple Frontera." *Publicación Electrónica del Programa de Estudios sobre saberes sobre el estado y elites estatales del IDES.* Accessed 3 November 2014. http://saberesdeestado.ides.org.ar/files/2014/10/Renoldi-IDES.pdf

Borders, Crime, and State Responses 115

Rey Balmaceda, Raúl. 1977. *Límites y fronteras de la República Argentina. Epítome Geográfico*. Buenos Aires: Oikos.

Sassone, Susana, G. Mares and D. Durado. 2001. "Política de frontera de la Argentina en la reestructuración territorial." *Publicación de V Jornadas argentinas de estudios de población*, Universidad de Luján, Argentina, 93–114.

Sassone, Susana. 2004. "Fronteras cerradas, fronteras abiertas en la Argentina: los desafíos de la integración en el Mercosur." In *La frontera: realidades y representaciones: actas de las jornadas multidisciplinarias llevadas a cabo en Buenos Aires, del 24 al 26 de agosto de 2004*, 221–239. Buenos Aires: IMHICIHU-Conicet.

Schiavoni, Lidia. 2005. "Trabajar en la calle: casos de prostitución y venta ambulante en Posadas, Misiones." In *Efecto de las políticas de ajuste en la década del 90*, edited by Myriam Barone and Lidia Schiavoni, 343–367. Posadas: EdUNaM.

Schulmeister, Gastón Hernán. 2009. "El creciente accionar del narcotráfico en la Argentina: Repercusiones internacionales e impactos en seguridad pública." Paper presented at Conferencia Subregional Retos a la Seguridad y Defensa en un Ambiente Político Complejo: Cooperación y Divergencia en Suramérica, Centro de Estudios Hemisféricos de Defensa, Cartagena de Indias, Colombia, July 27–31.

Sozzo, Máximo. 2008. "Inseguridad, prevención y policía. Ciudadanía y violencias." Vol. 4. Quito, Ecuador: FLACSO-Sede Ecuador.

Tarducci, Mónica. 2006. "Tráficos fronterizos." *Cadernos Pagu*, 26, 45–57.

Taylor, Peter. 1994. *Geografía Política. Economía-mundo-nación y localidad*. Madrid: Trama.

Trinchero, Hugo. 2000. *Los dominios del demonio. Civilización y barbarie en las fronteras de la Nación. El Chaco Central*. Buenos Aires: Eudeba.

Viñas, David. 1982. *Indios, Ejército y Frontera*. Mexico City: Siglo XXI.

Zsögön, María Cecilia. 2013. "Explotación sexual comercial infantil en la triple frontera entre Argentina, Brasil y Paraguay." *Revista do Centro de Educação e Letras*, 15 (2), 110.

Zusman, Perla. 2000. *Tierras para el Rey. Tres fronteras y la construcción colonial del territorio del Río de La Plata (1750–1790)*. Barcelona: Ediciones UB.

PART 1.3
STRATEGIC COUNTRIES

5 Guatemala's Border System

A First Approach

Beatriz Zepeda[*]

At the beginning of the twenty-first century Guatemala gained notoriety for the wave of violence that swept the country. Such violence, which was political in origin and a consequence of the armed conflict that ravaged the Central American nation for 30 years, was transformed and rendered more complex by the penetration of organized crime in state and social structures.[1] Empowered by globalization and the conditions it provides for transnational activities, both legal and illegal, transnational criminal actors have, thus, significantly contributed to the high levels of violence that characterized Guatemala during the past two decades.

As the largest country in Central America and an inescapable corridor between the north and south of the continent, Guatemala is the stage of fierce power disputes between transnational criminal groups, in addition to being the area through which people, capital, and goods flow in various forms between North and South America. This feature would in itself justify a rigorous study of Guatemala's borders and, in particular, its border system as conceived in this project (see "Introduction" in this volume). However, as noted for the general context (Carrión 2014, 1), up to this date there is scant research on Guatemala's borders that links these with either the legal or the illegal economy, or that discusses the diversity of the global, regional, and domestic phenomena that intertwine to create the country's border system.

The present exploratory work aims to offer a first contribution in that direction through the identification and discussion of some of the elements that compose Guatemala's border system. To this end, the chapter is divided into five sections. The first section reviews the existing literature on Guatemala's borders and the border-security connection in that geographical context. In order to identify the fundamental components of the country's border system, the second section provides a historical account of the process of border formation with the neighboring countries: Mexico, Belize, El Salvador, and Honduras, while the third section offers a general characterization of each of Guatemala's borders. In the fourth section, an initial and – by necessity, limited – attempt is made to identify the relationship between the characteristics of Guatemala's

DOI: 10.4324/9781003204299-10

borders and illegal flows. The fifth and final section puts forward some topics for a future research agenda aimed at enhancing our understanding of the role that the borders of Guatemala play in the articulation of transnational illegal flows.

The Border Issue in Guatemala: A Review of the Literature

Guatemala's borders have not been the object of much scholarly attention. The only existing work devoted to the characterization and analysis of Guatemala's borders and their links to illegal markets is Zepeda, González-Izás and De León-Escribano (2018; English edition forthcoming), that was produced in the context of the regional research project to which the present paper also belongs. Other than that, academic production on the borders of Guatemala has tended to focus on the extensive border with Mexico, and, for the most part, it has been developed from a "southern border" perspective by Mexican researchers.[2]

A noteworthy exception to this is Jacobo Dardón's (Coord.) *Caracterización de la frontera Guatemala-México* (2002), an exhaustive study on the physical and socio-demographic characteristics of the Guatemalan border departments. Because of the abundance of data it compiles, Dardón's book remains, to this date, the most important general work on the Mexico-Guatemala border. Two other salient general works must be mentioned: the bibliographic essay by Fábregas Puig and González Ponciano (2014) that offers a complete and systematic review of the literature produced on the subject between 1983 and 2013 and Castillo (1989), in which the Guatemalan author – by far the most prolific scholar on the Mexico-Guatemala border – outlined the complexity of the region well before other researchers even began to pay attention to it.

As regards the historical configuration of the Mexico-Guatemala border, academic production has been profuse. To mention but a few of the most significant works, Sepúlveda (1958) is a systematic, yet clearly Mexico-centric, account of the political process of territorial delimitation between the two countries since independence. A contrasting approach is De Vos's classic *Las fronteras de la frontera sur* (1993), which views the shape that Mexico's southern border ultimately took as the product of successive and competing geopolitical projects advanced by both native and external actors from pre-Hispanic times to the late nineteenth century. In turn, Castillo, Toussaint, and Vázquez Olivera's *Espacios diversos, historia en común* (2006) stands out for its careful and detailed historical reading of Mexico-Guatemala bilateral relations since the 1820s and, in that context, its thorough account of the configuration process of the two countries' shared border. Other, more specific, historical studies focus on the struggle for natural resources on the eastern section of the territory, which ultimately led to the formal

120   *Beatriz Zepeda*

demarcation of the border (De Vos 1978; Valdez 2006), while Tamayo Pérez (2015) provides an insight into the technical and political difficulties such demarcation entailed.

Another significant part of the literature on the Guatemala-Mexico border looks at cross-border economic and social integration. César Eduardo Ordóñez Morale's *Tendencias de la integración económica en Guatemala y el sureste de México* (2006) focuses on economic integration between northwestern Guatemala and southeastern Mexico and continues to offer the most complete interpretation to-date of the economic processes that configure that region as a cross-border one. Interestingly enough, most other works that approach cross-border economic transactions tend to highlight, instead, their informal character and the impact this has on cross-border life (see, i.a., Arriola 2005; Ordóñez Morales 2007; Clot 2013; Ruiz Juárez and Martínez Velasco 2015). In this context, Rebecca Galemba's *Contraband Corridor* (2018) stands out for its perceptive analysis of contraband as a way of life along the Chiapas-Huehuetenango border.

For its part, social cross-border integration has also been examined in various works. Arriola (1995) highlights Tapachula's role as the urban hub that articulates cross-border social life in the Soconusco region; Rodríguez-Castillo (2009) looks at the social construction of space, and Chavarochette (2014) dwells on the initial integration and subsequent process of differentiation between the populations of Comitán, Mexico, and Huehuetenango, Guatemala.

Of all the topics that have engaged Mexico-Guatemala border scholars' attention, perhaps the dominant one is migration. For one thing, circular migration of Guatemalan agricultural laborers has been a trademark of the border region since the late nineteenth century. For another, as the boundary between Central and North America, the Mexico-Guatemala border has been essential in the configuration of migration flows from Central and South America to the United States. Serrano and Martínez's (2009) coordinated volume tackles both migration types, while Anguiano and Trejo Peña (2007), Anguiano and Corona Vázquez (2009), Martínez Velasco (2014), and Rojas Wiesner (2017) discuss the intersection of the two kinds of human flows and the effects that Mexican policies aimed at curbing transit migration have had on the mobility of circular migrants, who are central to the local economy. More recent ethnographic studies, such as Ramos Rojas' (2015 and 2016) and Nájera Aguirre's (2020) focus, in turn, on circular migration and highlight the subjective mobility experiences of Guatemalan workers in Mexico's southern border.

The literature on transit migration has experienced a boom in the last few years. Pre-dating the most recent trends, Manuel Ángel Castillo has been publishing on this topic for decades now.[3] Other research in this area has sought to characterize and measure transit migration flows (Berumen et al. 2012; ITAM 2014; Nájera Aguirre 2016); outline migration routes (Casillas 2008; Martínez et al. 2015); highlight the role of gender and violence in the migrants' experience (Monzón 2006; Willers 2016; Cortés 2018); tackle the link between migration and security (Castillo 2005; Arriola 2009; Armijo Canto 2010; Castillo and Toussaint 2010; Benítez Manaut 2011; Villafuerte Solís and García Aguilar 2015), as well as portray the motivations, expectations and experiences of transit migrants from their own perspective (Brigden 2018). While much academic literature on the Central American migrant caravans that made the headlines from 2017 to 2019 is still in the making, Arriola (2019) and Comexi (2020) offer initial analyses of the causes, modus operandi, and policy implications of these unprecedented massive northbound human flows.

Finally, the geopolitical role of the Mexico-Guatemala border is a topic on which renewed academic interest can be ascertained. Daniel Villafuerte Solís' already classic *La frontera sur de México. Del TLC México-Centroamérica al Plan Puebla-Panamá* (2004), as well as his most recent *Tiempo de fronteras* (2017) have, in the last two years, been complemented by Basail (2018), Fuentes-Carrera (Coord.) (2020), and Heredia Zubieta (Coord.) (2020), all of which investigate different aspects of the Mexico-Guatemala border in the context of the Western hemisphere's changing geopolitics.

As already mentioned, Guatemala's borders with the other three neighboring countries have elicited significantly less scholarly attention. On Belize, a country with which Guatemala has an ongoing territorial dispute, Mónica Toussaint (1996) has produced an interesting historical review in which the origin and development of the territorial conflict are thoroughly discussed. The other topic related to the Guatemala-Belize border addressed by the academic literature is water and watershed management, and it has been amply explored in Kauffer Michel (2010) and García García and Kauffer (2011).

While Guatemala's borders with Honduras and El Salvador have not been studied individually, the region where the borders of these three countries converge has received attention from three different perspectives. The first one highlights its strategic nature throughout history. In this vein, MacLeod's historical study (1980) argues that insofar as this tri-border region connects the Atlantic and Pacific Oceans, it has been pivotal in the articulation of both licit and illicit trade circuits since colonial times. The second perspective, represented by Matilde González-Izás' works (2014a and 2014b), discusses the role that Guatemala's north and northeastern border territories have played in the constitution of new political (criminal) actors after the end of the armed conflict; while the third perspective identifies the tri-border region with a contemporary security problem related to high rates of violence and the presence of *maras* (gangs). The works of

122   *Beatriz Zepeda*

Emilio Goubaud (2008), Carolina Sampó (2013), and Douglas Farah (2011, 2013, and 2016) are particularly enlightening in this context.

By contrast, the literature on the Pacific coast, Guatemala's long maritime border, is, above all, historical and largely devoted to discussing the role of this territory and the characteristics of the societies that inhabited it during the pre-Hispanic era (Arroyo 2013; Demarest et al. 1991; Popenoe de Hatch and Alvarado Galindo 2010); while the region's economic history is reviewed in Regina Wagner's works (1994 and 2001).

As regards illegal flows and criminal actors involved in the circuits of illegality in Guatemala, the literature combines academic analysis and investigative journalism. Rodrigo Fernández Ordóñez's hemerographic research (n.d.) on the origins and development of drug trafficking in Guatemala offers a valuable historical account, while Julie López's investigations published in *Plaza Pública*[4] and Stephen Dudley's analyses for *InSight Crime*[5] are solid sources for the study of contemporary criminal activity in Guatemala. More scholarly inclined research includes Edgar Gutiérrez's analysis of drug-trafficking networks and parallel powers in Guatemala (2016 and 2013), Gutiérrez and Méndez's (2012) research on drug trafficking and money laundering, Arnson and Olson's (Eds.) (2011) work on organized crime in Central America and Mazzitelli's (2011) still relevant research on Mexican drug cartels' influence in Central America.

With reference to other illegal flows, the studies by Carmen Rosa De León-Escribano on arms trafficking (2014, 2011, and 2007) are obligatory sources, while Galembas' anthropological investigations (2012 and 2018) and Eduardo Stein et al.'s exploratory report on contraband (2015) must be highlighted as important contributions to an otherwise under-researched topic. As to human trafficking in Guatemala, whereas academic studies are yet to be produced, the country's record in this area is well portrayed in reports by UNICEF, ECPAT and ILANUD (2012), CICIG and Unicef (2016), and Procuraduría de los Derechos Humanos (PDH, 2016).

Prior to the publication in Spanish of Zepeda et al. (2018), the link between borders and illegal markets in Guatemala had only been the subject of Ralph Espach et al.'s study, *Criminal Organizations and Illicit Trafficking in Guatemalan Border Communities* (2011). Based on a case study methodology and focusing on the Sayaxché, Gualán, and Malacatán border communities, Espach et al.'s far reaching research highlights the role of borders in the articulation of transnational trafficking circuits and discusses social capital as a factor that influences how illicit trafficking ultimately impacts local communities.

The Historical Configuration of Guatemala's Border System

The roots of Guatemala's border system date back to the pre-Hispanic era, when the Mayan civilization (1000 BC–1200 AD) spread over the current territory of southeastern Mexico, almost all of Guatemala, Belize, and part of Honduras and El Salvador, forming a cultural, commercial, and political corridor between the North and South of the American continent. The collapse of this civilization, around 1200 AD, resulted in an important territorial reconfiguration, as the region was divided between cultures of Mayan origin that today remain settled in their ancestral territories. Eight centuries later, ancient trade routes are still recognizable in some of the patterns of informal exchange, and ethnic and cultural continuity characterizes much of the region's population on both sides of the border.

The Making of the Guatemala-Mexico Border Subsystem

In 1821, Guatemala declared its independence from Spain. Threatened by Mexico with military intervention, should it fail to do so, Guatemala joined the Mexican Empire in 1822 only to declare itself independent from Mexico a year later, when the empire's downfall was imminent. Under Mexican pressure, in 1824, Chiapas, which at that time belonged to Guatemala, voted to join the Mexican federation. However, Chiapas' southernmost region, Soconusco, continued to be a disputed territory and was imposed a status of "forced neutrality" until 1842 (De Vos 1993, 94–99; Fenner 2019), when, after the dissolution of the Central American Republic, it was finally annexed to Mexico by Antonio López de Santa Anna. This gave origin to a latent conflict between Guatemala and Mexico that would persist well into the late-nineteenth century.

Postcolonial geopolitics did not significantly change the established socio-cultural dynamics in the region. Especially in Soconusco, family ties, cultural practices, and trade with Guatemala continued to exist as they had done before. Politically, however, the repercussions were significant, as until the end of the nineteenth century, the boundary between Mexico and Guatemala remained undefined.

In 1881, an armed Guatemalan incursion to recover Soconusco was met with resistance by the population of Chiapas, putting Mexico and Guatemala on the brink of war (Pichardo Hernández 2012, 146). While the situation did not escalate to a full-scale military conflict, bilateral relations were rife with tension, a situation that was further compounded by the indeterminacy of the boundary line in the eastern part of the territory.

Indeed, the cartography of the period presented the Lacandon Jungle and the territory of Petén, Chiapas, Tabasco, and Campeche as "no man's land." This occurred as foreign lumber companies had begun to extract precious wood from the area along the basins of the Usumacinta, Lacantún, Pasión, and Chixoy rivers, which composed a coveted cross-border region. The lack of a clearly defined boundary led to allegations of trespassing by both governments and increased the tension between Mexico and Guatemala.

To put an end to hostilities, in 1882, the Herrera-Mariscal Treaty was signed. Its terms were clearly detrimental to Guatemala, which finally

124 *Beatriz Zepeda*

gave up its claims to Chiapas and Soconusco and lost about 15,540 square kilometers in the far North of Petén and the Lacandon Jungle, equivalent to 6% of its total territory (Castillo et al. 2006, 145). The treaty further established the Suchiate River as the boundary in the West, while stating that the demarcation of the rest of the line would be carried out by an ad-hoc binational commission.

Yet, boundary conflicts did not end with the signing of the treaty. Although the Binational Boundary Commission was formed in 1883, the delimitation process itself was the subject of multiple disputes (see Tamayo Pérez 2015). Additional logging permits, issued by the Guatemalan government to mostly foreign companies to lumber areas of the Lacandon Jungle, which, according to the 1882 treaty, belonged to Mexico (see De Vos 1978), generated more friction. It would not be until 1897, when the binational commission completed its work, that the shared border was clearly demarcated and ceased to be a matter of contention between Guatemala and its northern neighbor.

According to Valdez, the border arrangement between Guatemala and Mexico was, in fact, a negotiated settlement between transnational companies, including The Guatemalan and Mexican Mahogany and Export Company, whose manager at the time was the US engineer Miles Rock. The fact that Rock also headed the Guatemalan Boundary Commission highlights the link between the border agreement and private interests.

Moreover, since the Herrera-Mariscal Treaty was signed, significant investments in timber extraction began to flow from Belgium, the United States, Spain, France, and England into Guatemala, and in the 1890s American companies increased their investments in gum extraction activities. Thus, since the late-nineteenth and early-twentieth centuries, other contraband networks began to emerge, supported by timber exploitation and smuggling networks, which involved both private and state agents – often in interchangeable roles – (Valdez 2006, 130–173). They trafficked highly coveted products, such as archaeological pieces and wild animal and plant species, giving rise to a mode of smuggling that, despite the transformations of the border dynamics in recent decades, has been preserved until today (see Arriola 2005, 140–141).

The Making of the Guatemala-Honduras-El Salvador Border Subsystem

After the collapse of the Spanish monarchy in America, elites in the Central American provinces of the former empire sought emancipation, not only from Spain, but, more importantly, from Guatemala, which had been, until then, the center of colonial power in the region. Localism, regionalism, and rivalry between provincial elites became painfully evident with the dissolution of the short-lived Federal Republic of Central America (1823–1838/1841), in the context of which Honduras declared its independence in 1838 and, three years later, El Salvador seceded only to join Honduras and Nicaragua.

Guatemala's boundary with El Salvador was demarcated in 1856, after the latter became an independent state. In the case of the boundary with Honduras, the process was more complicated, for, although a treaty was signed in 1845, which stated that "the states of Honduras and Guatemala recognize[d] as their common boundary that laid down for the diocese of each in the Royal Ordinance of Intendentes of 1786" (Platt 1929, 323), the fact that such ordinance did not specify the dioceses' boundaries became a cause for constant tension until the 1930s. It would not be until 1933, after multiple failed negotiations, that the matter was subjected to international arbitration and the boundary was finally established on the right banks of the Tinto and Motagua rivers.

The Motagua was, in fact, a central piece in the configuration of Guatemala's border system. In colonial times, that river, which was then navigable, was essential to the establishment of the trade axis that connected – as it still does – the port of Santo Tomás de Castilla on the Atlantic with the port of San José on the Pacific. This East-West axis generated an intense commercial activity dominated, at first, by the Spaniards and later, by the Creoles and mestizos (*Ladinos*) settled in the eastern part of Guatemala (Izabal, Zacapa, Chiquimula, and Jutiapa). As González-Izás states: "Everyone, from the *corregidores* [chief magistrates] to the lieutenants of Chiquimula *corregimiento* [district], actively participated in the trade of cocoa, indigo, and cotton. Similarly, the most active merchants of the region held important posts in the colonial administration" (2014a, 33–34). Control over ports, customs offices, and law enforcement agencies granted these administrators a privileged position from which to pursue their commercial activities, which often included the trade of smuggled goods.

After independence, the process of international capital expansion that was experienced in Guatemala's border areas with Mexico in the late-nineteenth century, also took place in the eastern portion of the territory. In this case, however, the influence of the timber industry came from British investments in Belizean territory and from the concessions granted by the Guatemalan government to Bennett & Meany, as well as to the Eastern Coast of Central America Commercial and Agricultural Company (González-Izás 2014a, 119). This occurred in the same area where, years later, the United Fruit Company would erect its banana-producing enclave and where other American companies, such as the International Railroad of Central America and the Electrical Bond and Share Company, would concentrate their activities in the early-twentieth century. Once again, Guatemala's border regions became inextricably linked to private – mainly foreign – interests.

126   *Beatriz Zepeda*

Economic growth and the process of urbanization that Central America experienced in the 1950s brought about an increase in demand for consumer goods throughout the region. The drive to satisfy the demand of goods that were not locally available, or that could be purchased at more competitive prices elsewhere, encouraged both small and large-scale smuggling. Maritime ports on the Atlantic and the Pacific thus became nodal points for contraband, especially of textiles, packaged food, and household appliances. At about the same time, cattle theft and smuggling from and to Mexico, and between Guatemala, El Salvador, and Honduras became an important illegal activity that entailed creating clandestine transportation routes. Years later, those routes would prove equally functional to the trafficking of drugs and other illicit products.

The Absence of a Border with Belize

The territory of present-day Belize was under Spanish jurisdiction since 1493; however, it was the British who colonized the area. During the second half of the eighteenth century, Spain extended rights to private British loggers for the exploitation and export of timber from the Hondo River to the Belize River (1786). Although the accords did not grant it sovereignty, they facilitated the de facto possession of the territory by Great Britain. After Spain's defeat in the independence wars, both the Central American Federation and, later, independent Guatemala claimed, unsuccessfully, Belize's territory as their own.

In 1859, Great Britain and Guatemala signed the Aycinena-Wyke treaty, which recognized Britain's rights over the disputed territory, while setting the boundaries between the two jurisdictions. Article VII of the treaty further stipulated that Great Britain would build a road between Belize and Guatemala. Yet, the precise terms of this construction were not stated, and each of the countries interpreted its commitment differently (Toussaint Ribot 1996). Three years later, in 1862, Great Britain formally annexed Belize, which then became the colony of British Honduras.

Despite the numerous negotiations that took place throughout the following 80 years, aimed at enforcing article VII of the 1859 treaty, the road connecting Guatemala and Belize was never built. Guatemala blamed this on Britain, and in 1946, the Congress of Guatemala unilaterally declared the Aycinena-Wyke Treaty void and demanded the full restitution of Belize's territory.

This situation lasted until 1981, when Belize declared its independence. Ten years later, Guatemala recognized Belize's right to self-determination and statehood; however, the territorial and boundary dispute persisted. Moreover, in the following years, the absence of a clearly demarcated boundary caused several clashes – some of which threatened to escalate into full-blown military conflicts – and constituted a permanent source of tension in Central America (Orozco 2004).

In this context, the Organization of American States sought to mediate, and in 2008 Guatemala and Belize finally agreed to submit the dispute to the jurisdiction of the International Court of Justice (ICJ). As a previous step, however, the citizens of both countries were to express their consent via referenda. Guatemala's referendum took place on April 15, 2018 and Belize's on May 5, 2019. In both cases the, result was favorable to the submission of the dispute before the ICJ, thus making it possible to envisage, for the first time in years, a peaceful resolution to one of the longest-lasting boundary conflicts in the American continent.

Beyond the political implications of this dispute, the lack of definition of the territorial boundaries between the two countries, which continues at the time of writing, has given rise to a geographical space with scarce state presence. This situation has been exploited by criminal actors for activities such as logging, smuggling of animal species and archaeological pieces, migrant smuggling, and, especially, drug trafficking.

Guatemala's Borders: A Characterization

Located in northern Central America, Guatemala has a territory of 108,889 square kilometers. It borders Mexico to the North and Northwest, Belize and the Atlantic Ocean to the Northeast, Honduras and El Salvador to the East and Southeast, and the Pacific Ocean to the South. It is formed by 22 departments and 338 municipalities. Seven of these departments and 45 of these municipalities border one of the neighboring countries (Map 5.1).

According to the latest census, Guatemala's population is 14,901,286 inhabitants. 48.5% of them are men and 51.5% are women; 54% of the population is urban, 46% is rural, and predominantly young: 33.4% of the population is between 0 and 14 years old and 66% between 15 and 64 years old, the median age being 22.6 years. As regards ethnic self-identification, 56% of Guatemalans consider themselves mestizo, 41.7% Mayan, and 1.8% Xinca. 7,266,638 people, an equivalent to 48.7% of the total population, reside in border departments, while those who inhabit border municipalities are 2,479,211, which amount to 16.6% of the total population. Guatemala is a medium-low-income country: in 2018 GNI was $78.46 billion, and GNI per capita was $4,534.80. Unemployment in Guatemala is high: of the nearly ten million people above 15 years of age, only five million are economically active and among those who are employed, 70% belong to the informal sector (INE n.d.).

128 *Beatriz Zepeda*

While these figures offer a general depiction of Guatemala's sociodemographics, they obscure the significant differences that exist between the 22 departments and, especially, between border and non-border departments. Although it is not possible to exhaustively discuss such differences in this brief space, the following section attempts to highlight the main characteristics of Guatemala's border zones.

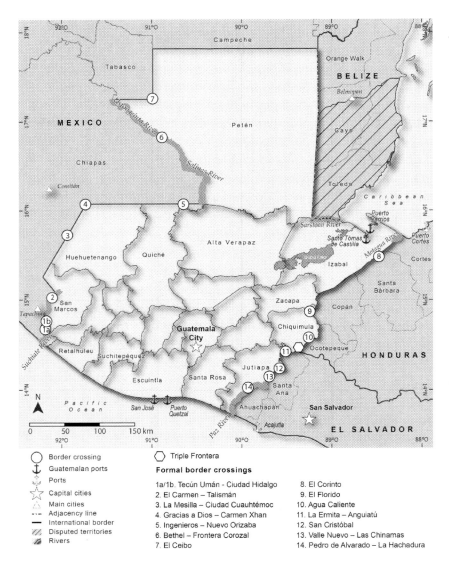

Map 5.1 The Borders of Guatemala

Map by Erika León

The Guatemala-Mexico Border

The Guatemala-Mexico border line stretches along 959.9 kilometers; 573.2 of these are land, 81.2 correspond to the Suchiate River, and 305.5 to the Usumacinta River (CILA 2018). Twenty-four municipalities of the departments of San Marcos, Huehuetenango, Quiché, and Petén border 22 municipalities of the Mexican states of Chiapas, Tabasco, and Campeche.

Nearly one fourth (24.8%) of Guatemala's total population lives in the border departments with Mexico. These four departments are predominantly rural, in percentages that fluctuate between 59.5, in the case of Petén, and 74.6, in the case of San Marcos; and two of them, Quiché and Huehuetenango, comprise a high proportion of indigenous population: 89% and 65%, respectively. The median age in these departments is lower than the national average, and ranges from 19.5 years in Quiché to 20.6 years in Petén. San Marcos, with a median age of 23.09 years, is an exception and lies above the national median (INE n.d.).

As regards economic conditions, all four departments present a lower economic participation rate (EPR) than the national average of 50.5%. While Petén, with 48% is close to the national rate, San Marcos, with only 38.6% is the department with the lowest EPR on this border (INE n.d.). Moreover, the four departments display high poverty rates, which, in all cases, significantly exceed the national one of 53.7%: San Marcos 60.2%, Petén 60.8%, Huehuetenango 73.8%, and Quiché 74.7% (INE 2015, 6). The latter are, in fact, the fourth and fifth poorest departments of the country.

Until 2003, there were only four formal border posts along this line: the two international bridges over the Suchiate River, which connect Tecún Umán with Ciudad Hidalgo, the El Carmen-Talismán international bridge (all three of them in the department of San Marcos), and La Mesilla-Ciudad Cuauhtémoc crossing, in Huehuetenango. In 2004, four new border posts were added: Gracias a Dios-Carmen Xhan in Huehuetenango, Ingenieros-Nuevo Orizaba in Quiché, Bethel-Frontera Corozal and El Ceibo, both of which are in Petén. In stark contrast with this meager number of official crossings, in 2018, the Mexican section of CILA, the binational boundary commission, registered 61 informal crossing points for vehicles along the international line (CILA 2018).

The Guatemala-Belize Adjacency Line

While not recognized as an official boundary by either Guatemala or Belize, the dividing line established by article 1 of the 1859 Aycinena-Wyke Treaty runs along 266 kilometers on the 89° West meridian, from the border with Mexico in the North to the Sarstoon River in the South, and from that point to the East along the Sarstoon until

130 *Beatriz Zepeda*

the latter flows into the Amatique Bay in the Atlantic Ocean. Both the departments of Petén and Izabal border Belize; however, whereas Petén's four municipalities of Melchor de Mencos, Dolores, Poptún, and San Luis share the entirety of the adjacency line's 266 kilometers with the three Belizean districts of Orange Walk, Cayo, and Toledo, Izabal only borders Toledo District along the brief segment of the Sarstoon River, before it joins the sea.

This border region is scarcely populated. Only 6.4% of Guatemala's total population inhabits the two border departments. This is also reflected in the low population density of the two departments: 45.22 people per square kilometer in Izabal and just 15.21 people per square kilometer in Petén, which is particularly striking when compared with the national population density of 136.8 inhabitants per square kilometer. Both Petén and Izabal are predominantly rural (59.5% and 59%, respectively); yet they display a much lower proportion of indigenous population than the national average: 30.1% in Petén and 28.9% in Izabal (INE n.d.). As in the rest of the country, EPR is low in these two departments: 44% in Petén and 50.7% in Izabal, while the poverty rate is considerably higher than the national one: 60.8% in Petén and 59.9% in Izabal (INE 2015, 6).

Although there is no official boundary line between the two countries, there is a formal crossing that connects the municipality of Melchor de Mencos in Petén with Benque Viejo del Carmen in Cayo District. As of 2015, two informal vehicle crossings existed on this border, one in Melchor de Mencos and another one in Poptún.[6] The fact that the demarcation line and a portion of Belize's territory are still disputed results in the lack of state presence in this area and renders it even more permeable to all sorts of flows of people and goods.

The Guatemala-Honduras-El Salvador Border

On the Central American Isthmus, Guatemala borders both Honduras and El Salvador and shares with them one common border at a point known as El Trifinio. The boundary with Honduras is 256 kilometers long, of which the last 15 correspond to the Motagua River before it flows into the Atlantic Ocean. The border with El Salvador, in turn, stretches along 203 kilometers, of which approximately seventy are marked by the Paz River and its mouth on the Pacific. From East to West, the departments of Izabal, Zacapa, Chiquimula, and Jutiapa border the Honduran departments of Cortés, Santa Bárbara, Copán, and Ocotepeque, as well as the Salvadoran departments of Santa Ana and Ahuachapán. Seventeen Guatemalan municipalities are found on this side of the border, while eight Honduran municipalities and nine Salvadoran ones lie across the international line.

Slightly over 10% (10.4) of the total population of Guatemala lives in the border departments with Honduras and El Salvador; however, while the population of Izabal, Chiquimula, and Jutiapa fluctuates between 408,688 in the case of Izabal and 488,385 in the case of Jutiapa, Zacapa has a much smaller population of 245,374. Even more striking is the difference between Zacapa and the rest of these departments regarding the percentage of indigenous population: whereas in the other three departments the indigenous population oscillates between 20.4% (in Jutiapa) and 28.9% (in Izabal), in Zacapa it is only 2.1% (INE n.d.).

Except for Jutiapa, where the percentage of urban population stands at 51.1, these departments are predominantly rural (between 55.8% and 62.6%) and display EPRs that range from 43.5% in the case of Chiquimula to 50.7% in the case of Izabal. As regards poverty, over 50% of the population in all four departments lives below the poverty line; notwithstanding, with a percentage of 70.6, Chiquimula stands out as the seventh poorest department in Guatemala (INE 2015, 6).

On the coasts of Izabal there are two international ports, Puerto Barrios and Santo Tomás de Castilla. Additionally, on the Guatemala-Honduras border, there are three official border crossings: El Corinto in Izabal, El Florido, and Agua Caliente, both in Chiquimula, as well as 18 informal crossing points for vehicles. In turn, on the Guatemala-El Salvador border there are four official border posts: Pedro de Alvarado-La Hachadura, Valle Nuevo-Las Chinamas, San Cristóbal, and La Ermita-Anguiatú, and 27 informal vehicle crossings, all of which are located in the department of Jutiapa. "Trifinio" is the point where the boundaries of the three countries meet and it is located in the southernmost point of the Concepción Las Minas municipality in Chiquimula. No official post of any of the countries exists here.

The Pacific Coastline

Six of Guatemala's departments border the Pacific Ocean: from South to North, Jutiapa, Santa Rosa, Escuintla, Suchitepéquez, Retalhuleu, and San Marcos; their combined shorelines build Guatemala's 254-kilometer-long Pacific coast. 23.7% of the country's total population lives in these coastal departments,[7] and of those which do not border another country, Escuintla, with 733,181 inhabitants is the most populated one. Escuintla is also one of the most urbanized departments of Guatemala. With 61.2% of its population living in cities, it surpasses the national average by 7.4% and San Marcos, the most rural department on the Pacific, by 35.8% (INE n.d.).

Of all the border zones, the Pacific one is the most densely populated. Except for Escuintla, whose population density is 30 people per square kilometer, all the other departments are inhabited by more than 130 people per square kilometer. Suchitepéquez, with 221 people per square kilometer, and San Marcos, with 272.3 inhabitants per square kilometer are among the most densely populated departments of the country,

132 *Beatriz Zepeda*

and they display the highest rates of indigenous population among the coastal departments: 38% in the case of Suchitepéquez and 38.8% in the case of San Marcos. This stands in sharp contrast with the rest of the departments, whose indigenous population is significantly smaller than the national average of 43.3%: 20.4% in Jutiapa, 16.2% in Santa Rosa, 15.8% in Retalhuleu, and only 5.2% in Escuintla (INE n.d.). Regarding economic participation, all the departments with a coast on the Pacific display slightly lower rates than the national average (between 49.6% and 47.4%), except for San Marcos, which with 38.6% is 11.9% lower than the average for the whole country (INE 2015, 6).

Currently, there are four ports on this coast: Puerto Quetzal, in Escuintla, which serves both international trade and international cruises, and is the sole official entry post on the Pacific coast; San José, also in Escuintla, which caters for domestic trade and the oil industry; Champerico, in Retalhuleu, once a vibrant port linked to the lumbering activities of the German Champer & Co. – hence its name – and nowadays used mainly by artisanal fishermen; and Ocós, located in San Marcos and only a few kilometers away from the border with Mexico, which, like Champerico, used to be an important import-export hub during the late nineteenth century and is now used mainly by local fishermen.

While there is only one formal entry post in Puerto Quetzal, the entire coast is dotted with a multiplicity of estuaries that flow into the sea and are totally navigable, in addition to being easily linked to the Inter-American highway that connects the country from east to west. This renders this "maritime border" extremely permeable and an important element in the articulation of Guatemala's borders and illicit flows.

Guatemala, Its Borders, and Illicit Flows

Which border dynamics prevail in Guatemala's borders? How do the characteristics of Guatemala's border territories influence the formation of transnational illegal flows? The response to these questions cannot be general but must rather address the important differences that exist between the various borders and border territories of Guatemala, which are, to a large extent, the product of longstanding historical processes.

In the case of the borders with Honduras and El Salvador, this is a territory characterized by its privileged location in one of the oldest and most important circuits of North Atlantic commerce. This circuit connects the trade flows (both legal and illegal) that circulate through the main ports located on the Atlantic coast (Omoa, Puerto Caballos, Santo Tomás de Castilla, and Puerto Barrios), the land borders between Guatemala, Honduras and El Salvador, and the port of Acajutla, located in El Salvador. This interconnection between the Atlantic and the Pacific, and between the three countries, forms the nucleus of what is now called the "Northern Triangle of Central America."

The strategic importance of this territory during the colony is widely documented (see Cabezas Carcache 1995) and largely explains why, in its early days, the border territory of Guatemala with Honduras and El Salvador was central to the disputes between European powers for control of the Atlantic-Pacific transoceanic trade corridor. As has already been said, this dispute was accompanied by and led to the proliferation of smuggling networks, often involving the very representatives of the colonial administration (MacLeod 1980). This factor ended up defining the characteristics that this border territory currently presents.

Events in more recent history have also marked the border territory of the Northern Triangle, particularly in its northeastern section. The important role played by the Northeast of the country as a scenario for counterinsurgency during the internal armed conflict (1960–1996), as well as the participation of local potentates in the fight against the guerrilla during the 1960s, encouraged the emergence of local actors, linked both to the army and border control, who, years later, would become the leaders and articulators of territorial criminal groups (González-Izás, 2014a). Arnoldo Vargas, Waldemar Lorenzana, and Haroldo Mendoza, all of whom have now been captured, are the epitome of such local criminal actors. Although their families no longer hold the almost monopolistic territorial power these leaders once wielded, they are still significant actors in the north and northeast of the country.

Currently, drug trafficking and the violence that has been associated with it have brought notoriety to this region of the country. After a period in which cocaine from Colombia was mainly trafficked northbound by sea along the Pacific coast, in the last three years, cocaine-trafficking land routes through the border with Honduras have become revitalized (Silva Ávalos 2021). Equally important, Izabal has become the "epicenter" of cocaine production in Guatemala, a criminal enterprise that includes both coca leaf production in large plantations and the establishment of laboratories to process the leaf into cocaine hydrochloride (Papadovassiliakis 2021; WDR 2020, 27).

The border with Mexico exhibits, in contrast, very different characteristics. On the one hand, the border territory between Petén and the Mexican states of Tabasco and Campeche, as well as the southeastern section of the state of Chiapas, are strongly marked by their jungle geography and low population density. These factors have long prevented the presence of state institutions – both Guatemalan and Mexican – and have made this territory a favorable environment for the development of illegal activities, among which illegal logging (since the end of the nineteenth century) and drug trafficking, in more recent times, stand out. Cannabis plantations abound in this area, as do clandestine airstrips used for the landing of small aircrafts that transport cocaine mostly from Venezuela, but also from Colombia (Sieff 2020). Once unloaded, the cocaine is transported by land across the border into Mexico. According

134   *Beatriz Zepeda*

to a 2018 report, no less than 65 illegal airstrips existed at the time in Petén (Chumil 2018).

On the other hand, the border area between San Marcos, on the Guatemalan side, and the state of Chiapas, specifically Soconusco, on the Mexican side, constitutes a deeply integrated region since colonial times, when, as argued above, these territories were even part of the same jurisdiction. After independence, economic integration continued, particularly from the mid-nineteenth century, when the development of coffee plantation agriculture in Chiapas and the ensuing demand for labor, gave rise to a significant flow of Guatemalan seasonal workers, that constitutes the nucleus of the vigorous labor market that exists to this day.

Together with the cross-border labor market that sustains this region, cross-border trade, much of which is carried out under conditions of informality, in the form of low-scale smuggling, energizes the economy of the border municipalities in San Marcos and Huehuetenango as well as in Chiapas (Ordóñez Morales 2006, 170–182), and it has managed to generate an infrastructural base of routes and modes of transport available for both legal and illegal activities.

Another factor that characterizes this territory is the intense flow of irregular Central American migrants that since the mid-1990s have crossed the border daily on their way to the United States, thus giving rise to an entire industry aimed at satisfying the needs of the population in transit. This industry, which includes transporters, moneychangers, middle-men, and *coyotes* (migrant smugglers), has proved enormously functional to the illegal and illicit businesses of narcotics trafficking and human trafficking.

As far as the Pacific coast is concerned, this is a territory that has not yet been conceived as a border, despite its important role in the development of Guatemala's export economy, particularly that of coffee, in the mid-nineteenth century (Wagner 2001). In addition to stimulating the coastal economy, the development of the coffee industry promoted the construction of the port of San José, through which coffee exports were to take place, and, later, the establishment of important communication routes – first the railroad and then the highway – that were to connect this port on the Pacific with Puerto Santo Tomás de Castilla on the Atlantic, thus configuring the transoceanic corridor of the modern era.

Because it offers numerous points of entry by sea into the country, the Pacific coast has become increasingly important in transnational illicit markets. While the lax control of cargo entering and leaving Puerto Quetzal has placed this port at the center of powerful smuggling and drug-trafficking structures (Cabria 2015), the geographic characteristics of the region, coupled with the high levels of poverty and marginalization of the local population, have rendered illegal activities, particularly the transport of narcotics, an economic alternative for many of the inhabitants of the Pacific coast. Accustomed to traveling by, and living off the sea, local fishermen offer drug traffickers motorboat transport services, support for the collection and small-scale transport of drug consignments, as well as warehouses for the storage of the goods. The drug traffickers, in turn, invest in local businesses, where they provide employment for the local population, thus creating local support networks for their illicit activities.

The diverse border dynamics just outlined are also mirrored by the differing violence indicators in the border territories. On a national scale, and based on data from 2019, Escuintla is the department with the highest homicide rate in the country: 78.8 homicides per 100,000 inhabitants. It is followed by Zacapa, with 77.7 homicides per 100,000 inhabitants, Chiquimula, with 70.3 homicides per 100,000 inhabitants and Izabal, with 56.8 homicides per 100,000 inhabitants.[8] These figures reveal that, while the department with the highest homicide rate (Escuintla) is on the Pacific coast, as a region, it is in fact the border with Honduras that stands out for the incidence of homicidal violence. By contrast, the border departments with Mexico display significantly lower homicide rates per 100,000 inhabitants: Huehuetenango 14.7, San Marcos 10.9, and Quiché 2.7. In this context, Petén constitutes an interesting exception, for while its departmental rate of 44.2 homicides per 100,000 inhabitants is not among the highest in the country, two of its municipalities, La Libertad on the border with Mexico and Melchor de Mencos, on the border with Belize, occupy the first and fifth places at the national level, with rates of 93.1 and 74.3 homicides per 100,000 inhabitants, respectively.

Topics for a Research Agenda

The preceding pages have only outlined the complexity inherent in the relationship between Guatemala's borders and transnational illicit flows. A deeper understanding of this relationship and its many facets requires further research to shed light on various unexplored issues.

First, more research that addresses Guatemala's border territories from a sociological perspective is needed. Overcoming the limitations entailed in state- and sovereignty-centric approaches and shifting our comprehension of borders from one that sees lines that contain and separate, to one that conceives of them as elements of articulation, can only contribute to a better understanding of cross-border phenomena (legal and illegal) and provide better inputs for public policy decision-making.

Second, much remains to be done to explain the impact that the features of specific border localities have on the forms that illicit flows take in border territories. In-depth small-scale analyses that consider the geography, infrastructure, demographic, economic, social, and cultural characteristics of each locality, as well as the way in which illicit flows

136   *Beatriz Zepeda*

intersect with and modify those peculiarities are necessary to advance in the knowledge of Guatemala's insertion in transnational illicit markets.

Third, it is necessary to look towards Belize. The absence of an officially recognized boundary between Guatemala and that country has led – perhaps inevitably – to a lack of attention to "border" issues (beyond the border dispute) on the part of academia. However, even when there is no demarcation line like with the other neighbors, the adjacency area with Belize displays many of the facilitating factors for illicit flows present in the other borders of Guatemala, enhanced, in this case, by the almost complete absence of state institutions, both on the Guatemalan and on the Belizean side.

Fourth, the relationship between borders, illegal markets, and violence must be problematized and further explored in Guatemala's case. While there is a high incidence of homicides in many of the border departments, violence is not spread evenly either among or within them. Moreover, whereas homicides appear to concentrate in specific municipalities, many of which are in fact on the border, not all border municipalities feature high homicide rates. Understanding the distribution of violence from a territorial perspective is therefore part and parcel of a more nuanced comprehension of the ways in which borders, illegal flows, and violence interlock in Guatemala.

Finally, one area of research that needs to be further developed is the constantly changing role of Guatemala's borders in transnational trafficking circuits. This endeavor, which requires approaching the issue from a broad geopolitical perspective that considers economic aspects and the distribution of power in the international system, is necessarily complementary to the local approach discussed above and, together with it, would contribute to illuminate the overlapping of borders and illegal markets in this part of the world.

Notes

* The author wishes to thank Adriana Castañeda Hernández and Diana Laura Robalo Rey for their invaluable research assistance.
1. For an interesting analysis of how this violence is supported and nourished by structures created during the armed conflict, see Briscoe (2009).
2. As this text is going to print, the project Región Transfronteriza México-Guatemala (RTMG) is reaching its conclusion. The project, which sought to understand the cross-border dynamics in the Mexico-Guatemala border regions, produced several books on topics such as the history, economy, demography, political institutions, and security of the region. While it has not been possible to include these works in this literature review, it is important to mention them as future references. For information on the RTMG book series, see http://www.rtmg.org/thematic/coleccion-rtmg.
3. Castillo's production is so abundant that selecting just a few of his works is as difficult as it would be unjust. For a list of this author's work on Central American transit migration through Mexico, see: https://scholar.google.com/citations?user=f34zxZYAAAAJ&hl=es

4. Available at https://www.plazapublica.com.gt/users/julie-lopez
5. Available at https://www.insightcrime.org/author/steven/
6. The data on informal crossing points on the borders with Belize, Honduras, and El Salvador was conveyed by a Guatemalan official in a 2015 personal communication with the author.
7. It is important to bear in mind that San Marcos and Jutiapa have also been considered as border departments with Mexico and El Salvador, respectively.
8. All the data on homicides were provided by Policía Nacional Civil.

References

Anguiano, María Eugenia and Alma Trejo Peña. 2007. "Políticas de seguridad fronteriza y nuevas rutas de movilidad de migrantes mexicanos y guatemaltecos." *Limina R. Estudios sociales y humanísticos*, V (2), 47–65. https://www.redalyc.org/pdf/745/74511236004.pdf

Anguiano Téllez, María Eugenia and Corona Vázquez,Rodolfo (Coords.). 2009. *Flujos migratorios en la frontera Guatemala-México*. Mexico City: INM, Colef.

Armijo Canto, Natalia. 2010. "Seguridad y migración en la frontera sur de México: De Guatemala a Belice." In *Seguridad y defensa en América del Norte: Nuevos dilemas geopolíticos*, coordinated by Raúl Benítez Manaut, 245–262. San Salvador: Woodrow Wilson International Center for Scholars, FundaUngo.

——— 2011. "Frontera sur de México: los retos múltiples de la diversidad." In *Migración y seguridad: nuevo desafío en México*, edited by Natalia Armijo Canto, 35–51. Mexico City: CASEDE. https://www.casede.org/PublicacionesCasede/MigracionySeguridad/cap2.pdf

Arnson, Cynthia J. and Eric L. Olson (Eds.). 2011. *Organized Crime in Central America: The Northern Triangle*. Woodrow Wilson Center Reports on the Americas #29. Washington, DC: Woodrow Wilson International Center for Scholars. https://www.wilsoncenter.org/sites/default/files/media/documents/publication/LAP_single_page.pdf

Arriola, Aura Marina. 1995. *Tapachula, "la perla del Soconusco" ciudad estratégica para la redefinición de fronteras*. Guatemala City: FLACSO-Guatemala.

Arriola, Luis Alfredo. 2005. "Agency at the Frontier and the Building of Territoriality in the Naranjo-Ceibo Corridor, Petén, Guatemala." PhD diss., University of Florida.

Arriola Vega, Luis Alfredo. 2009. "Seguridad y migración en el espacio fronterizo Tabasco-El Petén." *Migración y desarrollo*, 13 (second semester), 27–45. http://www.scielo.org.mx/pdf/myd/n13/n13a2.pdf

——— 2019. *López Obrador's Initial Policies Towards Central American Migrants: Implications for the U.S.* Rice University Institute for Public Policy. https://www.bakerinstitute.org/media/files/files/e9b6fe2c/mex-pub-amlomigrants-081419.pdf

Arroyo, Bárbara. 2013. "Comprendiendo los inicios de la complejidad social en la Costa del Pacífico y el Altiplano de Guatemala." In *Millenary Maya Societies: Past Crises and Resilience*, edited by M. Charlotte Arnauld and Alain Breton, 169–186. Papers from the International Colloquium. Accessed 25 October 2016. www.mesoweb.com/publications/MMS/11_Arroyo.pdf.

Basail, Alain. 2018. "Reconfiguraciones geopolíticas de la frontera sur de México. Crítica de sus gramáticas transnacionales." *Cuadernos de Nuestra América*, 27 (51), 103–136.

138 *Beatriz Zepeda*

Benítez Manaut, Raúl. 2011. "México, Centroamérica y Estados Unidos: migración y seguridad." In *Migración y seguridad: nuevo desafío en México*, edited by Natalia Armijo Canto. 179–196. Mexico City: CASEDE. https://www.casede.org/PublicacionesCasede/MigracionySeguridad/cap10.pdf

Berumen, Salvador, Juan Carlos Narváez and Luis Felipe Ramos. 2012. "La migración centroamericana de tránsito irregular por México. Una aproximación a partir de registros administrativos migratorios y otras fuentes de información." In *Construyendo estadísticas. Movilidad y migración internacional en México*, coordinated by Ernesto Rodríguez, Luz María Salazar, and Graciela Martínez, 83–134. Mexico City: Centro de Estudios Migratorios, UPM, SEGOB, INM, Tilde Editores.

Brigden, Noelle K. 2018. *The Migrant Passage. Clandestine Journeys from Central America*. Ithaca and London: Cornell University Press.

Briscoe, Ivan. 2009. "El Estado y la seguridad en Guatemala." *Working Paper/ Documento de Trabajo*, 88, FRIDE. Accessed 20 December 2014. http://fride.org/download/WP88_Guatemala_state_SPA_oct09.pdf

Cabezas Carcache, Horacio. 1995. "El comercio." In *Historia General de Guatemala*. Volume III. Guatemala City: Fundación para la Cultura y el Desarrollo.

Cabria, Elsa. 2015. "El puerto de la defraudación aduanera es por el que pasa más cocaína de Guatemala a México." *Nómada*. 2015 (April). Accessed June 4, 2015. https://nomada.gt/pais/el-puerto-de-la-defraudacion-aduanera-es-por-el-que-pasa-mas-cocaina-de-guatemala-a-mexico/

Carrión, Fernando. 2014. "Explorando la economía política de la violencia en los sistemas fronterizos de América Latina: Hacia una comprensión integral." Unpublished paper.

Casillas, Rodolfo. 2008. "Las rutas de los centroamericanos por México, un ejercicio de caracterización, actores principales y complejidades." *Migración y Desarrollo*, 10, 157–174. http://www.scielo.org.mx/pdf/myd/n10/n10a7.pdf

——— 2011. "Redes visibles e invisibles en el tráfico y la trata de personas en Chiapas." In *Migración y Seguridad: nuevo desafío en México*, edited by Natalia Armijo Canto, 53–71. Mexico City: CASEDE. https://www.casede.org/PublicacionesCasede/MigracionySeguridad/cap3.pdf

Castillo, Manuel Ángel. 1989. "La frontera México-Guatemala: un ámbito de relaciones complejas". *Estudios Latinoamericanos*, 4 (6–7), 128–137. http://dx.doi.org/10.22201/cela.24484946e.1989.6-7.47456

——— 2005. "Fronteras, Migración y Seguridad en México". *Alteridades*, 30 (15), 51–60. http://www.scielo.org.mx/pdf/alte/v15n30/2448-850X-alte-15-30-51.pdf

Castillo, Manuel Ángel and Mónica Toussaint. 2010. "Seguridad y migración en la frontera sur". In *Seguridad nacional y seguridad interior*, coordinated by Arturo Alvarado and Mónica Serrano, 269–300. Mexico City: El Colegio de México.

Castillo, Manuel Ángel, Mónica Toussaint and Mario Vázquez Olivera. 2006. *Espacios diversos, historia en común*. Mexico City: Secretaría de Relaciones Exteriores.

Chavarochette, Carine. 2014. "Identificaciones regionales entre las zonas fronterizas de Comitán, México y Huehuetenango, Guatemala. 1824–2001." *LiminaR. Estudios sociales y humanísticos*, 12 (2), 181–194. http://www.scielo.org.mx/pdf/liminar/v12n2/v12n2a12.pdf

Chumil, Katerin. 2018. "Suman tres las pistas clandestinas descubiertas en Petén en los últimos cuatro días." *El Periódico*, 27 March. Accessed 22 February 2020. https://elperiodico.com.gt/nacionales/2018/03/27/suman-tres-las-pistas-clandestinas-descubiertas-en-peten-en-ultimos-cuatro-dias/

Guatemala's Border System 139

Clot, Jean. 2013. "Acercamiento conceptual a las prácticas económicas informales en los pasos fronterizos entre México y Guatemala." *Diacronie*, 13 (1), 1–20. https://journals.openedition.org/diacronie/740

Comisión Internacional Contra la Impunidad en Guatemala (CICIG) and Unicef. 2016. *Trata de personas con fines de explotación sexual en Guatemala.* Guatemala City. http://www.cicig.org/uploads/documents/2016/Trata_Esp_978_9929_40_827_2.pdf

Comisión Internacional de Límites y Aguas entre México y Guatemala (CILA). Sección Mexicana. 2018. "Información general de la frontera entre México y Guatemala." Map.

Cortés, Almudena. 2018. "Violencia de género y frontera: migrantes centroamericanas en México hacia los EEUU." *European Review of Latin American and Caribbean Studies/Revista Europea de Estudios Latinoamericanos y del Caribe*, 105, 39–60. https://www.jstor.org/stable/pdf/26525008.pdf

Dardón, Jacobo (Coord.). 2002. *Caracterización de la frontera Guatemala-México.* Guatemala City: FLACSO-Guatemala.

De León-Escribano, Carmen Rosa. 2007. "La ebullición de la violencia armada y criminalidad común en Centroamérica y Panamá: El carácter transversal de la implementación de controles de armas pequeñas y livianas." In *Armas pequeñas y livianas: una amenaza a la seguridad hemisférica*, edited by Stella Sáenz Breckenridge, 257–334. San José: FLACSO.

―― 2011. "Tráfico ilícito de armas y municiones: Guatemala y la región centroamericana". *URVIO-Revista Latinoamericana de Estudios en Seguridad*, 10, 77–92.

―― 2014. "El tráfico de armas y su relación con el crimen y la violencia en Centroamérica." *Master's diss.*, UCAM. Murcia, Spain.

Demarest, Arthur A., Mary Pye, Paul Amaroli and James Myers. 1991. "Las sociedades tempranas en la Costa Sur de Guatemala." In *II Simposio de Investigaciones Arqueológicas en Guatemala, 1988*, edited by J. P. Laporte, S. Villagrán, H. Escobedo, D. de González and J. Valdés, 35–40. Guatemala City: Museo Nacional de Arqueología y Etnología.

De Vos, Jan. 1978. "La contienda por la selva Lacandona. Un episodio dramático en la conformación de la frontera sur, 1859-1895." *Historias*, 16, 73–98. https://estudioshistoricos.inah.gob.mx/revistaHistorias/wp-content/uploads/historias_16_73-98.pdf

―― 1993. *Las fronteras de la frontera sur. Reseña de los proyectos de expansión que figuraron la frontera entre México y Centroamérica.* Villahermosa: UJAT.

Espach, Ralph et al. 2011. *Criminal Organizations and Illicit Trafficking in Guatemalan Border Communities.* Arlington: CNA. https://apps.dtic.mil/sti/pdfs/ADA553572.pdf

Fábregas Puig, Andrés and Ramón González Ponciano. 2014. "The Mexico-Guatemala, Guatemala-Mexico Border: 1983-2013." *Frontera Norte*, 26, special number 3, 7–35. https://www.redalyc.org/pdf/136/13658129001.pdf

Farah, Douglas. 2011. "Organized Crime in El Salvador: Its Homegrown and Transnational Dimensions." *In Organized Crime in Central America: The Northern Triangle*, edited by Cynthia J. Arnson and Eric L. Olson, 104–138. Washington, D.C.: Woodrow Wilson Center for Scholars.

―― 2013. "Central America's Northern Triangle: A time for Turmoil and Transitions." *Prism*, 4 (3), 88–109. https://www.jstor.org/stable/pdf/26469830.pdf

140   Beatriz Zepeda

——— 2016. "Central American Gangs Are All Grown Up". *Foreign Policy*, 19 January. Accessed 3 February 2016. http://foreignpolicy.com/2016/01/19/central-americas-gangs-are-all-grown-up/

Fenner, Justus. 2019. *Neutralidad impuesta. El Soconusco, Chiapas, en búsqueda de su identidad, 1824–1842*. San Cristóbal de las Casas: CIMSUR.

Fernández Ordóñez, Rodrigo. n.d. "La larga ruta blanca. La evolución de la presencia del narcotráfico en Guatemala" (Parts I, II and III). Accessed 8 March 2016. https://issuu.com/s.sofia/docs/primera_parte; https://issuu.com/s.sofia/docs/la_larga_ruta_blanca__segunda_parte; https://issuu.com/s.sofia/docs/la_larga_ruta_blanca__tercera_parte

Fuentes-Carrera, Julieta (Coord.). 2020. *Entre lo político y lo espacial. Representaciones geopolíticas de la frontera México-Guatemala*. Mexico City: CentroGeo. http://www.rtmg.org/post/entre-lo-politico-y-lo-espacial-representaciones

Galemba, Rebecca B. 2012. "Corn is Food, not Contraband" The Right to 'Free Trade' at the Mexico-Guatemala Border." *American Ethnologist*, 39 (4), 716–748. https://anthrosource.onlinelibrary.wiley.com/doi/pdf/10.1111/j.1548-1425.2012.01391.x?casa_token=zSpbk_ZtXNYAAAAA:vXnVULILIWqvx5jJ5_0CZ1ajYg_P1QLgQpKtywItoa3u4rLfCCICU38dzfoeXfvvylqPklnI-wSu6Ws

——— 2018. *Contraband Corridor. Making a Living at the Mexico-Guatemala Border*. Stanford: Stanford University Press.

García García, Antonio and Edith F. Kauffer. 2011. "Las cuencas compartidas entre México, Guatemala y Belice: Un acercamiento a su delimitación y problemática general." *Frontera Norte*, 45 (23), 131–161.

González-Izás, Matilde. 2014a. *Territorio, actores armados y formación del Estado*. Guatemala City: Universidad Rafael Landívar.

——— 2014b. *Modernización capitalista, racismo y violencia en Guatemala*. Mexico City: El Colegio de México.

Goubaud, Emilio. 2008. "Maras y pandillas en Centroamérica." *Urvio. Revista Latinoamericana de Seguridad Ciudadana*, 4, 35–46. https://revistas.flacsoandes.edu.ec/urvio/article/view/35-46/1654

Gutiérrez, Edgar. 2013. "Guatemala: hábitat del narcotráfico." *Revista Análisis de la Realidad Nacional* (July–September), 184–203.

——— 2016. "Introducción". In *Élites y crimen organizado en Guatemala*, InSight Crime, 3–21. Accessed 2 September 2016. http://es.insightcrime.org/images/PDFs/2016/Guatemala_Elites_Crimen_Organizado.pdf

Gutiérrez, Edgar and Claudia Méndez. 2012. "Guatemala: narcotráfico, lavado de dinero e instituciones fallidas." In *Narcotráfico Corrupción y Estado: Cómo las redes ilícitas han reconfigurado las instituciones de Colombia, Guatemala y México*, edited by Eduardo Salcedo-Albarrán, Luis Jorge Garay Salamanca and Luis Astorga, 113–123. Mexico City: Editorial Grijalbo.

Heredia Zubieta, Carlos (Coord.). 2020. *Geopolítica en los tiempos de Trump: política internacional y aspectos institucionales de la relación México-Guatemala*. Mexico City: Centro de Investigación y Docencia Económicas. http://www.rtmg.org/post/geopolitica-en-los-tiempos-de-trump-politica-inte

Instituto Nacional de Estadística de Guatemala (INE) 2015. *República de Guatemala: Encuesta nacional de condiciones de vida*. Guatemala City: INE.

——— n.d. *Resultados del censo 2018*. Accessed January 3, 2020. https://www.censopoblacion.gt/.

Instituto Tecnológico Autónomo de México (ITAM). 2014. *Migración Centroamericana en tránsito por México hacia Estados Unidos: Diagnóstico y recomendaciones.* Mexico City: ITAM. https://www.comillas.edu/images/OBIMID/itam.pdf

Kauffer Michel, Edith F. 2010. "Migraciones y agua en la frontera entre México, Guatemala y Belice: aproximaciones en torno a una relación multiforme." *LiminaR. Estudios sociales y humanísticos,* 8 (2), 29–45.

MacLeod, Murdo. 1980. *Historia Socioeconómica de América Central Española 1520–1720.* Guatemala City: Editorial Piedra Santa.

Martínez, Graciela, Salvador David Cobo, and Juan Carlos Narváez. 2015. "Trazando las rutas de la migración de tránsito irregular o no documentada por México." *Perfiles Latinoamericanos,* 45, 127–155.

Martínez Velasco, Germán. 2014. "Inmigrantes laborales y flujo en tránsito en la Frontera Sur de México: dos manifestaciones del proceso y una política migratoria." *Revista Mexicana de Ciencias Políticas y Sociales,* 220 (January–April), 261–294. https://www.sciencedirect.com/science/article/pii/S0185191814708074

Mazzitelli, Antonio. 2011. *Mexican Cartels Influence in Central America.* Florida: Western Hemisphere Security Analysis Center. https://digitalcommons.fiu.edu/cgi/viewcontent.cgi?article=1044&context=whemsac

Monzón, Ana Silvia. 2006. *Las viajeras invisibles: Mujeres migrantes en la región centroamericana y el sur de México.* Guatemala City: PCM/CAMEX.

Nájera Aguirre, Jéssica Natalia. 2016. "El complejo estudio de la actual migración en tránsito por México: Actores, temáticas y circunstancias." *Migraciones Internacionales,* 8 (3), 255–266.

——— 2020. "Mercado de trabajo transfronterizo México-Guatemala: una construcción desde la experiencia de los trabajadores." *Estudios fronterizos,* 21, e055.

Ordóñez Morales, César Eduardo. 2006. *Tendencias de la integración económica en Guatemala y el sureste de México.* Guatemala City: Facultad de Ciencias Económicas de la Universidad de San Carlos de Guatemala, AVANCSO.

——— 2007. "Economía informal y sistema fronterizo en dos espacios locales situados en la frontera de Guatemala con México." *Revista de Geografía Agrícola,* 38, (January–June): 85–100. https://www.redalyc.org/pdf/757/75703808.pdf

Orozco, Gabriel. 2004. "Boundary Disputes in Central America: Past Trends and Present Developments." In *Boundary Disputes in Latin America Since the End of the Cold War,* edited by Jorge I. Domínguez, 1–32. Washington, D.C.: Interamerican Dialogue.

Papadovassiliakis, Alex. 2021. "Explorando a profundidad el crimen organizado en Guatemala y sus fronteras." Conference. *InsightCrime.* February 2, 2021.

Pichardo Hernández, Hugo. 2012. "Geografía y desintegración territorial en el México del siglo XIX." In *Geopolítica, relaciones internacionales y etnicidad. Aspectos de la construcción del Estado en América Latina durante los siglos XIX y XX,* coordinated by J. Benítez López et al., 127–151. Mexico City: Bonilla Artiga Editores, Universidad de Quintana Roo.

Platt, Raye R. 1929. "The Guatemala-Honduras Boundary Dispute." *Foreign Affairs,* 7 (2), 323–326. https://www.jstor.org/stable/pdf/20028693.pdf?casa_token=JzU87PxVT-IAAAAA:Jj57LoA3t6LDL_ZXwqt2Z2Etkcpd9XeXJRAQ7ROAeZyu8uDFzV5oij__kShNwZG2zY_QYn7ZU1YQAp0E2fHQZyaOb3pl90a_aAa5rn1tzJtx6Nisvm-9

142   *Beatriz Zepeda*

Popenoe de Hatch, Marion and Carlos Alvarado Galindo. 2010. "Rutas comerciales del Preclásico entre el altiplano y la costa sur de Guatemala: Implicaciones sociopolíticas." In *XXIII Simposio de Investigaciones Arqueológicas en Guatemala, 2009*, edited by B. Arroyo, A. Linares and L. Paiz, 11–25. Guatemala City: Museo Nacional de Arqueología y Etnología.

Procuraduría de los Derechos Humanos (PDH). 2016. *Informe de situación de la trata de personas en Guatemala, 2015*. Guatemala City. https://www.pdh.org. gt/documentos/seccion-de-informes/supervision-y-monitoreo/defensoria-de-persons-victimas-de-trata/informes-de-la-situacion-de-la-trata-de-personas/ 4990-informe-situacion-de-trata-personas-ano-2015/file.html

Ramos Rojas, Diego Noel. 2015. "Tácticas cotidianas de los trabajadores centroamericanos en las localidades limítrofes entre México y Guatemala." *Iberoforum*, 10 (20), 87–108. https://www.redalyc.org/pdf/2110/211043793004. pdf

—— 2016. "La movilidad transfronteriza México-Guatemala desde la representación cotidiana de los trabajadores centroamericanos." *Estudios fronterizos*, 17 (34), 21–40. https://doi.org/10.21670/ref.2016.34.a02

Rodríguez-Castillo, Luis. 2009. "La construcción social del espacio regional transfronterizo." *Economía, Sociedad y Territorio*, 29 (9), 221–227. http://www.scielo. org.mx/pdf/est/v9n29/v9n29a11.pdf

Rojas Wiesner, Martha Luz. 2017. "Movilidad de trabajadores agrícolas de Guatemala a la frontera sur de México en tiempos de control migratorio." *Entre Diversidades. Revista de Ciencias Sociales y Humanidades*, 8, 83–118. https:// dialnet.unirioja.es/servlet/articulo?codigo=6172173

Ruiz Juárez, Ernesto and Germán Martínez Velasco. 2015. "Comercio informal transfronterizo México-Guatemala desde una perspectiva de frontera permisiva." *Estudios Fronterizos*, 16 (31), 149–174. http://www.scielo.org.mx/pdf/ estfro/v16n31/v16n31a7.pdf

Sampó, Carolina. 2013. "Violencia en Centroamérica: Las maras en El Salvador, Guatemala y Honduras." *Revista Estudios de seguridad y defensa*, 2, 139–158.

Sepúlveda, César. 1958. "Historia y problemas de los límites de México: II. La frontera sur." *Historia Mexicana*, VIII (2), 145–174. https://www.jstor.org/stable/ pdf/25134953.pdf?casa_token=plrTKK9FQRoAAAAA:WzbiFtccxvU_ tRQslEWybriLwcnPf0vhycD6mEfPyf9LPZdP-Yo9jWF7S_f5f804bwU5h7N-- Ju75omB7BsaqS3T5g0hqEaCGTmVtRI2K-igVaruyGJ8

Serrano, Javier and Germán Martínez, coords. 2009. *Una aproximación a las migraciones internacionales en la frontera sur de México*. San Cristóbal de las Casas: ECOSUR.

Sieff, Kevin. 2020. "The Guatemalan Rainforest: Lush Jungle, Mayan Ruins and Narco Jets Full of Cocaine." *The Washington Post*. 5 July. https://www. washingtonpost.com/world/2020/07/05/guatemala-cocaine-trafficking-laguna-del-tigre/?arc404=true

Silva Ávalos, Héctor. 2021. "Explorando a profundidad el crimen organizado en Guatemala y sus fronteras." Conference. *InsightCrime*. February 2, 2021.

Stein, Eduardo et al. 2015. *Contrabando y defraudación aduanera en Centroamérica*. Guatemala City: Konrad Adenauer Stiftung, Red Centroamericana de Centros de Pensamiento e Incidencia. https://www.kas.de/c/document_library/ get_file?uuid=f5461a20-d8fc-44ce-7071-c4bba9b0274d&groupId=252038

Guatemala's Border System 143

Tamayo Pérez, Luz María Oralia. 2015. "La Comisión Mexicana de Límites y la definición de la frontera sur del país." *Revista de Geografia Norte Grande*, 60, 115–134. http://dx.doi.org/10.4067/S0718-34022015000100007

Toussaint Ribot, Mónica. 1996. *Belice: una historia olvidada*. Mexico City: Instituto Mora, Centro de Estudios Mexicanos y Centroamericanos. https://books. openedition.org/cemca/319

Unicef, ECPAT, ILANUD. 2012. *El delito de la trata de personas, especialmente de niños, niñas y adolescentes para la explotación sexual, comercial y otras modalidades. Guatemala, El Salvador, Honduras y Nicaragua: Una aproximación al sujeto activo del delito*. Guatemala City.

Valdez, Mario E. 2006. *Desencuentros y encuentro de fronteras: El Petén Guatemalteco y el Sureste Mexicano 1895–1949*. San Cristóbal de las Casas: Universidad Intercultural de Chiapas.

Villafuerte Solís, Daniel. 2004. *La frontera sur de México. Del TLC México-Centroamérica al Plan Puebla-Panamá*. Mexico City: Universidad Autónoma de México/Plaza y Valdez.

——— 2017. *Tiempo de fronteras. Una visión geopolítica de la frontera sur de México*. Tuxtla Gutiérrez: UNICACH.

Villafuerte Solís, Daniel and María del Carmen García Aguilar. 2007. "La doble mirada de la migración en la frontera sur de México: asunto de seguridad nacional y palanca del desarrollo." *LiminaR. Estudios sociales y humanísticos*, 5 (2), 26–46. https://doi.org/10.29043/liminar.v5i2.249

——— 2015. "Crisis del sistema migratorio y seguridad en las fronteras norte y sur de México." *Revista Interdisciplinaria de Movilidad Humana*, 44: 83–98. https:// www.scielo.br/j/remhu/a/sx644ywS9bxbmX6FcfPw9bP/abstract/?lang=es

Wagner, Regina. 1994. *Historia social y económica de Guatemala 1524–1900*. Guatemala City: Asociación de Investigación y Estudios Sociales.

——— 2001. *Historia del café de Guatemala*. Guatemala City: Villegas Asociados.

Willers, Susanne. 2016. "Migración y violencia: las experiencias de mujeres migrantes centroamericanas en tránsito por México." *Sociológica*, 89, 165–195. http://www.scielo.org.mx/pdf/soc/v31n89/0187-0173-soc-31-89-00163.pdf

World Drug Report (WDR). 2020. United Nations publication, Sales No. E.20. XI.6. https://wdr.unodc.org/wdr2020/index2020.html

Zepeda, Beatriz, Matilde González-Izás, and Carmen Rosa de León-Escribano (forthcoming). *Guatemala's Borders and Illegal Markets in the Age of Globalization*. New York: Routledge.

——— 2018. *Guatemala: fronteras y mercados ilegales en la era de la globalización*. Guatemala City: FLACSO-Guatemala, FLACSO-Ecuador, IDRC. https://biblio. flacsoandes.edu.ec/libros/digital/57003.pdf

6 Mexico's Cross-Border Subsystem

Cocaine Trafficking and Violence on the Northern Border

César Fuentes Flores and Sergio Peña Medina

Since the 1990s, most of the world's borders have moved from a binational logic of *complementary asymmetries* to a global border system that is part of the framework of illegal economies (Andreas 2004). In this context, Mexico's land borders[1] represent a paradigmatic example, because of their adjacency with the most developed country in the world to the north and, to the south, with less developed countries. Both vicinities condition the presence of a great amount of legal and illegal economic activities derived from the complementary asymmetries between the countries.

As a case in point, in the 1950s some illicit activities emerged at the Mexico-US border. The northbound flows included the contraband of liquor, drug trafficking, etc., whereas cigarettes, clothing, and household appliances flowed in the North-South direction (Alegría 1992). However, since the 1980s, as a consequence of the globalization process, borders stopped being spaces of place and became spaces of flows (Castells 2001a, Castells, 2001b). The presence of legal global economic activities, such as the maquila industry, tourism, etc., but also illegal economic activities, such as the smuggling of illicit substances (marijuana, heroin, cocaine) and arms smuggling, thus emerged and was further transformed to create global cross-border systems. These processes are part of a new logic of the administrative architecture of the "network of networks" (Carrión, in this volume). Illegal activities are more evident at the borders, as they take on a strategic role in the flows because of the configuration of the global space.

In the case of the trafficking of illegal drugs, such as cocaine, a global cross-border network has emerged, composed of producers, traders, distributors, and consumers (Flynn 1995, 122; Benítez 2002, 15). This cross-border network involves coca leaf producers in countries such as Peru, Bolivia, and Colombia, criminal groups in Honduras, El Salvador, and Guatemala involved in cocaine transport, drug cartels in Mexico and Colombia, who collaborate in the transport and distribution of cocaine, and finally consumers, mainly in the United States, Europe, and South America.

DOI: 10.4324/9781003204299-11

Mexico's Cross-Border Subsystem   145

The new structure of transnational drug-trafficking networks led to the strengthening of Mexican drug cartels and their accumulation of economic and firepower. This turned them into real threats to the country's security (Benítez 2009a, 28). As a result of internal divisions within the criminal groups, a process of fragmentation and diffusion took place, which led them to declare war on each other for the control of shipments, warehouses, transit routes, ports of entry to the United States and local markets, thus generating high levels of violence that resulted in thousands of homicides (Astorga 2005, 145). This violence was mainly concentrated in Mexico's northern border cities, such as Ciudad Juárez, Tijuana, Nogales, Nuevo Laredo, Reynosa, and Matamoros, in large part due to their role as strategic nodes for the traffic of narcotics.

The destructive power of organized crime groups was not limited to the violence they generated; it also included the capacity to infiltrate the security forces at different levels of the administration, and even to become de facto governments in order to control territories for their operation. This was interpreted by President Felipe Calderón's advisers as the "loss of territoriality" of the Mexican State (Benítez 2009b, 17). With this as a backdrop, in 2007, Felipe Calderón declared war on the drug cartels. One of the main combat strategies in such war was to increase the involvement of the armed forces in public security tasks (Benítez 2009a, 21).

Ciudad Juárez, Chihuahua was one of the places where the war between the drug cartels[2] for the control of routes, warehouses and the local drug market was most intense. From 2008 to 2011, this city experienced more than 8,246 intentional homicides, making it the most violent city in the world in 2010, with a homicide rate of 224 per 100,000 inhabitants (Observatorio de Seguridad y Convivencia Ciudadana 2012, 3).

The purpose of this chapter is to analyze the constitution of the global cross-border system of illegal economic activities from the angle of the process of production, commercialization, distribution, and consumption of cocaine and its impact on the violence experienced in Ciudad Juárez, Chihuahua from 2008 to 2012.

Borders and Globalization

To begin with, a comparative analysis of post-war international political economy regimes and those emerging from globalization will be carried out. This analysis will start from certain key concepts, which are relevant to understand international political economy regimes. The concepts used are *episteme*, territory, scales, space, and central actors.

Episteme and Borders

For the purposes of this work, the concept of *episteme* refers to the way knowledge about globalization and borders is produced. In the literature on international political economy, the predominant approach emphasizes the nation-state as the primary unit of analysis. Specifically, the realist approach, one of the dominant approaches to international relations, is based on the idea that the nation-state is the central actor in the system. The nation-state and its relationship to other nation-states are thus the focus of analysis of international relations (Morgenthau 2014; Starr 2006). Issues of high politics such as conflict, war, cooperation, alliances, trade in goods that are legally sanctioned by the nation-state, among others, dominate the production of scientific knowledge. In this form of knowledge production, borders are analyzed simply as lines that separate the internal from the external, the national from the foreign; in short, the cultural and legal limits of the nation-state. With globalization, this paradigm of producing knowledge (see Kuhn 1996) entered a crisis, since it is very limited in explaining the role and power that actors other than the state, are beginning to acquire; for example, multinational corporations, insurgent groups such as Al-Qaeda, among others. In addition, realism faces serious shortcomings in explaining the impact of the flows of investment, goods, and people, which turn borders not only into trade and logistics nodes, but also into production nodes.

Brenner (1999, 39) argues that a new way of producing knowledge, different from the state-centric approach, is needed to understand globalization. Critical theory, in particular, proposes an approach that allows to historically conceptualize economic, political, and spatial processes; an approach that, according to Brenner (1999, 39), has as a central element the historicity of the territory. Castells (1974, 17; 2011, 440) argues that each mode of production throughout history produces and structures its own space; space is articulated and organized to produce, circulate, exchange goods, and reproduce the processes of the dominant mode of production. In sum, the new way of producing knowledge about the international political economy must conceptualize globalization as a *spatial* reconfiguration of capitalism to ensure its *sine qua non* function – accumulation. From this critical geography approach, in the context of globalization, borders acquire a different and more complex connotation; they cease to be dividing lines and containers, and become functional spaces of third order[3] in the hierarchy of global cities (Sassen 2011, 147). The new way of generating knowledge around globalization must therefore understand the latter as a historical-temporal moment in the process of capitalist accumulation. Simultaneously, the international political economy of the illegal or the clandestine, as well as the legally sanctioned economy, undergoes a transformation of a spatial-organizational nature. According to Andreas (2004, 641), the illegal or clandestine political economy operates in a parallel or underlying way to the legal international political economy.

Territory and Sovereignty

A conceptual analysis of the territory and its transformation is necessary to understand the emergence and consolidation of criminal organizations that, in some instances, become a parallel power to the state. The concept of territory cannot, in fact, be separated from the concept of sovereignty (Sassen 1999, 3; 2007, 45; 2013, 21; Cox 2013, 46); the two of them stand in a symbiotic relationship.

Historically, this symbiotic relationship between territory and sovereignty can be traced back to the Peace of Westphalia (1648) that gave birth to the modern concept of the nation-state. According to some authors (Sassen 2007, 45; 2013, 21; Cox 2013, 46) territoriality is a legal construct that gives the state exclusive authority over a territory and is also known as sovereignty. This authority or sovereignty means that what is inside the container called nation is subject to prescribed rules and laws, rights, and obligations. Other political-territorial organizations such as states and municipalities (even if they are on the border) lack sovereignty in matters of agreements and treaties with foreign governments. International relations between nation-states are the exclusive domain of national governments, while the functions of the different levels of government are well marked and delimited. Legally speaking, borders are the clearly demarcated boundaries of the nation-state. The state assumes a panopticon role to ensure that flows that have not been legally sanctioned do not cross its borders.

Globalization substantially transforms state sovereignty. Brenner (1999, 39) describes globalization as a process of disassembling sovereignty. This disassembly of sovereignty means that, whether planned or unplanned, the state begins to lose or cede the monopoly power it has over the territory. Sovereignty is shared, either willingly or unwillingly, with other actors who need to control territory for their operations.

The literature on globalization revolves around those who think that sovereignty is an obsolete concept and, therefore, the nation-state begins to lose meaning, and others, such as Brenner (1999, 39; 2001, 591), Sassen (2007, 45), and Swyngedouw (1997, 137; 2000, 63), who argue that the nation-state only shares and adapts to the new needs of capitalism. Finally, neo-realists, such as Hollifield (1998, 595), argue that the nation-state has never lost sovereignty or control over territory. Furthermore, in this discussion we can include those studies on failed states (Helman and Ratner 1992, 3) that argue that the state loses the monopoly power of territorial sovereignty to actors that try to establish a new political-military/religious regime (e.g., ISIS in Iraq and Syria, Boko Haram in Nigeria), or those that simply want to exploit the advantages of state absence in their criminal economic activities (e.g., drug cartels, modern-day pirates, among others). Borders, in this context of

148   *César Fuentes F. and Sergio Peña M.*

sovereignty disassembling, become strategic points of both legal and illegal flows. Consequently, the control of this territory is critical to the political economy of clandestine flows (which generate exorbitant profits). Such control can be achieved through the complicity and corruption of the state, assuming that it still has some authority, or through open armed conflicts between groups, when the state has surrendered or lost its sovereignty completely.

Scales and Processes

Scale, according to Swyngedouw (1997, 137), is a particular geographical configuration and, at the same time, the result of socio-spatial processes that regulate and organize social power relations. In turn, Brenner (1999, 39) argues that scales are traditionally defined from a state-centric approach, which perceives space as a "container." From these works, two approaches can be identified on how to conceptualize scales. The first one analyzes them as processes; the second one sees them as "containers." Globalization has transformed the conceptualization of process scaling from a state-centered and container approach to a socio-spatial approach, where the power relations of sub and supranational actors are the main axis (Brenner 1999, 39).

Prior to globalization, scales were stable and characterized by a nested and hierarchical nature. Russian dolls, which are a fairly ubiquitous craft, are the best analogy to describe this kind of state-centric scale. The smallest doll is contained within a larger one. Translating the analogy to political-territorial scales, the smaller doll represents the local or municipal level while the larger doll represents the national level; each scale has a political territorial demarcation, functions, and mandates, which are clearly delegated[4] and indicated by law. Borders as political-administrative spaces are clearly marked and the control and surveillance functions are assigned to an agency and level of government, in most cases[5] to the federal sphere. The agencies in charge of border affairs are usually part of the ministry of foreign affairs; they are diplomatic in nature and have a counterpart from the neighboring country.

Globalization, it is argued (Brenner 1999, 39; Swyngedouw 1997, 137; 2000, 63), revitalizes not only the national scale, but also the sub and supranational scales, forming a "polymorphic" scalar structure, where functions are negotiated, and limits are difficult to determine. As a strategy of capitalist accumulation, globalization produces a dialectical process of deterritorialization and reterritorialization (Brenner 1999, 39; Brenner and Theodore 2002, 349); a compression of time and space by means of the erosion of barriers (physical, regulatory, tributary, etc.), and a reconfiguration of political territorial organizations (reterritorializing process), in such a way that scales are relativized. From this perspective, the configuration or conceptualization of borders changes from being lines and edges of territorial sovereignty, to acquiring a diffuse configuration and limits that are difficult to establish; the origin and destination of the processes do not necessarily correspond to the limits of national territorial sovereignty. Willingly or not, the nation-state relinquishes part of the control[6] of borders to facilitate globalization processes. From a political economy perspective, this deterritorializing and reterritorializing dialectic translates into the relationship between the market and the state: on the one hand, the market demands the destruction of barriers, while, on the other hand, the state seeks to maintain territorial sovereignty. Borders are not exempt from this dialectic (Spener and Staudt 1998, 15), which makes the border invisible to certain processes (foreign direct investment, capital, etc.), while reinforcing it for other undesirable processes (e.g., drug and human trafficking, to mention but two). In turn, trade barriers alter the costs of flows: they reduce the costs of legal flows, but increase those of clandestine ones, thereby creating economic opportunities for criminal activities.

Space and Globalization

It is also important to discuss how the meaning of space is transformed by the globalizing processes. Several authors (Lösch and Woglom 1954, 3; Christaller 1966, 16; Alonso 1964, 3; Richardson 1969, 15; Lefebvre 1991, 68; Soja 1996, 83; Brenner 1999, 17; Harvey 2006, 121; Castells 1974, 17; 2011, 440; Sassen 2011, 147) have addressed the issue of space, and several interpretations emerge from their works. For reasons of parsimony, these authors are grouped into two trends: classical and critical theory. From the perspective of political economy, space plays a fundamental role since it is there that the processes of globalization materialize.

The classical approach (Christaller, Lösch, Richardson, Alonso) conceptualizes space in an absolute way. According to Harvey (2006, 121) and Brenner (1999, 17), in the absolute approach, space is conceived as the Cartesian space. It is a "thing" that is pre-constituted and naturalized. It is, moreover, a static platform of social action. In sum, in this approach, space is fetishized. This spatial notion is compatible with the notion of the nation-state as a space that is "naturalized" by being perceived as something that gives form and identity to the nation. The national market is assumed to be a hierarchy of markets of different rank and threshold in the form of a beehive (each pentagon is a market). In this spatial notion, borders are deemed underdeveloped economic spaces, since political borders are an "unnatural" barrier that limits the range and threshold of potential markets. The underground economy will take advantage of the adjacency of differences (Alegría 1989, 53) to supply the potential or "natural" market that political barriers prevent from emerging, thus resulting in economies of agglomeration. Examples of this adjacency of differences are the variations

150   *César Fuentes F. and Sergio Peña M.*

in costs and/or laws that prohibit certain consumer goods on one side and allow them on the other. Borders render these differences adjacent and produce opportunities for trafficking and smuggling. By destroying these barriers to economic flows, globalization simply "naturalizes" the range and distance of the market and thereby erodes the benefits produced by the adjacency of differences.

In contrast, critical theory, particularly Brenner's proposal (1999, 50), conceptualizes space as a "geographic infrastructure," which is key to the development of capital. In addition, Castells (1974, 17; 2001, 440) points out that each mode of production produces and reconfigures space to facilitate capital accumulation; globalization as a stage of the capitalist mode of production reconfigures space into spaces of flows and networks. Flows have an origin and a destination; networks have nodes that articulate them. Unlike other views that argue that space loses meaning by becoming ubiquitous, critical theory maintains the notion that space continues to play a functional and hierarchical role in a new international division of labor. Maritime and land borders in this sense can be conceptualized as a "geographic infrastructure" of the global network; an infrastructure of a logistic nature that facilitates flows and, at the same time, also participates in the global production process by attracting foreign direct investment (FDI).

The underground economy is inserted in and takes advantage of the flows and networks produced by globalization; in other words, organized crime is globalized and reorganized on the basis of an international division of labor. For example, cocaine trafficking is reorganized and activities are segmented in a global context; some regions produce inputs (coca leaf, opium poppy, etc.), others specialize in processing, others in transport, others in distribution, and others, from the 1990s onwards, in money laundering.

Literature Review on Borders, Globalization, and Illegal/Illicit Activities

The review of the literature on Mexico's borders and illegal/illicit activities shows a great diversity of topics and approaches that can be grouped into six broad categories. The first one includes borders and organized crime and focuses on analyzing the threats and challenges posed to countries by transnational organized crime groups, whose strengthening and diversification threaten the stability of the border regions and, in some cases, that of countries as a whole. This group includes studies by Olson et al. (2010); Sandoval (2012); Dudley (2012); Block (2012); and Waldron (2014).

A second group of works focuses on analyzing the effects of drug trafficking on the security of countries, regions, and cities. Specifically, this literature emphasizes the effects of the fight among drug cartels for the control of markets and drug transportation routes that led to high levels of violence and thousands of deaths in some of Mexico's northern border cities. This category includes the work of Valdez and Sifaneck (1997); Rodríguez (2003); Longmire and Longmire (2008); Montana and Cooper (2009); Shirk (2010 and 2014); Krakau (2010); Aziz Nassif (2012); Garzón (2012); Mazzitelli (2012); and Medel et al. (2014).

The third set of studies is related to arms trafficking and smuggling across borders, particularly the northern border. Many of these firearms are used by organized crime groups to enforce their law in the territories they control and to confront other drug-trafficking groups, as well as the police or the military. These works also analyze the firearms market in the United States and its link to organized crime groups in Mexico. This line of research includes studies by Medel et al. (2014); Cook et al. (2009); Astorga (2010); Kai Miller (2010); Good (2010); Villarreal (2010); Goodman and Marizco (2010); Flores (2011); Kuhn and Bunker (2011); Goodman (2011); Young (2012); Lucatello (2012); Olson (2012); Dube et al. (2013); Finklea (2013); McDougal et al. (2013); Rodríguez (2014); and Kopel (2014).

The fourth group seeks to present the migrant smuggling networks between Mexico and the United States, their evolution over time, and the new threats faced by Central American migrants from organized crime throughout their journey through Mexico. In addition, they discuss some studies that prove that female migrants are kidnapped along the way with the purpose of human trafficking. Finally, other studies point to the need to protect migrants who have been victims of human trafficking. The studies by Ugarte et al. (2004); Cicero-Domínguez (2005); García et al. (2007); Meyer and Brewer (2010); Garza (2011); Casillas (2012); Cepeda and Nowotny (2014) can be grouped here.

The fifth set of academic work discusses the money-laundering strategies used by criminal organizations to maximize their profits and minimize the risk of detection. Additionally, some studies that show anti-money-laundering initiatives used as a strategy against organized crime are also included. Within this group of studies are the works of Ferragut (2012) and Realuyo (2012).

The final group focuses on the study of cross-border collaboration between Mexico and the United States in terms of security, particularly at border ports, to prevent the entry of terrorists into the United States through the border with Mexico. This group includes the work of Benítez and Rodríguez Ulloa (2010); Benítez (2009b); Ramos (2006 and 2013); Andreas and Wallman (2009); and Ashby (2014).

The Settlement of Mexico's Borders: Complementary Asymmetries

Mexico's northern border was settled in the mid-nineteenth century, after a war that caused the loss of half of its territory to the United States. The Treaty of Guadalupe Hidalgo was signed in 1848 and the Treaty of La Mesilla or Gadsden Purchase in 1853, thus defining the boundary

152   *César Fuentes F. and Sergio Peña M.*

between the United States of America and Mexico (Tamayo-Pérez 2014, 140). Currently, this border is 3,124.3 kilometers long and is defined in most of its extension by the course of the Río Bravo/Rio Grande, which functions as a natural limit. The Mexican border states from the Pacific Ocean to the Gulf of Mexico are Baja California, Sonora, Coahuila, Nuevo León, and Tamaulipas, and the US border states are California, Arizona, New Mexico, and Texas (Tamayo-Pérez 2014, 141).

In the nineteenth century, the cities located on both sides of the US-Mexico border were more integrated with each other than with the national centers of their respective countries.[7] At that time, contraband became a lucrative activity both for Americans and Mexicans in the region and flooded the Mexican market with goods from the United States. Contraband led to the movement of population to the border towns of Tamaulipas (Castellanos 1981, 32). In reaction to this, in 1858, the Mexican government decreed the free import of US products, thus changing the legal situation of the cross-border trade that had hitherto been considered contraband (Alegría 1992, 121) and creating a free trade zone in the northeast of the country. At that time, Mexico's northern border region was scarcely populated, and the Mexican government sought to promote its growth with the aim of curbing US expansionism.

Formal trade on the northern border began in 1880 with the establishment of the railroads and the aforementioned federal free zone policies. Poor economic conditions in commerce, industry, and agriculture prompted the border residents to revive the economy by boosting tourism and service activities. The "tourist" activities derived from the "prohibition era" in the United States encouraged the development of entertainment centers, especially nightclubs. The growth of cities depended increasingly on the arrival of American "tourists," who generated a strong economic spillover (Alegría 1992, 121).

From the beginning of the twentieth century until the 1930s, the population and economic activity of Mexican localities increased. In the case of the most recently formed cities, such as Tijuana and Ensenada, the free zone regime that comprised the territory of the Baja California peninsula and a part of Sonora was not created until 1939. As a result of the lack of road communication with the interior of the country, border populations intensified their "pattern of cross-border communication, strengthening asymmetric and dependent complementarities" (Alegría 1992, 122). In the 1960s, integration no longer occurred only through the flow of goods, but also of productive capital and labor. In this context, between both sides of the border "a complementary and asymmetric relationship [emerged] in which there was a selective brake, a form of expression of the structural differences that marked the character of Mexico's border towns" (Alegría 1992, 122).

Until the early twentieth century, the cities on the north side of the border, such as San Diego, El Paso, etc., were larger than their Mexican counterparts Tijuana and Ciudad Juárez. This situation would be reversed years later, when most Mexican cities grew in population, as a result of the attraction they exerted on inhabitants both from other regions of the country and abroad, many of whom sought to reach the United States and, when they failed to do so, settled in the border cities. Similarly, the population growth of Mexican border cities, which was influenced by migration flows, increased with the arrival of the maquila industry[8] and the large supply of jobs it brought with it.

By the 1960s, a cross-border urban system was consolidated, consisting of the so-called twin cities or binational pairs. Today, the twin cities from West to East are: Tijuana, Baja California and San Diego, California; Mexicali, Baja California and Calexico, California; Nogales, Sonora and Nogales, Arizona; Agua Prieta, Sonora and Douglas, Arizona; Ciudad Juárez, Chihuahua and El Paso, Texas; Ojinaga, Chihuahua and Presidio, Texas; Ciudad Acuña, Coahuila and Del Rio, Texas; Piedras Negras, Coahuila and Eagle Pass, Texas; Nuevo Laredo, Tamaulipas and Laredo, Texas; Reynosa, Tamaulipas and Mc Allen, Texas; and Matamoros, Tamaulipas and Brownsville, Texas (see Map 6.1).

As regards the final layout of Mexico's southern border, it was a conflict-ridden process. The 1842 Mexican annexation of Soconusco in the process of establishing the border with Guatemala, and the Caste War that

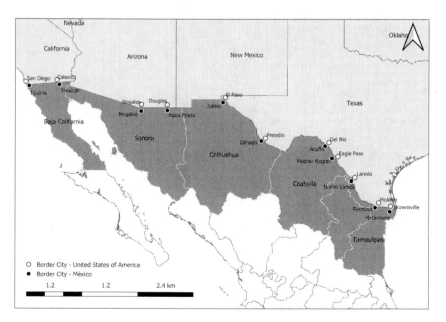

Map 6.1 Binational Pairs on the US-Mexico Border
Source: INEGI and USGS
Map by authors

devastated the eastern portion of the Yucatan Peninsula for half a century are clear examples of this. However, the processes that led to the definition of international boundaries with Guatemala in 1882, and with Belize (then British Honduras) in 1893, were different. The rivers Suchiate, Usumacinta, Chixoy, Azul, and Hondo are the natural boundaries on this area.

The border between Mexico and Guatemala is 962 kilometers long (Anderson 2003, 27), and comprises the current Mexican states of Chiapas, Tabasco, and Campeche, which border the Guatemalan departments of San Marcos, Huehuetenango, Quiché, and Petén (Castillo et al. 2006, 145). In sociocultural terms, the social groups living on each side of the border share a colonial heritage, as well as similar social, ethnic, and cultural characteristics. Currently, the border between the two countries has eight official ports of entry; seven in Chiapas: Ciudad Hidalgo, Talismán, Unión Juárez, Cuauhtémoc, Carmen Xhan, Frontera Corozal, Nuevo Orizaba; and one in Tabasco: El Ceibo (see Map 6.2).

Map 6.2 Formal and Informal Border Crossings on Mexico's Northern and Southern Borders

Map by the authors

Mexico's border with Belize was settled in 1893 through the Spencer-Mariscal Treaty. This treaty signed by Mexico and the British Crown recognized the colony of British Honduras and established the territorial configuration that Belize would later inherit when it obtained its independence in 1981. The Mexico-Belize border has an extension of 250 kilometers (Anderson 2003, 23) and the municipality of Othón P. Blanco of the state of Quintana Roo borders the Belizean districts of Orange Walk and Corozal (Castillo et al. 2006, 147). This border is ethnically, socially, and culturally heterogeneous and on the Belizean side its population is composed of people of Mayan, Chinese, African, Lebanese, and Indian descent.

Mexico's southern border is much more diverse in terms of its ecosystems, culture, ethnicity, historical processes, and productive strategies than the northern border. Another characteristic that distinguishes the region is the lack of economic development strategies on the part of the national government. "It was only in the 1980s that the Mexican government increased its presence on the southern border and created *ad hoc* institutions to address, through the Mexican Commission for Refugee Aid (COMAR), an unprecedented situation in the country" (Armijo 2009, 41).[9] Currently, there are two official crossing points between Belize and Mexico: in the towns of Subteniente López and La Unión, both in the state of Quintana Roo.

For several decades in the twentieth century, border dynamics and exchanges were constituted by the movement of border residents, temporary workers, local visitors, small-scale traders, among others, who apparently had freedom of movement, with or without documentation, and established family and commercial ties that persist to this day (Armijo 2009, 23).

Traditionally, cross-border exchanges have concentrated in the states of Chiapas and Quintana Roo. The state of Chiapas is an area of seasonal labor migration, mainly from Guatemala, that caters for coffee farms, as well as for construction activities and domestic work in the Soconusco region. In turn, the state of Quintana Roo borders Belize almost entirely and, in terms of its flows, it represents a much lesser migratory pressure for Mexico. On Mexico's southern border, Guatemalan workers can be found during the sugarcane cutting season. Additionally, constant flows for legal business activities and small-scale contraband across the Suchiate River take place all year long (Armijo 2009, 25).

Nowadays, the most serious security problems on Mexico's southern border are caused by drug, arms, and human trafficking. In 1998, the federal authorities implemented "Operation Sealing," a set of measures aimed at improving the interception of drugs in transit to the United States. This program was reinforced in 2000 with staff training and modern drug detection technology (Armijo 2009, 26).

156 *César Fuentes F. and Sergio Peña M.*

The Construction of the Cross-Border Cocaine-Trafficking Subsystem

Since the mid-1980s, internal and external borders have become more integrated into the globalization process through the establishment of global networks of the illegal economy (Andreas 2004). In that sense, as already mentioned, borders stopped being spaces of place and became spaces of flows (Castells 2001, 231). Drug trafficking, human trafficking, and arms trafficking are some of the illegal economic activities that clearly show the role that borders play in the constitution of the cross-border system of illegal activities. This process occurs in a new logic of the administrative architecture of the "network of networks" of criminal groups (Carrión, in this volume).

Although Mexico's borders are a space for the flow of a variety of illegal economies, the main security problem is caused by drug trafficking, especially marijuana, cocaine, and heroin. Drug trafficking became global because of the transnational relationship between production, transport, trade, and consumption networks (Flynn 1995, 23; Benítez 2002, 7). In the first stage, illegal drugs trafficking took place through a binational logic of *complementary asymmetries* between Mexico and the United States. Within this framework, Mexican cartels emerged when a consumer market for marijuana and heroin was consolidated in the United States after the Second World War (Astorga 2005, 143). Marijuana production was located in the "golden triangle" formed by the mountainous area of the states of Sinaloa, Chihuahua, and Durango, while opium poppy-producing areas were located in the mountainous areas of the state of Guerrero. At this stage, the production and trade of marijuana and heroin were carried out domestically by drug-trafficking groups such as the Tijuana and Juarez Cartels, whereas the consumer market was almost exclusively that of the United States. In order to carry out these activities, criminal organizations focused their strategy on controlling the main transportation routes and border crossings of Mexico's northern border cities. In this context, the growth of drug trafficking in Mexico was largely due to the inability of the Mexican government to control the borders, as well as to the weakness and corruption of the institutions responsible for security and the administration of justice (Benítez 2002, 25).

At the same time, from the 1980s onward, with the formation by the US government of the Southern Command's Joint Interagency Task Force South, the Caribbean routes used by the Medellín and Cali cartels for the transportation of cocaine to the United States market were closed. The Colombian cartels sought to replace these routes, and by the late 1980s and early 1990s, the new routes already included Panama, Honduras, El Salvador, Guatemala, and the Gulf of Mexico, as well as the Pacific Ocean corridor to Mexico and then across the border to the United States (Bagley 2012, 8). In order to accomplish this, the Colombian cartels had to negotiate and establish alliances with the Mexican cartels, and by the late 1990s, the South Pacific corridor became the main route for smuggling cocaine northwards from Colombia to the United States, although the Gulf of Mexico route also remained active (Bagley 2012, 17). The most important new routes for the entry of cocaine from Colombia are the South Pacific coasts of Oaxaca and Guerrero, as well as the Yucatan peninsula and Veracruz, for drugs arriving from Venezuela and Brazil. In land transit along the southern border, most narcotics enter through the Petén region of Guatemala (Benítez 2009b, 22).

This was the beginning of the constitution of the global cross-border system of cocaine transfer that includes the cultivation, production, transport, distribution, and consumption of cocaine. A first node in the system is constituted by the coca leaf growers of Peru and Bolivia, who were considered the main producers in the world from 1850 to the mid-1980s (Bagley 2012, 3). These two countries play an important role in planting, processing cocaine paste and, in some cases, refining it. A second node of the network is formed by Colombian drug traffickers, who buy the cocaine paste from Peruvian and Bolivian producers and in some cases process it in these countries, and, in other cases, transport it to their laboratories in Colombia for refining (Andreas 1995, 79). However, from the mid-1980s to the end of the 1990s, with the "success" of the interdiction policies implemented in the area by the United States government, part of the supply from countries like Peru and Bolivia was reduced, but Colombia's coca leaf production increased. According to information from the United Nations Office on Drugs and Crime (UNODC), coca leaf is currently produced in only three countries: Colombia (45%), Peru (35–40%), and Bolivia (15–20%). Figure 6.1 shows the participation of coca leaf production by country in the 2003–2012 period.

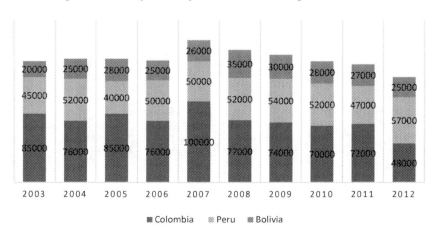

Figure 6.1 Coca Leaf Production by Country (2003–2012)

Source: UNODC (2010, 70)

A third node of the cross-border network is formed by Central American organized crime groups, which contribute, via logistics and protection services provided by the transporters, to cocaine shipments arriving by sea and air (Mazzitelli 2012, 17). The first airlifts linking Colombian and Central American transporters with their Mexican partners were established in the 1980s. By the late 1990s and in the wake of the strengthening of Mexican traffickers – the Sinaloa and Zetas cartels – air corridors from Colombia and Central America opened routes to southern Mexico. Today, these routes are located in the Caribbean countries of Honduras and Nicaragua, as well as Guatemala, and, more recently, Belize, and continue to be of fundamental importance to drug-trafficking groups:

> According to the Anti-Narcotic Division of the National Civilian Police of El Salvador, 20% of all cocaine shipments that transit through Central America are moved by air. From January to June 2010, air traffic control authorities reported 79 suspicious events, out of which 56 were directed to and originating from Central American locations. In 2009, the number of reported suspicious air trips totaled 192 events, of which 87 involved Central American locations. In 2008, 189 suspicious events were registered.
> (Mazzitelli 2012, 16)

Figure 6.2 shows the increase in cocaine seizures in Central American countries as an illustration of the role the region played in this system until 2012.

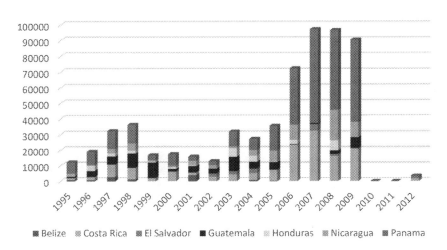

Figure 6.2 Cocaine Seizures by Country in Central America (1995–2012)
Source: UNODC (2010, 70)

A fourth node of the subsystem is constituted by the Mexican drug traffickers, who transport and distribute cocaine. This node emerged as a result of the Colombian drug traffickers' need to find new routes and negotiate with Mexican criminal groups for the use of the routes the latter had already established along the 3,152 kilometers of land border with the US drug-trafficking activities focused on key ports of entry, such as borders, that already had the infrastructure for illegal trade and a long history of smuggling of illicit substances (Ashby 2014, 485). According to Ramos (2006, 15), 90% of the cocaine, 100% of the marijuana, and 100% of the methamphetamines that reach the United States transit through Mexico.

As a result of the implementation of Plan Colombia in 1999, the two largest Colombian drug-trafficking groups, the Medellín and Cali cartels, were weakened. In turn, Mexican criminal organizations experienced a strengthening process, which led them to gradually monopolize the cocaine trade through the control of the Central American and Pacific Ocean routes (Rodríguez Beruff 2009, 287). This was also favored by the reduction of armies in Central America, which led to a low state presence in the territories, facilitating the establishment of drug routes in Honduras, El Salvador, and, mainly, in Guatemala (Felbab-Brown 2010, 42).

As a result, at the beginning of the twenty-first century, four large Mexican cartels were considered consolidated: the Sinaloa Cartel, led by Joaquín Guzmán Loera ("El Chapo"); the Tijuana Cartel, headed by the Arellano Félix family; the Gulf Cartel, with the Zetas as its armed wing; and the Juárez Cartel, headed by Amado Carrillo Fuentes (Benítez 2002, 18), each in control of different routes. For example, the Arellano Félix Cartel introduced cocaine into the Californian market; the Carrillo Fuentes cartel controlled the route from the center of the country to west Texas; while the Gulf Cartel controlled the route from the Guatemala-Mexico border to Tamaulipas and Texas (Benítez 2002, 19).

As happened in Colombia, Mexican cartels have recently suffered a process of fragmentation and diffusion of their criminal networks. This has rendered their dismantling by Mexican authorities much more difficult (Bagley 2012, 14). In 2000, the Sinaloa, Gulf, Tijuana, and Juárez cartels were the four largest and dominant drug-trafficking organizations in Mexico (Benítez 2002). Since 2000, after Vicente Fox's administration, at least three new drug-trafficking organizations emerged: the Familia Michoacana, the Beltrán Leyva Cartel, and the Zetas (Bagley 2012, 8).

In terms of diffusion, drug cartels have managed to increase their presence beyond their countries of origin, seeking to establish new routes and safe havens, opening corridors for the supply of all kinds of illegal products, laundering their assets and creating "zones" for commercial exchange. Therefore, they have created a new structure aimed at integrating local criminal factions into an international market, exploiting the advantages of the globalized world. In each case, organized crime is taking violence and corruption to new dimensions and territories (Garzón 2012, 22).

A fifth node of the subsystem is the cocaine distribution network within the United States. According to some sources, there is a whole distribution network in more than a thousand cities in the United States, commanded mainly by Mexicans or United States citizens of Mexican origin. The Sinaloa Cartel has a strong presence in Chicago, which is why this criminal group was declared enemy number one by the Chicago Crime Commission. The presence of Mexican cartels has also been detected in states such as Georgia, Kentucky, Illinois, Indiana, Michigan, Minnesota, Ohio, and Pennsylvania, among others. Officials from US agencies stated that, for these transnational networks to work, they need to have agents in Mexico as well as in the United States (Bagley 2012, 8).

The use of drugs has also become globalized. Although for many years cocaine use was concentrated in the United States and Europe, in the last decades it has grown rapidly in some Latin American countries. According to UNODC, in 2012, it was estimated that consumers in Latin America inhaled more than 200 metric tons of cocaine. Because of its size and population, Brazil has the largest number of consumers with approximately 900,000. However, the prevalence of cocaine use in Brazil among the general population is lower compared to Argentina and Chile (Bagley 2012, 10).

The rate of cocaine use in other regions of the world is also high. In Africa, the number of consumers is estimated at between 940,000 and 4.42 million, whereas Asia had an estimated number of users between 400,000 and 2.3 million (UNODC 2012, 256). The growth in cocaine use in South America and Europe increased global demand for this illicit product over the last decade. This led to the proliferation of new global trafficking routes (Bagley 2012, 12).

In parallel, there has been a continued decline in cocaine use in the United States since 1982, from 10.5 million users in that year to 5.3 million in 2008 (Bagley 2012, 15). Cocaine users in European Union countries doubled from 2 million in 1998 to 4.1 million in 2008 (UNODC 2010, 259).

The Cross-Border Subsystem of Illegal Economies and Violence on Mexico's Northern Border

The increase in violence in Mexico's northern border cities is mainly explained by three factors: (1) increase in common crime; (2) disputes between drug cartels for control of routes, warehouses, markets, etc.; and (3) the militarization of public security (Benítez 2009a, 29).

Mexico's Cross-Border Subsystem   161

Mexican drug cartels went from being associates, to being partners of the Colombian cartels and, finally, independent operators, which made them very powerful organizations (Mazzitelli 2012, 12). Mexican drug organizations became real powers in the country and the dispute over cocaine routes and local drug distribution markets triggered a fight between the different cartels for control of the *plazas* (territories): the cities where drugs are stored, the roads that connect the north of the country with the points of entry, the coasts and the borders with Guatemala and Belize. The contraband and distribution of this narcotic to North American, European and world markets is protected by conventional weapons, most of which are in the hands of criminal groups that deal in the illicit business (Lucatello 2012, 185).

In this context, a violence never seen before in Mexico was unleashed and, given their strategic location as nodes in the transfer of cocaine to the United States, some of the cities, especially on the northern border, saw the number of violent homicides increase dramatically. It is important to point out that since the terrorist attacks on the Twin Towers in New York City on September 11, 2001, the United States strengthened security on its border with Mexico, especially through the installation of aerial radars, which made it nearly impossible to introduce drugs across the border by means of short flights without being detected. Since then, most of the drugs are transported overland, increasing the importance of the control of routes and crossing points on the Mexico-US border.

Under these circumstances, cities like Ciudad Juárez, Tijuana, Nogales, and Nuevo Laredo became strategic for the crossing of drugs. A war between the different drug cartels for the control of these cities ensued, turning the streets into battlefields, where thousands of people died. The cartels' economic power was transformed into a mechanism to corrupt police, officials, and local authorities. For this reason, the municipal police corps quickly became institutions at the service of the mafias; while the federal government lacked the necessary police forces to deal with the situation in the whole country.

A paradigmatic case of the extreme level of violence generated among drug-trafficking groups was that of Ciudad Juárez, where a fierce fight began between the Juárez and the Sinaloa cartels for control of transport routes, warehouses, and the local drug market. The confrontation began in 2007 and, with it, the incidence of crime in the city increased. One of the crimes that grew the most was intentional homicide, whose rate has grown exponentially since then. In 2010 and 2011, the city reached 242 homicides per 100,000 inhabitants, making it the most violent city in the world. By 2012, however, the violence had declined and shifted to other cities such as Acapulco and Cuernavaca, where other organized crime groups were fighting for control of the *plazas*.

In 2006, as the confrontation between organized crime groups intensified, Felipe Calderón Hinojosa was sworn in as President of the republic. One of Calderón's priorities was to aggressively confront the drug cartels, for they had increased their level of violence and power in some areas of the country, including coastal states and those on the northern border (Olson and Wilson 2010, 23), where transnational flows of goods and people acquire a territorial quality. In 2007, President Calderón declared war on the cartels and stated: "It will be an all-out war because there is no longer any possibility of living with the drug cartels. There is no return; it is either they or us" (quoted in Benítez 2009a, 34). The strategy of the federal government was to mobilize the military forces, the Federal Police, and the Mexican Navy to some areas to dismantle the drug cartels and force them to operate outside of Mexico. In this process, 45,000 members of the army and federal police were mobilized to certain key points in the country, but mainly to cities on the northern border. Despite the deployment of the public force, the violence associated with organized crime grew exponentially. During President Calderón's term of office, from December 2006 to November 2012, more than 60,000 people were killed in the war between the cartels and in confrontations with the Mexican police and military forces (Benítez 2009b, 42). While not all victims were associated with the violence generated by the cartels, most were the result of competition between rival organized crime groups for control of strategic flow areas or markets.

As the violence increased, so did the concern of the US government. It focused, above all, on the possibility of violence spreading to its border cities with Mexico. In response to this threat, in March 2007, President George Bush met with President Felipe Calderón in Mérida, Yucatán, and the two agreed to significantly increase cooperation in the war against drug trafficking and the violence it generated. In that context, the Mérida Initiative was born. It entailed the United States providing Mexico with $1.4 million in equipment, training, and technical assistance over a three-year period (Olson and Wilson 2010, 25).

Cooperation between Mexico and the United States was put at risk after the "Operation Fast and Furious" incident, in which agents of the Bureau of Alcohol, Tobacco, Firearms, and Explosives (ATF) received orders to allow arms trafficking from the United States to Mexico in order to track down major drug traffickers (Lucatello 2012, 50).

In 2010 alone, almost 5,000 weapons were trafficked to Mexico, compared to an estimated 3,000 in 2007. According to information provided by Mexico's General Attorney's Office, around 2,000 weapons cross the border from the United States every day. The lack of strict controls at border points on either side allows so many weapons to enter undetected every day (Lucatello 2012, 51).

Arms trafficking did not only reach the drug cartels in Mexico, but also Central American countries such as Guatemala, Honduras, and El Salvador. The transport of arms in Central America is usually done through highways, where they travel hidden in secret compartments of trucks or other vehicles, inside tires or in fuel tanks. Traffickers usually use the main trade routes, such as the Pan-American Highway, which crosses all of Central America. The fact that there are few controls at border crossings facilitates overland transport. The other way of crossing illegal arms is the well-known "ant trafficking," that is to say small-scale trafficking, in which individuals transport small quantities from one country to another. Police investigations show that small arms (revolvers and pistols) destined for Guatemala enter that country through the border with Mexico by means of this mechanism. At the border between Nicaragua and Honduras, farmers exchange firearms for basic consumer products, and this system is also part of the "ant trafficking" pattern (Lucatello 2012, 52).

Conclusions

The cross-border subsystem of illegal economies, specifically cocaine-trafficking, is constituted by the articulation between production, marketing, distribution, and consumption (Benítez 2012). In this process, the first node is conformed by the farmers who cultivate the coca leaf in Peru and Bolivia. A second node is made up of the Colombian drug traffickers who buy the coca leaf and refine it in those countries or in laboratories in Colombia; the third node is made up of the Central American organized crime groups that transport and guard the drugs that come from Colombia and reach Mexico's southern border through their ports or clandestine airstrips. The fourth node is composed of the Mexican drug traffickers, who cross the northern border into the United States and distribute the drugs in a large number of US cities. In this process, the final node is constituted mainly by US consumers.

For the globalization of illegal/illicit activities to be possible, it was necessary for transnational organized crime to make use of the same technological advances that make the process of globalization of the legal economy possible: new digital technologies such as the Internet, fiber optics, smartphones that allow for rapid communication on a planetary scale, as well as the free flow of large amounts of money in search of investment opportunities and the emergence of new markets around the world.

In this new stage, transnational criminal organizations have managed to generate extraordinary profits, which have given them great economic power to distribute bribes among government officials and a great capacity to arm themselves to confront nation-states. However, in a parallel but opposite direction, the security policies of the United States have sought to reduce the spaces for the free flow of illegal substances and have made their transportation by sea and air much more difficult, thus rendering land borders strategic places for the crossing of drugs.

164 *César Fuentes F. and Sergio Peña M.*

Mexico's northern border cities were transformed into warehouses to store the large shipments of drugs arriving from other parts of the world that had to be transported in small quantities through border crossings. As a result, these cities became highly coveted flow areas and were involved in major confrontations between the various cartels for control of their transport routes, crossing ports, and the local drug market.

In this context, the cities on Mexico's northern border, such as Ciudad Juárez, were victims of the US security policies. Such policies sought to contain the flow of drugs, thereby inducing their storage in those Mexican cities and generating violence among organized crime groups. Mexico's northern border towns have also been the victims of the voracity of transnational organized crime, which seeks to make large profits by flooding the US drug market and uses those cities as spaces for the flow of small quantities of drugs, for whose transport city residents, usually young people, are often hired. Finally, border cities have also been affected by the damage that transnational organized crime causes by corrupting public institutions such as the police, the judiciary, and officials at different levels of government.

Notes

1. In this paper, land borders are understood as Mexico's borders with the United States, Guatemala, and Belize, while sea and air borders are referred to as internal borders.
2. The confrontation was between the Juárez Cartel and the Sinaloa Cartel.
3. According to Sassen (2011), there are command and control cities such as New York, London, and Tokyo, where capitalist strategic decisions are made. There are other secondary cities that play a logistical role in facilitating globalization at a regional level, such as São Paulo, Mexico City, Sydney, Buenos Aires, and Miami. There are also global cities of the third order where the productive processes take place, such as the northern border of Mexico and coastal areas in China, to mention a few. Finally, the fourth order cities are cities that have remained on the margins of globalization.
4. In the case of Mexico, the fight against drug trafficking (production, transport, trade, distribution, and consumption) belongs to the federal jurisdiction, even when these crimes occur in a local space. In federalist and decentralized systems such as the United States, local institutions have mandates to act.
5. In Mexico and the United States, the Constitution establishes that the only authority to sign agreements and treaties of an international nature is the federal government. In the case of Mexico and the United States, there are bilateral commissions to deal with border issues such as the International Boundary and Water Commission (IBWC).
6. The North American Free Trade Agreement (NAFTA) is an example of a deterritorialization process that facilitates trade flows between Mexico, the United States, and Canada. Along with trade agreements, new ways of managing the borders between Mexico and the United States

Mexico's Cross-Border Subsystem   165

are emerging and binational commissions are created with personnel from both countries working together. A good example is the Border Environment Cooperation Commission (BECC).

7. It is important to mention that it was only until 1940 that the center of the country was able to communicate with the border of Baja California by rail and until 1946 by road (Alegría 1992, 132).

8. In the case of Mexico's northern border, the establishment of the Border Industrialization Program meant the arrival of the maquiladora industry in 1965. This program permits the realization of industrial assembly activities through the free import of supplies – mainly from the United States – the processing of the inputs and the repackaging of the final product, before sending it to the country of origin for sale.

9. Editors' note: This "unprecedented situation" was the arrival of thousands of Guatemalan refugees, who, in the context of the civil war, fled the repression they were being subjected to by the Guatemalan army.

References

Alegría, Tito. 1989. "La ciudad y los procesos transfronterizos entre México y Estados Unidos." *Frontera Norte 1* (2), 53–90. https://doi.org/10.17428/rfn.v1i2.1654

———— 1992. *Desarrollo urbano en la frontera México-Estados Unidos, una interpretación y algunos resultados.* Mexico City: Consejo Nacional para la Cultura y el Arte.

Alonso, William. 1964. *Location and Land Use.* Cambridge, MA: Harvard University Press.

Anderson, Ewan. 2003. *International Boundaries: A Geopolitical Atlas.* New York: Routledge.

Andreas, Peter. 1995. "Free market reform and drug market prohibition: US policies at cross purposes in Latin America." *Third World Quarterly 1* (16), 75–87.

———— 2004. "Illicit International Political Economy: the Clandestine Side of Globalization." *Review of International Political Economy 11* (3), 641–652.

Andreas, Peter and Joel Wallman. 2009. "Special issue on illicit markets and violence." *Crime Law and Social Change 52* (3), 225–336.

Armijo, Natalia. 2009. "Vulnerabilidad de seguridad en la relación México-Centroamérica." In *Atlas de seguridad y la defensa en México 2009,* coordinated by Raúl Benítez, Abelardo Rodríguez and Armando Rodríguez, 171–174. Mexico: Colectivo de Análisis de la Seguridad con Democracia.

Ashby, Paul. 2014. "Solving the border paradox? Border security, border integration and the Merida Initiative." *Global Society 18* (4), 483–508.

Astorga, Luis. 2005. "El tráfico de drogas, la seguridad y la opción militar." In *Globalización, Poderes y Seguridad Nacional,* coordinated by Alberto Aziz Nassif and Alonso Sánchez. Mexico: Porrúa/CIESAS.

————2010. "El tráfico de armas de Estados Unidos hacia México. Responsabilidades diferentes." In *International Drug Policy Consortium.* Accessed 3 September 2014. https://www.urosario.edu.co/urosario_files/53/53893403-66d0-430e-90c5-47ce43c7f4ea.pdf

Aziz Nassif, Alberto. 2012. "Violencias en el norte de México: el caso de Ciudad Juárez." *Iberoamericana 48* (12), 143–155.

166   *César Fuentes F. and Sergio Peña M.*

Bagley, Bruce. 2012. *Drug Trafficking and Organized Crime in the Americas: Major Trends in the Twenty First Century.* Washington, DC: Woodrow Wilson International Center for Scholars, Latin American Program.

Benítez, Raúl. 2002. "Crimen organizado; fenómeno transnacional, evolución en México." *Centrales,* 215, 7–12.

—— 2009a. "La crisis de inseguridad de México." *Nueva Sociedad.* 220, 173–189.

—— 2009b. *La nueva seguridad regional: Amenazas irregulares, crimen organizado y narcotráfico en México y América Central.* Mexico City: Fundación para las Relaciones Internacionales y el Diálogo Exterior.

—— 2012. "The Geopolitics of Insecurity in Mexico-United States Relations". In *The State and Security in Mexico. Transformation and Crisis in Regional Perspective,* edited by Brian Bow and Arturo Santa Cruz, 33–46. New York: Routledge.

Benítez, Raúl and Carlos Rodríguez Ulloa. 2010. "Seguridad y fronteras en Norteamérica: del TLCAN a la ASPAN." In Seguridad *y Defensa en América del Norte: Nuevos dilemas geopolíticos,* edited by Raúl Benítez, 221–244. Mexico: Colectivo de Análisis de la Seguridad con Democracia.

Block, Steven. 2012. "Characteristics of Internationally Trafficked Stolen Vehicles along the U.S.-Mexico Border." *Western Criminology Review* 13 (3), 1–14.

Brenner, Neil. 1999. "Beyond State-Centrism? Space, Territoriality, and Geographical Scale in Globalization Studies." *Theory and Society* 28 (1), 39–78. https://www.jstor.org/stable/3108505

—— 2001. "The Limits to Scale? Methodological Reflections on Scalar Structuration." *Progress in human geography* 25 (4), 591–614. https://journals.sagepub.com/doi/pdf/10.1191/030913201682688959

Brenner, Neil and Nik Theodore. 2002. "Cities and the Geographies of Actually Existing Neoliberalism." *Antipode* 34 (3), 349–379.

Casillas, Rodolfo. 2012. "La mundialización del delito. Redes de tráfico y trata de personas en México." *New Society* 24, 122–132.

Castellanos, Alicia. 1981. *Ciudad Juárez: la vida fronteriza.* México: Nuestro Tiempo Editores.

Castells, Manuel. 1974. *La Cuestión Urbana.* México: Siglo Veintiuno Editores.

—— 2001a. "Information Technology and Global Capitalism." In *On the Edge: Living with Global Capitalism,* edited by Will Hutton y Anthony Giddens, 52–74. London: Jonathan Cape.

—— 2001b. *The Rise of the Network Society: The Information Age: Economy, Society, and Culture.* New York: John Wiley & Sons.

—— 2011. *The rise of the network society* (Volume 12). New York: John Wiley & Sons.

Castillo, Manuel Ángel, Mónica Toussaint, and Mario Vázquez Olivera. 2006. *Espacios diversos, historia en común.* Mexico: Secretaría de Relaciones Exteriores.

Cepeda, Alice and Kathryn Nowotny. 2014. "A Border Context of Violence: Mexican Female Sex Workers on the U.S.–Mexico Border." *Violence Against Women* 20 (12), 1506–1531.

Christaller, William. 1966. *Central places in southern Germany.* New York: Prentice-Hall.

Cicero-Domínguez, Salvador. 2005. "Assessing the U.S.-México Fight Against Human Trafficking and Smuggling: Unintended Results of U.S." *Northwestern Journal of International Human Rights* 303 (4), 35–47.

Cook, Philip J., Wendy Cukier, and Keith Krause. 2009. "The Illicit Firearms Trade in North America." *Criminology and Criminal Justice* 9 (3), 265–286.

Cox, Kevin. 2013. "Territory, Scale, and Why Capitalism Matters." In *Territory, Politics, Governance* 1 (1), 46–61.

Dube, Arindrajit, Oendrila Dube and Omar García-Ponce. 2013. "Cross-Border Spillover: U.S. Gun Laws and Violence in Mexico." *American Political Science Review* 107 (3), 397–417.

Dudley, Steven. 2012. *Transnational Crime in Mexico and Central America: Its Evolution and Role in International Migration*. Washington, DC: Migration Policy Institute.

Felbab-Brown, Vanda. 2010. *Shooting up: Counterinsurgency and the war on drugs*. Washington, DC: Brookings Institution Press.

Ferragut, Sergio. 2012. *International Security Programme Paper 2012/01 Organized Crime, Illicit Drugs and Money Laundering: the United States and México*. Chatham House. International Security Programme Paper (01).

Finklea, Kristin. 2013. *Southwest Border Violence: Issues in Identifying and Measuring Spillover Violence*. Congressional Research Service.

Flores, Carlos. 2011. *¿Es posible detener el tráfico de armas?* Mexico: Centro de Estudios de Derecho e Investigaciones Parlamentarias.

Flynn, Stephen. 1995. "Globalización del narcotráfico: las drogas y el crimen organizado." *Revista Occidental* 12 (3), 35–54.

García Vázquez, Nancy Janett, Elisa Guadalupe Gaxiola Baqueiro and Arnoldo Guajardo Díaz. 2007. "Movimientos transfronterizos México-Estados Unidos: Los polleros como agentes de movilidad." *Confines* 5 (3), 101–113.

Garza, Rocío. 2011. "Addressing Human Trafficking Along the U.S.-México Border: The Need for a Bilateral Partnership." *Journal of International and Comparative Law* 413 (19), 413–452.

Garzón, Juan Carlos. 2012. "El futuro del narcotráfico y de los traficantes en América Latina." In *Atlas de seguridad y defensa en México 2012*, edited by Sergio Aguayo and Raúl Benítez, 31–38. Mexico: Colectivo de Análisis de la Seguridad con Democracia. Security and Coexistence Observatory.

Good, Beverly. 2010. *Preventing Bulk Cash and Weapons Smuggling into Mexico: Establishing an Outbound Policy for the Southwest Border for Customs and Border Protection*. Naval Postgraduate School.

Goodman, Colby. 2011. *Update on U.S. Firearms Trafficking to México Report*. Washington, DC: The Woodrow Wilson International Center for Scholars.

Goodman, Colby and Michel Marizco. 2010. "U.S. Firearms Trafficking to México: New Data and Insights Illuminate Key Trends and Challenges." In *Shared Responsibility: U.S.-Mexico Policy Options for Confronting Organized Crime*, 167–203. Working Series Paper on U.S.-Mexico Cooperation. Washington, DC: The Woodrow Wilson International Center for Scholars.

Harvey, David. 2006. *Spaces of Global Capitalism: Towards a Theory of Uneven Geographical Development*. New York: Verso.

Helman, Gerald and Steven Ratner. 1992. "Saving Failed States." *Foreign Policy* 89, 3–20. https://doi.org/10.2307/1149070

168　*César Fuentes F. and Sergio Peña M.*

Hollifield, Frank. 1998. "Migration, Trade, and the Nation-State: The Myth of Globalization." *International Journal of Law & Foreign Affairs* 3 (2), 595–636. https://www.jstor.org/stable/45302102

Kai Miller, Benjamin. 2010. "Fueling Violence Along the Southwest Border: What More Can Be Done to Protect the Citizens of the United States and Mexico From Firearms Trafficking." *Houston Journal of International Law* 32, 163–199.

Kopel, David. 2014. "Mexico's Gun-Control Laws: A Model for the United States?" *Texas Review of Law & Politics* 18 (1), 27–95.

Krakau, Philipp. 2010. *Narco-Negocio y seguridad en México: Conceptos, efectos y posibilidades de cooperación con los Estados Unidos.* Mexico: Friedrich Ebert Foundation.

Kuhn, David A. and Robert J. Bunker. 2011. "Just Where Do Mexican Cartel Weapons Come From?" *Small Wars & Insurgencies* 22 (5), 807–834.

Kuhn, Thomas. 1996. *The Structure of Scientific Revolutions.* Chicago: University of Chicago Press.

Lefebvre, Henri. 1991. *The Production of Space.* Oxford: Blackwell.

Longmire, Sylvia and John Longmire. 2008. "Redefining Terrorism: Why Mexican Drug Trafficking Is More than Just Organized Crime." *Journal of Strategic Security* 1 (1): 35–52. https://www.jstor.org/stable/26462950

Lösch, August and William Woglom. 1954. *The Economics of Location.* New Haven: Yale University Press.

Lucatello, Simone. 2012. "El desafío del tráfico de armas en México y Centroamérica." In *Atlas de seguridad y la defensa en México 2012*, coordinated by Sergio Aguayo and Raúl Benítez, 47–54. Mexico: Colectivo de Análisis de la Seguridad con Democracia. Security and Coexistence Observatory.

Mazzitelli, Antonio. 2012. "Mexican Cartel Influence in Central America." In *Atlas de seguridad y la defensa en México 2012*, coordinated by Sergio Aguayo and Raúl Benítez, 19–24. Mexico: Colectivo de Análisis de la Seguridad con Democracia. Security and Coexistence Observatory.

McDougal, Topher, David A. Shirk, Robert Muggah and John H. Patterson. 2013. *The Way of the Gun: Estimating Firearmas Traffic Across the U.S.-México Border.* Igarapé Institute and University of San Diego.

Medel, Monica, Yongmei Lu and Edwin Chow. 2014. "Mexico's Drug Networks: Modeling the Smuggling Routes Towards the United States." *Applied Geography* 60, 240–247. http://dx.doi.org/10.1016/j.apgeog.2014.10.018

Meyer, Maureen and Stephanie Brewer. 2010. *A Dangerous Journey through Mexico: Human Rights Violations Against Migrants in Transit.* Washington, DC: Washington Office on Latin America.

Montana, Salvador and Stephen Cooper. 2009. "Mexico's Drug Wars: Implications and Perspectives from California and California's San Joaquin Valley." *The International Journal of Continuing Social Work Education* 12 (2), 45–56.

Morgenthau, Hans J. 2014. "A Realist Theory of International Politics." *The Realism Reader* 53, 12–53.

Observatorio de Seguridad y Convivencia Ciudadana. 2012. "Estadísticas de homicidios en Ciudad Juárez, Chihuahua." Universidad Autónoma de Ciudad Juárez, 1–10.

Olson, Eric and Christopher Wilson. 2010. "Beyond Merida: The Evolving Approach to Security Cooperation." *Working Paper Series on U.S.-Mexico Security Cooperation.* Washington, DC: Woodrow Wilson International Center for Scholars.

Mexico's Cross-Border Subsystem 169

Olson, Erick. 2012. *Considering New Strategies for Confronting Organized Crime in México*. Washington, DC: The Woodrow Wilson International Center for Scholars.

Olson, Erick, David Shirk and Andrew Selee. 2010. *Shared Responsibility: U.S.-Mexico Policy Options For Confronting Organized Crime*, 1–30. Washington, DC: The Woodrow Wilson International Center for Scholars.

Ramos, José María. 2006. "La seguridad en la frontera con Estados Unidos: de la ineficacia a políticas estratégicas." In *Atlas de seguridad y la defensa en México 2009*, coordinated by Raúl Benítez, Abelardo Rodríguez and Armando Rodríguez, 159–161. Mexico: Colectivo de Análisis de la Seguridad con Democracia.

——— 2013. "Relaciones México-Estados Unidos y dilemas en seguridad ciudadana fronteriza." *Fronteras: rupturas y convergencias*, coordinated by Fernando Carrión and Víctor Llugsha, 169–186. Quito: FLACSO-Ecuador-IDRC.

Realuyo, Celina. 2012. *It's all about the Money: Advancing Anti-Money Laundering Efforts in the U.S. and Mexico to Combat Transnational Organized Crime*. Washington, DC: The Woodrow Wilson International Center for Scholars and University of San Diego.

Richardson, Harry. 1969. *Regional Economics. Location Theory, Urban Structure and Regional Change*. New York: Praeger.

Rodríguez, Daniel. 2014. *2001–2011. Estrategias de una relación compleja: Tráfico ilícito de armas y frontera entre México y Estados Unidos*. Quito: FLACSO-Ecuador.

Rodríguez, John. 2003. International Drug Trafficking: Police Corruption on the US/Mexico Border. Master of Science in Criminal Justice, University of Texas-Pan American.

Rodríguez Beruff, Jorge. 2009. "La seguridad en el Caribe en 2008: Huracanes, crimen, rusos y soft power." In *Seguridad Regional en América Latina y el Caribe. Anuario 2009*, coordinated by Hans Mathieu and Paula Rodríguez, 24–56. Bogotá: Friedrich Ebert Stiftung. https://biblio.flacsoandes.edu.ec/shared/biblio_view.php?bibid=124446&tab=opac&oai.flacsoandes.org.124446

Sandoval, Efrén. 2012. "Economía de la fayuca y del narcotráfico en el noreste de México. Extorsiones, contubernios y solidaridades en las economías transfronterizas." *Desacatos* 38, 43–60.

Sassen, Saskia. 1999. *Losing Control? Sovereignty in an Age of Globalization*. New York: Columbia University Press.

——— 2007. *A Sociology of Globalization*. New York: W.W. Norton & Co. www.scielo.org.co/pdf/anpol/v20n61/v20n61a01.pdf

——— 2011. *Cities in a World Economy*. New York: Sage Publications.

——— 2013. "When Territory Deborders Territoriality." *Territory, Politics, Governance* 1 (1), 21–45. https://doi.org/10.1080/21622671.2013.769895

Shirk, David. 2010. "Criminal Justice Reform in Mexico: An Overview." *Mexican Law Review* 3 (2), 189–228.

——— 2014. "A Tale of Two Mexican Border Cities: The Rise and Decline of Drug Violence in Juárez and Tijuana." *Journal of Borderlands Studies* 29 (4), 481–502.

Soja, Edward. 1996. *Third Space: Journeys to Los Angeles and Other Real-and-Imagined Places*. Oxford: Blackwell.

Spener, David and Kathleen Staudt. 1998. *The US-Mexico Border: Transcending Divisions, Contesting Identities*. Boulder: Lynne Rienner Publishers.

170 *César Fuentes F. and Sergio Peña M.*

Starr, Harvey. 2006. "International Borders: What They Are, What They Mean, and Why We Should Care." *SAIS Review* 26 (1), 3–10.

Swyngedouw, Erik. 2000. "Authoritarian Governance, Power, and the Politics of Rescaling." *Environment and Planning: Society and Space* 18, 63–76. https://disaster-sts-network.org/sites/default/files/artifacts/media/pdf/swyngedouw.pdf

———— 1997. "Neither Global Nor Local: 'Glocalization' and the Politics of Scale." In *Spaces of Globalization: Reasserting the Power of the Local*, coordinated by Kevin R. Cox, 137–166. New York: The Guilford Press. https://www.research.manchester.ac.uk/portal/en/publications/neither-global-nor-local-glocalization-and-the-politics-of-scale(65af1505-dde1-4d7f-a730-c069b2f40918).html

Tamayo-Pérez, Luz María. 2014. "Las fronteras de México: apuntes para su demarcación científica y técnica en el siglo XIX." *Revista Colombiana de Geografía* 2 (23), 139–157.

Ugarte, Marisa B., Laura Zárate, and Melissa Farley. 2004. "Prostitution and Trafficking of Women and Children from México to the United States." *Journal of Trauma Practice* 2 (3–4), 147–165.

United Nations Office on Drugs and Crime (UNODC). 2010. *World Drug Report: Executive Report*. New York: United Nations Organization.

————. 2012. *World Drug Report*. New York: United Nations Organization.

Valdez, Avelardo and Stephen Sifaneck. 1997. "Drug Tourists and Drug Policy on the U.S.–Mexican Border: An Ethnographic Investigation of the Acquisition of Prescription Drugs." *Journal of Drug Issues* 27 (4), 879–897.

Villarreal Palos, Arturo. 2010. "Tráfico de armas entre Estados Unidos y México ¿existen soluciones posibles?" *Letras jurídicas* (11), 1–24.

Waldron, Sean. 2014. *Transnational Organized Crime Groups and Their Impact on Economic Crime on the US–Mexican Border*. ProQuest LLC. https://www.proquest.com/openview/e573f074602437ee0e9bfa0e2f2645db/1?pq-origsite=gscholar&cbl=18750

Young, Stewart M. 2012. "Going Nowhere 'Fast' (or 'Furious'): The Nonexistent U.S. Firearms Trafficking Statute and the Rise of Mexican Drug Cartel Violence." *Journal of Law Reform* 46 (1), 1.

PART 1.4

MULTIFUNCTIONAL COUNTRIES

7 Projecting Borders across the Atlantic
The Case of Italy from a Latin American Perspective

Federico Alagna[*]

Located in the center of the Mediterranean Sea and with more than 7,000 kilometers of coastline, the Italian Peninsula has been a crossing point for people and goods between Europe and the rest of the Mediterranean for millennia.

At first sight, devoting a chapter to Italy – both to its borders and to the illegal activities that cross them – in a book that presents a state of the art of the border system in Latin America may seem to require a justification. In fact, in the context of a comparative and introductory study, this chapter aims: (a) to offer some reflections on the global border system and the countries that compose it, even outside Latin America; (b) to understand some of the characteristics of a multifunctional country, which is the destination of multiple forms of trafficking (also) coming from Latin America; (c) to deepen our understanding of the specific case of migrant smuggling and the policies that Italy is implementing to address it, at a time when all these dynamics are becoming increasingly salient and often politicized at a global level, not least in the Americas.

Italy and Latin America are firmly interconnected when it comes to criminal activities and trafficking, also in the light of the deep-rooted links between Italian mafia-type organizations[1] and South American syndicates. A case in point is drug trafficking from Colombia, which makes Italy one of the main places of transit and destination for South American cocaine, as evidenced by the numerous operations conducted by the police forces (DCSA 2019; see also Forgione 2009). Within this perspective, understanding the characteristics of the Italian border system and the illegal trafficking that takes place throughout the Italian territory plays a fundamental role in the analysis, not only of the criminal flows that originate in Latin America, but also of the global border system as a whole.

The main objective of this chapter is, thus, to understand the state of the Italian border question and – taking into account the historical evolution of Italy's territorial boundaries – to identify the basic characteristics of its border system, in particular in relation to criminal activities and their connections with Latin America.

DOI: 10.4324/9781003204299-13

Projecting Borders across the Atlantic 173

In this vein, the first section of the chapter will focus on the aspects of definition of Italy's borders over time; the second section will analyze the existing literature on the border issue in Italy, in order to understand how and in what terms this topic has been problematized in debates of – but not limited to – an academic nature; the third section will list the main characteristics of the relationship between the Italian border system and the criminal flows that cross the territory. In this section, the Mediterranean border will take on the greatest importance, and will be further explored in a fourth section, in particular relation to the issue of migrant smuggling and the Italian and European policy responses thereto. In turn, air border issues will not be considered, not because they are not important in the analysis of Italian cross-border criminal flows (on the contrary, see for instance, DCSA 2019, 38, 44; Ministero dell'Interno 2019), but because of their merely analytical marginality in approaching the border issue from its physical and relational aspects.

The approach chosen for this chapter is necessarily multidisciplinary, considering a historical and geographical perspective in the evolution of Italian borders, a criminological perspective referring to the illegal flows, and a more policy-oriented one regarding the way in which Italy has sought to manage these phenomena, particularly in its Mediterranean border. Throughout the chapter I will seek, whenever possible, to present these considerations in relation to the issue of borders and cross-border crimes in Latin America, understanding and exploring – it is worth stressing again – how the Italian case can be significant in this perspective.

A Genealogical Introduction: From the Border Definition to the Construction of an Inter-Border System

After territorial and state redefinitions both in Italy and in the neighboring territories, Italian land borders coincide today with the mountain range of the Alps, which separates the country – from northwest to northeast – from France, Switzerland, Austria, and Slovenia (see Map 7.1). What remains are the maritime borders and two enclaves, i.e., the states of San Marino and Vatican City. These two latter cases, however, will not be discussed in this chapter.

To simplify the matter in a way that is functional to this state of the art, it can be assumed that, in the definition of the Italian borders, from the unification of the country in 1861 to the present day, four main phases have occurred: (a) the progressive annexation of the various states, city-states and territories that would eventually form the Kingdom of Italy (1861–1870); (b) the new structure after the First World War, with the expansion of the country toward the Balkans (1918–1921); (c) the new structure after the Second World War, following the resolution of the issues concerning the eastern and northeastern borders, as well as the consolidation of other borders (1945–1975); (d) the process of functional

174 *Federico Alagna*

Map 7.1 Italy and its Borders
Map by the author with mapchart.net

redefinition of internal borders in the European Union (EU) – and with some neighboring countries, including Switzerland (1985–present): this culminated in the abolition of customs, in 1993, and border controls for persons, with the entry into force, in 1995, of the Schengen Agreement and the associated Convention implementing the Schengen Agreement of June 14, 1985 (the Schengen Convention) (see Olivi and Santaniello 2015).

This section will not attempt to provide an exhaustive analysis of the evolution of Italian borders.[2] Instead, it seems more relevant, in the perspective of this book, to focus mainly on the last two phases, which respectively mark the current territorial definition of Italy after the Second World War and the function and characteristics assigned to the borders through the process of European integration.

Except for some marginal variations, the history of the evolution of Italy's borders ends on November 10, 1975. On that date, the signing of the Treaty of Osimo put an end to the territorial disputes between Yugoslavia and Italy, representing the *de jure* ratification of a condition that had existed *de facto* since the London Memorandum of 1954, when

Projecting Borders across the Atlantic 175

British troops separated the occupation zones with barbed wire. The independence of Slovenia and Croatia in 1991 did not alter the validity of the treaty.[3] In fact, the Slovenian (formerly Yugoslavian) front is undoubtedly one of the most controversial cases in the definition and evolution of the Italian borders, due to the different interests at stake and the marked presence of minorities on both sides of the demarcation line.

The case of the Austrian border is similar. The dispute should have been solved, along with all the others that emerged in the continent after the Second World War, thanks to the negotiations that took place among the new states that were born after the war. The 1946 so-called De Gasperi-Gruber Agreement apparently went in this direction, consigning Alto Adige/South Tyrol to Rome, while Italy committed to protecting the German-speaking minorities, who had been the object of attempts at assimilation during the Fascist period (Steininger 2003, 97–111).

However, Austria's reunification in 1955 and the establishment of its status of international neutrality gave origin to new territorial disputes around the country. Simultaneously, a violent separatist movement developed in Alto Adige/South Tyrol. By the end of the 1950s and the beginning of the 1960s, a wave of attacks against institutions, police forces and infrastructure plunged Alto Adige/South Tyrol into a state of extreme tension. The recognition of a "second" special autonomy for the region of Trentino-Alto Adige/South Tyrol in 1972, and a parallel process – that saw the main autonomist party, the Südtiroler Volkspartei, fully enter into the Italian political dynamics through government agreements in local administrations (see Pallaver 2017) – contributed to the decrease of the tensions and their violent manifestations (see Woelk et al. 2008).

To complete the overview of the evolution of the land borders, on the French front, the 1947 Treaty of Paris ultimately solved some of the territorial disputes, by assigning to France small parts of Piedmont and Liguria, thus ending Italy's territorial claims (see Costa Bona 1995). The border between Italy and Switzerland, in turn, experienced only minor modifications over the decades since the Italian unification (Bazzocco 2011).

Once the political borders were re-established after the end of the war, another process of great significance was initiated, with the dismantling of trade and economic barriers between some European countries. This process – which began with the Messina Conference of 1955 and was consolidated with the Treaty of Rome of 1957 and the creation of the European Economic Community – led to the elimination of trade barriers between Italy and most of the Western European states, and progressively also entailed a continental political integration. After some complicated years, the process gained new momentum with the Single European Act of 1986 and culminated in the Maastricht Treaty of 1992, which not only abolished limitations on the movement of capital and services, but also those on the movement of persons. This treaty also eliminated regular controls on goods and adopted a common customs system for the entire European Union (Olivi and Santaniello 2015, 199–235). The internal borders of the EU were further revolutionized when the Schengen Agreement and the Schengen Convention came into force, as they established that "[i]nternal borders may be crossed at any point without any checks on persons being carried out"[4] (Article 2 of the Schengen Convention), thus constituting the so-called Schengen Area (see Map 7.2).

Nevertheless, this system would not be able to cancel all the borders, which continued to exist. First, this was the case in terms of the applicable legislative framework – as for some aspects of the fight against

Map 7.2 The Schengen Area

Map by the author with mapchart.net

Projecting Borders across the Atlantic   177

organized crime or for the asylum system – both of which are particularly relevant to this chapter (Fletcher et al. 2017; Mitsilegas 2016). Second, exceptional situations have also contributed to border persistence, with the possibility to re-establish border controls for political reasons – as in the case of France or Austria, to stop migratory movements from Italy – or for emergency reasons, as recently happened with the COVID-19 pandemic (see, among others, Liga 2020; Montaldo 2020; Schacht 2019). The result is the maintenance of borders; yet, the way in which they are perceived is radically modified, and so are the characteristics of cross-border flows.

Finally, in parallel to the creation of a Schengen Area and an area of free movement, which coincide only in part (see Council of the EU 2018), the mirroring creation of a space that is non-Schengen and non-free movement took place. These are the foundations of Fortress Europe and the construction of the more marked and insurmountable external border of the EU, which will be reviewed in more detail in the rest of the chapter. For the time being, it is worth noting how this determines, with regard to the Italian case, the structurally different condition of the maritime border, in comparison to the other borders, as it coincides with part of the external border of the EU.[5]

Putting all this into a more general framework, and closer to the perspective of this book, the Italian maritime border becomes important as a transit point for the global movement of people and goods, although only through natural gateways located outside Italian borders, such as Suez and Gibraltar.

Thus, the Mediterranean Sea becomes a crossroads for the flows of people and products, and connects with the distant Latin America, as well as with the closer areas of Africa and the Middle East by means of the flows directed (also, but not exclusively) toward the Italian peninsula, this being the starting point for the dispersion along the vast interior of Europe.

General Aspects of the Italian Border Question in the Literature

Taking as the period of interest the one that begins with the conclusion of the Second World War – when, as was mentioned in the previous section, the current territorial configuration of Italy and its borders was completed – some specific aspects have drawn scholarly attention and will be briefly explored below. These are, generally speaking, exceptions within a literature that does not seem to be excessively rich either in quantitative or qualitative terms (i.e., the breadth of perspectives on the subject).

The border with Yugoslavia/Slovenia has probably been the object of the most abundant production in terms of a literature, which is mainly

178 *Federico Alagna*

linked to the events concerning the definition of the territorial boundaries, particularly at the end of the Second World War (for an overview of the issues concerning this border, see Cattaruzza 2017). More specifically, a large part of the literature has been dedicated to analyzing the issue of the Italian displaced people who left Istria and Dalmatia – as well as the historical and political controversy over the responsibility for war crimes in the region during and after the Second World War (1939–1945) and the issue of *foibe*[6] (Ballinger 2003; Sluga 2001).[7] In a way, it is not surprising that this border is the most frequently considered from a historical perspective, due to its relatively more recent and, at the same time, more complicated evolution. Studies on cross-border flows of goods and people, connected to the 1990s wars, to criminal trafficking and forced migration are particularly worth mentioning (Irrera 2006; Limes 2000; Strazzarri 2008).

As for the rest of the land borders, the literature concerning the evolution of the borders with France, Switzerland, and Austria is somehow marginal and limited in relation to the objectives of this book. There are however interesting exceptions – also beyond the sources that were already mentioned in the previous section – such as Woelk's (2013) institutional approach to the Austrian border, and his focus on the issue of the autonomy of Alto Adige/South Tyrol. The case of the Austrian border has also been discussed with particular interest with regard to the relationship between the existence of physical boundaries and the process of cultural elaboration of the borders (Mikes 2010; Steininger 2003; Woelk et al. 2008). On the border with Switzerland, some of the main topics which have been considered include cross-border labor and financial flows, as well as the overall perspective of the Swiss-Italian border region (Baruffini 2011; Chopard and Garofoli 2014; Kuder 2004, 2012; Mazzoleni and Mueller 2017). In the French case, Vedovato (1996) offers an interesting – albeit dated – overview, while Casella Colombeau (2017, 2020), Giliberti (2017), and Martini and Palidda (2018) tackle the issue of migration and its criminalization, a topic on which interest has grown enormously in recent years (Liga 2020).

More generally, migration and international security have occupied a central place in the literature on the process of functional and cultural redefinition of the internal borders of the EU and the Schengen Area, as well as on the strengthening of the common external border. Here it seems important to highlight those studies concerning the evolution of the meaning and function of the borders within the Schengen Area (O'Dowd 2002; Bueno Lacy and Van Houtum 2015).

Furthermore, as we saw in the previous section, the mirroring aspect of this process unfolds in the construction of a common external border. Among the many works, we can mention Armstrong (2020), Engelbert et al. (2019), Jünemann et al. (2017), Ruiz Benedicto and Brunet (2018) and, more specifically on border externalization policies, Gebrewold

(2007) and Zaiotti (2016). Many newspaper articles, reports and grey literature – produced by institutions such as the European Commission or the European Parliamentary Research Centre (and with different degrees of not only critical capacity, but also influence on the policy process) – complete a very rich and interesting picture. Still within the framework of the EU securitization literature, Ceccorulli (2019) and Evrard et al. (2020) consider the crisis of the Schengen Area, while the literature dealing, more generally, with the course of European integration and the progressive redefinition of borders and their functions is potentially infinite. In the Italian language literature (and perspective), it is worth mentioning Olivi and Santaniello (2015), Bruno (2012), Fauri (2006) – the latter with an economic approach. In the English language literature, among the many existing works, we can refer to Wiener et al. (2018) for a theoretical framework of the integration, Dinan (2014) for a historical perspective and De Vries (2018) with a view to the future and the theme of Euroscepticism.

Illegal Activities in the Italian Border System and the Connections with Latin America

Countless types of illegal activities take place at the Italian borders, in several directions. In numerous cases, these are either directly or indirectly connected with Latin America, especially when it comes to cocaine trafficking. This is shown, among others, by the analyses of the Direzione Centrale per i Servizi Antidroga (DCSA)[8] (DCSA 2019, 16–19), or by the six-monthly report of the Direzione Investigativa Antimafia (DIA),[9] which offers an up-to-date picture of the situation in its 688 pages (in Italian), including an analysis of the most relevant trends (Ministero dell'Interno 2019). This section will emphasize just a few specific aspects within this very extensive general framework, before devoting more attention to the issue of migrant smuggling in the Mediterranean.

Literature on organized crime in Italy abounds, and several works are worth mentioning before delving into current trends and analyses. Beyond those publications that address the issue from a historical perspective (such as Ciconte 2008) and those examples of institutional reports that offer a detailed and up-to-date view of the situation (such as DCSA 2019; Frontex 2020; Ministero dell'Interno 2019), works such as that of Di Gennaro and La Spina (2018) are central to a general understanding of the macro-issue of organized crime in a criminological and criminal law framework. Becucci (2006) and Fiandaca and Visconti (2010) have also proposed several interesting analyses on cross-border crime in Italy and the presence of foreign criminal groups.

Considering in more detail the main cross-border illegal activities and the way in which they connect Italy to the wider global border system,

180 *Federico Alagna*

it is easy to identify the maritime border (central Mediterranean Sea and Adriatic Sea) as the center of multiple illegal economic circuits, by virtue of the specific characteristics this area presents. The volume and variety of criminal phenomena in the Mediterranean Sea are widespread. It could not be otherwise if, as the European Commission has pointed out, 81% of illegal trade worldwide takes place by sea (Legambiente 2013, 2). Nonetheless – it is worth stressing – this does not mean that land borders are not relevant in this perspective. Much to the contrary, they are extremely important, given the fact that all borders are crossed by multiple types of illicit activities, including drug trafficking, arms trafficking, and money laundering (see Ministero dell'Interno 2019, 479–490).

In relation to drug trafficking, for example, land borders are points of entry of all the main types of drugs: cocaine and heroin (French and Austrian borders), cannabis (hashish through the French border and marijuana through the Swiss one), and synthetic drugs. However, in all cases, although to a different extent, despite being important entry (and exit) points, land borders appear to be marginal in comparison to the maritime border – with the aforementioned important connections with Latin America in cocaine trafficking. In this context, synthetic drugs are an exception, as they tend to enter mainly through the air border (DCSA 2019, 26–67).

Delving deeper into the different land borders and from a more general viewpoint, in the case of the Swiss border, financial crimes are particularly relevant, with black money flowing in both directions: after extraction abroad, re-introduction often occurs, with the aim to put the hidden money into circulation. In 2012 alone, the Italian financial police seized, at the border of Como, more than €50 million (VareseNews 2012). Both ordinary citizens and Italian organized crime seem to be involved in these processes, beyond the border region (Federal Office of Police 2019, 16–17; Ministero dell'Interno 2019, 487). Figures revealed in past years indicate that entry and exit flows are practically equivalent and that, generally speaking, individuals avoid resorting to accomplices for the transport of money, preferring to do it themselves (Del Frate 2014). On the same border, interesting processes related to drug trafficking have recently been detected on the Netherlands-Switzerland-Italy route (Ministero dell'Interno 2019, 61).

The internal borders with France, Austria, and Slovenia also present interesting features. As mentioned, a harmonization process is taking place at the legislative level, and judicial and police cooperation is increasing within the EU – we recall, for instance, the harmonization of confiscation policies (although with some missed opportunities, see Alagna 2015), as well as the regulations on organized crime, the European arrest warrant, the institution of offices such as Europol and Eurojust (for an overview of Justice and Home Affairs policies in the EU, see Ripoll Servent and Trauner 2017). Yet, legislative borders still exist, pending full

Projecting Borders across the Atlantic 181

harmonization. This is not an insignificant problem in the face of organized crime, since, on the one hand, this situation guarantees the free movement of goods and persons (including illegal goods and members of criminal organizations), while, on the other hand, it does not give full circulation to control instruments (for a general analysis and considerations of possible policy options, see Carrera et al. 2016).

In an overall view, it is worth noting, for example, the strong presence of organized crime, especially the Calabrian 'ndrangheta, in areas bordering France. This is particularly the case in the regions of Piedmont and Liguria, which are considered strategic, since they provide "an easy access to France; the same entrance passage that, as early as in the 1970s, led many members of the 'ndrangheta to frequent part of the Côte d'Azur, where they built real logistic networks for assisting prominent figures that were on the run, taking advantage of the close relationship with the criminality of Marseille" (DNA 2014, 149;[10] see also Ministero dell'Interno 2019, 479–480). Among the various types of trafficking, we can recall, once again, the trafficking of narcotics in the France-Italy direction, with cargoes coming from the Moroccan-Spanish route (DCSA 2019, 26, 54; EMCDDA and Europol 2013, 46).

The border with Slovenia, in turn, displays several interesting characteristics in relation to various forms of trafficking, including cigarette smuggling. Two different trends can be identified: the large transnational organizations choose to use the Adriatic maritime border, with the possibility of being assisted by an adequate logistic network; on the other hand, a "strategy of Eastern European organizations oriented toward a partitioning of cigarette cargoes and the massive use of cars for transport" (DNA 2014, 455–456) seems to be asserting itself.

Yet, as already said, beyond these cases related to land borders, which are summarized in reports such as those by the DCSA (2019) and the DIA (Ministero dell'Interno 2019), addressing the Italian border question from a global perspective, and with a special regard to the connections with Latin America, the most interesting case has to do with maritime borders, to which I have already briefly referred.

Trafficking in illegal and counterfeit products is undoubtedly one of the most relevant activities. In order to understand the various forms of trafficking in illegal products, the data released by the customs agency (Agenzia delle Dogane e dei Monopoli 2019) seem interesting, especially if read in conjunction with the main investigative findings in the DIA reports (Ministero dell'Interno 2019). Furthermore, a study by the Italian non-profit organization Legambiente, based on 155 national and international police investigations on illegal trafficking by sea, in the period 2011–2012, is also particularly useful. The report shows that 71% of the investigations carried out focused on counterfeit goods and protected species, 19% on waste trafficking and 10% on agri-food fraud. The country that was most often involved in illegal routes to and from

182 *Federico Alagna*

Italy was China, whose ports have been identified as points of departure or arrival of illegal flows within the scope of 39 investigations. In second place is Greece, followed by Albania, North Africa, the Middle East, and Turkey (Legambiente 2013, 2–4). In this sense, the port of Naples plays a central role and the relations established between Chinese criminal groups and the Neapolitan Camorra have been of crucial importance (UNICRI 2011, 98–99).

In this area, criminal associations demonstrate a great organizational capacity and the complicity they enjoy: UNICRI (2011, 105), for example, has revealed that "[s]hipments usually passed through countries like Spain, Greece, Hungary or Austria to dissimulate their origin and make them appear at the eyes of the Italian custom authorities as an intra-EU shipment: corruption was often used for this purpose. Once the goods reached Italy, they were stored in several different places all over the country."[11]

Drug trafficking is equally important. Here too, incoming flows stand out. Even more than in other cases, the existence of criminal organizations in Italy, who are deeply rooted in the territory and in a position to maintain relations with institutional, political, and financial actors of great importance at the global level, plays a fundamental role (DCSA 2019, 15–16). The Calabrian 'ndrangheta is especially important in this context, if one considers its ability to deal on a par with South American drug traffickers, obtaining generous amounts of drugs through trust, cash payments, and with the capacity to organize advanced logistical transport networks, from Latin America to major European ports (see Forgione 2009).

According to EMCDDA and Europol (2013, 32), in the context of heroin trafficking, Italy represents "a key location because of its extensive coastline, air and maritime transport infrastructure, large consumer market for heroin and concentration of organized criminal groups." In fact, Italy is a crossroads for multiple trafficking activities, related to different substances (cocaine, heroin, cannabis, synthetic drugs) and managed by a number of national and international criminal organizations (see DCSA 2019; Ministero dell'Interno 2019).

In this sense, the role of the Mediterranean border is crucial, as it is subject to a "complete and absolute dominion" by the 'ndrangheta, the main organization dedicated to drug trafficking worldwide, in the port of Gioia Tauro (one of the busiest container ports in Italy), where, "through a penetrating conspiracy activity, it manages to obtain broad, continuous, and almost inexhaustible internal support." It should not be surprising, then, that the port of Gioia Tauro has historically been "the main gateway for cocaine in Italy. It is enough to note that only during the reference period (June 2012–July 2013) almost half of the cocaine seized in Italy […] was intercepted in Gioia Tauro" (DNA 2014, 419–420).

Projecting Borders across the Atlantic 183

Indeed, in the 2010s, the port of Gioia Tauro represented one of the main channels for the entry of cocaine into Europe, also confirming that "maritime shipments pose the greatest problem because large quantities can be transported at any one time, and detection is difficult" (EMCDDA and Europol 2013, 45). In the last years, however, there has been a significant reduction in seizures in this port and a relative increase in other ones, such as Genoa and Livorno, demonstrating, once more, the capacity of criminal organizations to readjust and control various entry points (DCSA 2019, 16–39).

The Italian maritime border also plays a key role in the entry of heroin and cannabis derivatives (DCSA 2019, 40–60). In this case, the Adriatic coast is the privileged one, due to the close relations between the criminal groups and associations of the Apulia region and the criminal groups of the Balkans: "the Salento area is therefore consolidated as a reference point for the traffics coming from Albania (especially heroin and marijuana), and so it represents, in this sector, an important reference point for the other mafias at a national level" (DNA 2014, 422). Data on heroin and cannabis seizures confirm the central role of the Apulia coast in this type of activity (DCSA 2019, 22, 56, 191, 212; DNA 2014, 422; Ministero dell'Interno 2019).

Arms trafficking is also particularly interesting, and Italy, once again, represents a country of transit and destination at the same time, with flows moving from the Balkans to Italy and the EU and in a two-way street between Italy and North Africa (Savona and Mancuso 2017, 56–58). On this subject, an interesting, though not too recent, publication by Finardi and Tombola (2002) can be highlighted, while the chronicles of the last years report numerous relevant cases, sometimes handled by the same organizations dealing with drug trafficking (Ministero dell'Interno 2019, 266, 355, 359). Regarding the issue of waste trafficking, some interesting and updated data and reflections can be found in the specific focus on "mafias and waste" in the DIA report (Ministero dell'Interno 2019, 580–662).

Finally, with regard to illegal activities related to migration processes, there are cases of both migrant smuggling and cross-border human trafficking[12] (Militello and Spena 2019). Smuggling will be discussed in more detail in the following pages. As far as transnational trafficking is concerned, its extreme relevance and salience in the Italian case are addressed in the works of Antonopoulos et al. (2019) and Palumbo (2016). A recent study published by the Italian Ministry of Interior points at the established patterns and emerging trends, including the type of trafficking, the nationality of victims and perpetrators, their modus operandi (Ministero dell'Interno 2021). The book authored by Ciconte and Romani (2002), albeit quite dated, is also worth mentioning.

184 *Federico Alagna*

The (Myth of the) Italian and EU Fight against Migrant Smuggling[13]

Among the different illegal activities undertaken across the Italian Mediterranean borders, migrant smuggling has been met with special interest over the past years, not only in academia, but also in the political discourse and general debate.

Although reliable and complete data related to undocumented migration and migrant smuggling across the Mediterranean (and anywhere else) are, by definition, difficult to obtain, some of the most accurate estimates indicate an exponential growth of flows in the years 2014, 2015, and 2016, and a dramatic decrease of these figures from 2017 and 2018 onward (UNHCR 2018; 2020; Villa et al. 2018). This is due to a number of factors that include the governmental disengagement from search and rescue (SAR) operations and the policing of humanitarian actors in the Mediterranean; push-back and externalization policies through agreements with transit countries, in spite of international law obligations and human rights concerns;[14] a rise in numbers on other routes, as well as on "invisible" landings (Furlanetto 2019; UNHCR 2020).[15]

Academic and grey literature, judicial proceedings, and practitioners acknowledge that all these migration flows in the Mediterranean Sea are connected, to different extents and in diverse ways, to migrant smuggling (see Aloyo and Cusumano 2018, 12–14; De Bruycker et al. 2013; Fargues and Bonfanti 2014; Pastore et al. 2006). For this reason, and in light of the structural characteristics of Italy's maritime borders, it is fair to move from this assumption.

In so doing, a very first issue to consider is how different this phenomenon may be, depending on the characteristics of the smuggler: from small-scale, family-run and loosely coupled groups to big mafia-type organizations; from "altruistic" smugglers to "evil" criminals (Alagna 2020c; Sánchez and Achilli 2019).

In the case of the Italian Mediterranean border, organized crime networks may get involved along specific segments of most migration routes, in particular within Libya, even though this is not always the case, and the extent of their involvement varies substantially (see Campana 2018, 2020; Militello and Spena 2019). In migration movements which involve the crossing of the Mediterranean Sea, the situation of those people in charge of steering the vessel or assisting the boat skipper, by using the compass or the satellite phone to call the rescuers, is particularly delicate. Evidence has shown that these people – who, once arrived in Italy, are eventually accused of being smugglers – in most cases hardly fall within any criminal organization. On the contrary, they often are migrants themselves, forced to perform such duties at the time of boarding.[16] Such differentiation, however, is often neglected in judicial and law enforcement practices (Alagna 2020b,

Projecting Borders across the Atlantic 185

82–88) and is hardly visible in law enforcement agencies analyses and reports (e.g., Europol 2020; Frontex 2020).

Criminal organizations active in this field are mostly based outside Italy and do not have any stable connection with Italian mafia-type organizations (Campana 2018; Militello and Spena 2019, 15–16). They also tend to show high degrees of resilience and responsiveness to changes in the political and institutional settings, as well as in the policy framework to tackle migrant smuggling (National Deputy Anti-Mafia Prosecutor, interview with the author, April 17, 2019).

In the framework of this chapter, besides the specific characteristics of smuggling flows across the Mediterranean border of Italy, some policy aspects appear to be particularly relevant, especially in a comparative perspective with Latin America. The overall trend witnessed throughout the last 30 years in Europe is effectively summarized in the concept, recalled throughout the chapter, of Fortress Europe (Engelbert et al. 2019), – which was laid down in the process leading to the Schengen Convention of 1990, with the overall idea that the progressive disappearance of internal border controls should be accompanied by a strengthening of the external borders. This included the introduction in national laws of the offence of facilitation of undocumented immigration and the so-called "carriers liability regime," *de facto* outsourcing border control to transport carriers (Scholten 2015). The outsourcing nature of border management in Europe – which is also evident in the case of Italy's Mediterranean border – is further confirmed by the growth in externalization practices, which delegate to third countries (Libya, but also Niger and beyond, see Akkerman 2018) the implementation of policies depicted as anti-smuggling, but which often reveal the ultimate goal of curbing migration movements, regardless of human rights and international law obligations (Council of Europe Commissioner for Human Rights 2019, 2020). As an UNODC officer put it, referring to the EU approach to the fight against migrant smuggling and its shortcomings, this is "the sliding effect that has resulted from using it as a migration management instrument, which it is not. [...] The intent, rather than fighting smuggling, is to manage migration better" (UNODC officer, Skype interview with the author, April 25, 2019). Also, the promotion of a strong humanitarian rhetoric ended up facilitating the disguise of harsh migration management policies, producing a smokescreen around the Mediterranean border (Cusumano 2019; Cuttitta 2018; Garelli and Tazzioli 2018). An active role on the part of Italy and, even more so, of the European Union as a stable actor in shaping long-term and comprehensive Mediterranean policies, based on the respect of human rights of migrants, is yet to come (see Alagna 2020a).

This system also involves a number of private actors, from transport carriers to NGOs active in SAR operations (cf. Cusumano and Pattison

186 *Federico Alagna*

2018; Scholten 2015), who are *de facto* forced, at times, to participate in border governance and in anti-smuggling activities. Outsourcing, externalizing, and shifting out (or "shifting South") policies matter; not only for what they tell us about the Italian and European approaches to smuggling, migration, and human rights, but also because, from a broader perspective, they show the patterns of a spatial and political redefinition of borders, that move far from where they lie on maps: a trend which can be interesting in a comparative approach with the migration and smuggling movements across the Americas.[17]

One last aspect that is worth mentioning in this context relates to the interconnection between different borders. The way in which changes at one border impact other borders – in terms of policy adoption or implementation, in smuggling practices, etc. – shows the intrinsic systemic nature of these cross-border movements and, more broadly, of borders themselves. This is further reaffirmed by the connection between inbound and outbound migrant smuggling movements through different Italian borders (Militello and Spena 2019, 20). More broadly, and more relevantly from a Latin American perspective, this whole process shows that migrant smuggling and undocumented migration trajectories appear to be connected at a global level, and so – as one example among many – harsher border policies at the Mediterranean border can have an impact on the growth of African migration to and through the Americas, exposing migrants to even greater risks, endangering their lives and producing more violent forms of smuggling (see Bonello 2019; Sur 2019; Yates 2019).

A Global and Latin American Approach to the Italian Borders

This chapter has tried to offer an overview of the Italian case, with some insights from a Latin American perspective and within a broader understanding of the global border system. My hope is that, throughout these pages, it has been possible to appreciate the importance of such an approach, by also understanding the characteristics of a multifunctional country, and grasping the global projection of some illegal activities, which also involve Latin America. In the last section of the chapter, I have sought to delve into the EU and Italian approach to migrant smuggling. In so doing, I have tried to highlight how what is happening in the Mediterranean can also say something when the focus is oriented toward Latin America.

Much more can and should be said about these issues, and this chapter offers but a series of initial reflections on the subject, mostly emphasizing and referring to existing studies and publications. For the time being, I believe that the fundamental conclusive remark – from which successive reflections may arise – is the peculiarity and the global relevance of the Italian case in terms of the border-crime profile, both in absolute terms and, even more importantly, when looking at it from a Latin American perspective. An overview of Latin American border dynamics cannot dispense with an analytical relationship – since it empirically exists – with external cases, in order to stimulate the understanding of processes that cannot be isolated from their structurally global context. This has been the ultimate purpose of this chapter.

Notes

* I wish to thank Federico Giamperoli, Kasia Fantoni, and Rodrigo Bueno Lacy for their extremely generous and valuable inputs. I am also particularly grateful to the book editors for their attentive support and their insightful comments and suggestions.

1. Considering the broad approach of this chapter in relation to organized crime in Italy, I will not delve into detailed differentiations among the various Italian mafia-type criminal organizations. It suffices to highlight their structural difference from ordinary criminal organizations and the coexistence of common patterns with different specifications among them (see Santino 2011; Sciarrone and Storti 2014).
2. For a general account, see Mack Smith (2000) and the more specific geographical works considered in the rest of this chapter.
3. On these developments and the more general Italian eastern border question, see Cattaruzza (2017).
4. I have sought to include all textual quotations from official documents in their official English version. When not available in English, they have been translated from Italian or Spanish.
5. Monar (2018), among others, explains the projection of the internal security of the EU on its external border.
6. The term *foibe* usually refers to the massacres perpetrated against the Italian population of Venice Julia and Dalmatia, during the Second World War and immediately after its conclusion. The name is derived from the large karst caves, known in Venice Julia as *foibe,* where the bodies of many victims were disposed of.
7. See also Oliva (2003, 2005, 2006), who has addressed the issue of Italian responsibility for war crimes during the occupation of Yugoslavia.
8. The DCSA is a specialized inter-force agency, conducting anti-drug trafficking investigations and law enforcement operations.
9. The DIA is an inter-force agency, tasked with investigative and law-enforcement duties related to the fight against organized crime. Every six months, the Minister of Interior presents a report to Parliament regarding the main activities performed by the DIA and the most relevant investigative achievements. These bi-annual reports represent an invaluable source of information about organized crime activities in Italy.
10. The DNA (*Direzione Nazionale Antimafia e Antiterrorismo*) is the National Anti-Mafia and Anti-Terrorism Prosecutor's Office, in charge of coordinating the organized crime and terrorism-related investigations conducted by the District Anti-Mafia Prosecutor's Offices (*Direzioni Distrettuali Antimafia*) throughout the national territory.
11. For more details on the connections between product counterfeiting and transnational crime, see Ministero dello Sviluppo Economico and UNICRI (2012).
12. Buckland (2009) provides a useful explanation of the differences and overlaps between the two phenomena.

13. This section is partially based on my doctoral dissertation (see Alagna 2020b). The interviews and informal conversations referred to and cited in this paragraph were conducted in the framework of my PhD research. Interviewees' names are not mentioned for the sake of anonymity, as mutually agreed at the time of the interview.
14. See Villa (2018), and, specifically on the latter aspects, Council of Europe Commissioner for Human Rights (2019, 2020).
15. This was confirmed by a National Deputy Anti-Mafia Prosecutor, in interview with the author, on April 17, 2019.
16. A report of Oxfam Italia, Borderline Sicilia Onlus, and Tavola Valdese (2016) defines them as *"presunti scafisti,"* i.e., "alleged smugglers/boat drivers" (see also Alagna 2020b, 82–84). This aspect was further discussed with and confirmed by several practitioners, in the context of various interviews (Sicily-based lawyer 1, phone interview with the author, September 26, 2018; Sicily-based judge, informal conversation with the author, October 17, 2018; Sicily-based lawyer 2, phone interview with the author, October 17, 2018 and National Deputy Anti-mafia Prosecutor, interview with the author, April 17, 2019).
17. For an overview, see the dedicated chapters in the volume edited by Triandafyllidou and McAuliffe (2018).

References

Agenzia delle Dogane e dei Monopoli. 2019. *Libro Blu 2018: Organizzazione, statistiche, attività.* https://www.adm.gov.it

Akkerman, Mark. 2018. *Expanding the Fortress: The Policies, the Profiteers and the People Shaped by EU's Border Externalisation Programme.* Amsterdam: Transnational Institute & Stop Wapenhandel. https://www.tni.org/

Alagna, Federico. 2015. "Non-conviction Based Confiscation: Why the EU Directive Is a Missed Opportunity." *European Journal on Criminal Policy and Research*, 21, 447–461. https://doi.org/10.1007/s10610-014-9252-8

——— 2020a. "From Sophia to Irini: EU Mediterranean Policies and the Urgency of 'Doing Something'." *IAI Commentaries*, no. 20/32, Istituto Affari Internazionali, May 2020. https://www.iai.it/sites/default/files/iaicom2032.pdf

——— 2020b. *Shifting Governance: Making Policies against Migrant Smuggling across the EU, Italy and Sicily.* PhD dissertation. Radboud University & University of Bologna. https://hdl.handle.net/2066/222053

——— 2020c. "Understanding the Complexity of Migrant Smuggling: The 'Smuggling Spectrum' as Comprehensive Analytical Framework." *International Journal of Migration and Border Studies*, 6 (4), 298–318. https://doi.org/10.1504/IJMBS.2020.10034099

Aloyo, Eamon and Eugenio Cusumano. 2018. "Morally evaluating human smuggling: the case of migration to Europe." *Critical Review of International Social and Political Philosophy.* https://doi.org/10.1080/13698230.2018.1525118

Antonopoulos, Georgios A., Andrea Di Nicola, Atans Rusev, Fiamma Terenghi. 2019. *Human Trafficking Finances. Evidence from Three European Countries.* Cham: Springer.

Armstrong, Ashley Binetti. 2020. "You Shall Not Pass! How the Dublin System Fueled Fortress Europe." *Chicago Journal of International Law*, 20 (2), Article 13. https://chicagounbound.uchicago.edu

Projecting Borders across the Atlantic 189

Ballinger, Pamela. 2003. *History in Exile: Memory and Identity at the Borders of the Balkans*. Princeton and Oxford: Princeton University Press. https://doi.org/10.2307/j.ctv301g0z

Baruffini, Moreno. 2011. "Cross-border Commuting in the Swiss-Italian Region; Labour Market Effects of Progressive Integration." In *Measuring Geographical Mobility in Regional Labour Market Monitoring: State of the Art and Perspectives*, edited by Christa Larsen, Ruth Hasberg, Alfons Schmid, Marc Bittner, Franz Clément. Munich and Mering: Rainer Hampp Verlag.

Bazzocco, Adriano. 2011. *La frontiera comune. La frontiera tra Italia e Svizzera*. Embassy of Switzerland in Italy and Directorate-General for the International Affairs of the Italian Ministry of Education, University and Research. http://www.italiasvizzera150.it/

Becucci, Stefano. 2006. *Criminalità multietnica; i mercati illegali in Italia*. Roma-Bari: Laterza.

Bonello, Deborah. 2019. "From Africa to Mexico. How Far Would You Go for the American Dream?" *The Telegraph*. https://www.telegraph.co.uk/news/african-migrants-in-america/

Bruno, Fernanda. 2012. *Stati membri e Unione Europea. Il difficile cammino dell'integrazione*. Turin: Giappichelli.

Buckland, Benjamin S. 2009. "Human trafficking & smuggling: Crossover & overlap." In *Strategies against Human Trafficking: The Role of the Security Sector*, edited by Cornelius Friesendorf, 137–165. Geneva & Vienna: National Defence Academy and Austrian Ministry of Defence and Sports.

Bueno Lacy, Rodrigo and Henk Van Houtum. 2015. "Lies, Damned Lies & Maps: The EU's Cartopolitical Invention of Europe." *Journal of Contemporary European Studies*, 23 (4), 477–499. https://doi.org/10.1080/14782804.2015.1056727

Campana, Paolo. 2018. "Out of Africa: The Organization of Migrant Smuggling across the Mediterranean." *European Journal of Criminology*, 15 (4), 481–502. https://doi.org/10.1177/1477370817749179.

——— 2020. "Human Smuggling: Structure and Mechanisms." *Crime and Justice*. https://doi.org/10.1086/708663

Carrera, Sergio, Elspeth Guild, Lina Vosyliūtė, Amandine Scherrer and Valsamis Mitsilegas. 2016. "The Cost of Non-Europe in the Area of Organised Crime". *CEPS Paper in Liberty and Security in Europe*, no. 90, April 2016.

Casella Colombeau, Sara. 2017. "Policing the Internal Schengen Borders – Managing the Double Bind between Free Movement and Migration Control." *Policing and Society*, 27 (5), 480–493. https://doi.org/10.1080/10439463.2015.1072531

——— 2020. "Crisis of Schengen? The Effect of Two 'Migrant Crises' (2011 and 2015) on the Free Movement of People at an Internal Schengen Border" *Journal of Ethnic and Migration Studies*, 46 (11), 2258–2274. https://doi.org/10.1080/1369183X.2019.1596787

Cattaruzza, Marina. 2017. *Italy and Its Eastern Border, 1866–2016*. New York and London: Routledge.

Ceccorulli, Michela. 2019. "Back to Schengen: The Collective Securitisation of the EU Free-Border Area." *West European Politics*, 42 (2), 302–322. https://doi.org/10.1080/01402382.2018.1510196

Chopard, René and Gioacchino Garofoli. 2014. *La Banca ticinese e l'impresa del nord Italia. Opportunità d'integrazione transfrontaliera*. Milan: Franco Angeli.

190 *Federico Alagna*

Ciconte, Enzo. 2008. *Storia criminale: La resistibile ascesa di mafia, 'ndrangheta e camorra dall'Ottocento ai giorni nostri*. Soveria Mannelli: Rubbettino.

Ciconte, Enzo and Pierpaolo Romani. 2002. *Le nuove schiavitù, il traffico di esseri umani nell'Italia del XXI Secolo*. Milan: Editori Riuniti.

Costa Bona, Enrica. 1995. *Dalla guerra alla pace: Italia-Francia 1940–1947*.Milan: Franco Angeli.

Council of Europe Commissioner for Human Rights. 2019. *Lives Saved. Rights Protected. Bridging the Protection Gap for Refugees and Migrants in the Mediterranean*, June 2019. https://rm.coe.int/lives-saved-rights-protected-bridging-theprotection-gap-for-refugees-/168094eb87.

―――― 2020. "Letter to the Minister of Foreign Affairs and International Cooperation of Italy," 13 February 2020. https://rm.coe.int/letter-to-mr-luigi-di-maio-minister-of-foreign-affairs-and-internation/16809c8262

Council of the EU. 2018. *Schengen. Your Gateway to Free Movement in Europe*. Luxembourg: Publications Office of the European Union. https://doi.org/10.2860/290668

Cusumano, Eugenio. 2019. "Straightjacketing Migrant Rescuers? The Code of Conduct on Maritime NGOs." *Mediterranean Politics*, 24 (1), 106–114. https://doi.org/10.1080/13629395.2017.1381400

Cusumano, Eugenio and James Pattison. 2018. "The Non-governmental Provision of Search and Rescue in the Mediterranean and the Abdication of State Responsibility." *Cambridge Review of International Affairs*, 31 (1), 53–75. https://doi.org/10.1080/09557571.2018.1477118

Cuttitta, Paolo. 2018. "Delocalization, Humanitarianism, and Human Rights: The Mediterranean Border between Exclusion and Inclusion." *Antipode*, 50, 783–803. https://doi.org/10.1111/anti.12337

DCSA–Direzione Centrale per i Servizi Antidroga. 2019. *DCSA 2019*. https://antidroga.interno.gov.it/

De Bruycker, Philippe, Anna Di Bartolomeo and Philippe Fargues. 2013. *Migrants Smuggled by Sea to the EU: Facts, Laws and Policy Options*. MPC RR2013/06, Robert Schuman Centre for Advanced Studies, San Domenico di Fiesole (FI): European University Institute. http://cadmus.eui.eu

De Vries, Catherine E. 2018. *Euroscepticism and the Future of European Integration*. Oxford: Oxford University Press.

Del Frate, Claudio. 2014. "Il traffico di valuta cambia verso. I soldi dalla Svizzera all'Italia." *Corriere della Sera*, 28 March 2014. http://www.corriere.it

Di Gennaro, Giacomo and Antonio La Spina (Eds). 2018. *Mafia-type Organisations and Extortion in Italy. The Camorra in Campania*. New York & London: Routledge.

Dinan, Desmond. 2014. *Origins and Evolution of the European Union*. Oxford: Oxford University Press.

DNA–Direzione Nazionale Antimafia. 2014. *Relazione annuale sulle attività svolte dal Procuratore nazionale antimafia e dalla Direzione nazionale antimafia nonché sulle dinamiche e strategie della criminalità organizzata di tipo mafioso nel periodo 1° luglio 2012 – 30 giugno 2013*. January 2014. http://www.stampoantimafioso.it

EMCDDA – European Monitoring Centre for Drugs and Drug Addiction and Europol. 2013. *EU Drug Markets Report: A strategic analysis*. Luxembourg: Publications Office of the European Union. http://europol.europa.eu

Engelbert, Jiska, Isabel Awad and Jacco van Sterkenburg. "Everyday Practices and the (Un)Making of 'Fortress Europe': Introduction to the Special Issue." *European Journal of Cultural Studies*, 22 (2), (April 2019): 133–143. https://doi.org/10.1177/1367549418823055.

Europol. 2020. *European Migrant Smuggling Centre. 4th Annual Report – 2019*. https://europol.europa.eu

Evrard, Estelle, Birte Nienaber and Adolfo Sommaribas. 2020. "The Temporary Reintroduction of Border Controls Inside the Schengen Area: Towards a Spatial Perspective." *Journal of Borderlands Studies*, 35 (3), 369–383. https://doi.org/10.1080/08865655.2017.1415164

Fargues, Philippe and Sara Bonfanti. 2014. *When the Best Option Is a Leaky Boat: Why Migrants Risk Their Lives Crossing the Mediterranean and What Europe Is Doing about It*. MPC 2014/05, Robert Schuman Centre for Advanced Studies, San Domenico di Fiesole (FI): European University Institute. http://cadmus.eui.eu

Fauri, Francesca. 2006. *L'integrazione economica europea*. Bologna: Il Mulino.

Federal Office of Police. 2019. *Annual Report Fedpol 2019*. https://www.fedpol.admin.ch/

Fiandaca, Giovanni and Costantino Visconti (Eds). 2010. *Scenari di mafia*. Turin: Giappichelli.

Finardi, Sergio and Carlo Tombola. 2002. *Le strade delle armi*. Milan: Jaca Book.

Fletcher, Maria, Ester Herlin-Karnell and Claudio Matera (Eds). 2017. *The European Union as an Area of Freedom, Security and Justice*. New York and London: Routledge.

Forgione, Francesco. 2009. *Mafia Export*. Milan: Baldini e Castoldi.

Frontex. 2020. *Risk Analysis for 2020*. Luxembourg: Publications Office of the European Union.

Furlanetto, Valentina. 2019. "Sbarchi fantasma, così arriva in Italia l'80% dei migranti con barchini e contatti Facebook." *Il Sole 24 ore*, 29 September 2019. https://www.ilsole24ore.com/

Garelli, Glenda and Martina Tazzioli. 2018. "The Humanitarian War against Migrant Smugglers at Sea." *Antipode*, 50 (3), 685–703. https://doi.org/10.1111/anti.12375

Gebrewold, Belachew. 2007. *Africa and Fortress Europe, Threats and Opportunities*. Aldershot: Ashgate Publishing Limited.

Giliberti, Luca. 2017. "La criminalizzazione della solidarietà ai migranti in Val Roja: note dal campo." *Mondi migranti*, 3, 161–181. https://doi.org/10.3280/MM2017-003008

Irrera, Daniela. 2006. *Gli Stati Criminali. Un possibile modello esplicativo*. Milan: Giuffrè Editore.

Jünemann, Annette, Nikolas Scherer and Nicolas Fromm (Eds). 2017. *Fortress Europe?*. Wiesbaden: Springer.

Kuder, Martin. 2004. "Portare i soldi in Svizzera: contrabbando di capitali ed evasione fiscale nell'Italia del boom." *Contemporanea, Rivista di storia dell'800 e del '900*, 4, 609–622. https://doi.org/10.1409/18620

——— 2012. *Italia e Svizzera dal 1945 al 1970. Commercio, emigrazione, finanza e trasporti*. Milano: Franco Angeli.

Legambiente. 2013. *I mercati illegali. Traffici illeciti di rifiuti, merci contraffatte, prodottiagroalimentari e specie animali. Numeri, storie e scenari della "globalizzazione in nero"*. Rome, 12 February 2013. http://www.legambiente.it/

192 Federico Alagna

Liga, Aldo. 2020. "Les politiques migratoires en France, en Italie et en Espagne. Un système complexe d'interdépandances internes et régionales." *Études de l'Ifri*, June 2020. https://www.ifri.org/

Limes. 2000. *I Quaderni speciali di Limes: Gli stati mafia.* QS/2000, 11 March 2000. https://www.limesonline.com/

Mack Smith, Denis. 2000. *Storia d'Italia.* Roma-Bari: Laterza.

Martini, Francesca and Salvatore Palidda. 2018. "Continuità e mutamenti delle migrazioni nel confine tra l'Italia e la Francia." *Altreitalie. Rivista internazionale di studi sulle migrazioni italiane nel mondo*, 56, 117–129. https://www.altreitalie.it/

Mazzoleni, Oscar and Sean Mueller. 2017. "Cross-Border Integration through Contestation? Political Parties and Media in the Swiss–Italian Borderland." *Journal of Borderlands Studies*, 32 (2), 173–192. https://doi.org/10.1080/088656 55.2016.1195698

Mikes, Tony. 2010. "Inclusive Minority Governance in Finland, South Tirol and Slovakia." *ALPPI Annual of Language & Politics and Politics of Identity*, 4, 59–73.

Militello, Vincenzo and Alessandro Spena. 2019. *Between Criminalization and Protection.* Leiden: Brill. https://doi.org/10.1163/9789004401723

Ministero dello Sviluppo Economico and UNICRI. 2012. *La contraffazione come attività gestita dalla criminalità organizzata transnazionale. Il caso italiano.* Rome: Ministero dello Sviluppo Economico. http://www.unicri.it/

Ministero dell'Interno. 2019. *Relazione del Ministro dell'Interno al Parlamento. Attività svolta e risultati conseguiti dalla Direzione Investigativa Antimafia. Gennaio-Giugno 2019.* http://direzioneinvestigativaantimafia.interno.gov.it/

——— 2021. *La tratta degli esseri umani in Italia. Focus.* Rome, March. http://www.interno.gov.it/

Mitsilegas, Valsamis. 2016. *EU Criminal Law after Lisbon: Rights, Trust and the Transformation of Justice in Europe.* Oxford & Portland, OR: Hart Publishing.

Monar, Jörg. 2018. "The External Shield of Internal Security." In *The Security Dimensions of EU Enlargement*, edited by David Brown and Alistair J.K. Shepherd. Manchester: Manchester University Press. https://doi.org/10.7765/9781526130860.00011

Montaldo, Stefano. 2020. "The COVID-19 Emergency and the Reintroduction of Internal Border Controls in the Schengen Area: Never Let a Serious Crisis Go to Waste." *European Papers.* European Forum, 25 April 2020: 1–9. https://doi.org/10.15166/2499-8249/353

O'Dowd, Liam. 2002. "The Changing Significance of European Borders." *Regional & Federal Studies*, 12 (4), 13–36. https://doi.org/10.1080/714004774

Oliva, Gianni. 2003. *Foibe. Le stragi negate degli italiani della Venezia Giulia e dell'Istria.* Milan: Mondadori.

——— 2005. *Profughi. Dalle foibe all'esodo: la tragedia degli italiani d'Istria, Fiume e Dalmazia.* Milan: Mondadori.

——— 2006. *Si ammazza troppo poco": i crimini di guerra italiani 1940-43.* Milan: Mondadori.

Olivi, Bino and Roberto Santaniello. 2015. *Storia dell'integrazione europea.* Bologna: Il Mulino.

Oxfam Italia, Borderline Sicilia Onlus and Tavola Valdese. 2016. *Presunti scafisti: le vittime invisibili del traffico di esseri umani.* Progetto #OPENEUROPE.

Pallaver, Günther. 2017. "The Südtiroler Volkspartei. Success through Conflict, Failure through Consensus." In *Regionalist Parties in Western Europe. Dimensions of Success*, edited by Oscar Mazzoleni and Sean Mueller, 107–134. London and New York: Routledge.

Palumbo, Letizia. 2016. *Trafficking and Labour Exploitation in Domestic Work and the Agricultural Sector in Italy*. Robert Schuman Centre for Advanced Studies, Global Governance Programme, Research Project Report, June 2016. San Domenico di Fiesole (FI): European University Institute. http://cadmus.eui.eu

Pastore, Ferruccio, Paola Monzini and Giuseppe Sciortino. 2006. "Schengen's Soft Underbelly? Irregular Migration and Human Smuggling across Land and Sea Borders to Italy." *International Migration*, 44 (4), 95–119. https://doi.org/10.1111/j.1468-2435.2006.00381.x

Ripoll Servent, Ariadna and Florian Trauner (Eds). 2017. *The Routledge Handbook of Justice and Home Affairs Research*. Abingdon: Routledge.

Ruiz Benedicto, Ainhoa and Pere Brunet. 2018. *Building Walls. Fear and Securitization in the European Union*. Barcelona: Centre Delàs d'Estudis per la Pau, Transnational Institute & Stop Wapenhandel. https://www.tni.org/

Sánchez, Gabriella and Luigi Achilli (Eds). 2019. *Critical insights on irregular migration facilitation: Global perspectives*. Florence: European University Institute. http://doi.org/10.2870/111653

Santino, Umberto. 2011. "Studying Mafias in Sicily". *Sociologica*, 2. https://doi.org/10.2383/35872

Savona, Ernesto U. and Marina Mancuso (Eds). 2017. *Fighting Illicit Firearms Trafficking Routes and Actors at European Level*. Final Report of Project FIRE. Milan: Transcrime – Università Cattolica del Sacro Cuore.

Schacht, Kira. 2019. "Border checks in EU countries Challenge Schengen Agreement." *Deutsche Welle*, 12 November 2019. https://www.dw.com/en/

Scholten, Sophie. 2015. *The Privatisation of Immigration Control through Carrier Sanctions*. Leiden: Brill – Nijhoff. https://doi.org/10.1163/978900429 0747

Sciarrone, Rocco and Luca Storti. 2014. "The Territorial Expansion of Mafia-type Organized Crime. The Case of the Italian Mafia in Germany." *Crime, Law and Social Change*, 61, 37–60. https://doi.org/10.1007/s10611-013-9473-7

Sluga, Glenda. 2001. *The Problem of Trieste and the Italo-Yugoslav Border: Difference, Identity and Sovereignty in Twentieth-Century Europe*. Albany, NY: State of New York University Press.

Steininger, Rolf. 2003. *South Tyrol: A Minority Conflict of the Twentieth Century*. New Brunswick, NJ: Transaction Publishers.

Strazzarri, Francesco. 2008. *Notte Balcanica, guerre, crimini e stati falliti alle porte dell'Europa*. Bologna: Il Mulino.

Sur, Priyali. 2019. "Why Record Numbers of African Migrants Are Showing Up at the U.S.-Mexican Border." *Foreign Policy*, 26 June 2019. https://foreignpolicy.com/

Triandafyllidou, Anna and Marie McAuliffe (Eds). 2018. *Migrant Smuggling Data and Research: A global review of the emerging evidence base, Volume 2*. Geneva: International Organization for Migration.

UNHCR. 2018. "Refugees and Migrants Arrivals to Europe in 2017." 16 February 2018. http://www.unhcr.org

194 *Federico Alagna*

—— 2020. "Refugee and Migrant Arrivals to Europe in 2019 (Mediterranean)." 18 March 2020. http://www.unhcr.org

UNICRI. 2011. *Counterfeiting: A Global Spread, a Global Threat*. Turin: UNICRI. http://www.unicri.it

VareseNews. 2012. "Un fiume di denaro clandestino dalla Svizzera all'Italia." *VareseNews*, 19 December 2012. http://www.varesenews.it

Vedovato, Giuseppe. 1996. "Cooperazione trasfrontaliera tra Italia e Francia." *Rivista di Studi Politici Internazionali*, 63 3 (251), 371–389. https://www.jstor.org/stable/42737680

Villa, Matteo. 2018. "Sea Arrivals to Italy: The Cost of Deterrence Policies." *Ispi – Italian Institute for International Political Studies*, 5 October 2018. https://www.ispionline.it/en/

Villa, Matteo, Elena Corradi and Antonio Villafranca. 2018. "Fact Checking: migrazioni 2018." *Ispi – Italian Institute for International Political Studies*, 7 May 2018. https://www.ispionline.it/en/

Wiener, Antje, Tanja A. Börzel and Thomas Risse (Eds). 2018. *European Integration Theory* (3rd ed). Oxford: Oxford University Press.

Woelk, Jens. 2013. "South Tyrol Is (Not) Italy: A Special Case in a (De)federalizing System." *L'Europe en Formation,* 3 (369), 126–137. https://doi.org/10.3917/eufor.369.0126

Woelk, Jens, Francesco Palermo and Joseph Marko. 2008. *Tolerance through Law: Self Governance and Group Rights in South Tyrol*. Leiden & Boston: Martinus Nijhoff Publishers.

Yates, Caitlyn. 2019. "As More Migrants from Africa and Asia Arrive in Latin America, Governments Seek Orderly and Controlled Pathways." *Migration Information Source*, Migration Policy Institute, 22 October 2019. https://www.migrationpolicy.org/

Zaiotti, Ruben (Ed.). 2016. *Externalizing Migration Management*. London: Routledge, https://doi.org/10.4324/9781315650852

Interviews

1. Lawyer, Sicily, September 26, 2018 (phone)
2. Judge, Sicily, October 17, 2018 (informal conversation)
3. Lawyer, Sicily, October 17, 2018 (phone)
4. National Deputy Anti-mafia Prosecutor, April 17, 2019
5. UNODC officer, April 25, 2019 (Skype)

8 Brazil and Its Borders

History and Limits of a Sovereign State

Letícia Núñez Almeida, Agnes Félix, Rafael Masson, Nathan Bueno, and Jennifer Silva[†]

Introduction

Regardless of the existence of walls, borders always exist on maps. Borders promote socio-cultural processes of exchange or coexistence across international demarcation lines. In Brazil, this phenomenon can be observed in urban centers and rural areas, where negotiations and disputes of interests occur in the dichotomy *close to* and *over* the limit; a limit that brings closer and, at the same time, draws apart, thus creating sociabilities that are typical of these continuity and discontinuity relations.

According to Golin (2002), the Brazilian border strip is an abstraction that stems from conceptions of national defense and territory; that is to say, as a strategic area of the state. However, the border zone is real and is constituted by complex relations and dynamics, which are often invisible and disqualified as peripheral by the nation-state.

Unlike the idea of a border zone, which is difficult to demarcate, "flexible according to the socio-territorial arrangements of opposing force-fields" (Cataia 2007, 6), demarcation lines are established by a political decision and can be drawn, measured, and memorized. Although these zones represent a certain reality, they are essentially indeterminate, and their existence does not depend exclusively on direct political decisions. Cataia further explains that the zone gives rise to the border line, while the border as a line is the product of an always transitory movement, precisely because of its historical nature. The argument suggests that borders are not only the result of space, but also of time. Thus, their extension and duration constitute a concept of limit. According to the author:

> It is the time that gives meaning to form; that is to say, the process of border formation is more important than the actual shape of borders. As historical phenomena, borders are the result of choices; hence we state the inexistence of natural borders. Borders, even those supported by natural frameworks, are the result of social choices and

DOI: 10.4324/9781003204299-14

196 *Letícia Núñez Almeida et al.*

not of natural impositions. In fact, at the dawn of history, natural elements conditioned men and their activities, imposing physical barriers. A mountain, a desert, or a forest could mean (zonal) limits to circulation; nevertheless, technical developments made it possible to overcome the barriers and, as the latter began to fall one by one, other barriers, which were no longer natural, but rather political, were erected.

(Cataia 2007, 7)

Each geopolitical and social context creates its own representation of borders, both in theory and in matters of the state. This distinction is addressed by Dorfman, who refers to the different constructions of geographical thought: "[...] Border theory, even when produced in a positivistic environment of natural and universal science expectations, identifies the political, unnatural character of the border, as well as its varied material forms" (2013, 4).

In this sense, the notion of border is polysemic, as Albuquerque (2010) explains, and can represent both the political and the legal boundary between certain territories, as well as an imprecise region of cultural hybridism, a place of flows and mixtures. For this author, borders are symbolic identity markers of different ethnic, linguistic, and religious groups. They indicate, from fronts of economic expansion on certain empty spaces of the national territory, to metaphorical boundaries that delimit different areas of knowledge. Regardless of the landscape in which they are operationalized, borders always refer to the possible relationship between limits and approaches; they question the extent to which there is distance and proximity between different poles. The border is that measuring space where the continuities and discontinuities of social and individual dynamics in a territory can be observed. Whether symbolic or not, such territory is always delimited, even in an abstract way, and is theoretically constructed in a multidisciplinary way.

Geographical and Socio-Political Borders

Brazil has approximately 17,000 kilometers of borders. Eleven of its states and 588 of its municipalities have borders that cover a total area of about 8.5 million square kilometers (see Table 8.1). Brazil borders ten countries in South America: Argentina, Uruguay, Paraguay, Peru, Bolivia, Colombia, Venezuela, Suriname, Guyana, and French Guiana; that is, every South American country, except Chile and Ecuador. Since the nineteenth century, Brazil has governed its border strip by means of special regulations,[1] according to which, such border strip stretches 150 kilometers from the demarcation line along the land border. Approximately ten million people inhabit this border territory.

Machado (1998) maintains that the municipalities on the border strip can be divided into three arcs: Northern, Central, and Southern. The distribution of the 588 municipalities along the border strip and, consequently, of their population, is quite uneven, with a strong concentration (418 municipalities) in the Southern Arc (see Map 8.1). Rio Grande do Sul is located within this arc, with 197 municipalities, followed by Paraná and Santa Catarina, with 139 and 82 municipalities respectively, totaling 71.1% of the municipalities on the border strip. The Northern Arc, which comprises the sates of Amapá, Amazonas, Acre, Pará, and Roraima, has only 71 municipalities on the border strip. They represent 12.1% of all municipalities on that strip (Alvarez and Salla 2010). Only

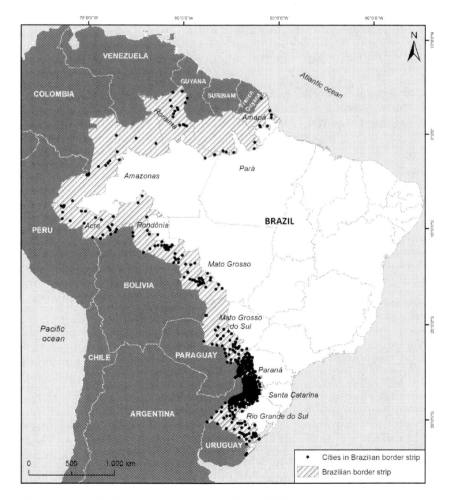

Map 8.1 Brazil's Border Strip Municipalities (2000)

Map by the authors based on data by Retis, 2002

198   *Letícia Núñez Almeida et al.*

Table 8.1 Brazil: States and neighboring countries

State	Neighboring countries
Rio Grande do Sul, RS	Uruguay, Argentina
Santa Catarina, SC	Argentina
Parana, PR	Argentina, Paraguay
Mato Grosso do Sul, MS	Paraguay, Bolivia
Mato Grosso, MT	Bolivia
Rondonia, RO	Bolivia
Acre, AC	Bolivia, Peru
Amazonas, AM	Peru, Colombia, Venezuela
Roraima, RR	Venezuela, Guyana
Pará, PA	Suriname
Amapá, AP	French Guiana

Source: Almeida (2014)

three state capitals are located in this area – Boa Vista, Rio Branco, and Porto Velho – and only two municipalities have an average population between 300,000 and 400,000 inhabitants. In other words, the municipalities on the border strip can be considered small, since most of them (81%) have a population that does not exceed 20,000 inhabitants.

These dimensions suggest that the Brazilian border strip is composed of many borders, which are different from each other. While in some states all the municipalities are located on the border strip, as in the case of Roraima and Acre, others have triple river and land borders, such as Amazonas, Paraná, and Rio Grande do Sul. Some municipalities are small towns of two or three thousand inhabitants; others have a larger population of 20,000 or 30,000 inhabitants, when the number of inhabitants of the cities on either side of the border is added. Other municipalities are even larger, with about 90,000 inhabitants on the Brazilian side, such as Sant'Ana do Livramento. Some cities have no road, but only river access, such as the Amazonian municipality of Tabatinga, which forms a triple border with Leticia (Colombia) and Santa Rosa (Peru). From Manaus, the capital of the state of Amazonas, it takes seven days – upstream – to get to Tabatinga, and three days – downstream – to return. Furthermore, the binational bridge between Brazil and French Guiana and only road over the Oiapoque River, which connects (but also separates) the municipalities of Saint-Georges (France) and Oiapoque (Brazil), was completed in 2011 but has not yet been opened to the public. This delay, in addition to preventing integration between the two countries, puts at risk the migrants who cross the border by river, as well as through the Amazon Forest, in search of informal job opportunities in clandestine mines and illegal trade (Almeida 2015).

In order to better understand the characteristics and differences between Brazil's multiple borders, in what follows we will review the main historical events that shaped the 17,000 kilometers of borders Brazil currently sports.

Brazil's Borders: A Brief Historical Tour

Brazil's Borders with Argentina

Currently, the border between Brazil and Argentina stretches along 1261.3 kilometers, a total of 25 kilometers of land and 1,236 kilometers of watercourse (Almeida 2015). The border strip comprises a total of 38 cities, the main one being the municipality of Foz do Iguaçu. Located on the triple border with Argentina and Paraguay, Foz do Iguaçu is known for the Friendship Bridge, that links Paraguay and Brazil, and the Fraternity Bridge, which connects Brazil and Argentina, and is a symbol of the integration of these three States (Clemente 2013; Nogueira 2004). Along this dividing line, there are 12 official border crossings.

One of the emblematic moments in the history of the border between Brazil and Argentina was the *Questão de Palmas*, a dispute between the two countries related to Argentina's claim to the western territory of the states of Paraná and Santa Catarina. In the last decade of the nineteenth century, an attempt was made to put an end to the *Questão de Palmas* through the 1890 Treaty of Montevideo (Bueno 1995).

Although the purpose of the treaty was to end the intrigues resulting from the *Questão de Palmas*, the new republic resisted its ratification and ended up rejecting the terms of the treaty in 1891. Brazil's reluctance derived from its interest in continuing to own the geopolitically strategic region known as Misiones in the Northwest of Rio Grande do Sul (Campos 2007). In view of the difficulty to reach an agreement, Brazil and Argentina resorted to the arbitration of the United States, whose arbitral award ended up deciding the issue in Brazil's favor. The current borders between Brazil and Argentina were largely consolidated after that period by the Treaty of Limits between Brazil and Argentina, signed in October 1898.

One of the most important events for the consolidation of the borders at the beginning of the twentieth century was the demarcation process of the obelisks of the Triple Frontier. Located on the triple border with Argentina and Paraguay, these monuments are a symbol of integration between the three states (Martins 2010). Later, some modifications were introduced by the Declaratory Articles on the Demarcation of the Borders between the United States of Brazil and the Republic of Argentina, signed in October 1910. The purpose of this agreement was to demarcate the islands in the fluvial courses of the border areas between both states, which were mainly located in the Uruguay River. The 1997 Brazil-Argentina Complementary Boundary Convention helped to define the borders in relation to the Brazilian Island, located at the mouth of the Quaraí River in the triple border between Argentina, Brazil, and Uruguay (LNCC 2012). Since then, there have been no official alterations in that region.

200 *Letícia Núñez Almeida et al.*

Southern Brazil hosts the largest group of twin cities with major urban centers on the border strip. This is the border line with the Mercosur countries,[2] which encompasses 69 municipalities and an estimated population of 1,438,206 inhabitants (Silva and Rückert 2009). It is also here that urban "border" social relations are most easily observed, since border dynamics become apparent in the activities of *sacoleiros* (Rabossi 2004), *cambistas* (Almeida 2014), *chiveros and paseros* (Diez et al. 2012), and *laranjas* (Barros 2008)[3] around the geographical limit itself. In this sense, informality and illegality can be observed in the daily life of urban centers, as the economy of these region's municipalities lives off the dividing line and the exchange and financial possibilities it creates.

The Brazil-Uruguay Border

The border between Brazil and Uruguay is 1,069 kilometers long, of which 320 kilometers are on land and 749 kilometers are waterways. This border comprises 1,174 border markers (small constructions that identify the limit of a border line), a number only inferior to that of the border between Brazil and Venezuela (Almeida 2015). The border line runs through the entire south of the state of Rio Grande do Sul and the north of the Uruguayan departments of Artigas, Rivera, Cerro Largo, and Rocha.

Brazil's border with Uruguay has always been innovative in all senses: it was the first to have its own legal formation perfectly defined by an international agreement (1851); the first to be demarcated (1852/1862) and the first to be formally characterized (from 1920) (LNCC 2012).[4]

With a turbulent history, Brazil and Argentina were of great importance in the formation of Uruguay. Due to various conflicts arising from territorial disputes, the region where Uruguay is located was once part of both Brazil and Argentina, whose rivalry became manifest during the Cisplatin War, when both countries fought over the Uruguayan territory. At the end of that war, Uruguay attained its independence and formal recognition from Brazil and Argentina through the 1828 Treaty of Montevideo (Fagundes 2010).

Uruguay's borders had been set since the end of the Cisplatin War, when the fluvial delimitations that separate Uruguay from Argentina and Brazil were recognized. The Treaty of Limits between Brazil and the Oriental Republic of Uruguay, signed in October 1851, consolidated the border between the two countries by establishing the first official delimitation. It is worth remembering that said treaty legitimized part of the borders that had been defined after Uruguay's independence.

Other relevant agreements for the delimitation of the territories of Uruguay and Brazil were the Treaties of Laguna Merín, signed in October 1909, and the Convention of Arroyo San Miguel, of May 1913, which sought to modify the borders in Laguna Merín and the Yaguarón River, establishing the general principles of trade and navigation in that region, in order to promote greater cooperation between the two states.

In relation to the latest treaties aimed at characterizing the border, much was done in the third and fourth decades of the twentieth century, through the Joint Commission on the Limits of the Brazil-Uruguay Border. The commission's work resulted in the resolution of the Chuy Stream question and therewith laid the ground for the delimitation of the maritime border. In addition, the commission carried out engineering works and projects in the Chuy region and began to perform inspections of the border markers (LNCC 2012).

In this region, the absence of salient geographical features or other spatial characteristics facilitates the inhabitants' free movement between the two countries, for even over the fluvial borders there are binational bridges (Almeida 2015). Another relevant factor that contributes to understanding the harmonious relationship between Brazil and Uruguay regarding borders are the natural characteristics of the border line, for instance, its few landforms and even terrain. In fact, after the official delimitation of the border between Brazil and Uruguay was completed, there were almost no regional or localized conflicts arising from territorial disputes between these two states. This bears witness to the peaceful nature of these spaces. The current border with Uruguay is classified by the Brazilian government as a synapse,[5] a category that highlights the potential for integration between the two states.

The Brazil-Paraguay Border

The border line between Brazil and Paraguay stretches along 1,366 kilometers, of which 437 kilometers are on land and 929 kilometers are composed of rivers and lakes (Almeida 2015). Border relations between the two countries had their genesis in the Treaty of 1872 and the Complementary Treaty of 1927, which were responsible for the demarcation of the areas between the two countries. The Treaty of Limits, signed on January 9, 1872, defined the Brazil-Paraguay border, starting at the mouth of the Apa River and ending at the mouth of the Iguaçu River, thus designing the current Brazilian states of Mato Grosso do Sul and Paraná. On May 21, 1927, the Complementary Treaty marked the border between the mouth of the Apa River and the outflow of the Bahia Negra and identified the tripartite point where the borders of Brazil, Paraguay, and Bolivia meet (LNCC 2012). For that border, the Protocol of Instructions, dated May 9, 1930, which directly and specifically established the format for the process of border delimitation by the states, continues to be a regulatory instrument. As a result of this protocol, 910 markers were built between the countries by the Joint Commission of Limits and Characterization of the Brazil-Paraguay Border, created in 1930 (Almeida 2015).

202 *Letícia Núñez Almeida et al.*

One of the main symbols of connection between Brazil and Paraguay is the International Friendship Bridge. Built in the 1950s and 1960s, the bridge is the link between Foz do Iguaçu and Ciudad del Este, and is currently the third largest free trade zone in the world and Brazil's best-known border.

The border demarcation between Brazil and Paraguay was the result of a regional war that took place in the 1860s, when the Triple Alliance (Argentina, Brazil, and Uruguay), with support from the British government, fought against Paraguay. From December 1864 to March 1870, bloody battles were fought, including one on the bank of the Riachuelo Stream, tributary of the Paraguay River, in the Argentine province of Corrientes. The conflict revolved around landlocked Paraguay's aspiration to have access to the sea, and therefore, Paraguay's troops occupied areas under the jurisdiction of both the Empire of Brazil and Argentina, that today belong to the state of Mato Grosso do Sul. For the Paraguayan government, winning the war would have meant achieving the desired maritime freedom through the Paraguay River; however, this objective was elusive. Despite making momentary advances, such as dominating the current state of Rio Grande do Sul, Paraguay's actions ultimately failed, and the Brazilian and Argentine forces ended up defeating Paraguay, which, in 1870, was declared the loser of the war that has ever since borne its name.

Fausto (2013) argues that Paraguay was devastated by the conflict, particularly as a result of the loss of territory to Brazil and Argentina, as well as the suspension of the country's modernization process that had been underway prior to the war. As a final balance, the most reliable estimates indicate that half of the Paraguayan population died, representing a pronounced demographic loss: from approximately 406,000 inhabitants in 1864 to 231,000 in 1872, with most of the survivors being elders, women, and children (Fausto 2013, 185).

Nowadays, the border with Paraguay is classified by the Brazilian government through the model of synapse, used to characterize twin cities featuring areas with high levels of exchange between the border populations (SEBRAE 2009). This type of intense cross-border exchange can be exemplified by the question of the *brasiguayos/Braziguayans* (Albuquerque 2010), a term used to describe Brazilians – mainly from Paraná and Rio Grande do Sul – and their descendants, who have lived in Paraguay since 1960, when they were prompted by the agricultural development policies of the two states during the construction of the Itaipu Dam's hydroelectric power plant. In 1967, the Paraguayan government lifted the ban on the purchase of land by foreigners, and thus the small Brazilian producers who received compensation for their plots, which were part of the Itaipu water mirror, began to buy land at lower prices in the neighboring country.

Consequently, during that time, the number of Brazilians in Paraguay increased exponentially and boosted the region's economy. However, relations between the three population groups (Brazilians, *Braziguayans,* and Paraguayans) gradually became the focus of conflicts with a xenophobic slant. Since then, Paraguayans have accused immigrants of illegally occupying and monopolizing land, as well of violating environmental laws through the use of certain chemicals. From this perspective, Brazilians appear as the actors who have negatively affected the original citizens of that area.

Currently estimated at 350,000, *Braziguayans* are found mainly in the regions of Canindeyú and Alto Paraná, in southeast Paraguay. These regions are now showing a reverse migration flow, as Brazilians are returning to Brazil for fear of threats from Paraguayan armed militias and invasions by social groups (Estrada 2015). Economic growth structured on the basis of land redistribution policies caused Brazil and Paraguay to face an informal redesign of the border lines. In return for growth, the phenomenon triggered the aforementioned social impasses (Cammarata 1993).

The Brazil-Bolivia Border

Brazil's border with Bolivia comprises 3,423.2 kilometers, of which 2,609.3 kilometers run along rivers and canals, 63 kilometers stretch along lagoons and 750.99 kilometers along land routes (LNCC 2012). This area was delimited through the treaties of 1867, 1903, 1928, and by Roboré's Diplomatic Notes of 1958.

In 1941, the Brazil-Bolivia Mixed Demarcation Commission was created for the establishment of the border milestones and was made responsible for erecting 438 border markers (Almeida 2015). Yet, the 1867 Treaty, on which the commission's work was based, had been negotiated in a context in which the geographical situation of the rivers in the Amazon Basin was not concretely known and, therefore, gave rise to some boundary disputes. In fact, the lack of technical resources to understand the configuration of the Amazon Basin generated misinterpretations in the markings and it was only in 1928 that an area which, according to the 1867 Treaty belonged to Bolivia, but that had hitherto been inhabited by Brazilians, was regulated. That area, known today as the state of Acre, was officially under Bolivian jurisdiction; however, that territory had long hosted a significant number of Brazilians, who did not recognize the Bolivian government. Under these circumstances, Brazil carried out a military occupation until, encouraged by a fine paid to Anglo-American tenants, it achieved the pacification of Acre.

In 1903, Brazil proposed a land exchange to Bolivia that would allow it to keep Acre as a Brazilian territory. Through the Treaty of Petrópolis, Bolivia ceded Acre in exchange for territorial compensations at several border locations, the construction of a railway by the Brazilian State,

204 *Letícia Núñez Almeida et al.*

freedom of transit through the region's rivers to the Atlantic Ocean, and a financial compensation of £2 million.

Because of the significant extension of that border area, delimitation and marking occurred in different ways over time. The first part was carried out between 1870 and 1879 and was in charge of a Brazilian commissioner. In turn, the drawing of the border lines in the Amazon region took somewhat longer, having begun in 1907 and culminated in 1914. Thus, demarcation occurred largely through decoupled practical initiatives. It was not until 1941 that the two states reconciled their directives to conclude the process through the Mixed Demarcation Commission.

The last observation regarding the definition of the border was raised by the Diplomatic Note no. 1 C/R, which was part of the 1958 Roboré Agreement (approved by the National Congress only ten years later, in 1968). The analysis of the border area between Brazil and Bolivia would finally come to an end in 1979. In 1990, with help of helicopters, the Brazil-Bolivia Mixed Demarcation Commission carried out inspections in the border areas and surveyed the territory from the state of Acre to the Brazil-Bolivia-Paraguay Tripartite Point (LNCC 2012). As a result of these inspections, the Mixed Commission recommended the reconstruction of some of the main markers and the identification of new complementary milestones to enable a more efficient the recognition of the land border.

The Brazil-Peru Border

The border that divides Brazil and Peru is 2,822 kilometers long and 67% of this border is constituted by rivers. On the Brazilian side, the states of Acre and Amazonas border the Peruvian departments of Loreto, Ucayali, and Madre de Dios. The negotiations between the two states to establish their borders date back to 1826, and the first treaty was signed in July 1841. It should be noted that this agreement was not specifically about border delimitation, but is rather known as a treaty of peace, friendship, trade, and navigation.

Another important moment in the history of border relations between Brazil and Peru is the 1851 Convention, which sought to regulate trade and navigation on the Amazon River and its tributaries. The most important effect of this convention was the free trade of products, goods, and vessels between Peru and Brazil in their rivers and borders. Furthermore, although it was not intended to delimit boundaries, the convention, along with the 1841 agreement, helped legitimize the Brazil-Peru border. The main personality who contributed to the consolidation of the border between Brazil and Peru was Baron of Rio Branco, who, on September 8, 1909 in Rio de Janeiro signed the definitive treaty of limits with Peru.

Brazil's border with Peru has several blind spots along the rivers in the Amazon region that are used for drug trafficking. The recurrent problem of cocaine trafficking is so pronounced that in 2014 it gave rise to the first declaration of state of emergency due to drug trafficking in Peru. This allowed security forces to invade private homes without a warrant and facilitated the arrest of people and the expulsion of foreigners.

The cities of Ramón Castilla and Yavarí, which border the cities of Leticia in Colombia and Tabatinga in Brazil, are good examples of this phenomenon. Reports from the United Nations Office on Drugs and Crime show that this border region was responsible for 6% of cocaine production in Peru and indicate that more than 80 people were accused of trafficking in the same year in the region's largest city, Caballococha. In 2009, Peru became the world's leading producer of coca leaf, surpassing Colombia, which registered 103,000 tons according to the United Nations Office on Drugs and Crime (UNODC 2013).

The Brazil-Colombia Border

The border between Brazil and Colombia comprises a total of 1,644.2 kilometers, with 835 kilometers of land border and 809 kilometers of river border (Almeida 2015, 58). It is located in the Brazilian state of Amazonas, while on the Colombian side, it stretches along the departments of Amazonas, Vaupés, and Guyana. There are only four official crossing points along those more than 1,600 kilometers: Yauarete (Colombia) and Iauaretê (Brazil); La Pedrera (Colombia) and Ipiranga (Brazil); Tarapacá (Colombia) and Vila Bitencourt (Brazil); and Leticia (Colombia) and Tabatinga (Brazil). Tabatinga and Leticia, together with Santa Rosa in Peru, conform a triple border, and are twin-city conurbations. These are also the cities with the largest population concentration on the Brazil-Colombia border, adding up, between both of them, about 50,000 inhabitants (Nogueira 2004, 2).

The border delimitation between Brazil and Colombia has been the subject of a long process, which began with the emancipation movement of the Spanish viceroyalties in America in 1821, while Gran Colombia, formed by the current territories of Venezuela, Colombia, Ecuador, and Panama, still existed. After independence, there were countless attempts to demarcate the borders through treaties of limits. One of these attempts took place in 1826; however, it failed, as every common idea of the bases of negotiation was lacking (Goes 2013, 40). The second attempt at delimiting the border between Colombia and Brazil occurred in 1853 and was led by Brazil's plenipotentiary, Miguel María Lisboa. On this occasion, the efforts failed again, because the Congresses of both countries were against delimiting the borders by the principles of *uti possidetis* (Goes 2013, 41). Afterward, there were two more attempts to establish a

206 *Letícia Núñez Almeida et al.*

boundary line between Brazil and Colombia: one in 1867, when Brazil appointed Councilor Joaquim Maria Nascentes de Azambuja to negotiate a border agreement in Bogotá, an endeavor in which he did not succeed; and another in 1880/1882, when Minister Próspero Pereira Gamba was sent to the state of Rio de Janeiro, as Colombia's delegate, for a new attempt to demarcate the lands that constituted the border between the two countries. Once again, the mission failed (Lins 1965, 371).

During this period of border demarcation attempts, a dispute between Venezuela, Brazil, and Colombia emerged. It derived from the Treaty of Limits and River Navigation signed in 1859 by the Brazilian and Venezuelan governments, which was contested by the Colombian government, for – it alleged – said treaty divided Colombian lands. Brazil resolved this dispute by applying the rule of negotiating with the country that had jurisdiction over the territory (Goes 1991, 133).

After all these attempts, Baron of Río Branco sent the plenipotentiary Enéas Martins as minister to negotiate the territorial limits with Colombia. Together with Alfredo Vázquez Cobo (Colombia), Martins signed the Vázquez Cobo-Martins Treaty, in the city of Bogotá on April 24, 1907 (Garzón Nieto 1982, 5). The treaty established that the border between Brazil and Colombia would be located between the Piedra de Cucuhy on the Río Negro and the mouth of the Agapóris River on the left bank of the Japurá or Caquetá River (Garzón Nieto 1982, 6). At the time of this demarcation, there was a region under dispute between Colombia, Ecuador, and Peru; however, its delimitation was decided years later with the 1928 Treaty of Limits and River Navigation. Thus, it was the Vázquez Cobo-Martins Treaty, along with the Treaty of Limits and River Navigation that determined the limits between Colombia and Brazil, which are preserved until today.

After the long history of litigation around the Brazil-Colombia border, and despite the current relationship of friendship and reciprocity between the two countries, there are still some conflicting issues, mainly due to the actions of the Revolutionary Armed Forces of Colombia (FARC), as well as to the trafficking of arms and drugs that takes place on these borders (Guzzi 2008, 54).

Brazil's border with Colombia is critical to understanding international border systems, as it differs from Brazil's southern borders in that it does not encompass many urban settlements or twin cities. Most of its extension is in the Amazon rainforest. The same is the case of Brazil's borders with Venezuela, Guyana, Suriname, and French Guiana.

The Brazil-Venezuela Border

Located in the northern region is the border between Brazil and Venezuela, which is 2,199 kilometers long, all of them on land (Almeida 2015, 58). This border is part of the Brazilian states of Amazonas and

Roraima, and it comprises eight border municipalities: Uiramutã, Pacaraima, Amajari, Alto Alegre, Iracema, Barcelos, Santa Isabel del Rio Negro, and San Gabriel de Cachoeira. On the Venezuelan side, the departments of Amazonas, Bolívar, and a disputed region between Venezuela and Guyana, known as Território Esequibo, border Brazil.

The history of the border between Brazil and Venezuela, as did that with Colombia, began with the emancipation movement of Gran Colombia against the Kingdom of Spain, which culminated in 1829. During the first attempts to delimit the borders, the issue had to be dealt with jointly by Brazil, Colombia, and Venezuela, since, after the independence of Colombia and Venezuela, the boundaries between the two countries were not defined (Goes 2013, 38–39). As already mentioned, in 1859, the Venezuelan and Brazilian governments signed the Treaty of Limits and River Navigation on the principle of *uti possidetis,* which gave Brazil juris-diction over the upper Rio Negro and Venezuela over the Fort of San Carlos, a demarcation that was objected to by the Colombian government (Goes 1991, 133). This territorial dispute between Colombia and Venezuela would only be resolved in 1891 by the Spanish Queen María Cristina, who determined that Venezuela had no jurisprudence on the territory between the Memachi River and the source of the Rio Negro (Brazil n.d., 3).

In 1878, the Brazilian Minister of Foreign Affairs, Baron de Villa Bela, appointed a commission to demarcate the border between Brazil and Venezuela, headed by Lieutenant-Colonel Francisco Xavier Lopes de Araújo. In 1880, this commission, along with its Venezuelan coun-terpart, began to delimit the territory between the Memachi, the Tomo, and the Maturacá rivers. The demarcation was concluded on February 17, 1883, and the work of the Joint Demarcation Commission derived in the First and Second Protocols of 1905, whereby the border delinea-tion made by the commission was approved (Brazil n.d., 3). Two further agreements were signed to determine milestones along the border: the Third Protocol signed on February 29, 1921, in Caracas, and the Fourth Protocol, which was ratified in Rio de Janeiro on July 23, 1928.

Due to Venezuela's lacking budget, the Mixed Demarcation Commission suspended activities for some years. It resumed its work in 1938 with new instruments, such as aerial reconnaissance. On August 23, 1973, the commission announced that the division between the two countries could be legitimately signed and concluded that the length of this boundary was approximately 2,199 kilometers.

Today, this border is of fundamental importance for the understand-ing of multi-ethnic dynamics and its relations with public security pol-icies, both at the municipal and national levels. The state of Roraima and its capital, Boa Vista, are almost entirely on the border line. In addition, 70% of its territory is inhabited by indigenous people and is therefore subject to special legislation that limits the actions of the state (Almeida 2014).

The Brazil-Guyana Border

The border between Brazil and Guyana is located in the northern region of Brazil and south and southwest of Guyana. The border line is 1,606 kilometers long, out of which 908 kilometers are on land and 698 kilometers are composed of lakes and rivers (Almeida 2015, 58). The largest part of this border is located in the Brazilian state of Roraima, while a shorter segment is in the state of Pará. There are urban centers on the border strip and along the border line, as well as twin cities, especially in the state of Roraima. The cities on the border strip are Boa Vista (capital of Roraima), Cantá, Faro, Mucajái, Rorainópolis, São João da Baliza, and São Luiz. In turn, the cities that are on the border line are: Caracarái, Caroebe, Iracema, Normândia, Oriximiná, and Uiramutã. In addition to these, Bonfim must be mentioned, as it constitutes a twin city with the Guyanese city of Lehtem.

Goes (1991) states that conflicts in this border region began in the post-colonial period. According to Oliveira (2015), from 1837 to 1838, the border became the object of a dispute between Brazil and the United Kingdom, when one of the borders was occupied by naturalized English dispatcher Robert Herman Schomburgk. The specific region in question was the military post on the Pirara River. Goes (1991, 155) asserts that there was a growing movement within British society that insisted in the legitimacy of the occupation of the lands that had been left vacant by the Brazilian state. Since 1842, several attempts were made to solve this territorial issue, but no effective agreements were reached. In the 1890s further efforts were made to resolve the dispute, and in 1898, the United Kingdom, through its Prime Minister, proposed a new demarcation for the region. This was not accepted by Brazil, who argued that the new formation would be detrimental to its interests (Goes 2013, 103).

After these frustrated attempts to resolve the dispute, Brazil and the United Kingdom agreed that the territorial issue should be resolved through international arbitration. To that effect, they chose King Victor Emanuel III of Italy as arbitrator. The 1904 ruling favored the United Kingdom with 60% of the territory, leaving the remaining 40% to Brazil (Goes 2013, 104–105). According to Menck (2009, 477) although the outcome was unfavorable to Brazil, it was a good option, as it averted the consolidation of the British occupation in the region.

The General Treaty of Limits between Brazil and Great Britain, signed in London on April 22, 1926, brought about the current configuration of the border, and established its three geographical markers: Mount Roraima, Mount Yakontipu, and the source of the Tacutu River, in Mount Wamuriaktawa (Brazil 1906). The treaty also details the possibilities of international arbitration for the resolution of future disagreements. Finally, during the 1930s, other documents that dealt with the border were agreed upon, such as the Protocol of Instructions of March 18, 1930, the exchange of diplomatic notes of 1932, and the 11th Conference of the Joint Commission of 1939 (Retis n.d., 2).

The Brazil-Suriname Border

The border between Brazil and Suriname has a territorial extension of 593 kilometers, all of which are on land (Almeida 2015, 58). Most of the border stretches along the state of Pará with a shorter section in the state of Amapá. The Brazilian municipalities that belong to the border strip between these two countries are Alenquer, Almeirim, Óbidos, Oriximiná, and Laranjal do Jari, which also borders French Guiana. There are, however, no twin cities or cross-border conurbations. In fact, the cities are mostly located at the opposite end of the border between Suriname and Brazil, making urban cross-border interactions difficult.

The regulatory framework for the delimitation of this border was adopted in 1906, when the treaty that settled the borders between Brazil and the Kingdom of the Netherlands was signed. According to this document, the border is defined by the land section between French Guiana and British Guiana, from East to West and, from North to South, between the basins of the Amazon River and the basins of the waters that run into the Atlantic Ocean (Brazil 1906). In 1931, the Protocol of Instructions signed on April 27 of the same year established the markers, which were formalized between 1935 and 1938 (Retis n.d., 2).

Yet, the history of the boundaries between Suriname and Brazil goes back to earlier times. According to Steiman (1998, 105), the population in the border region is linked to the state's activities during colonial times, especially to the drive to create settlements along the fortifications that were built to defend the territory. In this sense, the first record of this region is identified by the Retis Group in relation to the Dutch West India Company that administered the colonial regions of Esequibo, Demerara, and Berbice in the eighteenth century (Retis n.d., 2). In 1775, there was a territorial expansion by the Portuguese and the construction of the Fortification of San Joaquin. Later, in 1777, through the Treaty of San Ildefonso, the Brazilian borders specified in the Treaty of Madrid were reinstated. Historical records show that between 1781 and 1783 a first Mixed Demarcation Commission, to which Captains of Frigate Antonio da Silva Pontes and Ricardo Franco de Almeida Serra belonged, undertook inspections of the territory. Thanks to that commission's work, the watershed of the Paracaima range was identified and the delimitation could be carried out following the line of ridges to the Sierra de Tumucumaque (French Guiana) (Retis n.d., 2). Another milestone in the configuration of Suriname's borders occurred in 1903, when part of what was then Dutch Guiana, which included the colonies of Esequibo, Demerara, and Berbice, was appropriated by the United Kingdom.

210   *Letícia Núñez Almeida et al.*

After these events, Suriname's border with Brazil took a very similar shape to its current one. According to the records of the First Brazilian Boundary Demarcation Commission of the Ministry of Foreign Affairs, the following documents constitute the historical background for the current demarcation of the Brazil-Suriname border: (a) Brazil-Netherlands Boundary Treaty of May 5, 1906; (b) Decree No. 7,133 of September 24, 1906, responsible for executing the previous treaty; (c) Protocol of Instructions for the Demarcation of the Border between Brazil and the Colony of Suriname of April 27, 1941; (d) Note No. 1.130/40, from the Minister of the Netherlands, of September 22, 1931; and, finally, (e) Note from the Brazilian Government to the Minister of the Netherlands, of September 22, 1931, approving the Protocol of Instructions (Brazil n.d., 1).

From these documents, it is clear that the demarcation of the territory and boundaries between Brazil and Suriname did not face major difficulties. On the contrary, in 2011, the first conference of the Brazil-Suriname Mixed Boundary Commission took place in Belém. Based on this conference, the governments of the two countries proposed a schedule for the inspection of markers at the border and other cooperation mechanisms on border issues (Brazil 2011).

The Brazil-French Guiana Border

The border between Brazil and French Guiana is located in the north of the Brazilian territory and in the south and southeast of the French overseas department. It has an extension of 730 kilometers, of which 303 kilometers are on land, and the other 427 kilometers correspond to rivers and lakes (Almeida 2015, 58). The whole of this border is in the Brazilian state of Amapá. The cities of Amapá, Calçoene, Ferreira Gomes, Pedra Branca do Amapari, Pracuúba, and Serra do Navio compose the border strip, while the municipality of Laranjal do Jari is located on the border line between French Guiana and Suriname. The city of Oiapoque has a twin city configuration with the French city of Saint-Georges-de-l'Oyapock. However, with this exception, the urban centers of the municipalities on the border area are concentrated on the opposite side of the dividing line.

According to Silva and Rückert (2009), the current configuration of this border is the result of centuries of conflict between the Portuguese and the French. In 1637, the Captaincy of the Northern Cape was created as a way of securing the country's northern borders, especially between the Orange and Northern capes, as a response to the creation of the Compagnie du Cap Nord by France in 1634 (Goes 2013, 93). According to Goes (2013), there were several later attempts to assert the territory, and, in 1700, an agreement was reached to neutralize the territory of Macapá, occupied by the French since 1688. After signing the Treaty of Utrecht in 1713, Portugal and France went on to define the boundaries between their colonial territories from the Oiapoque River (Silva and Rückert 2009). Goes (2013) describes how from 1725 there was opposition from the French to the demarcation. In 1797, under Napoleon's pressure, Portugal and France signed another treaty on the region (Goes 2013, 94). In 1801, by the Treaty of Badajoz, Portugal agreed to the demarcation of the border by the River Araguari (Goes 2013); however, in 1806, John VI of Portugal considered the agreements signed after the Treaty of Utrecht invalid. In 1815, during the Congress of Vienna, Portugal agreed to reestablish the borders proposed by the Treaty of Utrecht (Goes 2013, 95).

Years later, France felt pressured to review and expand its territory. This led to the construction of a military post in the region, albeit on the Brazilian side (Brazil 2008a). The resolution of this issue involved the English, with their claims to secure the territory of British Guiana and prevent French advances. According to Brazil's official records (Brazil 2008a), an opposition movement took hold of the Brazilian population, and, in 1840, under British pressure, the French vacated the region.

The Brazilian Empire then began to build a military post called Dom Pedro II (Brazil 2008a). Nonetheless, the dispute continued throughout the century, and worsened after the discovery of gold deposits in the region that attracted much international interest (Brazil 2008a). Official records show that, as a reaction, both France and Brazil instituted local governments in the region in the 1890s; this led to the beginning of a new phase of conflict that caused deaths for both countries. To resolve the dispute, the countries opted for international arbitration by the Swiss Federal Council, which issued its ruling in favor of Brazil on December 1, 1900 (Goes 2013; Retis n.d.). At the end of the twentieth century, in 1981, the Treaty of Paris on the maritime delimitation between Brazil and French Guiana was signed. It established the current configuration of the border based on the Treaty of Utrecht and the 1900 arbitration awards (Brazil 2008b). Nevertheless, the controversial processes and disputes between countries are part of the history of this region, and, in a certain way, still affect attempts at integration. An example of this is the already mentioned case of the binational bridge over the Oiapopque River that connects the two municipalities. The bridge was completed in 2011 and there are still no concrete prospects of its being opened to transit, especially due to the obstacles in the process of paying for its construction (Almeida 2015, 54; Lissardy 2016).

Boundaries and Border Approaches

Brazilian borders are not only about integration, multiplicity, meeting of identities, and cross-border agreements, but also about differences, conflicts, and local logics of cross-border disputes. Grimson (2005)

212 *Letícia Núñez Almeida et al.*

propounds that the richness of thematizing borders lies in the possibility of showing the contingency and historicity of limits, although that does not imply emphasizing only the porosity of borders or losing sight of power struggles and persisting stigmas. According to the author, "[...] political borders offer a terrain, an especially productive territory, not only because populations that supposedly ascribe to different nationalities coexist there, but also because they are spaces of peculiar interest to and intervention of state power" (Grimson 2005, 2).

According to Grimson, rethinking sociological problems from the perspective of borders breaks with a centralist tradition, since, in his view, histories and political processes are commonly thought from the large cities, considering the top-down and center-periphery nation-building process. Thus, recovering the agency dimension of border regions, instead of universalizing their supposed resistance to the nation-state, opens the possibility of analyzing how relations between border societies and the nation-states of which they are part are articulated.

In Magnoli's view (1986), states fear the social complexity of border regions. According to the geographer, the reasons for this can be found in the classic definition of French geographer Jacques Ancel: "Border is a political isobar that sets the balance between two pressures. Isobar, in maps and charts, is the line that separates areas of different atmospheric pressure; along its route, the pressure is constant" (Magnoli 1986, 10). Little is known about Brazilian borders, even about the criminal circuits of traffic and contraband that end up characterizing them as a risk for the defense of the national territory. The border is, thus, the result of discursive and non-discursive practices, not a fact for analysis. For this reason, it is not reduced to a geographic limit, but includes other faces like the border of civilization, border of cultures, ethnic groups, and the historicity of man (Martins 2009). In Martins' words:

> [...] I take the border as a privileged place for sociological observation and knowledge about the conflicts and difficulties inherent in the constitution of the human being, in the encounter of societies that live on their limits and on the threshold of history. It is at the border that we can better observe how societies are formed, disorganized, or reproduce.
>
> (Martins 2009, 10)

It is possible to assert that the border is not a sociological concept; rather, it is a native construction that can have different meanings depending on the look of the observer. However, in the case of borders between countries, these would not exist if there were no limits determined by law; they are abstract constructions that create their own social dynamics. Even in regions where the demarcation line succeeded the existence of local communities, it is believed that there is a real exchange, where the limit plays a fundamental role in everyday relations. This is especially the case in those relations that develop in what can be called "border economies," i.e., dynamics that stem from the asymmetries between countries.

Spaces of pressure, tensions and disputes, no-man's-lands, and lawless territories are some of the ways in which Brazilian borders are commonly portrayed by the media and even by the state in speeches and government policies. For Silveira (2012), media coverage and "national public security" are intertwined in the process of constructing a securitized and criminal image of Brazilian borders and *favelas*. As the author explains:

> On the one hand, media coverage develops its competence to report facts to which risks to public security, patrimony, and the tax order are attributed, thus eliciting the public's interest. It does so by closely following those who, on the other hand, are the agents who currently make up the National Public Security Force. We consider that the news broadcast encourages this relationship and assumes the role of producer of fire alarms by articulating two different situations, which involve events located at the national borders and those that occur in *favelas*.
>
> (Silveira 2012, 2)

There is also a host of stigmatizing news about the borders of Brazil's southern region, which has the highest population density in the country. It is also the area where 197 out of the 588 border municipalities are located, in contrast to the larger part of the border strip territory, which is characterized by low population density and difficult access to the boundary markers. Due to the difficulties in installing markers at certain points on the border, especially in the Amazon rainforest, the placing of each marker has been a victory for the teams of the Ministry of Foreign Affairs' Brazilian Boundary Demarcation Commission.

The inevitable diversity of this region is constantly neglected by the common census and the media whenever "Brazilian borders" is the topic. Rather, the spotlight is put on the Triple Frontier, composed of Ciudad del Este in Paraguay, Foz do Iguaçu in in Brazil, and Puerto Iguazú in Argentina. This triple border is always characterized by the Brazilian press as a site for drugs and arms trafficking, money laundering, illegal cigarette sales, and has gained the appellatives of "smugglers' paradise," "a sanctuary for corruption, impunity, and crime," "a transit area for *sacoleiros* (drug mules)," and "a haven for Arab traffickers and terrorists" (Albuquerque 2010, 20). As Albuquerque states:

> [...] all sorts of calamities are attributed to Ciudad del Este, from arms trafficking to child trafficking, training of "sleeper" terrorist cells, contraband, crime, high rate of street violence, etc. This vision

214 *Letícia Núñez Almeida et al.*

extends to Foz do Iguaçu, which is considered to have a very high level of insecurity and criminality (one of the highest in Brazil). [...] The mass media (radio, television, newspapers, and internet) spread the most negative image possible of the Triple Frontier around the world, joining a campaign aimed at justifying possible interventions in the region.

(2010, 39)

The diffusion of this limited image[6] is transferred to the other borders, as if a specific region could represent the socio-cultural reality of the others, which is impossible, as Grimson explains:

Borders are spaces of condensation of socio-cultural processes. These tangible interfaces of national states unite and separate in various ways, both in material and symbolic terms. There are borders that only appear on maps and others that have steel walls, borders where nationality is a diffuse notion, and others where it constitutes the central category of identification and interaction.

(Grimson 2005, 3)

The fact that border issues have always been a matter of national defense and the competence of public security authorities, in addition to the images constructed around the Triple Frontier, have created – and recreated – an imagery of the region as a Wild West landscape; a lawless desert, where crime reigns and people are divided between the bandits (the population) and the good guys (the state). Since little is known about the former, and they end up being invisible, the latter feed the discourse of "lawless lands," as if the state were not present in those spaces.

Final Considerations

As the result of an historical process, the border emerges as the limit of territories that are continuously redefined, and disputed by different human groups, depending on where it is located. It has a dynamic character and it articulates multiple exchanges; yet it is also a catalyst for conflicts that escape the strict control of the nation-state. The countries' border areas possess peculiar characteristics that render borders spaces of tension and, simultaneously, of integration. This duality reveals the need to establish separations and limits, which take into account cultural differences and the preservation of state sovereignty, while allowing for the exercise of common social practices and exchanges. Borders are, at the same time, areas of separation and approximation, barrier line, and polarizing spaces (Max and Oliveira 2009). They are areas of circulation between countries or states that build on existing socio-cultural inequalities, levels of cooperation and social interaction both in the symbolic and in the political and economic fields. According to Pesavento,

> There is, without doubt, a tendency to think about borders from a conception that is anchored in territoriality and developed in politics. In this sense, the border is, above all, the closure of a space, the delimitation of a territory, the fixing of a surface. [...] Even in that approach fixed by territoriality and geopolitics, the concept of border already advances toward the domains of that symbolic construction of belonging that we call identity, and that corresponds to an imaginary reference framework that is defined by difference.
>
> (Pesavento 2002, 36)

The border space brings in itself a third dimension beyond the *limes,* a way between two territories that does not belong to either one, but to both of them, thus opening the perspective of a third glance between the singularity of the local and the universalizing ideas of the border (Leenhardt 2002). In this understanding, the border is not a territory, but a dynamic and historically constructed social space. As proposed by Golin:

> I will suggest a definition of space: we should take the territory through a dynamic notion, that is, the used territory. That which is scientific is not territory, it is the used territory. And space, which is a way of seeing the territory as well, is formed by systems of objects and actions in an indissoluble and dialectic union.
>
> (Golin 2002, 23)

In the case of Brazil, we assume that the border region has its complex exchange and mobility networks. This does not imply that its existence does not depend entirely on the state. In fact, it is only because of the latter that the border can be explained, especially if we take its products into account. The examples are endless; they are distinct processes of historical and geopolitical formation, identities, political disputes, and regional development. Yet, this is far from asserting that there is nothing in common along the 17,000 kilometers of Brazilian borders. From North to South, the economic activity at the borders is based on agricultural production, plant and mineral extraction, and formal and informal trade. The industrial sector has no presence in these regions, hence there seems to be a "border economy" common to the Brazilian border region (Almeida 2012), even though the municipalities located in the same border arc have an infinite number of different social dynamics, for example, the diversity of the Amazon agricultural frontiers, the conflicts of interest and planning programs of the state of Rondônia, the territorially based movements of Medio Solimões, etc. (Aubertin 1988).

216 *Letícia Núñez Almeida et al.*

Regions that are stigmatized as "lawless lands" or "no man's land" only exist because of legislation and the presence of the state. It is from the latter that cross-border flows are articulated and transform those territories into alive spaces, which are constituted by diverse forms of power. The borders of Brazil – territory and population – along with the borders of other South American countries, have been associated by the media and public opinion to a negative agenda, where crime and violence are constant labels (Silveira 2012).

Border areas articulate legal and illegal networks that are still little known from a sociological perspective. Border regions are traditionally seen as violent places (Waiselfisz 2010), especially because of the institutionalization of some criminal activities, such as drug and arms trafficking. However, in the case of Brazil, there is no evidence to prove that such activities are the cause of the stigmatizing violence that the media and the state attribute to border areas. And yet, some illegal activities, such as arms contraband, can indeed be a source of violence in large urban centers, since they bring arms into the country. This will be investigated later in this study when we delve deeper into border systems and their relations with the illegal markets.

Notes

1. The main legal instruments that regulate the occupation and development of the Brazilian border strip are: Law No. 6,634 of May 2, 1979 and Decree No. 85,064 of August 26, 1980, which consider the border strip as an indispensable area for national security.
2. Southern Common Market, a free trade bloc formed by Brazil, Argentina, Paraguay, Uruguay, Venezuela, and Bolivia.
3. They are all categories native to different segments of the southern borders, which refer to the people who transport goods from one country to another, exchange currency, and provide smuggling-related services.
4. LNCC – Borders and Limits of Brazil is a website that has a compilation of histories and treaties on Brazilian borders. The page index is available at http://www.info.lncc.br/.
5. The term "synapse" is an integral part of the typology of cross-border interactions present in the Promotion Program for the Development of the Border Strip (PDFF) of the Ministry of National Integration. In the field of cross-border interactions, border situations are not the same along the international (continental) border of the country due to geographical differences, the differentiated treatment it receives from government bodies, and the type of relationship established with neighboring countries. The PDFF incorporates the following typologies of cross-border interactions for the Brazilian case: margin, plug zone, front, capillary, and synapse.
6. It is a very rich region in many ways: Brazilians, Argentineans, Paraguayans, Indians, Palestinians, and Lebanese all live here together. Guarani is recognized as an official language and is taught in schools. Likewise, there are binational schools that teach Portuguese, Spanish, and Arabic. The Binational Hydroelectric Plant of Itaipú and the Iguaçu Falls are located in this region.

References

Albuquerque, Jose Lindomar. 2010. *A Dinâmica das Fronteiras: os Brasiguaios na Fronteira entre o Brasil e o Paraguai*. Brazil: Annablume.

Almeida, Letícia Núñez. 2012. *Resenha: espacios urbanos y sociedades transfronterizas en la Amazonia*. Colombia: IMANI-Instituto Amazónico de Investigaciones; Universidad Nacional de Colombia-Sede Amazonia. CuadernosCeru (USP) 23, 9–25.

——— 2014. *O que há de comum nas fronteiras brasileiras? Distâncias e aproximações entre as fronteiras do Brasil com o Uruguai e com a Venezuela*. IV Encontro Internacional de Ciências Sociais: espaços públicos, identidades e diferenças. Brazil: *Anais*. http://www2.ufpel.edu.br/ifisp/ppgs/eics/trabalhos.htm. Accessed 3 April 2016.

——— 2015. *O Estado e os ilegalismos nas margens do Brasil e do Uruguai: um estudo de caso sobre a fronteira de Sant'ana do Livramento (BR) e Rivera (UY)*. Brazil: Universidade de São Paulo.

Alvarez, Marcos César and Fernando Salla. 2010. *Violência e Fronteiras no Brasil: tensões e conflitos nas margens do Estado-nação*. Brazil: 34 Encontro Anual da ANPOCS GT 37-Violência, Criminalidade e Justiça Criminal no Brasil.

Aubertin, Catherine. 1988. *Fronteiras*. França: ORSTON.

Barros, Ariadne dos Santos de. 2008. "A informalidade dos *laranjas* na fronteira Brasil/Paraguai." *História na Fronteira*, 1 (1), 61–88.

Brazil, Ministério das Relações Exteriores. 1906. *Tratado entre os Estados Unidos do Brasil e os Países Baixos, estabelecendo a fronteira entre o Brasil e a Colônia do Suriname (assinado no Rio de Janeiro, em 05/05/1906. Sancionado pelo Decreto n 7.133, de 24/09/1906 e transcrito conforme redação original.)*, Brazil.

——— 1926. *Tratado Geral e Convencão Complementar de Limites*. Conceção Especial e Complementar de Limites: O Brasil e a Gran-Bretanha. Brazil. http://dai-mre.serpro.gov.br/atos-internacionais/bilaterais/1926/b_23/. Accessed 20 April 2016.

——— 2008a. *Primeira Comissão Brasileira Demarcadora de Limites: 3.0 – Resumo Histórico*. Brazil. http://sistemas.mre.gov.br/kitweb/datafiles/Pcdl/ptbr/file/Fronteiras/França/Resumo.pdf. Accessed 22 April 2016.

———2008b. *Primeira Comissão Brasileira Demarcadora de Limites: 4.0 – Copia dos Tratados de Limite*. Brazil. http://sistemas.mre.gov.br/kitweb/datafiles/Pcdl/pt-br/file/Fronteiras/França/Cópia%20dos%20Tratados%20de%20Limites.pdf. Accessed 22 April 2016.

——— 2011. "Comissão Mista Brasil-Suriname de Limites: Ata da Primeira (1ª) Conferência." http://sistemas.mre.gov.br/kitweb/datafiles/Pcdl/ptbr/file/Documentação%20Oficial/Suriname/Densificação/1a%20Conferência%20Português.pdf. Accessed 26 April 2016.

——— n.d. *Listagem da documentação oficial*. Brazil: Ministério das Relações Exteriores. http://sistemas.mre.gov.br/kitweb/datafiles/Pcdl/pt-br/file/Fronteiras/Suriname/2_0-%20Documentação%20Oficial.pdf. Accessed 22 April 2016.

Bueno, Clodoaldo. 1995. "Idealismo e rivalidade na política externa brasileira da República: as relações com a Argentina (1889-1902)." In Anais do Simpósio O Cono Sul no contexto internacional, 41–46. Porto Alegre: EDIPUCRS.

Cammarata, Emilce Beatriz. 1993. "Migraciones Guaraníes Contemporáneas". Unpublished paper.

218   *Letícia Núñez Almeida et al.*

Campos, Luciano Rodrigues. 2007. *A Controvérsia Em Torno Do Chamado Território Das Missões.* http://www.webartigos.com/artigos/a-controversia-em-torno-do-chamadoterritorio-das-missoes/4876/ Accessed 17 April 2016.

Cataia, Márcio. 2007. "A relevância das fronteiras no período atual: unificação técnica e compartimentação política dos territórios." *Revista Electrónica de Geografia y Ciencias Sociales.* Universidad de Barcelona XI (245), 21.

Clemente, Isabel. 2013. "Sociedades y prensa local en la frontera Uruguay-Brasil: desde la depresión a la segunda pos-guerra." Paper presented at the XII Jornadas de Investigación de la Facultad de Ciencias Sociales, Udelar, Montevideo.

Diez, Carolina et al. 2012. "Chiveros, paseras, paquitos: intercambios en los bordes. Economía y frontera en Misiones, Argentina". Paper presented at GT 02, 28. Reunião Brasileira de Antropologia, July 5.

Dorfman, Adriana. 2013. "A condição fronteiriça diante da securitização das fronteiras do Brasil." In *Fronteiras em perspectiva comparada e temas de defesa da Amazônia*, edited by Durbens Nascimento y Jadson Rebelo, 96–124. Belém: EDUFPA.

Estrada, Marcos. 2015. *The impact of land policies on international migration: The case of the Brasiguaios.* International Migration Institute: University of Oxford. http://www.imi.ox.ac.uk/publications/the-impact-of-land-policieson-international-migration-the-case-of-the-brasiguaios. Accessed 16 April 2016.

Fagundes, Pedro Ernesto. 2010. "O Uruguai e o Mercosul: novos desafios de José Mujica." Meridiano, 47 (114), 51–53.

Fausto, Boris. 2013. *História do Brasil.* 13 ed. Brazil: EDUSP.

Garzón Nieto, Julio. 1982. *Arreglo de límites entre la república de Colombia y la república de los Estados Unidos del Brasil.* Bogotá: Imprenta Nacional de Colombia.

Goes, Sydesio Sampaio Filho. 1991. *Navegantes, bandeirantes, diplomatas: Aspectos da descoberta do continente, da penetração do território brasileiro extra Tordesilhas e do estabelecimento das fronteiras da Amazônia.* Brasilia: Fundação Alexandre de Gusmão.

——— 2013. As Fronteiras do Brasil. Brasilia: Fundação Alexandre de Gusmão. http://funag.gov.br/loja/download/1030-as-fronteiras-do-brasil.pdf. Accessed 16 April 2016.

Golin, Tau. 2002. *A fronteira.* Brazil: L&PM Editores.

Grimson, Alejandro. 2005. "Fronteras, estados e identificaciones en el Cono Sur." In *Cultura, política y sociedades: Perspectivas latino-americanas*, compiled by Daniel Mato, 127–142. Buenos Aires: CLACSO.

Guzzi, André Cavaller (2008). "As Relações EUA-America Latina: Medidas e Consequências da Política Externa Norte-Americana para combater a produção e o tráfico de drogas ilícitas." Master's thesis. Programa Interinstitucional (PUC-SP/UNESP/UNICAMP), São Paulo. http://repositorio.unesp.br/bitstream/handle/11449/96289/guzzi_ac_me_mar.pdf?sequence=1. Accessed 16 April 2016.

Leenhardt, Jacques. 2002. "Fronteiras, fronteiras culturais e globalização." In *Fronteiras culturais: Brasil, Uruguai e Argentina*, coordinated by Maria Helena Martins, 27–34. Cotia:: Ateliê Editorial.

Lins, Alvaro. 1965. *Rio-Branco (O Barão do Rio-Branco): Biografia pessoal e História Política.* 2. ed. Sao Paulo: Companhia Editora Nacional.

Brazil and Its Borders 219

Lissardy, Geraldo. 2016. "A ponte entre Brasil e Guiana Francesa que ninguém pode cruzar." *BBC Brazil*, January 3, 2016. http://www.bbc.com/portuguese/noticias/2016/01/160103_ponte_brasil_guiana_francesa_rb. Accessed 24 April 2016.

LNCC. 2012. "Fronteiras e Limites do Brasil." *Fronteiras e limites do Brasil*. http://www.info.lncc.br/. Accessed 16 April 2016.

Machado, Lia. 1998. "Limites, fronteiras e redes." In *Fronteiras e espaço global*, organized by T. M.Strohaecker et al., 41–49.Porto Alegre: AGB Porto Alegre.

Magnoli, Demétrio. 1986. *O que é geopolítica?* Brazil: Brasiliense.

Martins, José de Souza. 2009. *Fronteira: a degradação do outro nos confins do humano*. Sao Paulo: Hucitec.

Martins, Lavínia Raquel Martins de. 2010. "O Turismo na História de Foz do Iguaçu." Masters dissertation, Universidade do Vale do Itajaí.

Max, Cláudio Zarate and Tito Carlos Machado de Oliveira. 2009. "As relações de troca em região de fronteira: uma proposta metodológica sob a ótica convencionalista." *Geosul* 24 (47), 7–27.

Menck, José Theodoro Mascarenhas. 2009. *A Questão do Rio Pirara (1829–1904)*. Brasilia: Fundação Alexandre de Gusmão.

Nogueira, Ricardo José Batista. 2004. "Território de fronteira: Brasil/Colômbia." Paper presented at Congresso Luso-Afro-Brasileiro De Ciências Sociais, Coimbra. *A questão social no novo milênio*. Portugal: Centro de Estudos Sociais. http://www.ces.uc.pt/lab2004/pdfs/RicardoNogueira.pdf

Oliveira, Samara Mineiro. 2015. "Formação das Fronteiras Brasileiras: Uma abordagem geo-histórica." Bachelors dissertation, Universidade de Brasília. http://bdm.unb.br/bitstream/10483/11473/1/2015_SamaraMineiroOliveira.pdf Accessed 19 April 2016.

Pesavento, Sandra Jatahy. 2002. "Além das fronteiras." In *Fronteiras culturais: Brasil, Uruguai e Argentina*, coordinated by Maria Helena Martins, 35–40. Cotia: Ateliê Editorial.

Rabossi, Fernando. 2004. "Dinámicas económicas en la Triple Frontera (Brasil, Paraguay y Argentina)." In *Seguridad, planificación y desarrollo en las regiones transfronterizas*, coordinated by Fernando Carrión, 167–193. Quito: FLACSO-Ecuador / IDRC-CRDI.

Retis. 2002. "Terra Limitânea: Atlas da Fronteira Continental do Brasil." http://www.retis.igeo.ufrj.br/atlas_de_fronteira/altas/paginainicio.htm. Accessed 19 April 2016.

——— n.d. "Processo de Demarcação da Fronteira Continental do Brasil." http://www.retis.igeo.ufrj.br/atlas_de_ fronteira/pdf/DELIMITAOFRONTfinal4.pdf. Accessed 19 April 2016.

SEBRAE. 2009. "Faixa de fronteira: Programa de Desenvolvimento da Faixa de Fronteira – PDFF." http://ois.sebrae.com.br/wpcontent/uploads/2013/06/cartilha-faixa-de-fronteira.pdf. Accessed 16 April 2016.

Silva, Gutember and Aldomar Rückert. 2009. "A fronteira Brasil-França: Mudança de usos político-territoriais na fronteira entre Amapá (BR) e Guiana Francesa (FR)." *Confins* 7. https://confins.revues.org/6040?lang=pt. Accessed 19 April 2016.

Silveira, Ada Cristina Machado da. 2012. "A cobertura jornalística de fronteiriços e favelados: narrativas securitárias e imunização contra a diferença." *Intercom, Rev. Bras. Ciênc. Comum., São Paulo* 35 (1), 75–92.

Steiman, Rebeca. 1998. "A Geografia das Cidades da Fronteira Norte: um perfil." In *Fronteiras e espaço global: III Colóquio Internacional de Estudos Fronteiriços.* Porto Alegre: Associação dos Geógrafos Brasileiros Seção Porto Alegre.

UNODC, United Nations Office on Drugs and Crime. 2013. *Drug World Report 2013.* New York: UNODC

Waiselfisz, Julio Jacobo. 2010. "Mapa da violência 2010: anatomia dos homicídios no Brasil." Instituto Sangari. http://institutosangari.org.br/mapadaviolencia/MapaViolencia2010.pdf. Accessed 22 April 2016.

PART 2
THEMATIC AXES

9 Illegal Markets

A New Institutional Architecture and Its Territorial Expression in Latin America

Fernando Carrión Mena

> *I assure you, and forgive me for being so frank, that here, at this meeting, there are many people who are being paid by drug traffickers and who are informing the narcos of what is happening in real time.*
>
> Juan Manuel Santos, President of Colombia[1]

Introduction

Very little importance has been given to the issue of illegal economies in academic studies of cities and borders. Perhaps this is so, because such economies have not been seen as an increasingly significant component of economic and territorial development, but also because the "war on drugs" policy – in force since 1971 – has sought to veil them under moral, legal, political, and cultural considerations. Nor can it be ignored that economic science itself has not generated methodologies, indicators, and sources to approach them; so much so, that the few existing ones have proved insufficient when it comes to measuring and, above all, knowing illegal economies. Additionally, it cannot be ruled out that this might be due to the interpretation of illegal economies as if they were a simile or part of informal economies, although it is fair to say that economic analysis has already begun to distinguish the two of them.

Informal economies are mainly conceived as a modality conformed by a structural dualism – inherent to developing countries – which is expressed in the formal and informal, legal and illegal, marginal and integrated dichotomies. The common explanation was that popular entrepreneurship was external to modernity; that in the labor market, self-employment led to underemployment; that capital had low productivity due to low technological development and a high labor share, and that those markets were poorly regulated and displayed little control and competitiveness. This set of characteristics led to an association of what was then conceived as an equation: informal economy equals – mainly urban – poverty. In reality, this "confusion" still operates, since illegal economies mix with and mimic informal markets, so that illegal markets

DOI: 10.4324/9781003204299-16

224 *Fernando Carrión Mena*

reproduce themselves camouflaged within informality and the logic of illegality is subsumed into the logic of informality.

To be clear, informal economies are those economic activities with low productivity and high tax evasion, which are not recorded in national accounts, and are characterized by precarious employment – no social security, low wages – as well as a lack of compliance with urban, commercial, and labor standards (Portes and Haller 2004). By contrast, illegal economies are those production, distribution, and consumption activities that are directly typified as criminal. They are unlawful and, therefore, each of their phases is punishable. Moreover, these phases are linked to each other under the logic of an "inter-criminal system;" that is to say, no phase can be understood, if not in relation to the others.

These definitions are, nonetheless, insufficient, which is why it is essential to differentiate the concept of illegal economy from that of informal economy, for they depict, in fact, different realities. Moreover, the amount of economic resources that illegal economies mobilize is increasingly significant, due to their links with both the legal and informal markets, be it through money laundering, or the logic of subsuming what is informal to what is illegal, and both of them to what is legal.

The resources that infiltrate the state under the guise of "silver" (corruption), "lead" (intimidation), and "democracy"[2] (elections), cannot be dismissed either, as they seek to undermine the state through the reduction of its policies' efficiency and the loss of institutional legitimacy. As a result, the notion of "failed state" emerges, and operates, less as an analytical concept, than as a certification policy of the actions of the state to combat drug trafficking.

Today in Latin America, it is very difficult not to feel the presence of the illegal economies related to drug trafficking,[3] arms trafficking,[4] contraband,[5] or human trafficking.[6] They are, in fact, ubiquitous, due to the magnitude of their transactions and high profitability, in addition to being linked – in different ways – to the legal and formal areas of the economy (tourism, construction, trade). Moreover, they are also visible because they generate not only illegalities in different areas of the economy (front men, usury, bribery, or illegal taxes), but also a set of criminal acts with high levels of violence, such as contract killings and kidnappings, among others.

Another characteristic of illegal economies and related crimes is connected to their new territoriality. Today, there are three strategic places where these economies are strongly expressed: First, the borders, where illegal economies have an astounding level of growth, where homicide rates are the highest, and from where illegal economies are projected toward the world (platforms or hubs). Second, the cities, preferred places of the new economy, of mass consumption, of the growth of violence, and – as it happens with the borders – of their conversion into structuring nodes of cross-border regions, both because markets and the related crimes tend to concentrate in the cities, and because they assume the function of universal platforms. Finally, tax havens, broad spaces, where global economic transactions take place. The three of them are reconstituted with globalization, development, technology, and the reform of the state, which act syncretically.

This work seeks to raise awareness of the weight of the illegal economy, its links to the new criminal reality, and the formation of an unprecedented territorial organization in Latin American countries. In other words, it points to the need to study in greater depth this new problem, which has implications in various areas. This chapter is a first approach to the subject and, for the time being, it is linked to questions and hypotheses rather than to answers that clarify the relationship between illegal markets, violence, and territories.

The Context of Illegal Markets

Since the last decades of the twentieth century, a process of economic transformation was unleashed throughout the world, to an extent that many authors, such as Castells (2001), and institutions, such as the OECD,[7] began to speak about the existence of a new economy, characterized by the expansive growth of created wealth, the presence of this phenomenon on a planetary scale, and the existence of a variety of interconnected sectors of the economy. In this process, two main elements stand out: on the one hand, the new information and knowledge technologies (Castells 2001); and, on the other hand, the presence of new actors that embody modern management models. Undoubtedly, illegal economies are part and parcel of this transformation, thanks to their new and mutual interconnections with legal economies.

This explains why a fundamental transformation in crime in Latin American can be perceived. It is a moment of change from a criminal situation constituted by traditional violence, stemming from social asymmetries, recreational cultures, and the survival strategies of certain population sectors, to a modern violence, characterized by an explicit predisposition to commit criminal acts, that leads to both the division of labor within an organization and the internationalization of criminal operations, and that is sustained mainly by the economic logics of illegal economies. It is modern violence that operates as a structuring element for all types of violence, including the traditional one, for the ultimate reason for its existence is the procurement of economic benefits by illegal means.

For instance, every stolen or illegally produced object must be integrated into the legal market to be commercially viable, producing thereby a very clear division of labor. On one side, there are those who carry out the theft operations and, on the other side, those who introduce the stolen object into the market. The key in this process is the issue of stolen

226 *Fernando Carrión Mena*

products circulation, for which there are two forms that arise at the two ends of the circuit: depending on whether the actor is the one who steals or the one who trades, each one establishes relations with the other, either as a mediator or as a contractor.

This process is carried out by criminal networks displaying two characteristics. First, each network specializes in different lines of business (jewelry, cell phones, drugs); and second, they are structured from the supply side with the contacts that the thieves possess to introduce the stolen goods into the market, or from the demand side, based on pre-established contracts proposed by the merchants of stolen goods (Ávila and Pérez 2011). Moreover, this is a mechanism through which the illegal market uses the informal one to obtain monetary liquidity. Hence, a good security policy must go hand in hand with good economic policies that attack each of the links and circuits of the overall production process.

The change was foreshadowed since the 1980s, when Latin America underwent a process of reconstitution of violence and crime, from the traditional to the modern one, due – among other things – to three particular factors. First, the reform of the state, linked to the promotion of the market economy (privatization, deregulation, competitiveness, and open trade), encouraged the expansion of illegal economies, while weakening the state, which relinquished the possibilities of regulating the market, reducing socio-economic inequalities, and representing the "general interest." The situation is so complex that, as Manwaring (2009) points out, "Mexico is a country where political power is migrating from the state to small non-state actors, which are organized into broad networks with private armies, their own revenues, charitable services, and the capacity to make alliances and conduct wars." Additionally, the state lost the ability to control violence, because it lagged the high flexibility and dynamism of crime, and because it was penetrated by the illegal markets.

The privatization of production and the free commercialization of weapons, security technology, and private security,[8] fostered, for one thing, the commodification of the service.[9] The universal right to protection, which should be guaranteed by the state, became, thus, a commodity that must be paid for, and imposed an inequality of access to protection. It is estimated that private security services cover less than 5% of the European population and, what is worse, "the degree of security obtained is proportional to the price paid" (Petrella and Vanderschueren 2003). For another thing, it is necessary to understand that the state's monopoly of force is lost to the private sector. This is the case of the industry of private guards that employs twice as many police officers as public police forces in Latin America.[10]

It must be mentioned that economic liberalization promoted the dynamization of the world economy and the parallel articulation of the legal economy with the illegal one. Furthermore, the offshore logic[11] gained increasing importance because of the generalization and strengthening of the benefits and services provided by tax havens,[12] where legal and illegal markets meet, as well as because of the significance of transfer prices that produced a tax loss of $361 billion for nation-states (Christian Aid 2009).

Second, and in parallel, security policies underwent a substantial change after the 9/11 attacks in the United States. From that moment on, it became clear that security policies can, in certain cases, produce more violence than protection. For instance, one could mention the legitimacy acquired by the concepts and practices of "preventive war" (Bush), "necessary war" (Obama), or "extraterritoriality of justice" (Uribe) that have resulted in so many deaths and continue to produce so much devastation. It is in this context that the US invasions of Afghanistan and Iraq took place, as did Colombia's attack on the Amazonian hamlet of La Angostura in territory of Ecuador.

From that moment onward, there was an offensive of international development aid aimed at reforming the whole of the criminal system in Latin America (police,[13] justice,[14] and prisons[15]), in order to face what was defined as the three global threats: terrorism, migration, and drug trafficking. Therewith, our countries lost their "sovereignty over crime," for these policies were designed to reduce threats to the national security of other countries and not to improve the citizen security of ours. According to the Transnational Institute and WOLA,

> Latin American countries have not always had such harsh drug laws; rather, these latter have been adopted in recent decades. Although in countries such as Argentina and Brazil such laws came into force in the context of authoritarian regimes, generally in the region *the shift toward punitive drug laws came in response to international pressure*, specifically stemming from the three major drug conventions adopted under the aegis of the United Nations, which promoted stiffening sanctions for drug offenses. These treaties required that the countries modify their domestic legislation so as to criminalize all acts – except use – related to the illicit market in controlled substances. In some cases, the legislation went beyond what the treaties required. *The Andean countries in particular submitted to the pressures of the "war on drugs" waged by the U.S. government, which conditioned economic assistance and trade benefits on the acceptance of its drug strategy.*
>
> (Transnational Institute and WOLA 2010, 5; emphasis added)

It is striking that in our countries there is no direct relationship between the crimes reported by the population and the citizen security policies implemented by governments. In Ecuador, as in other countries, crimes reported by the population are not prosecuted, as evidenced by

228   *Fernando Carrión Mena*

the following data: In 2005, complaints for crimes against property were 61.1% of the total, and only 0.66% were crimes involving narcotics; however, 62% of the prison population had been charged with crimes involving drugs. Two years later, in 2007, the trend continued: complaints of crimes against property (robbery, theft) and persons (homicide, sexual crimes) accounted for 72.45% of the total, yet only 4.42% of all inmates were imprisoned for these crimes. In turn, while complaints about narcotics were 0.34% of the total, they led to 71.78% of the convictions. Moreover, not only are national crimes not prosecuted, but this policy, which favors a type of crime that is often not reported, has led to the crisis of the prison system in Ecuador and in many other countries of the region.[16]

Finally, the scientific-technological revolution in the field of communications generated greater connectivity and mobility of production factors, which led to the integration of the legal and illegal markets through money laundering, electronic transactions, and the constitution of new supra-territorial management modalities (reduction of distant territories). Additionally, new crimes have emerged, such as cybercrime or trafficking in human organs. This latter is possible thanks to the advancement of medicine, the incorporation of highly qualified personnel into the circuits of the illegal markets, and the possibility of transferring the organs in good conditions of refrigeration and asepsis. Perhaps one of the components most favorable to the illegal markets' boost on a global scale is the Internet, as it is a decentralized, flexible, and integrated group of real-time communication networks, without any unified and institutional form of service management.[17]

In sum, the illegal economy has a sense (objectives), organization (social subject), association between different criminal actors (networks), and a strategic definition of the whole set of criminal actions (planning, criminal intelligence). Therefore, it can be said that the beginning of the twenty-first century was marked by the presence of important organizations of illegal networks in the economy, society, the territory, and the state. In other words, there was an increase in crime, which was proportional to the weakening of both the state and the sense of public life. As a result, there has been a worrying rise in the levels of distrust among citizens toward public institutions: distrust toward the police in Latin America increased from 30% in 1996 to 39% in 2007 and from 41% to 51% in the case of the Armed Forces, while it slightly decreased from 33% to 30% in the case of the judicial system (Corporación Latinoabarómetro 2007).

The New Criminal Architecture

The newly emerging economy originates, among other elements, from a general restructuring of the logics of production of the illegal markets on a planetary scale, giving rise to three distinctive signs of the new

Illegal Markets 229

architecture. In the first place, the internationalization of the management of all the circuits and chains of the new criminal organizations stems from the high levels of connectivity, which accelerate the integration of distant territories and facilitate the mobility – therefore, the articulation – of production factors. This, in turn, provides a material basis for the real-time interaction of all the units at a gigantic level. In Sassen's words, "the geography and composition of the global economy changed so as to produce a complex duality: a spatially dispersed, yet globally integrated organization of economic activity" (1991, 3).

In second place, there is the emergence of a new productive architecture based on globally organized companies, designed to manage the different stages of the value chain more efficiently. A global decomposition of the productive processes is evidenced, not only in the territory (dispersed spaces), but also in each one of the activities pertaining to the phases of the general process, by resorting to the modalities of outsourcing,[18] franchising,[19] or holding.[20] These modalities are used according to the conditions of each place (local), constituting an organizational system composed of networks and nodes structured at world level (global),[21] and they display a unique quality: when the parts are attacked by the police, for instance, the rest of the system is neither contaminated nor affected. The outsourcing and franchising modalities operate in dispersed locations, while in the global context, the holding company operates in such a way as to have a highly efficient organizational structure that is immune to the actions of the judicial system, since outsourcing and franchising dynamics also operate as security valves or fuses that trip after an attack by the police. When the police dismantle a gang, cartel, or criminal mafia, the organization itself immediately replaces it (another local group or fraction of it) or reconstitutes itself thanks to its high flexibility (it changes routes), in order to continue functioning undisturbed. This is the advantage of this large holding structure.

Finally, the integration of illegal markets with legal ones led to the boundaries between them becoming "liquefied," much more so in countries or localities with service economies that have low institutional quality and markets with high levels of international insertion. That is why this network of networks forms free zones that allow for integration at different levels: inter-criminal links (arms with drugs, for example), links between the illegal and the legal (such as money laundering), cross-border relations, and articulations between what is locally dispersed and what is globally integrated. These free zones are not only functional to the integration of illegal activities, but also to the protection of crime and criminals (trust, organization, and civic culture), due to the fact that illegal capital acquires privileged economic and political power in these exceptional places.

All this is possible because of the new actors behind the process. The criminal institution transits from isolated organizations (organized

230 *Fernando Carrión Mena*

crime)[22] to an integrated system of international organizations, in the shape of a network of global networks. Networked organizations are managed from the virtual space, as well as from low vulnerability and risk areas, which are strategically located between production and consumption territories, following the most common routes of legal commercial exchange. Thanks to this strategy, criminal organizations have achieved an unprecedented level of penetration of the territory, the state, the economy, and society, which has given them significant economic weight to become more politically influential on all the scales and areas in which they operate.

However, it remains a task for the future to study the direction of the flow of command within the organization. It would be different if the headquarters of the network originated in Colombia, Peru, or Mexico (or if it were controlled from any territory in the world by criminal groups from those countries), that if it were in the countries of the global North. The question then arises, whether a Latin American cartel holding is emerging to dominate the illegal drug and trafficking economy. If so, the profits from sales to the final consumer would be distributed differently, benefiting the headquarters of the holding company.

The Expansion of Illegal Economies

Illegal economies are changing the global system through the amount of economic resources they mobilize, their presence within states, their investing in legal markets, and by their rootedness in society (culture).

The money mass that illicit markets mobilize is estimated to be of an enormous magnitude.[23] According to Moisés Naím,

> The financial industry, which exploded in the 1990s, has not been spared in the onslaught. Quite the contrary: money laundering and tax evasion have grown in proportion to the ballooning size of the international financial system, or faster. In 1998 the then director of the International Monetary Fund, Michel Camdessus, estimated the global flow of dirty money at 2 to 5% of the global economy, a figure he called "beyond imagination." Yet more recent estimates place the flows of laundered money at up to 10% of global GDP.
>
> (2005, 16)

This means that in six years, the flow of dirty money doubled, thus showing an impressive upward trend. If this trend continued to our day, what would the contribution of illegal markets to the world economy be?

At the beginning of this century – 2002 – in Latin America there was a flow of illegal economic resources of 6.3% of the GDP, which represented an amount of no less than $70 billion. In 2012, Mexico,[24] Brazil, and Argentina alone laundered around $20 billion each; Colombia,

Illegal Markets 231

Table 9.1 Illegal markets in relation to GDP and population

Country	GDP (billions of dollars)	Illegal markets (billons of dollars)	Illegal markets/ GDP	Population	Illegal markets (dollars per person)
Mexico	1,150	37.0	3.22%	114,793,341	322.3
Brazil	2,477	20.0	0.81%	196,655,014	101.7
Argentina	448	20.0	4.46%	40,764,561	490.6
Central America and the Caribbean	355	25.0	7.04%	79,904,215	312.9
Colombia	333	10.0	3.00%	46,927,125	213.1
Chile	249	10.0	4.02%	17,269,525	579.1
Peru	180	4.0	2.22%	29,399,817	136.1
Ecuador	78	2.2	2.81%	14,666,055	150.0
World	699,800	600	0.10%	6,974,242,787	86.03

Sources: GDP: CEPALSTATS. The data corresponds to 2011. Population data by the World Bank. The data corresponds to 2008–2011.

Chile, and Peru – according to the Attorney General – around $10 billion each;[25] Ecuador $2.2 billion, and the whole of Central America around $25 billion. For all these reasons, it can be said that in the early 2010s, the figure in the region was well over $120 billion.[26]

As shown in Table 9.1, the weight of illegal markets in relation to the country or region's GDP is greater at the destination (Argentina and Chile) or near it (Mexico, Central America, and the Caribbean). The high relative weight in Central America may respond to the fact that 82% of the South American cocaine transits through there, as well as to the low weight of its GDP. Brazil's case, in turn, appears to be related to the large size of that country's economy. It is undoubtedly a significant weight and, most seriously, one that is growing.

However, it is also related to the fact that the amount of laundered money is directly proportional to the price of the narcotics. In Colombia, where it is produced, a kilo of cocaine is worth $1,800; in Panama, which is part of the route, it is worth $3,000; on the border between Mexico and the United States, the price climbs to $50,000, and, on the streets of New York, where it is consumed, it is worth over $100,000. That is why, according to studies by the University of Florida, it is estimated that 80% of the resources remains in the United States and Europe, while the rest stays in the production and transit areas (routes). The price of drugs is, therefore, not determined by production activities – where value is added – but by those of circulation (risk) and proximity to demand (consumption).[27] What remains to be studied is who controls the accumulation process, regardless of the price in each of the places and phases of the process.

232 *Fernando Carrión Mena*

Where is the money? Among which economic sectors is this money distributed? To answer these questions, it is necessary to resort to international experiences on which studies have been carried out. For 2009, Forgione (2010) estimated at $446 billion the amount linked to cocaine trafficking; the other drugs (marijuana, chemicals, opium) must be added to this, as well as the other sectors of illegality (trafficking, arms, contraband, tax evasion).

According to the same author, in Italy, the mafia's annual turnover is between €120 and €180 billion. Between 40% and 50% of this money is used to reproduce illicit activities through the payment of bribes, drugs, technology, weapons, salaries, and hit-men, among other items (Forgione 2010), while between 50% and 60% of this sum enters the legal economy. An amount of this magnitude – no less than $300 billion worldwide – leads to the dynamization of the legal economy with fresh resources and, more clearly, to the blurring of the boundaries between legal and illegal markets.

This large money supply penetrates the economy, society, and the state. Economic activity is intensified by money intended to reproduce illicit activities, as well as by money invested in the less regulated legal markets, which have quick cash flows and are relatively functional to the reproduction of illicit markets. This is the injection of fresh money that boosts economic sectors such as tourism (restaurants, hotels), construction (housing), commerce (shopping centers), and certain services (transport, finance). However, it should be noted that in each country or region these processes adapt to particular local conditions, in order to make laundering possible. This is why criminal networks cannot be understood outside the set of relationships between legal and illegal actors and those who participate directly and indirectly in criminal activities.

New cultures have developed that are linked to quick and easy profits, new forms of consumption, new content in *narco* soap operas and music (*narcocorridos*),[28] as well as to a new capacity to generate employment, which is one of the greatest social buffers and sources of support and legitimacy for criminal groups. Colombia, Mexico, and the United States, among other countries, have produced an infinite number of films related to drug trafficking which, in turn, have brought about a vivid public debate and novel academic studies, with Colombian soap operas probably arousing the greatest interest, not only among viewers, but also among academics.

The state is also object of the penetration by illicit actors and activities that can take place in four possible ways: first, by crossing country borders and generating international problems; second, by encroaching on state structures, wearing them down and making them permissive to illegality through the use of economic resources (corruption) or intimidation (extortion); third, by creating parallel military forces that dispute

Illegal Markets 233

the power of the state; and fourth, by using the existing democratic procedures to gain direct representation.[29] In short, state institutions are undermined by corruption and by the creation of parallel power structures, something that has led to the expression "failed state," which is nothing more than a form of "certification" by powerful governments of the anti-drug policies of the countries where a large part of the narcotics is produced.

This economic movement can be explained, among other things, by the significant change that the narcotics sector is undergoing in the world economy. It is one of the largest, most dynamic, and, probably, most modern sectors on the planet. It is therefore possible to say that illegal economies feed the global economic system, which means that the twenty-first century will continue to be characterized by the presence of mafia networks in the economy.

The Territories of Illegal Economies

The social production of the space of illegal economies has been profoundly transformed, following, in some way, the logic of the legal economy and the large global companies. This is so, because legal and illegal economies are related, and the latter are somehow part of the former. Illegal economies have experienced a change in their social subject: from local criminal organizations, sustained by planning (criminal intelligence) and the division of labor in the commission of criminal acts (specialization), to organizations composed of global networks that operate as integrated systems of spaces of different scales. It is, then, a process of qualitative change that produces the unprecedented fact of a global organization that carries out local actions.

Within this duality – already mentioned by Sassen – new management models are constituted where dispersed (local) spaces meet strategic conditions within the general (global) structure, such as the reduction of vulnerability thanks to the existence of institutions with limited control (weak) and good location in the productive chain (connectivity, positioning, comparative advantages), thus reducing risk and boosting productivity.

The traditional territorial separation between narcotics producing, consuming, and transit countries tends to be transformed due to factors, such as technological development, which allows for new varieties of coca, for instance, whose seeds can be planted in different habitats and are immune to glyphosate spraying. There is also the presence of a multiplicity of drugs that are produced industrially in any place and, therefore, independently of the conditions of a natural habitat.[30]

No less important is the international decomposition of production processes and the globalization of consumption, which can be seen in the

234 *Fernando Carrión Mena*

fall in demand for cocaine in the United States in recent years, and its increase in Europe and Latin America. According to Gratius,

> There are 8.4 million cocaine users in the Americas, 68% in the U.S., 29% in South America and 3% in Central America. These figures show that there has been a worrying increase in cocaine consumption in South American countries, especially in Brazil, where demand is the second highest in the Americas, followed by Argentina and Chile. Mexico is the only country where heroin use is high.
>
> (2012, 6–7)

Today, marijuana (cannabis) can be grown in different climates and on different scales. It is produced in the United States and Europe, as well as in Latin America and Africa, while cocaine processing is gradually being released from production areas to relocate to places closer to the sites of demand. For this reason, the old spatial distinction between producing and consuming countries tends to be diluted and to fade away; so much so, that the design of differentiated policies between supply and demand, typical of the "war on drugs," has lost meaning today. If they ever had any chance of having positive effects, under the new circumstances, such differentiated policies appear outdated.

The focus of anti-narcotics policies on the production and circulation phases generated high levels of violence in the places where these phases take place, and practically none in the sites of demand. The expression "we put the dead and you put…" the weapons, the policies, and the economic accumulation, uttered by authorities in Mexico, Guatemala, Colombia, and El Salvador became recurrent. In its 2013 report on drugs, the Organization of American States points out that "[t]he intensity of the violence associated with drug trafficking – especially in countries affected by the production, transit, and trafficking of illegal drugs – has been the principal factor in driving the concern of senior level officials in becoming more actively engaged in this debate" (OAS 2013, 5). However, it fails to mention that this violence originates in the policies of war promoted by the same institution, precisely in those places, and not where the demand for narcotics is concentrated.

Currently, three unique situations converge: (a) the high level of diffusion of drug use on a global scale, to the extent that it is possible to speak of the globalization of consumption; (b) demand for opiates and cocaine continues to be concentrated, first, in the United States and, second, in Europe; and, finally, (c) the maintenance of the territorial division of labor according to the phases of production, circulation, and consumption of drugs throughout the world.

Yet, while marijuana is the drug whose consumption is more widespread (more addicts, more countries, greatest quantity) in the world, cocaine represents the largest share within the structure of illegal economies, due to its high price and its production-accumulation logic. Clearly, a process of globalization of a very wide menu of natural and industrial drugs has developed, where cocaine works as the functional articulation nucleus of the whole of the narcotics market, as well as of the illegal markets of, for example, human trafficking or commercialization of firearms.

The global space in which illegal drug markets operate is constituted by a productive and financial institutional machinery that follows the organizational logic of formal companies, such as Nike or General Motors, whose structures, characterized by high territorial dispersion and territorial division of labor, are not very different from those of the Sinaloa Cartel or the N'drangheta. In fact, modern global corporations are neither about a parent company with multiple subsidiaries in different markets, nor about taking advantage of low production costs in different locations. They are, just like drug cartels, networked organizations, led and facilitated by the technological and communications revolutions.

The spread of economic activities around the planet which follow the logic of improving monetary benefits in contexts of lower relative risk (security for the illegal system) to obtain greater comparative advantages in each of the phases of the productive process is evident. In the case of the Sinaloa Cartel, a weak state (Mexico) can help guarantee criminal activities, because it reduces the risk incurred in with criminal operations, whereas in the case of N'drangheta, a country with large open markets (Italy), with a requirement for fresh money, labor outsourcing, and scant regulation, becomes particularly attractive for money laundering, foreign investment, and the development of certain illegal activities.

The explanation of organizational similarity goes hand in hand with two key elements. For one thing, the articulation between the legal and the illegal markets born of mutual necessity. In order to "exist," illegal markets must launder money in the legal markets; in turn, to be able to compete, reproduce and expand, legal markets need fresh money. For another thing, both types of market adopt the logic of integration based on the modalities of holding, outsourcing, and franchising, thus providing illegality with a greater degree of efficiency in all circuits and phases; and, above all, designing a security system that is deactivated in each of its parts, when law-enforcement attacks it, without affecting the whole. This is a structure with shields or fuses that isolate the constitutive parts when they are hit, so that the system as a whole continues to function. In this sense, it is a model that reduces risk.

The case of the Sinaloa Cartel provides a good illustration of these groups' metamorphosis, as this organization ceased to be both a cartel, and – strictly speaking – from Sinaloa. This grouping changed its

236   *Fernando Carrión Mena*

management logic, and increasingly resembled other global giants, albeit with much greater flexibility, thanks to its status as a holding company that articulates countries and companies of different types and precedence, both for economic and security reasons. That is why they even changed their original name from the Sinaloa Cartel to the Federation.[31] Today, the Sinaloa Cartel is, rather, a network of networks-type organization, which transcends its original spatial anchorage in the Mexican state of Sinaloa in order to, first, manage a larger territory in Mexico; second, control the Pacific route to the United States; and, third, insert itself in the most dynamic region of the world economy: the Asia-Pacific Basin. That is why, nowadays, this organization is also known as the Pacific Cartel.

To be sure, these changes come hand in hand with the new economy; however, they are also related to the impact of Plan Colombia, the star project of the war on drugs' policy designed by the United States, which had a budget of around $10 billion from US aid, and a similar additional amount for covert activities, as we now know thanks to the *Washington Post* (cited in *El Mundo* 2013).[32]

This initiative took off at the beginning of the twentieth century and followed the typical postulates of targeted security and anti-narcotics policies, promoted by international development aid organizations, be they multilateral or bilateral. Targeted policies are strategic actions that can be directed at social subgroups (secondary or tertiary prevention), a criminal type (such as drug trafficking), or a territory (region, area). In general, practice has shown that targeting tends to sustain heterogeneity and increase, in the short and medium terms, the dynamics, flexibility, and degrees of criminal violence, within a criminal integration framework that tends to fragment society, break social ties, and stigmatize populations. It also tends to deepen the inter-delinquency logic (as a criminal system) and deny the meaning of the "place effect" as the space where crime exists: the local articulated to a global organizational logic.

Plan Colombia generated some visible effects. On the one hand, in Colombia, there are the three most publicized issues of the supposed efficiency and goodness of the proposal: the contraction of drug cultivation areas – although it is also worth mentioning that this generated an increase in productivity; the significant reduction of some indicators of violence such as homicides, kidnappings, and related crimes; and, finally, it cannot be ignored that the internal blows in Colombia, product of police and military repression, typical of the war on drugs, also caused the disappearance of the large territorial cartels (Cali and Medellín) along with the erosion of strong and personalized leaderships (Pablo Escobar, Rodríguez Gacha). This also led to the emergence of smaller cartels or criminal gangs (Bacrim) that are more functional to the new context of the global drug market.

Illegal Markets 237

In addition, there are some impacts that are not widely discussed, such as the environmental costs and the violation of human rights caused by the chemical eradication of drugs in the geographical areas where these are cultivated, to the point that environmental pollution has unleashed a humanitarian crisis in those places.

There have also been forced displacements of civilian population by armed actors, whether the Autodefensas Unidas de Colombia (AUC) or other paramilitary groups, law enforcement agencies, and irregular armies. The Internal Displacement Monitoring Centre (IDMC) estimated that between 4.9 and 5.9 million Colombians were displaced by violence, making Colombia the country with the highest incidence of internally displaced population in the world. Mexico, in recent times, is also suffering from the same circumstances.

On the other hand, additional, outward, impacts must also be considered. They regard not only the increase in related crimes, or the rise in the levels of violence, but also the re-articulation of illegal markets in general. In order to understand these consequences, it is necessary to consider two expressions: the so-called "balloon effect," which occurs when the policies manage to contain the phenomenon they wish to control in the sites where they are implemented, yet they generate, in turn, a bulge in the surrounding space; and the "flea effect," in which the implementation of a policy in one place causes the problem to "leap" to another space (new routes), another time (another day or another hour), or other activities (from robbery to contract murder).

Both the balloon effect and the flea effect result from targeted policies. However, they differ in a fundamental aspect: while the first one is a direct product of the articulation between the space of policy implementation and that of influence, the latter represents, rather, a seemingly unrelated leap from one crime to another, from one space to another, and from one time to another. In any case, both effects tend to render criminal activities highly dynamic and flexible, while also evidencing the opposite side; namely, that public policies are characterized by high rigidity and no universalization.

In the case of focalized anti-drug policies, which are the central foundation of the "war on drugs," they were first directed toward the production sphere, mainly located in the Andean countries (Plan Colombia) and, later on, toward the sphere of the circulation-route phases, when the problem spilled over into Mexico and Central America (Plan Mérida). This policy achieved very little in the sites of demand or consumption (U.S., Europe), because the strategy was to attack production. It is due to this policy that today there is an increasing globalization of drug consumption with emphasis on Latin America, where Brazil is positioned as the second country of cocaine consumption and the first of crack use. Additionally, the pressure on cultivation areas led to the displacement of cocaine production in Colombia toward Venezuela, Bolivia, Peru, and

238   *Fernando Carrión Mena*

Brazil, as well as to the relocation of processing laboratories to the most important routes or directly to consumption sites.

Due to the balloon effect, Plan Colombia brought about the articulation of the different phases of narcotics production (cultivation, processing, routes, consumption) through a set of actors (gangs, cartels, or mafias) controlled – for the time being – by the Mexican cartels (Sinaloa, the Gulf). In this case, the atomization of the large Colombian cartels was highly functional to the world-wide restructuring of the sector, since Mexican cartels knew how to position themselves within an international organization supported by a network of networks, an important division of labor between the different nodes spread throughout the globe. This integration increased the narcotics' productivity level, expanded the diversified supply of different types of drugs and established important links with other types of crime (arms, human trafficking) and other markets (legal, informal). In other words, from the flea effect, that leaps to another place or another product, to the balloon effect, which generates the complete readjustment of the narcotics sector at the regional, and even at the global level, several sectors of illegality were linked (narcotics, human trafficking, arms, precursors), and were connected to different territories, where production, circulation, and consumption of narcotics takes place.

Hence, nowadays there are high-tech cocaine processing laboratories located closer to the routes and, above all, to the sites of demand, modifying and pluralizing the destinations of consumption. In this way, competitiveness has improved, thanks to technology and the reduction of transportation costs of precursor chemicals. Today there are fixed laboratories, on different scales, as well as mobile laboratories, which can process high quality cocaine at a moderate cost, moving around previously defined territories. In short, these are suitable vehicles for mobile production in any place deemed convenient.

If years ago, the Colombian cartels used to export cocaine – which had some added value – today, they export the raw materials to later add value in the places closest to the demand. In this way, the region enters the usual economic logic of providing commodities or raw materials, so that the more developed countries industrialize production and achieve greater capital accumulation.

Two additional situations must be considered: crack and base paste, which are the residues of the production process, are aimed at the consumption of the poorest population and countries of the region, while the best quality products are aimed at high-income places. Moreover, when cocaine arrives in Europe or the United States, a yield of more than four times the initial amount can be obtained through processing it in laboratories.

Before the implementation of Plan Colombia, the Colombian cartels were the large, organized structures that controlled all phases of the cocaine process (production, processing, commercialization trafficking) because the production phase was the organizing axis of the entire process. This is why the Colombian cartels were territorial in origin, as the Medellín Cartel and the Cali Cartel, among others, prove. Additionally, they controlled the routes and the entry to the largest market in the world: the United States, through Florida. Thus, these cartels became both the "central command" and the "functional nucleus" of the whole process and, therefore, the direct beneficiaries of the drug-trafficking business. Today, this situation has changed: those who obtain the greatest benefits are those actors closest to the places of consumption – within the value chain – and who control a greater share within the holding (central command).

However, since the implementation of Plan Colombia, a much more complex structure has taken shape, where the Colombian cartels and their productive-territorial base lost the central articulating role they used to have, forcing them to reinvent themselves, at a time when Mexican cartels had already begun to control the business from the new routes and consumer markets they operated. In other words, it is no longer the production of cocaine that determines the price of the product, but the cost of risk and transportation that comes from the traffic and the characteristics of the demand (micro-trafficking).

In this context, the entry routes into the United States, the country with the largest demand, are relocated: from Florida, which is managed by the Colombian territorial-productive cartels, to the Mexico-United States border, dominated by the Mexican cartels. This entails, in turn, a rearticulation of the Andean production zones (Colombia, Peru, and Bolivia) with the strategic locations along the routes (Central America, Mexico), toward the sites of higher demand (United States).[33] This alliance exponentially boosts the Federation, the Pacific Cartel or the Sinaloa Cartel, thanks to the control it is beginning to exert over the multi-destination corridors for products such as drugs, chemical precursors, arms, migrants, and contraband, among others. This is also the case, because the economic and organizational base of the Mexican cartels, allied to the Colombian and other countries' criminal gangs, is beginning to push its integration into the Asia-Pacific Basin market, as the most dynamic region in the world economy.

Today, the Sinaloa Cartel is one of the richest and largest economic groups in the world; even *Forbes Magazine* once listed its main boss, "El Chapo" Guzmán, as one of the wealthiest men on the planet (Sevilla 2015). Most importantly, according to *The Economist*, this "global federation" manages more than 3,500 companies in about 50 countries located on four continents: the United States and Canada in North America; Spain, Italy, Germany, and Russia in Europe; China, Japan, and five more countries in Asia; several countries in Africa, and practically every country in Latin America (Reveles 2010).[34]

240 *Fernando Carrión Mena*

This expansion process is based on the reconstitution of the cartels through alliances or conquests that lead to oligopolistic concentration. Thus, for example, the Beltrán Leyva brothers, partners of both the Zetas and the Gulf cartels, submit to the Federation. La Familia Michoacana, in turn, has reinvented itself in the Knights Templar Cartel becoming the third most powerful Mexican cartel. Something similar happened in the Colombian context, where the Calle Serna brothers, the Tres Comba, formerly members of the Rastrojos, surrendered to justice, thus leaving the organization in a weak condition, which made it possible for it to be absorbed by the Urabeños. These latter also sought the link with the Pacific Basin, articulated to the Federation, and, thereby, entry into the great world markets. The recomposition of these Mexican and Colombian groups follows the trend to globalize, as is the case with the Calabrian N'drangheta, which carries out activities in 32 countries around the world, including 8 in South America, 14 in Europe, 4 in Africa, in the United States, and in Canada (Forgione 2010).

It is necessary to consider examples of autonomously born targeted policies that could be a positive factor in radiating the virtuous qualities of a new policy and not the perverse effects of the old one. One such policy is the legalization of marijuana in Uruguay and in the US states of Colorado and Washington, which have recognized these changes as a starting point for building a new anti-drug policy, even over the OAS proposal to "begin to discuss" the issue (OAS 2013) or the policies of the International Narcotics Control Board (INCB) and the United Nations Office on Drugs and Crime (UNODC). These latter are, in fact, held hostage by the US "war on drugs"-policy, designed more than 40 years ago, with negative and regressive results.

It is this global territory within which these new criminal organizations operate. In Latin America, such organizations have two strategic and privileged places: cities and borders, with border-cities' being the most privileged of them all.

The Borders

Borders are key places in the process, insofar as they become nodes or global platforms for integration and projection of illegal economies. In the case of borders, the central logic stems from complementary asymmetries; this means that the differences between neighboring states allow for the integration of illegal activities (contraband) and the separation of the legal ones.

In that perspective, two elements are key: first, border economies grow because the separation between states facilitates crime and slows down the legal world; and, second, because with the restructuring of the global economy, national borders have become a global border

Illegal Markets 241

system, in which, for instance, the Mexico-Guatemala border is closely linked to the México-US border, since weapons produced in distant places, or drugs destined for distant sites of demand can pass through them.

Furthermore, in this context, a change in the key social subject of the process takes place: the classic smuggler (organized crime), typically, a local merchant who takes advantage of the differences in exchange rates, prices, and products, to introduce merchandise from one country to another without respecting local legislation (taxes, quotas), gives way to the global trafficker (global network), typical of the logic of organization based on a global holding company that welcomes local border groups (outsourcing).[35]

In Latin America, it is evident that the integration-separation of borders takes shape from bi- or trinational urban systems, adopting the form of a zipper, as in the case of the United States-Mexico border cities. This latter interurban system is composed of 22 intermediate cities, 11 on each side, where the Ciudad Juárez-El Paso binomial stands out, operating in the manner of a metropolis, where the dividing line merely indicates where Ciudad Juárez ends, and El Paso begins. Nonetheless, each of this urban units' constitutive parts is different, so much so, that Ciudad Juárez has a rate of 148 homicides per 100,000 inhabitants, while El Paso's homicide rate is less than one per 100,000 inhabitants.

There are also borders where three states coincide through their respective cities. A conspicuous case is that of the Triple Frontier formed by Foz do Iguaçu in Brazil, Ciudad del Este in Paraguay, and Puerto Iguazú in Argentina. The only thing that separates these three cities is the Paraná River, whereas they are bound by illegal economic dynamics: drugs, smuggling, arms, and stolen products.

Another interesting border is that along four countries with an urban base composed of four cities: Manaus in Brazil, Iquitos in Peru, Leticia in Colombia, and Sucumbíos in Ecuador. Unlike the previous example, these four cities form a multinational urban system, which is born from the river and has become the material basis of local integration. Brazil's search for the Pacific allows us to think of a common future for the four cities, due to the Manaus-Manta highway, but also to the need to control the flow of narcotics into Brazil, today, the second largest consumer of cocaine in the world.

With the worldwide expansion of the new economy, cities form a territoriality constituted by a global network that unfolds throughout the planet. Within this network, each city functions as a center of coordination, control, and services of the world capital (Sassen 1991, 2–3). This implies that each one of them positions itself according to the conditions that it offers for capital optimization and the security of illegal markets. At present, the most attractive region is undoubtedly the Asia-Pacific Basin, where legal and illegal capital is jointly directed.

242 *Fernando Carrión Mena*

The economic sectors where this capital tends to concentrate vary greatly, depending on the society in question, although most of them are urban based. For example, the real estate sector is an economic activity where such capital has high incidence. At present, the largest cities in Latin America exhibit a significant growth in this sector that is alternatively depicted as a bubble, an oversupply, or a real estate boom that is difficult to explain.[36] The commercial, automotive, and tourism sectors are also attractive for laundering assets from illegal economies.

The Cities

Cities and business are strongly linked. Cities produce wealth, attract foreign investment, and concentrate masses of consumers. In markets with a high presence of illegality, such as those we have discussed in this chapter, it is not difficult for this money to be incorporated into the urban economy, both formal and informal.

As an example, we can point out three highly striking cases, where these illegal economies are promoted in the cities: First, in the area of informal trade, located in certain typical places of our cities, we must highlight, for example, La Merced in Mexico City, Polvos Azules in Lima (3,200 vendors), or Las Bahías in Guayaquil. The case of the San Andresitos, in Bogotá, is very revealing: In 2004, over $2.5 billion were traded there. These are places where informality and illegality meet, as both smuggled and stolen goods are sold there under conditions typical of informality: no rent payment, taxes, or fees.

A second example are the drugs that circulate in Brazil's domestic market, which are administered and controlled by the *comandos*, criminal structures that operate from detention centers (Garzón 2008). One of the most emblematic cases is that of the First Command of the Capital (PCC), which, from the prison of São Paulo, manages the drug trade for the inmates themselves, as well as in the *biqueiras* (drug-selling points). In response to a 2006 attempt at inmate relocation, the PCC organized, from the prison, the shutdown of São Paulo, the largest city in Latin America, resulting in the death of around 80 people, the burning of at least 30 buses, and widespread looting.[37] Prisons in Latin America have become the most violent places in society and the node from which an important segment of the illegal markets is organized.

In turn, the *jogo do bicho* is a kind of popular lottery played with animal symbols, rather than numbers, that emerged as a funding mechanism for the Rio de Janeiro Zoo in 1892. It soon became popular, and now, more than a century later, it is controlled by illegal organizations known as *bicheiros*. These groups' popularity grew thanks to their deep social links, which stem from their role as of samba schools' sponsors and other philanthropic activities. This allowed them to expand the lottery market and, above all, to diversify their economic activities with the trafficking of drugs, arms, the promotion of parapolice militias and slot machines, among others. Today the *bicheiros* is a criminal organization that operates in 25 of Brazil's 26 states.

An interesting case of outsourcing are the so-called "collection offices," which were originally born in Medellín and were promoted by Pablo Escobar. The initial objective was to have a semi-autonomous body of the Medellín cartel to provide services in certain "dirty" tasks of the organization, without its structures being violated, its image deteriorated, or its legitimacy eroded. The members of this body were demobilized soldiers, paramilitaries, or members of the drug trade, who, until the 1990s, worked exclusively for the Medellín Cartel; however, they later became independent and began to provide services to the highest bidder, thus succeeding at expanding their activities throughout Colombia, and even reaching Mexico, Guatemala, Brazil, and Spain.[38]

The variety of services these groups provide is very broad, ranging from the collection of all kinds of debts (monetary, settling of accounts), kidnapping of people to later sell them, guaranteeing the routes of the various traffics, extortion, murder (hitmen), burning buses, setting fire to shops or houses, distributing drugs, to propaganda distribution. Each of these services causes a negotiated fee that is the basis for a rapid and copious accumulation of capital.

Generally speaking, in these cases of penetration into informality (fairs, markets, and *jogo de bicho*) and the development of an outsourcing scheme within the general structure of drug trafficking (collection offices), there is rapid capital turnover, high profitability, and total liquidity. In all three examples, there is great capacity for criminal groups to generate employment and, therefore,[39] to legitimize themselves, as well as strong links with the global systems of illegality. This clearly demonstrates that illegal economies penetrate both formal and informal markets.

In other words, illegal markets prosper through their links with other segments of the market (informal and legal). To this end, they engage with protection services, mechanisms of corruption, extortion and intimidation, the provision of minimum logistics, the development of activities that give them legitimacy in the eyes of the population (employment, housing, carnival, football), and the "clearing of the road" (social cleansing). All these actions are illegal and many of them lead to violence.

The rise of commercial illegalities and the restructuring of the latter's productive architecture generate a set of related crimes, that give rise to violence: the new cybercrime, contract killings, kidnappings, the strong dispute of markets, human rights violations, and the application of hardline policies. As a result, Latin America's homicide rate has doubled in 20 years and, what is more serious, the levels of violence have increased. Thus, for instance, in Honduras 62%, in Colombia 47%, and in Ecuador 17% of the registered homicides are the result of contract killings. If the

244 *Fernando Carrión Mena*

trend continues, contract killing will soon become the main cause of violent death in the region.

Moreover, not only is there an increase in the number of homicides, but also – according to 2010 *Latinobarómetro* – the demands for citizen security have increased at a greater rate: in 2000, they were in fourth place; in 2005, they moved up to second place; by 2010, citizen security was solidly positioned as the first demand of Latin American society (Carrión 2012).

Illegal markets are like King Midas: where illicit activities reach, the economy grows to a threshold, and its sustainability is achieved thanks to violence. Mexico lost more than 110,000 people during the six-year term of Felipe Calderón's government (2006–2012), due to its policy of war on drugs. This policy was imported from Colombia, although it was originally conceived in the United States. Fear and insecurity have become the main imageries of Latin American cities (Silva 2003), and security, the primary demand of the population.

Conclusions

Currently, illegal economies generate related crimes and violence; yet criminal actions are undertaken in an organized manner and with an international scope. A key space for this expansion is directly related to borders, as spaces that separate-integrate two or more states under the dynamics of a global border system. Today, many of these border regions are experiencing a paradox: an economic boom that attracts population and generates growing levels of violence, both of which are higher than national averages.

Since the beginning of the twenty-first century, border regions have become strategic locations for the world's most profitable illegal markets, such as narcotics, arms, human trafficking, chemical precursors, and smuggling, among others. From this moment on, borders have become "places" that perform functions like those of an integration node, where products (narcotics), supplies (chemical precursors), or services (health, sanctuary) that come/go, from/to different parts of the planet, enter and leave in real time. The place becomes a force field where social agents, institutional actors, and things exist and relate to other borders (system).

Today, borders are not only bi- or multinational. They are global borders that integrate illegal markets thanks to three key factors: their strategic position in the new logic of illegal economies, institutional fragility, and their distance from the centers of power. Because of the amounts of money they manage and the global logic of their actors, it can be stated that illegal economies modify the dynamics of the world economic system, to such an extent that the twenty-first century can be considered that of the mafia networks of the economy, because of their impact on states (lead, silver), legal markets (investment), and informal economies (mimesis). This situation has rendered criminal networks "more international, wealthier, and more politically influential than ever before" (Naím 2005, 13).

The neoliberal criticism of the state prevented us from seeing the consolidation of an ever-stronger mafia economy. It limited itself to looking at corruption and not at what was happening in the formal markets. Nor did it make a self-critique of the role that the process of privatization and economic liberalization played in the growth of this new economy and its related crimes.

Illegal groups generated a global presence by following the logic of dispersion of activities throughout the territory and the integration in the cyberspace network. They prospered in territories where there were weak public and private institutions and good services (logistics, connectivity). On the basis of this general dynamics, the Latin American territory became integrated as a provider of commodities, services, and products in demand on a global scale.

The best policy to confront these networks is not the use of the police, no matter how internationalized it might be, but rather we should think about fundamental elements: on the one hand, integration to generate, for example, a decrease in the complementary asymmetries between countries, to promote legal penal harmonization in regional blocks, and, on the other hand, an economic policy that eliminates tax havens, improves income distribution, decentralizes taxes (border tariffs), and acts on all phases of the drug production cycles.

Notes

1. Speech by the President of Colombia to his peers at the International Conference in Support of the Central American Security Strategy, June 2011.
2. The presence of money from illegal economies for the financing of electoral campaigns has been detected in several countries in the region, as well as the presentation of candidates from criminal ranks.
3. According to James Petras (2001), international banks receive no less than $500 billion a year from illicit markets.
4. Eric Berman, from Small Arms Survey (2012), states that the arms trade has doubled in the last four years and that business is now over $10 billion a year.
5. Mexico is the first country in Latin America, and the fourth in the world, after Russia, China, and India, in terms of contraband and counterfeiting. According to the Organization for Economic Cooperation and Development (OECD), during 2005 smuggling in border areas amounted to, approximately, $200 billion (quoted in Posada García 2007).
6. "Slavery is just one facet of a global trade in human beings across borders that affects at least 4 million people every year, most of them women and children, for an estimated value of $7 to $10 billion" (Naím 2005, 14).
7. The OECD created the New Economy Forum to discuss this new economy's scope and characteristics with leading economists and institutions from around the world.

246 *Fernando Carrión Mena*

8. The private security sector offers a range of no less than 50 types of services, among which are arms, insurance, intelligence, body guarding, transfer of valuables, alarms, protection, armoring, risk management, ransom negotiation, and technology.
9. According to Frigo (2003): "In Latin America, private security is a rapidly expanding economic sector [...] In the last 15 years, private security has gained a place of relevance both in the world and in our region [...] The world market for private security was worth $85 billion last year, with an average annual growth rate of 7 to 8% [...] In Latin America, growth is estimated at 11%."
10. In addition to the 1.6 million formally registered guards, there may be an additional 2 million informal ones. In Latin America, therefore, there would be about 4 million people working in the private security sector, a number that is growing by 6% to 8% every year" (Frigo 2003).
11. The offshore logic refers to the extraterritoriality of investments, company incorporation, and the opening of bank accounts, among others, thanks to the existence of advantages, such as tax benefits, light bureaucratic burdens, privacy, and banking secrecy, over those conditions available at the place of habitual residence.
12. The OECD estimates the amount of money mobilized by tax havens at $7 billion, of which $1.6 billion comes from illegal markets. There are about 74 tax havens in the world.
13. The so-called "Police Reform" took place in this context, following the systematic efforts at social delegitimization that was undertaken against police corps all around Latin America. This reform had two, exogenously produced, main ingredients: privatization and militarization.
14. "Criminal populism" made a strong entrance with profound reforms to the criminal codes, which expanded the criminal types, substantially increased the penalties, and lowered the age of criminal responsibility, among other things. In addition, the codes of criminal procedure were substantially modified through the inclusion of the oral system or the councils of the judiciary.
15. Prison privatization spread throughout the region as a failed attempt to resolve the prison crisis, which stemmed mainly from criminal policies and the war on drugs.
16. "The severity of current drug laws has contributed significantly to increasing incarceration rates and prison overcrowding in the countries studied. In seven of these countries for which it was possible to obtain data for the 15 years from 1992 to 2007, the incarceration rate increased, on average, more than 100%. With some differences among countries, incarceration for drug offenses shows an upward trend in every case" (Transnational Institute and WOLA 2010, 5).
17. Although this was a strength for the new communication technologies and social networks, today it is threatened by the security policies implemented by the great powers, especially the United States through the NSA and the large world operators (Facebook, Google), who have complied with them.
18. In the narcotics sector, this economic figure is widely used to carry out specialized tasks in certain sections of the routes, in processing (laboratories) and in the marketing phase (known as micro-trafficking), as it seeks familiarity with the location, efficiency, and, above all, risk reduction.
19. This entails granting economic rights under a general model or logic, so that the administration of certain isolated activities is autonomous, but with rigid general parameters established by the holding company.

Illegal Markets 247

20. This refers to the conglomeration of companies that makes it possible to improve economies of scale, divide labor to improve productivity, integrate dispersed actors, break with the rigid hierarchy and – in this particular case – link legal and illegal markets.
21. It is not by chance, for example, that the Urabeños or the Colombian Rastrojos currently have links and international relations with Italian, Mexican, Ukrainian, Russian, and Spanish criminal groups.
22. Article 2a of the United Nations Palermo Convention defines organized crime as "a structured group of three or more persons, existing for a period of time and acting in concert with the aim of committing one or more serious crimes or offences established in accordance with this Convention, in order to obtain, directly or indirectly, a financial or other material benefit" (UNO 2004, 5). This article covers three characteristics: number of persons (minimum three), stability of actions (certain time), and a (financial) benefit. Today, this definition falls short; there is an internal and an external division of labor, internationalization is clear, the articulation to the legal economy is a requirement, and the amount of money involved is enormous.
23. According to Braslavsky (n.d.), "estimates indicate that some $600 billion is laundered from illicit businesses worldwide every year."
24. In Mexico "drug cartels have an estimated income of $37 billion per year" (Gratius 2012, 7).
25. "The $10 billion that is laundered in Chile every year is equivalent to 10% of the total in Latin America and a little less than a year of our exports" (Comisión de Hacienda del Senado, Chile).
26. ECLAC estimated that in 2011, Latin America received an external investment of $137 billion.
27. Alejandro Gaviria and Daniel Mejía (2011) state that only 2.6% of the total value of Colombian cocaine sold on the streets of the United States returns to the former country.
28. Editors' note: *Narcocorridos* can be translated as "drug ballads" and are comparable to "mafioso raps."
29. "The results of the October 2011 elections show that the political structures linked to the Bacrim, parapolitics and drug trafficking, [...] won the governorship in ten out of [Colombia's] thirty-two departments, as well as numerous mayoralties" (Ávila and Velasco 2012).
30. According to the report of the Andean Parliament's Commission on Foreign Affairs (Comisión de Asuntos Exteriores del Parlamento Andino 2012), 110 new industrial psychoactive substances were identified in Europe between 1997 and 2009.
31. A federation is an institutionalized grouping of relatively autonomous entities.
32. According to *El Mundo*'s report on the *Washington Post* article, this secret program in Colombia "is one of the largest undercover intelligence actions developed by the United States since the September 11, 2001 attacks. The aid to combat the guerrillas had an additional budget of about $9 billion from U.S. military aid under Plan Colombia, which began in 2000."
33. It should be noted that the processing laboratories were also moved to Peru from Ecuador and Venezuela. In Bolivia and Brazil, cultivation and consumption became more widespread.
34. "The Pacific Cartel is today a true confederation, a perfectly globalized criminal organization that operates with a pyramidal structure of a prosperous enterprise" (Reveles 2010, 42).

248 *Fernando Carrión Mena*

35. In some places, border economies are experiencing an economic boom, which stems, precisely, from the weight that illegal markets have acquired. This gives rise to a paradox: the highest homicide rates and largest migration balances in Latin America are found in these territories. In other words, there would appear to be a fatal attraction to these zones of violence.
36. Probably the most striking case is that of Panama, where the free circulation of the dollar, and the tax and financial incentives – given its status as a tax haven – are very attractive for the purchase and sale of real estate. The volume of construction is clearly larger than the local market's demand.
37. The same thing happened in the Envigado prison where Pablo Escobar, or "Don Berna" was held. It continues to happen in the prisons of Mexico, Colombia, Venezuela, Guatemala, Chile and Ecuador, among many others.
38. The Zetas emerged in Mexico in the late 1990s as an armed group directly linked to the Gulf Cartel. Its membership is drawn from the elite groups of the Mexican and Guatemalan armies. Eventually, they separated from the Gulf Cartel because, with the information they had, they believed they could form their own organization. However, they did not control the ports or direct routes to the United States; nor did they have the contacts that concentrated the demand for the drug. These limitations forced them to carry out violent acts to finance themselves. This example shows the limits of the model and the reason why, in Colombia, the collection offices kept to their own.
39. According to Forgione (2010), between the legal, illegal, and submerged sectors, the mafia industry employed 27% of the working population in Calabria, 12% in Campania and 10% in Sicily; practically, almost 10% of the working population in the main regions of the Italian Mezzogiorno.

References

Ávila, Ariel and Bernardo Pérez. 2011 *Mercados de criminalidad en Bogotá.* Bogotá: Arco Iris.

Ávila, Ariel and Juan David Velasco. 2012. "Injerencia política de los grupos armados ilegales." In *Y refundaron la Patria... de cómo mafiosos y políticos reconfiguran el Estado colombiano,* edited by Claudia López Hernández, 79–214.Bogotá: Random House Mondadori.

Braslavsky, Guido. n.d. "Qué son los paraísos fiscales. Los paraísos fiscales ocultan un tercio de todos los fondos del sistema bancario mundial." Accessed 27 June 2013. http://www.gestiondelriesgo.com/artic/discipl/disc_4011.htm

Carrión, Fernando. 2012. "¿Prevenir o gobernar la violencia?" In *Ciudades, una ecuación imposible,* edited by Mireia Belil, Jordi Borja and Marcelo Corti, 209–228. Buenos Aires: Café de las Ciudades.

———— 2013. *Asimetrías en la frontera Ecuador-Colombia, entre la complementariedad y el sistema.* Quito: FLACSO-IDRC.

Castells Manuel. 2001. *La era de la información: economía, sociedad y cultura.* México: Siglo XXI Editores.

Christian Aid Report. 2009. "False Profits: Robbing the Poor to Keep the Rich Tax-Free." Accessed 13 May 2012. www.christianaid.org.uk/images/false-profits.pdf

Comisión de Asuntos Exteriores del Parlamento Andino. 2012. *Informe Europa y América Latina: la lucha contra el narcotráfico.* Accessed 21 August 2012. www.europarl.europa.eu/activities/committees/studies.do?language=EN

Corporación Latinobarómetro. 2007. *Informe Latinobarómetro 2007.* Accessed 25 September 2013. www.latinobarometro.org

Illegal Markets 249

—— 2010. *Informe Latinobarómetro 2010*. Accessed 27 September 201.3 www.latinobarometro.org

El Mundo. 2013. "Ayuda de la CIA fue adicional al Plan Colombia: Washington Post." 23 December 2013.

Forgione, Francesco. 2010. *Mafia export*. Barcelona: Anagrama.

Frigo, Edgardo. 2003. "Hacia un modelo de seguridad privada en América Latina." Paper presented at Primer Congreso Latinoamericano de Seguridad Privada, Bogotá, September 24–26. Accessed 18 November 2012 http://www.segured.com/Index.php?od=2&article=S26

Garzón, Juan Carlos. 2008. *Mafia & Co*. Bogotá: Planeta.

Gaviria, Alejandro and Daniel Mejía. 2011. *Políticas antidroga en Colombia: éxitos, fracasos y extravíos*. Bogotá: Universidad de los Andes.

Gratius, Susanne. 2012. *Europe and Latin America: Combating Drugs and Drug Trafficking*. Brussels: European Union.

Manwaring, Max. 2009. *A 'New' Dynamic in the Western Hemisphere Security Environment: The Mexican Zetas and Other Private Armies*. Carlile, PA: Strategic Studies Institute.

Naím, Moisés. 2005. *Illicit: How Smugglers, Traffickers, and Copycats Are Hijacking the Global Economy*. United States: Doubleday

Organization of American States (OAS). 2013. *The drug problem in the Americas*. Accessed 12 January 2014. http://fileserver.idpc.net/library/OAS-Analytical%20Report_The-drug-problem-in-the-Americas.pdf

Petras James. 2001. "Estados Unidos, un imperio financiado con dinero sucio." http://www.voltairenet.org/article120085.html

Petrella, Laura and Franz Vanderschueren. 2003. "Ciudad y violencia." In *La ciudad inclusiva*, compiled by Marcello Balbo, Ricardo Jordán and Daniela Simioni, 215–236. Santiago: CEPAL.

Portes, Alejandro y William Haller. 2004. *La economía informal*. Santiago: CEPAL.

Posada García, Miriam. 2007. "México, cuarto lugar mundial en venta de piratería y contrabando." *La Jornada*, 4 July 2007.

Reveles, José. 2010. *El cartel incómodo: el fin de los Beltrán Leyva y la hegemonía del Chapo Guzmán*. México: Grijalbo.

Sassen, Saskia. 1991. *The Global City. New York, London, Tokyo*. New Jersey: Princeton University Press.

Sevilla, Ramón. 2015. "Forbes encumbró en su lista a El Chapo." *24 Horas*, July 15. Accessed on 17 July 2012. http://www.24-horas.mx/forbes-encumbro-en-su-lista-a-el-chapo/

Silva, Armando. 2003. *Bogotá imaginada*. Universidad Nacional de Colombia: Convenio Andrés Bello. Editora Aguilar, Altea, Tauros, Alfaguara.

Small Arms Survey. 2012. *Small Arms Survey 2012: Moving Targets*. Cambridge: Cambridge University Press.

Transnational Institute and WOLA. 2010. *Systems Overload. Drug laws and prisons in Latin America*. Amsterdam and Washington: WOLA.

United Nations Organization (UNO). 2004. *United Nations Convention Against Transnational Organized Crime and the Protocols Thereto. Vienna*. New York: United Nations.

10 Cross-Border Urban Complexes

The Urban Morphology of a Global Structure

Fernando Carrión Mena and
Víctor Llugsha Guijarro

Cities are places of great heterogeneity amid large population concentrations. This diversity brings with it a series of elements that render the use of space particularly complex. Traditionally, the limits of the city were linked to the functional characteristics of production: the notions of the medieval city, the industrial city, and the garden city account for this. Nowadays, economic development and the advance of information technologies make it possible to surpass the traditional limit, moving from the segregation of space by activities and people, to a networked city (Carrión 2014), where flows substitute places (Castells 1997) and distances shrink. In this context, cities find the opportunity to link with a national environment, with options for global articulation to other cities in the world. This is the case of border cities, which, due to their geographical proximity, are directly connected to their counterparts on the other side of the demarcation line.

Cities with less than 500,000 inhabitants are very heterogeneous; they range from urban concentrations with rural characteristics, to agglomerations that have been able to develop an important economic fabric based on the exploitation of natural resources and their competitive advantages (UN-Habitat 2012, 26). In economic terms, small border cities appear to be more competitive, especially because of the dynamism that allows them to benefit from industrial investments, as is the case of cities located on economic corridors or at the periphery of conurbations (UN-Habitat 201, 39). As a result of globalization, cities have increased their international trade. The political, tax, and legal conditions that small and intermediate cities can generate in the process of competitiveness are, in this context, of great importance.

Border cities develop on the boundary (edge) of the nation, a space that is not usually conceived of from the point of view of integration. The borders' purpose of separation takes precedent over integration, an antagonistic element of the public space, which is, in turn, the articulator of the city. Border cities that work and live together in an interconnected way have managed to build, out of the symbolic sphere, common spaces that articulate diverse actions, turning from the limit to the border zone.

DOI: 10.4324/9781003204299-17

The present chapter takes as its starting point the analysis of urban growth in Latin America. In so doing, it emphasizes the role of border cities as economic and population attraction poles; as spaces that, due to their morphology, make it possible to configure a typology of agglomerations that are articulated in urban border complexes in the region, and that, due to their specific features, develop a specific type of violence, which responds to their dual character: urban and border. This discussion is complemented with an analysis of the development of public policies that refer to border areas in Latin America.

Urban Violence, Border Violence

One of the most evident changes in violence throughout history is the one relating to criminal geography, which arises from the special conditions of the social production of the space of violence, as well as from security policies (Carrión 1996). Hence, there are currently two places where these conditions are displayed in a privileged way: cities, due to the urbanization of violence; and borders, due to their conversion into an advantaged space for transnational crime, sustained by the weight that illegal economies have acquired.

Border cities maintain this double territorial condition, as they combine the two types of space, and because the urban system that we find there structures the cross-border region as a field of variable attraction forces (Carrión 2013, 23). In the last 20 years, the overall average of homicides in Latin America has doubled (Briceño-León 2007, 35), with both cities and borders displaying the highest rates (Carrión 2013). However, in border cities both types of space are concentrated: the urban space and the border condition, and they act simultaneously. This has led to higher homicide rates than national averages in most border cities.

This new reality is shaped by the historical leap that borders in Latin America are experiencing, as they move from the space of *places,* typical of binational contraband, to the territory of *flows,* induced by organized international trafficking (Castells 1997), which is the expression of global crime that operates through networks, organizations, and holdings. Thus, although border violence is localized, it has global repercussions.

Cross-Border Urban Complexes

Latin America encompasses 43 countries that are home to a population of 625 million, (CEPAL 2016). In 1950, 41% of the region's population was concentrated in cities; today, the urban population is over 80% and is estimated to reach 90% by 2050 (UN-Habitat 2012, 20). These figures point to a process of rapid and widespread urbanization, which has made Latin America the most urbanized region in the world (Bárcena 2001).

252 *Fernando Carrión Mena and Víctor Llugsha Guijarro*

However, the distribution of the population has not been balanced throughout the territory of the continent. Much to the contrary, urbanization has been concentrated, unequal, and exclusive, and has therefore led to a significant polarization: while 63 cities with more than one million inhabitants concentrate 41% of the population, the cities considered small – between 2,500 and 500,000 inhabitants – contain the remaining 49% (Arriagada 2000). In other words, Latin American urbanization has not spread homogeneously, so that accelerated urban growth has gone hand in hand with unsatisfied social demands. In addition to poverty, the region suffers from serious and persistent inequality: "There is a considerable deficit of employment and abundant labor informality, [...] inequality manifests itself in socially and spatially divided cities, despite the multiple opportunities for economic and social development offered by urbanization" (UN-Habitat 2012, 39).

Since the end of the twentieth century, there has been a major change in the pattern of urbanization in Latin America, consisting of: (a) the significant upsurge in the number of cities (over 16,500 in the region); (b) the population increase in cities; and (c) the outward territorial redirection of the population both toward the borders and as international migration flows (Lates 2001). These components have undoubtedly contributed to the faster growth rate that border cities now display, when compared to other cities in the same country and urban growth rates in the past. Historically, Latin America and the Caribbean have been characterized by the concentration of population in a few cities, "which generally also monopolize wealth, income, socio-economic and administrative functions, and, in most cases, political capital" (UN-Habitat 2012, 25). With the growth of the urban population, and the change in traditional destinations of rural-urban migration, urbanization tended to be widespread throughout the continent.[1] In the second half of the twentieth century, the cities, initially located on the Pacific or Atlantic coasts, began to spread more evenly throughout the countries' interior and, in many cases, to neighboring areas.

Cities cannot exist in isolation, so much so, that their origins are inextricably linked to the countryside (Ruiz and Delgado 2008). Nowadays, cities can only be understood in their interurban essence. This is evident in the case of cross-border regions, as the reason for their existence is the connection to the city on the other side, thus forming an urban system that operates under the logic of a "zipper." This logic is based on the dynamics of mirror cities: a city is born on one side and, simultaneously, another city is born on the other side of the border. In this way, systems of small but global cities are formed. These cities are, in turn, highly conflictive, and prone to displaying high rates of crime and violence.

A case in point is the United States-Mexico border. The cities on either side of this border act in relation to each other under the logic of a mirror.[2] However, due to the transformation of the figure of the smuggler

Cross-Border Urban Complexes   253

into that of the trafficker, this relationship moved from being exclusively binational to being global (Sassen 1991). In that context, the logic of the magnet (according to which territories attract each other as if they were magnetic fields) is what prefigures interurban integration.

This urban attraction faces, notwithstanding, the political, legal, and economic provisions derived from each of the country's make up, displaying themselves as asymmetries that are complemented by the condition of each side of the border. These complementary asymmetries are exploited on a different scale and become an ideal space for the emergence of illegal economies.

Urban systems rely on border economies and local powers, which give them international prominence, in a context where nation-states are losing weight to cities, both internationally and transnationally. The system of cities within emerging regions, such as borders, manages to mark out, articulate, and project an urban-regional subsystem with international insertion. The organization of this subsystem is produced, first, thanks to the logic of complementary asymmetries across borders and, second, to the conversion of borders into global platforms that generate interesting spaces of multinational integration, where cities and their governments acquire greater international significance.

The logic of complementary asymmetries existing across national borders is enhanced by three conditions that these regions currently fulfill: economic growth, attraction of population, and their condition of international platforms. Nonetheless, there is a negative counterpart at the borders: the high homicide rates linked to illegal markets. Despite this ambivalence, interesting spaces of multinational integration have emerged, where cities and their governments acquire a significant role. In Latin America, the most distinctive and significant urban border complexes can be typified as follows:

a) Bordering cities (nuclear): They are structured around the dividing line between countries. They are urban localities with an integrated (continuous) urban sprawl. These cities form an urban unit, albeit separated by the political-administrative demarcation line between different states. This creates a sort of supranational urban fragmentation or segregation. This is the case of cities that extend over more than one national territory, and can take one of the following shapes: *binuclear or binary cities,* structured between two countries (for example, Tulcán-Ipiales on the Colombian-Ecuadorian border or Tacna-Arica on the border between Peru and Chile); *trinuclear or trinary cities,* stemming from relations between three countries (Ciudad del Este-Foz do Iguaçu-Puerto de Iguazú, on the border between Paraguay, Brazil, and Argentina) and *metropolitan cities,* composed of a central city that articulates peripheral urban spaces, such as Ciudad Juárez-El Paso, on the Mexico-United States border.

b) Border cities (nuclear): They are located on different sides of the dividing line but are contiguous to urban border localities on the other side, which share traits that reflect each other (like mirrors), despite not having territorial continuity between them. In other words, they are cities that lack adjacent spaces, but are integrated by the common logic of the functioning of border regions (Puerto Asís in Colombia and Sucumbíos in Ecuador exemplify this modality).

c) Cross-border cities: They are structured in a single multinational region contained by the integration of the different borders of adjoining countries. In this case, binational or multinational urban systems are formed (for example, Manaus in Brazil, Leticia in Colombia, Iquitos in Peru, and Sucumbíos in Ecuador, where Ecuador and Brazil are not adjacent, yet are connected by a waterway).[3] In this type of complex, various forms of governance can be found, which are shaped over time and according to the each of the regions' particular conditions. Among them are the following:

- The *commonwealth of municipalities*, which consists of an agreement between two or more local governments for the joint administration of one or more competencies (services, infrastructure), without creating a new institutional framework. This is the case of solid waste and environmental management between the cities of Tulcán in Ecuador and Ipiales in Colombia, which was born, precisely, as diplomatic relations between the two countries had been severed. Similar cases exist between Ecuadorian and Peruvian cities, or between cities in Argentina and Chile and, to a larger extent, between border cities in Guatemala, Honduras, and El Salvador (Trifinio) (Quintero 2006).
- The *twinning*, which stems from the integration of different cities with common interests, in order to strengthen ties and promote joint projects. This is a mechanism for horizontal cooperation that allows successful policies to be transferred from one municipality to another. The most emblematic case is, probably, that of Manaus in Brazil, Iquitos in Peru, Leticia in Colombia, and Nueva Loja in Ecuador, for the development of international infrastructure and to address the issue of drug trafficking (Sierra 2013, 188).
- The *association*, an entity with legal status, formed by a group of municipal partners to pursue a common goal in a stable manner. For instance, in the association between municipalities that operates since the signing of the Peace Accords between Peru and Ecuador (1998), a rotation of the top management was established, and a legal status is being sought for the so-called Binational Association of Municipalities of Southern Ecuador and Northern Peru (ABIMSENOP). The case of the Trifinio

Region, where 45 border municipalities with 670,000 inhabitants in Guatemala, El Salvador, and Honduras pursue a Tri-National Border Development Plan (Organization of American States 1988) is also worth mentioning.

- The *metropolitan area*, consisting of an urban region with a central city with which other cities are articulated. The formation of metropolitan areas emerges from the logic of a mirror. For example, in the so-called Triple Frontier between Foz do Iguaçu (Brazil), Ciudad del Este (Paraguay), and Puerto Iguazú (Argentina).

These four cases of municipal integration show that the local sphere is highly flexible in dealing with integrated urban development, even in the context of international tensions, as occurred during the Ecuador-Peru conflict or the Ecuador-Colombia crisis and the ensuing severance of diplomatic relations.

Typology of Border Towns

To illustrate this typology of cities and local governments, we present the following significant cases:

Bordering Cities

Binuclear Bordering Cities

An example of a binuclear border city is Santana do Livramento-Rivera, located on the Brazil-Uruguay border, which is 1,068 kilometers long. Around this space, the cities on each side of the border structure a zipper-shaped system to form the border region. In this border area, there are two cities that form an urban unit with 185,957 inhabitants (Goulart et al. 2017): Santana do Livramento, located in Brazil, and Rivera, located in Uruguay. The two cities are separated only by an urban road that demarcates the national territories and the symbolic patriotic universes, while they constitute a unique and bilingual community.

Paradoxically, concern about local violence in these cities appears to be a justification for states, for investing in the defense of sovereignty, instead of investing in in citizen security, to strengthen the cities, their local governments, and the development of the border strip. Considering these cities as violent has led to the design of policies aimed at combating the diversity of criminal activities that take place there, such as contraband, cattle rustling, drugs, and arms trafficking, among others, that even impact the economies of large cities located elsewhere (Montevideo and São Paulo).

Santana do Livramento and Rivera form one of the main binational urban centers in the format of bordering cities, where the local

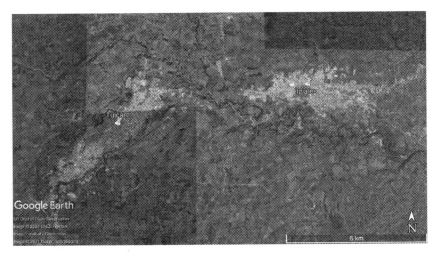

Figure 10.1 Binuclear City: Tulcán and Ipiales
Source: Google Earth (2021a)

population does not need a passport or other formalities to live, work, and move around that space, which is known as the "Peace Border." In fact, although the origin of these cities is linked to the interests of national defense, the needs of border populations promoted the construction of a border culture, which fostered the integration of the two cities. The only thing that separates them is a street, which marks, at the same time, the geographical boundary between the two countries.

As Figure 10.1 shows the cities of Tulcán in Ecuador and Ipiales in Colombia, constitute a conurbation with a very solid and expanding border economy, fueled by the contraband of gasoline and gas to Colombia, and textiles and technological goods to Ecuador, as well as migrant smuggling, arms and drugs trafficking, and the supply of services and goods to irregular groups. During the Colombian conflict (1990–2002), drug trafficking and common crime were the motor of the border economy. In this context, the cities of Ipiales and Tulcán constitute an interesting example of cooperation in adversity, translated into low relative homicide rates in the border region. In these cities, there is an intermunicipal association for the joint management of solid waste and the environment, which, as already mentioned, was created even as diplomatic relations between Ecuador and Peru were strained.

Cross-Border Binuclear Cities

Cúcuta and San Antonio, on the Colombia-Venezuela border, form a cross-border binuclear complex, concentrating around 700,000 inhabitants, to which San Antonio contributes only about 10% of the total population. Although they are not physically contiguous, the two cities function under a logic of complementarity, as if they were one.

Contraband is an important component of the economy of the border region, especially at this moment because of the exchange rate and the differences in economic policies between the two countries. In fact, due to the gasoline subsidy in Venezuela, the cost of this fuel is 60 times lower than in Colombia; in turn, the border free zone is used to supply Venezuela with all types of products. This zone also has a strong presence of drug traffickers, irregular groups, and the Colombian military. The homicide rate per 100,000 inhabitants in Cúcuta is 35 (Consejo Ciudadano para la Seguridad Pública y la Justicia Penal 2019), whereas San Antonio's is 3 (FUNDAREDES 2021).

Cross-Border Trinuclear Cities

An example of a trinuclear city is the one formed by Ciudad del Este, Foz do Iguaçu, and Puerto de Iguazú, in the triple border between Argentina, Brazil, and Paraguay (see Figure 10.2). In 1961 the joint population of the three cities was around 60,000 inhabitants; nowadays it is around 700,000 (Devia and Ortega 2019). This growth is the result of the construction of the Itaipu dam and the development of illegal markets that have been thriving in the region since the end of the twentieth century (Cardin 2013, 256). Illegal markets are the main form of sustenance of this trinuclear city, where the trafficking of drugs (cocaine,

Figure 10.2 Triple Frontier: Ciudad del Este, Foz do Iguaçu, and Puerto de Iguazú

Source: Google Earth (2021b)

marijuana) articulates the circulation of arms, ammunition, explosives, medicines, and counterfeit money, among other illicit flows.

Cross-Border Metropolitan Cities

The metropolitan agglomeration of Ciudad Juárez-El Paso is probably one of the most complex in the American continent and the one with the greatest potential, provided violence and illegality are brought under control. In terms of concentrated population, it is the largest border city in Latin America with about two million people (Fuentes and Peña 2017). In fact, although both cities have twinning agreements, Ciudad Juárez and El Paso constitute a single metropolitan space as shown in Figure 10.3.

In the early 2010s, the Mexican border of Ciudad Juárez came to be considered the most violent in the world (Ramos 2013, 170). In 2010, all Mexican border cities together had an average homicide rate of 96 per 100,000 inhabitants. By contrast, that same year in Ciudad Juárez, the homicide rate rose to 229 per 100,000 inhabitants, that is, ten times the national rate of 22.9. On the other hand, on the US border, the homicide rate was 3.6 per 100,000 inhabitants, and the national rate was 4.8. In the Ciudad Juárez-El Paso metropolitan area, the former is one of the most violent cities in Mexico, while El Paso is one of the most peaceful in the United States, because of the exploitation of complementary asymmetries. Due to the concentration of flows and actors that interact in this space, this is a global border, through which arms

Figure 10.3 Ciudad Juárez-El Paso Metropolitan City
Source: Google Earth (2021c)

and ammunition, as well as drugs and migrants from all over the world transit.

Cross-Border Urban Systems

Polarized Urban Systems

An example of cross-border cities that create an integrated urban system is the region conformed by Manaus in Brazil, Leticia in Colombia, Iquitos in Peru, and Sucumbíos in Ecuador, with a structuring axis in the Putumayo River (see Figure 10.4). The tetra-border is a little-known multinational cross-border region. Until now, the attention it has received has been mainly reduced to highlighting its negative conditions related to a low presence of state institutions, and the public sector in general, as well as a precarious social capital. Nonetheless, the region has a very strong gravitational mass of attraction linked to the Brazilian market, which allows it to constitute an integrated territory under the form of an urban system.

The Manta-Manaus road infrastructure is a multimodal corridor that seeks to link the port of Belem on Brazil's Atlantic coast with the port of Manta on Ecuador's Pacific coast, to boost trade between the two coasts of the South American subcontinent and Asia. Thus, their twinning allows the four cities to obtain advantages to face problems, such as drug trafficking, and, at the same time, to promote common

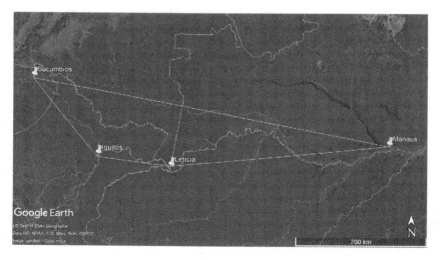

Figure 10.4 Manaus, Leticia, Iquitos, and Sucumbíos Border
Source: Google Earth (2021d)

initiatives of international character, such as developing the transcontinental transport axis.

Regional Urban System

The Peruvian-Ecuadorian urban axis, Huaquillas-Aguas Verdes, articulates the binational inter-municipal association of 45 municipalities constituted after the signing of the Peace Accords between the two countries in 1998. The association has benefited from significant resources from international development aid and has managed to strengthen relations both at the local and national levels, although there is now a growing economy nourished by Peru's new status as the world's leading cocaine producer. In these cities, contraband and drug trafficking are the structuring elements of local conflicts.

The other regional urban system that should be highlighted is Trifinio, formed by Esquipulas (Guatemala), Metapan (El Salvador), and Ocotepeque (Honduras) around the Montecristo Massif. The Trifinio region covers 7,584 square kilometers, has a population of over 670,000 (Comisión Trinacional del Plan Trifinio 2015), and is the object of a Tri-National Border Development Plan, a constitutive part of the Central American Integration System (SICA).

Urban Border Policies

Border policies such as Plan Colombia, Plan Ecuador, the Binational Development Plan for the Peru-Ecuador Border Region, among others mentioned in this book, present similar features that have been reproduced in the region and can be characterized along three general lines: (a) they are unilateral, and fail to take into account the cross-border reality; (b) they are homogeneous, because they do not distinguish the differences existing along the borders; and (c) they are conceived and executed from the centers of power, distant from the reality of the borders (Espinosa 2013, 32; Gómez 2013, 113).

Unilateralism tends to strengthen complementary asymmetries, because national policies designed by each country end up increasing the differences between them; for example – and especially – economic policies in the monetary (parity, exchange rate), tax (tariffs), international trade (trade balance), and financial (credits) fields. Economic policy tends to be more effective when it is implemented with a certain minimum of consensus among countries or, at least, with a certain degree of agreement in the regions or cross-border zones on certain sensitive issues, such as oil derivatives (management of subsidies on a regional scale) or tariffs, which should not only be a concurrent tax base between the local and the national, but also an element that reduces inequalities within states. Nevertheless, it is also important to stimulate public investment in these territories, with the aim of strengthening local institutions, promoting an alternative regional development to that of illegal markets, and reducing the weight of national and public security policies in benefit of citizen security.

The extreme case of unilateralism is represented by the construction of physical barriers or walls that further separate countries and increase illegality and the unavoidable interaction problems. Border regions should not be understood from one side only (unilateralism), but in the light of the cross-border dynamics in which they are inscribed.

The homogeneity of border policies is a second component to be discussed. Never has the design of homogeneous policies brought positive effects on heterogeneous realities, even less so in the case of borders that are not only intrinsically different on each side, but also within each country.

The centralist logic of policies is also highly pernicious, because not only does it ignore local governments as key partners, but it also fails to consider border societies. Policies are aimed at the defense of sovereignty and rely on military presence (national security), internal public order with police control (public security), immigration control (visas), and the customs burden (tariffs, quotas), which are not functional to the new role of borders at this moment in time. Generally, national policies tend to produce physical, virtual, or tariff barriers, as well as safeguards, through military-police presence and the construction of walls that create greater opportunities for illegal integration, while producing obstacles for legal activities.

Ultimately, the dominant view of borders is anchored to the military, customs, and immigration, with no role assigned to the local population or government. In this sense, the demand for citizen security implies not only strengthening local institutions, but also generating a new productive structure to replace the dominant one of illegal markets. This means raising the hierarchy of public policy in the field of prevention through (a) decentralization, which transfers resources and powers to municipalities; and (b) integration, which promotes the development of the entire cross-border region.[4]

Border towns suffer daily from violence, while the illegal and legal economies that develop in these areas tend to benefit the country through money laundering, low prices, and good products.[5] This is increasingly so now, when the effects of global violence are local, and because security policies are designed exogenously to the region, without listening to the voices of the main actors: producers, traders, women, and young people living at the borders.

Conclusions

Border urban growth has generated poles of economic attraction. These are spaces that, due to their morphology and use of complementary asymmetries, have given rise to a diversity of cities that constitute cross-border urban complexes based on their form and relations. The cross-border logic stemming from local/national competition must be imposed over the border, so that integration and decentralization act as prevention policies.

With territorially isolated borders and on the margins of decision-making spaces, security policies may exclude the counterpart state and the inhabitants of the region itself, which is why designing strategies without incorporating the other implies ignoring reality and contributing to greater violence. As long as security policies that build greater distances and differences between neighboring states continue to be applied, the actors of violence will develop unified cross-border territories for crime. Additionally, treating those who are unequal in a similar way deepens the differences and therefore increases the structural conditions of violence.

In border cities, two of the drivers of violence are related to inequalities; for one thing, neighboring states with complementary asymmetries. For another thing, border territories are determined by the distance and proximity to the center of national political and economic power. It is for these reasons that security policies must be of decentralization and integration, as opposed to centralization and separation.

These types of inequalities construct illegalities that give way to "border violence" – concentrated in border cities – not in terms of the traditional social and economic imbalances within a city or society, but in the relationship of two or more countries that both meet and are separated at the borders.[6] The paradox of this situation is that border areas – at least the most dynamic ones – have positive migration balances, because border economies begin to operate as a gravitational mass that attracts the population, even if, in some cases, the violence reaches a threshold that operates as a negative externality (Carrión 2013, 28).

Citizen security strategies imply focusing on the population as well as on interpersonal relations, since the state is the guarantor of peaceful coexistence. In other words, alone the consideration of these strategies already implies a process of decentralization, because the inhabitants of the border areas become the main subjects of policy. A proposal of this type runs against hegemonic policies that are deployed in border areas, where national security (territorial sovereignty) is the main interest. Since these strategies have, as a rule, not been aimed at strengthening public and private institutions (social capital), they have fallen prey to organized crime, whose actors aim to subject them to their interests.[7]

Border areas require policies to promote security. Such policies should consider: (a) integration between neighboring countries.[8] In this perspective, integration should not only be considered between neighboring countries but also at the regional level, because the combat of international crime demands it. A case in point would be the proposal to promote the legal harmonization in the criminal field throughout South

Cross-Border Urban Complexes 263

America; (b) decentralization within states is an unavoidable consideration. Strengthening local and regional governments in border areas, establishing a tariff policy that benefits the development of local society, making public investments and a material base (infrastructure) that strengthens the cross-border region; and (c) building a network of border cities, where local governments promote exchange ties in different areas, in favor of intermunicipal cooperation; a structure similar to that of the Union of Ibero-American Capital Cities (UCCI), emphasizing the particularities of urban border spaces, since border cities do not represent the political power of the state to which they belong and, in many cases, not even that of their provinces or departments. The role of border cities within the regional economy is extremely important; such is the case of Ciudad Juárez, which, "without being the political capital, is the main economic engine of [the state of] Chihuahua [...]" (Alarcón 2014, 261).

The violence generated in the asymmetries that develop at the border (what has been characterized here as "border violence"), can be diminished by means of development initiatives that prioritize decentralization and integration, thus allowing the consolidation of border areas, where local governments and the population benefit from their condition as border inhabitants. Common spaces between border cities, such as the International Plaza in the so-called Peace Border (Rivera-Santana do Livramento), which promote the encounter of diversity in the public environment, will strengthen border citizenship.

Notes

1. As the cycle of rural-urban migration closes, two more cycles open simultaneously: urban-urban migration and international migration, in a context of significant reduction of natural population growth, leading to reduced rates of urbanization (UN-Habitat 2012, 28).
2. The most striking case is that of Ciudad Juárez, Chihuahua and El Paso, Texas, which form a transnational metropolitan area; while the first has a rate of over 100 homicides per 100,000 inhabitants, the second has less than one.
3. Similarly to the category of border cities, each country occupies its own sovereign space within the legally established limits; however, due to their geographical location and their activities, they create a particular unit in the form of a sub-region.
4. The example of economic policy is a central point, which should not eliminate the possibility of promoting a process of legal harmonization in the criminal field.
5. In 1996, the San Andresitos – informal sale stalls – in Bogotá generated more than $2 billion (*El Tiempo* 1997).
6. As mentioned, violence is not explained by attributes, but by relationships.
7. Border policies must be constructed from a complementary perspective; a border meeting between finance ministers would probably be better than just a meeting of defense ministers.
8. Asymmetries create distances for the legal and proximities for the illegal.

References

Alarcón Gil, César. 2014. "Ciudad Juárez: Sociedad, criminalidad y violencia transnacional." In *Ciudades en la encrucijada: violencia y poder criminal en Río de Janeiro, Medellín Bogotá y Ciudad Juárez*, 249–329. Medellín: Corporación Región.

Arriagada, Camilo. 2000. *Pobreza en América Latina, nuevos escenarios y desafíos de política para el hábitat urbano*. Santiago: CIESPAL.

Bárcena, Alicia. 2001. "Evolución de la urbanización en América Latina y El Caribe en la década de los noventa: Desafíos y oportunidades." *Información Comercial Española. Revista de Economía*, 790 (February–March), 51–61.

Briceño-León, Roberto. 2007. *Sociología de violencia en América Latina*. Quito: FLACSO, Municipio del Distrito Metropolitano de Quito, Corporación Metropolitana de Seguridad.

Cardin, Eric. 2013. "Mecanismos de contrabando y tráfico en la triple frontera." In *Fronteras: rupturas y convergencias*, complied by Fernando Carrión and Víctor Llugsha, 255–266. Quito: FLACSO, IDRC.

Carrión, Fernando. 1996. "Violencia urbana, nuevos escenarios." *Revista Latinoamericana de Comunicación CHASQUI*, 53, 43–46. https://revistachasqui. org/index.php/chasqui/article/view/1004/1034

—— 2013. "La violencia fronteriza." In *Seguridad, planificación y desarrollo en las regiones fronterizas*, edited by Fernando Carrión, 23–44. Quito: FLACSO, IDRC.

—— 2014. "El espacio público no es un espacio, es una relación." Paper presented at the seminar Espacio Público, Bogotá.

Castells, Manuel. 1997. *La era de la información, economía, sociedad y cultura, III*. Madrid: Alianza Editorial.

CEPAL. 2016. "La población de América Latina alcanzará 625 millones de personas en 2016, según estimaciones de la CEPAL". Accessed 2 June 2021. https://www.cepal.org/es/noticias/la-poblacion-america-latina-alcanzara-625-millones-personas-2016-segun-estimaciones-la

Comisión Trinacional del Plan Trifinio. 2015. "Descripción de la región." Accessed 10 June 2021. http://www.plantrifinio.gob.hn/plan-trifinio/descripcion-de-la-region

Consejo Ciudadano para la Seguridad Pública y la Justicia Penal. 2019. "Metodología del ranking (2019) de las 50 ciudades más violentas del mundo." Accessed 3 June 2021. http://www.seguridadjusticiaypaz.org.mx/sala-de-prensa/ 1589-metodologia-del-ranking-2019-de-las-50-ciudades-mas-violentas-del-mundo

Devia, Camilo and Ortega, Dina. 2019. "Características y desafíos del crimen organizado transnacional en la Triple Frontera: Argentina-Paraguay-Brasil." *Revista Criminalidad*, 61 (1), 9–28. Accessed 9 June 2021. http://www.scielo.org.co/scielo. php?script=sci_arttext&pid=S1794-31082019000100009&lng=en&tlng=es

El Tiempo. 1997. "Sanandresitos lavan US$878 millones." El Tiempo (Bogota D.C.). 4 July 1997. Accessed 6 June 2021. https://www.eltiempo.com/archivo/ documento/MAM-627228

Espinosa, Roque. 2013. "Discursos de seguridad." In *Fronteras: rupturas y convergencias*, complied by Fernando Carrión and Víctor Llugsha, 31–41. Quito: FLACSO, IDRC-CRDI.

Fuentes, César and Sergio Peña. 2017. "Las fronteras de México: Nodos del sistema global de las drogas prohibidas." México: El Colegio de la Frontera Norte: Facultad Latinoamericana de Ciencias Sociales: IDRC-CRDI. Accessed 9 June 2021. https://biblio.flacsoandes.edu.ec/libros/digital/56999.pdf

Cross-Border Urban Complexes 265

FUNDAREDES. 2021. "Curva de la violencia." Accessed 3 June 2021. https://www.fundaredes.org/2021/04/26/informe-primer-trimestre-curva-de-la-violencia-2021/

Gómez, Andrés. 2013. "Análisis comparado de las políticas de seguridad de Ecuador y Colombia respecto a su zona de frontera." In *Asimetrías en la frontera Ecuador-Colombia: entre la complementariedad y el sistema*, complied by Fernando Carrión, 23–44. Quito: FLACSO, IDRC.

Google Earth. 2021a. "Binuclear City: Tulcán and Ipiales." Accessed June 10. https://earth.google.com/web/@0.81223652,-77.68604288,16551.57658174a,0d,35y,0.0163h,2.1549t,0r?utm_source=earth7&utm_campaign=vine&hl=es-419

—— 2021b. "Triple Frontier: Ciudad del Este, Foz do Iguaçu, and Puerto de Iguazú." Accessed 10 June 2021. https://earth.google.com/web/@-25.5280445,-54.57243742,-91277.94166065a,110373.9205667d,35y,-1.0267033h,2.41235699t,0r?utm_source=earth7&utm_campaign=vine&hl=es-419

—— 2021c. "Ciudad Juárez-El Paso Metropolitan City." Accessed 10 June 2021. https://earth.google.com/web/@31.75170879,-106.44210921,-28931.62962135a,50695.67108922d,35y,0.02225727h,0.54431818t,0r?utm_source=earth7&utm_campaign=vine&hl=es-419

—— 2021d. "Manaus, Leticia, Iquitos, and Sucumbíos Border." Accessed 10 June 2021. https://earth.google.com/web/@-1.43394473,-69.03607292,1823900.59019757a,0d,35y,-0.1432h,0t,0r?utm_source=earth7&utm_campaign=vine&hl=es-419

Goulart, S., Misoczky, M. C., and Flores, R. K. 2017. "Contradições e dinâmicas sociais e econômicas na Fronteira da Paz." *Desenvolvimento Em Questão*, 15 (38), 7–43. https://doi.org/10.21527/2237-6453.2017.38.7-43

Lates, Alfredo. 2001. "Población urbana y urbanización en América Latina." In *El regreso a la ciudad construida*, complied by Fernando Carrión, 49–76. Quito: FLACSO.

Quintero, Rafael. 2006. *Asociativismo municipal en América Latina: gobiernos locales y sociedad civil*. Quito: Abya Yala/FLACMA-DFID/GTZ.

Ramos, José. 2013. "Relaciones México-Estados Unidos y dilemas en seguridad ciudadana fronteriza." In *Fronteras: rupturas y convergencias*, complied by Fernando Carrión and Víctor Llugsha, 169–186. Quito: FLACSO, IDRC-CRDI.

Ruiz, Naxhelli and Javier Delgado. 2008. "Territorio y nuevas ruralidades: un recorrido teórico sobre las transformaciones de la relación campo-ciudad." *EURE*, 34 (102), 77–95. Accessed 8 February 2016.

Sassen, Saskia. 1991. *The Global City*. New Jersey: Princeton University Press.

Sierra, Jorge. 2013. "Desafíos de la frontera México-Estados Unidos." In *Fronteras: rupturas y convergencias*, complied by Fernando Carrión, and Víctor Llugsha, 187–201. Quito: FLACSO, IDRC.

UN-Habitat. 2012. *Estado de las ciudades de América Latina y El Caribe 2012. Rumbo a una nueva transición urbana*. Brazil: United Nations Human Settlements Programme.

11 A Gender Perspective in the Study of Latin American Border Systems

María Amelia Viteri and Iréri Ceja

Introduction: The Importance of a Gender Perspective

This chapter highlights some of the ways in which gender structures operate to enable and justify certain types of violence, along with the illegal and interdependent markets in a localized context and territory.[1] In doing so, it addresses both the theoretical and methodological importance of applying a gender-focused approach – mainly gender anthropology – to the issues at hand. This is achieved by situating the category of gender within a framework of structural violence (Bourgois 2010; Farmer 1996).

In applying this theoretical framework, we regard the category of gender as elastic and understand it as a verb, as opposed to a noun. We are interested in mapping the processes through which gender is produced and defined, while stressing that an analysis that ignores a gender perspective, or that uses "gender" as a synonym for woman, overlooks the multiplicity of factors that enable violence in Latin America's global border system.

For a brief conceptual review, we begin by mentioning Eveline and Bacchi (2005), who examine from a gender mainstreaming perspective how one of the initial premises of the term "gender" was the distinction of sex as a biological trait, from gender as a set of social attributes, norms, and socially learned behaviors, which allowed a discourse that favored equal opportunities for men and women and demystified the "woman equals mother" equation.

This distinction has been confronted by theorists such as Judith Butler (2004, 2006), who views the body itself as having been imbued with social characteristics, behaviors, and expectations based on stereotypes and assumptions around constructions of "the feminine" and "the masculine," which migrate between bodies and are not inherent to anyone. Thus, authors such as Connell and Messerschmidt (2005) explain how this differentiation is a problem for both women and men. Categories of analysis such as "hegemonic masculinities" have been very useful in observing how such constructs benefit one group to the detriment of the

DOI: 10.4324/9781003204299-18

other (Carrigan et al. 1985). As Judith Butler (2006) argues, it is not that sex shapes gender, but that gender constructs sex. Moreover, Moi (1999) urges us to think about social problems from the perspective of the body and its experiences, using Simone de Beauvoir's phenomenology (2005). In any case, gender, like theory, is not a fixed structure, but a contingent and localized process with specific power effects (Eveline and Bacchi 2005, 501).

Understood as a verb, the notion of gender acknowledges that it is the body that informs relations of power and privilege; that is, gender becomes a body and the body is marked by gender; thence the body occupies specific roles, which, to a certain extent, are predetermined not only by gender but also by national, geographical, ethnic, class, age, sexual, and migratory status.[2] The way in which bodies and their functions are represented in the media plays a fundamental role in the proliferation of inequalities around those that strengthen power structures within societies.

Throughout this analysis, some of the questions we address are: (a) which processes allow us to incorporate gender as a category of analysis in the global border system? (b) who are the enabling actors of the gender-based violence that is produced and reproduced at the border? and (c) how does a gender studies and anthropology-based approach allow us to broaden the analysis of borders and border-related illegalities and routes?

Within this framework, the chapter is divided into two main sections. The first is a theoretical discussion that conceptually addresses gender mainstreaming and is, itself, divided into two subsections: one problematizing borders and the body and the other focusing on illegal markets, actors, and violence. The second section seeks to broaden the analysis of border crimes and interpersonal violence by incorporating the gender perspective into the study of feminicide, migrant smuggling, and the trafficking of drugs, organs, and sex. In this latter section, we highlight some notable Latin American examples of this illegality: feminicide in Mexico, migrant smuggling in Central America and Mexico, and human trafficking in Ecuador and Colombia.

Gender, Body, Borders

Contemporary places, spaces, policies, and practices celebrate certain bodies by making them visible, while erasing, denying, and exploiting others. Among these denied bodies are those of women in conditions of forced labor and sex trafficking at the borders.

There have been several approaches to the study of borders. In spatial terms, their boundaries are evidenced in political-legal agreements through concepts such as territory, time, and space (Fawcett 1918; Montañez and Delgado 1998); in other words, borders are the places

268 *María Amelia Viteri and Iréri Ceja*

where the state exercises its power and sovereignty. Borders have also been conceived as social constructions of political interest (Anderson 1993; Balibar 2005). From this perspective, borders are the space where the limits of an ideologically orchestrated national identity are drawn as spaces of subjectivity (Faret 1997), as social continuums between two nations that constantly permeate each other (Redfield 1941) while in permanent tension to maintain their identities. In this sense, and stemming from the idea of a nation, "borders have been constructed as social dimensions that delimit the territory 'geopolitically,' while inflaming the culture that gives way to a national identity" (Betanzos Núñez 2014, 9).

The classical view that permeated border studies for many years was that of the German geographer Ratzel (1987), who understood borders as rigid dividing lines that, like an epidermis, protected the nation from the outside world. However, with the development of capitalism in its neoliberal phase, the proliferation of multinational companies, the trans-nationalization of resources and production processes, and the displacement of developed countries' industries to underdeveloped countries, this concept came to be questioned. As Fernández states, "the imposition of the economic border on the political and legal border became evident, as did the transformation of the latter into a fictitious geographical delimitation" (1980, 18).

In this way, due to the circulation of capital, products, and people, and their importance in the global economy, there was a shift from the notion of a rigid border to one of a porous border, and from the notion of the delimitation and periphery of the nation-state to one of the border as a global center and space (Garduño 2003). Thus, border regions display economic and social dynamics with the border zone of the neighboring country with which, despite their differences, they are interconnected (Ordóñez 2007). Concepts such as "overflows" resort to frameworks of anthropology of gender to study borders, bodies, and their categories in their intersectionality, highlighting how borders are constructed as they are transformed (Viteri 2014). In so doing, they redefine notions of belonging and citizenship.

According to Carrión et al. (2013), borders are heterogeneous realities with diversified economies – both legal and illegal. These economies are generally asymmetrical and functional to one another, as "what is legal here is illegal there; what exists here does not exist there, or what has a higher price here is cheaper there; therefore, there is a trade flow that generates a system of illegalities where the economy of one side spills over into the other side, in the manner of communicating vessels" (Carrión et al. 2013, 206–207). Thus, the particularity of borders is that they respond to a different logic than the rest of the country. It is a logic that operates as the inverse of that of the border of the neighboring country, since "the more differentiated factors are imposed (walls, tariffs), the greater asymmetries are created, increasing risks and, therefore, prices and violence" (Carrión et al. 2013, 206).

It is precisely the asymmetry that facilitates the flow of goods and capital, and that allows illicit markets to operate in global networks. This same logic of asymmetry has proved to be an investment process, in which the growing securitization of borders has led to an increase in people's vulnerability, as the former become strategic spaces in the global economy, where the movement of products and capital is prioritized, and the movement of people is restricted.

Again, this chapter does not approach gender as a fixed or biological identity, but as a category of differentiation between subjects; a category that, when intersecting with other categories such as age, class, and ethnicity, generates double or triple hierarchies, making subjects and their bodies more vulnerable in particularly violent territories of global capitalism. We therefore refer conceptually to the edges that accentuate the fluidity and mobility of categories, overlapping forms of belonging, and contesting, along the way, borders understood solely as territory (Viteri 2014).

Several factors result in the development and proliferation of violence in general, and gender violence in particular, such as the impunity established by drug-trafficking mafias and organized crime, which often includes the police and different state institutions (Revelo 2005, 150). The case of Ciudad Juárez, the Mexican city bordering the United States, is a clear example of these processes. In that city (with the highest rates of feminicide in the world), there appears to be a direct relationship between capital, violence, and death. Ciudad Juárez's dynamics changed with the advent of *maquiladoras*, i.e., transnational capital factories where (foreign) products are assembled, allowing companies to evade the higher taxes they would have to pay in other countries while paying their workers (usually female internal migrants and mestizo women) according to the host-country's relatively low wage scale.

Maquiladoras experienced exponential growth in Mexico as a result of the North American Free Trade Agreement (NAFTA) signed by Mexico, the United States, and Canada in 1994. In Ciudad Juárez, there is a direct relationship between the accumulation of deregulated capital for transnational companies and the violation of the local population's rights, as well as between the increase in economic capital for some and the sacrifice of poor and mestizo women, "where monetary and symbolic economy, control of resources and power of death are articulated" (Segato 2004, 3). According to Segato, in Ciudad Juárez:

> Illegal trafficking of all kinds of goods to the other side of the border includes the goods produced by the work extorted from the *maquiladora* workers, the surplus value added by the capital gain extracted from that work, in addition to drugs, bodies and, in short, the sum of

270 *María Amelia Viteri and Iréri Ceja*

> the considerable capital that these businesses generate south of paradise. Their illicit circulation is similar to granting constant refunds to an unjust, voracious and insatiable taxpayer who, at the same time, hides his demands and ignores the seduction he exercises. The border between misery-of-excess and misery-of-lack is an abyss.
>
> (Segato 2004, 4)

The *maquiladora* industry unleashes a migration of and by gender conditions, increasing the already existing vulnerability of – usually single and young – working-class women who are deprived of their social, community, and socio-affective networks (Cerbino and Macaroff 2010).

The normalization of gender-targeted violence at the borders has reached such a high degree that sexual abuse is "expected" by undocumented migrant women, who take contraceptives prior to their migrant crossing in order to at least avoid a forced pregnancy (Álvarez 2015, 123–124). This is part of the migratory knowledge and what Peggy Levitt (1996) calls "social remittances."[3]

According to Alvarez's study (2015), on Mexico's southern border with Guatemala, the standard practice for some women, who must use their bodies "as currency" in order to continue the migration route that involves numerous crossings, is equally violent and involves the additional risks of abduction for forced labor or sex work and encountering too many individuals who expect money in exchange for enabling the crossing or providing momentary protection.

Within this framework, and as evidenced by the previous examples, it is the body, differentiated by material and symbolic cultural understandings around gender, that enables these types of violence and the differentiated vulnerabilities of certain bodies in relation to others. It is important, therefore, to examine the context of illegal economies and how certain places, spaces, policies, and practices celebrate certain bodies, while erasing and denying others (Casper and Moore 2009).

At the same time, an anthropological perspective allows us to recognize the agency of women at the borders by questioning identity categories thought of as static (Anzaldúa 2012) and by localizing the body against surveillance politics and violence (Varela 2017). This perspective acknowledges cross border productivity and reproducibility dynamics that mobilize the economy and remain outside of the stereotypes of Latin American borders and transnational crime (Guizardi 2020).

Illegal Markets, Actors, and Violence from a Gender Perspective

The growing complexity of the borders is evident in the very diversification of both illicit markets and the services offered by criminal groups, as well as in the complex relations they have with the state. In this regard, Sansó-Rubert (2010) points out that organized crime has become

A Gender Perspective 271

all-encompassing since, geographically, it has acquired global dimensions; ethnically and culturally, it has taken on transnational dimensions; in its structure it has become multiform – forging agreements with political and social sectors –, and in addition, it has become pluriproductive, due to the abundance of both licit and illicit goods and services.

Illicit is what is outside the law; that is to say, its definition comes from the state's own frameworks. De Sousa and Ferreira (2004), citing Adler-Lomnitz (1994), define illicit markets as a system that depends on at least three characteristics: corruption, violence, and the value of trust. The same authors refer to corruption as that process "which is related to the use of public offices with a view to favoring the private economy of those involved in an illicit transaction" (De Sousa and Ferreira 2004, 152). Social relations generated by illegal markets are also contractual relations that function and are fulfilled outside the framework of the law (Ghezzi and Mingione 2003), and they do so thanks to the value of trust placed on the other party (Adler-Lomnitz 1994), as well as to the use of illegitimate violence in the event of non-compliance by one of the parties. Thus, illegitimate violence and corruption are the resources that make agreements and the operation of illegal markets viable.

As Tilly (1985) points out, the state and organized crime are in a constant dispute to control the means of violence. Organized crime makes rational use of violence to maintain the economic transactions and flow of capital and products that feed these markets. When we speak of rational use, we do so in terms of Weber (2001); that is, not as an antonym for irrationality, but rather as a means to an end.

Organized crime actors are in conflict over key territories, territories that connect two states, but also territories that are linked with global economies, both legal and illegal. Hence, disputes over control of these markets – by criminal groups and the state – translate into disputes over the control of the territory as well as the bodies that inhabit that territory. Women's bodies become testimonies of what Revelo (2005) calls cultural systems of social inequality, in which multiple forms of gender-based violence are rooted.

In these spaces of struggle for territorial control, violence is key. This violence responds to the very structural frameworks that make illegal markets possible and does so under gender-differentiated logics. A gender-studies perspective makes it possible to determine and analyze what these differential logics are, how they are produced, and how they function for the development of control regimes over territorial borders and bodies at various scales. One of these forms of violence is feminicide, as described in the following section.

Localized Violence: Feminicide

Mexican feminist Marcela Lagarde coined the term *femicide* from Diana Russell and Jill Radford (1992); however, the Mexican feminist went from the literal translation "femicide" to feminicide, since the first meaning

272 María Amelia Viteri and Iréri Ceja

was homologous to homicide, while the idea of feminicide refers to all forms of violence against women. According to Lagarde, "Feminicide is made up of the set of misogynistic violent acts against women that imply the violation of their human rights, threaten their security, and put their lives at risk" (2006, 33). As the author highlights, the continuity of these crimes stands on the weakness or the absence of the rule of law, which allows unlimited violence, and unaccountable murders to be reproduced. In this sense, it is a fracture of the state that favors impunity, which is why, for the author, "feminicide is a state crime" (Lagarde 2006, 33) that can be perpetrated in conditions of war and peace.

Feminicides have been particularly evident in territories in conflict. Hernández Castillo (2006) illustrates how, in patriarchal systems, gender violence objectifies women, turning them into prizes or "spoils" of war. The author further explains that gender analyses from militarized regions, such as Davida Wood's work on Palestine (in Hernández Castillo 2006) or Dette Denich's research (1995) on Sarajevo shows that in contexts of political-military conflict, female sexuality tends to become a symbolic space of political struggle and rape is instrumentalized as a way of demonstrating power and domination over the enemy. Hernández Castillo adds that, "from a patriarchal ideology, which continues to regard women as sexual objects and as the repositories of family honor, rape and sexual torture are an attack on all the men of the enemy group" (2006). Along the same line, Segato (2012) argues that new forms of conflict involve a need to attack women and children in particular, in order to show how unlimited violence is. This is, therefore, an expressive violence that would seem to have no immediate utility, but which transmits a clear message to the powerful and a challenge to others who regard women's bodies as subject to male guardianship.

Media and public policy continue to present gender-based violence as a domestic problem that occurs within the family and the home. But these crimes are not limited to the private sphere, even though judicial reports repeat this *ad nauseam* (Segato 2012). The unintelligible nature of gender-based crimes at the border does not allow us to understand, at first glance, that these crimes are precisely the product of patriarchal structures and differential categories that render certain bodies, such as those of women, vulnerable. At work here is the same logic of global capitalism and border dynamics, especially the commercial logic of illegal markets; it is a logic that, for women, translates into vulnerability. Worse still, the unintelligibility of the facts and the homogeneity of interpretations come together to exacerbate this vulnerability.

As a congresswoman, Lagarde managed to have the term "feminicide" integrated into Mexico's Federal Criminal Code in 2007, making this the first time these types of acts were criminalized in the Americas. However, due to the increase in violence against women – particularly in the case of Mexico, where it is defined in terms of criminal offenses –,

A Gender Perspective 273

Segato (2012) insists on a more granular criminalization of the different types of violence against women that would distinguish those that stem from interpersonal relationships and those that do not. The idea is not to deny that any type of violence against women is a product of structural gender relations, but to acknowledge that finer categorizations will allow for more effective criminal investigations. When categorizing crimes involving violence against women, Segato (2012) alludes to feminicide as a category to be used within the ambit of state law to encompass all gender crimes committed at the border. That includes crimes that occur in interpersonal contexts as well as those perpetrated by agents whose motives are directed within the context of a systemic order.

Regarding developments in other countries, the Latin American Network for Security and Organized Crime (Relasedor), attached to FLACSO-Ecuador, reports that in the case of Ecuador 1,628 women were murdered between 2007 and 2012. The Latin American Association for Alternative Development (ALDEA), part of the Alliance for Mapping and Tracking Femicides in Ecuador, reports that 748 women were murdered between 2014 and 2020. Moreover, as reported by Ecuador's Special Commission for Security, Justice, Crime and Transparency Statistics, 935 women have been violently murdered[4] between August 10, 2014 and May 31, 2019. Responding to the ongoing violence and the pressure exerted by feminist groups and human rights advocates (both organizations and individuals), Ecuador's *Código Orgánico Integral Penal* (COIP) (Comprehensive Organic Criminal Code), which was signed into law in 2015, defines feminicide as a criminal offense and provides for prison sentences of up to 25 years for those found guilty of committing this crime. The high-profile case of the 2013 rape and murder of Karina del Pozo led to a struggle for this classification.[5]

The Survey on Family Relations and Gender Violence against Women (2001), conducted by Ecuador's Ministry of the Interior, in coordination with the Transition Commission toward the Council for Women and Gender Equality, shows that in Ecuador, out of a total of 1,800 women, 53.9% suffered psychological violence, 30% physical violence, 25.7% sexual violence, and 53.3% property violence (Carcero 2011). In other words, six out of every ten women in the country have experienced some type of gender-based violence, this being more common among indigenous women (67%) and women of African descent (66.7%). Moreover, according to research conducted by the Transition Commission toward the Council for Women and Gender Equality (2011), among Ecuadorian women, 92% of violent deaths are feminicides or suspected feminicides, and 64% of feminicides are committed by partners or former partners in the home of the victim or the perpetrator (Carcero 2011). Yet in Ecuador, only 36% of the violent deaths of women are classified as feminicides, even though an estimated 93.7% are committed by intimate partners or former partners (Fiscalía General del Estado 2019, 14).

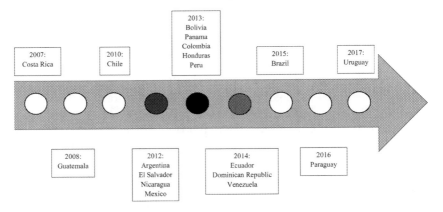

Figure 11.1 Femicide/Feminicide National Legislation by Country, Including Year

Source: OECD (2019), SIGI Country Profiles (genderindex.org), and UN Women (2018)

Figure 11.1 shows when each of the countries listed below first enacted laws that address femicide/feminicide. Addressing the enactment of these laws becomes important when looking at current femicide rates and comparing them to gender-based homicides committed prior to these laws' enactment. Here, it is important to consider how, by whom and where the requirements for investigating the homicide of a woman as a femicide/feminicide were established. Thus, even though the enactment of these laws and new categories constitutes progress in the fight for women's rights, the patriarchal system continues to kill feminized bodies.

Tables 11.1 and 11.2 show the figures and rates of femicides and feminicides in eight Latin American countries between 2014 and 2019. The data obtained from CEPAL uses the categories of femicide/feminicide[6] to refer to the homicide of a woman because of her gender. In several cases, the figures are incomplete due to the limitations with which public institutions in each country categorize homicides: (lack of) knowledge

Table 11.1 Latin America: Number of femicides/feminicides

Year	Mexico	Guatemala	Colombia	Ecuador	Peru	Bolivia	Argentina	Brazil
2014		225		27	100		225	
2015	411	189		55	103	96	235	
2016	609	193	57	67	105	104	254	1663
2017	741	218	208	102	116	110	251	1582
2018	891	172	228	59	142	130	255	1851
2019	983	160	226	67	128	117	252	1941

Source: Gender Equality Observatory for Latin America and the Caribbean (2019)

A Gender Perspective 275

Table 11.2 Latin America: Rate of femicides/feminicides per 100,000 women

Year	Mexico	Guatemala	Colombia	Ecuador	Peru	Bolivia	Argentina	Brazil
2014				0.3	0.6		1	
2015	0.7	2.4		0.7	0.7	1.8	1.1	
2016	1.6	2.4	0.2	0.8	0.7	1.9	1.1	1.6
2017	1.5	2.7	0.8	1.2	0.7	2	1.1	1.5
2018	1.5	2.1	0.9	0.7	0.9	2.3	1.1	1.7
2019	1.5	1.9	0.9	0.8	0.8	2	1	1.8

Source: Gender Equality Observatory for Latin America and the Caribbean (2019)

and legislation concerning gender-based crimes, for example, in cases involving violent deaths, the logic of the forensic medical system, the precariousness of the civil registry process and related morgue systems, including the possibilities of extracting DNA samples and performing autopsies.[7]

While the numbers are relative to the total population, the femicide/feminicide rates show the magnitude of the problem in each of the listed countries. The most alarming statistics are found in Guatemala (with an apparent downward trend), Mexico and Brazil (with an upward trend), although these trends could also be explained by changes in rates of reporting or the application of these penal categories.

Localized Violence: Smuggling of Persons and Human Trafficking for Labor, Sex, and Other Forms of Exploitation

The conceptualizations of "human trafficking" and "migrant smuggling" used by nation-states and implemented in security policies are taken from the United Nations Protocol to Prevent, Suppress and Punish Trafficking in Persons, Especially Women and Children, supplementing the United Nations Convention against Transnational Organized Crime, also known as the 2000 Palermo Convention.

The difference between the two concepts lies in the means whereby persons are recruited, as human trafficking – be it for the purposes of sexual exploitation, labor exploitation, or organ trafficking, among others – is carried out by means of coercion, abuse, or deception, whereas illicit smuggling is carried out with the consent of the persons concerned. While "smuggling ends with the arrival of the migrant at his destination, human trafficking involves the exploitation of the victim by the traffickers after arrival in order to obtain some benefit or profit through exploitation" (UNODC 2014). As stipulated in the same convention, the smuggling of persons is always transnational, as it involves crossing from at least one state to another, while human trafficking may not be, as movement and exploitation may occur within national borders.

276 *María Amelia Viteri and Iréri Ceja*

Critical literature on migration points out that the politics underlying these categories are rooted in a security perspective that criminalizes mobility and promotes surveillance practices (Domenech 2013; Feldman-Bianco 2018), undermining the life of forcibly displaced populations. The latter ignores the role of the states in enabling conditions of illegality (De Genova 2002) and exposing migrants to trafficking and smuggling networks (Viteri et al. 2017; Mansur 2015).

There are two feminist approaches to the issue of human trafficking. The first one is inscribed within the field of human rights and looks at prostitution as legitimate work. Nonetheless, it must be stated that, from this perspective, sexual work as a product of trafficking, as well as work in *maquiladoras*, constitute what Kevin Bales (2012, 2009) has called "new slavery." The author documents the contemporary proliferation of these "new slaves" and how they are directly connected to the global economy. Likewise, Bales highlights and problematizes human trafficking and slavery present in countries such as the United States, pointing to and denouncing their networks, forms of production and main actors. The second point of view is represented by the Coalition Against Trafficking in Women, which considers all types of prostitution as a violation of women's rights.

Many sex workers' rights activists have been concerned about the impact that these conceptual divergences might have on sex workers, as anti-trafficking measures have historically been used to regulate sex work and thereby women's bodies, including those of migrant women. In that sense, Bernstein (2014) emphasizes how debates over the meanings and treatment of prostitution are intertwined with debates about geographical, national, and moral boundaries (Ruiz 2015). Based on her research on Ecuador's southern border, Ruiz problematizes the imagery of "genuine" or "true" sex relations in the intimacy of sex work. The author further illustrates how not only sex workers, but also groups of immigrant women, engage, through sporadic sexual exchanges, in transnational relationships where sex, intimacy, affection and material exchanges are mixed, as a way of dealing with economic precariousness (2015, 16–18).

Doezema (2002) has problematized definitions of human trafficking, pointing out that making all women victims homogenizes them as a group and silences them as individuals, thus ignoring the multiple dimensions which overlap in each case, and leaving them in a relationship of dependence on and vulnerability before the laws and decisions of the state, its resources, and those who design public policy.

In many cases governments conceal, under the mantle of combating human trafficking, a moralistic struggle against any form of sex work. One way of avoiding this problem is to reject both the neo-abolitionist approach, which denies women the possibility of consenting to sex work and being regarded as legitimate (as opposed to immoral) workers, and the neo-regulatory perspective that condemns forced prostitution but fails to ensure sex workers' rights. This would allow gender relations in the sex industry to be conceived not simply as an issue of women being exploited by male oppressors but rather as one in which men, women, and transgender people are understood to occupy various positions that place them at different levels of power, at the same time, as clients or sex workers. It would also avoid making a neocolonial distinction between women from industrialized as opposed to non-industrialized countries, granting them possibilities of autonomy and agency normally seen as belonging to non-migrant women in industrialized countries.

Another important issue is the relationship between sex work and migration. It is necessary to think about the migration phenomenon that, whether linked to trafficking networks or not, exposes migrants to illicit markets and constant sexual abuse. Migration, which in principle is based on the free choice of people to move, is often driven by the need to escape different types of physical or economic violence, often directly threatening the migrants' physical integrity or life. The migration process itself exposes people, particularly women, who are susceptible to sexual abuse along the way, to various crimes. As stated earlier, Central American migrants who cross Mexico to get to the United States take birth control (contraceptives) as a means of preventing pregnancy, given the high probability of being raped or needing to exchange sex for support at some point along their journey. In this sense, although figures continue to speak of a higher proportion of male in comparison to female migrants, the figures are becoming increasingly balanced. Thus, it is important to consider migration in a manner that is differentiated and beyond the data (Ángeles and Rojas 2000).

Another concrete example that allows us to address the complexity of these phenomena is that of Ciudad Hidalgo, on the southern border of Mexico. As documented by Álvarez (2015, 132), brothels on the borders are marginalized spaces. Due to their location, they facilitate impunity, illegality in their functioning, global trafficking, sex trade based on undocumented migration, and trafficking networks, where members of different police departments, immigration agents, and the military (in addition to drug traffickers, *coyotes*, and similar criminal actors) pay for the services of undocumented sex workers. This creates complex relationships between undocumented migrants, who become undocumented sex workers and may also become mules or trafficking victims, to name but a few of the activities in which they are involuntarily involved.

Studies of women trafficking on the Mexico-Guatemala border have shown that while trafficking in Honduran women is mostly for sexual exploitation, trafficking in Guatemalan women tends to be for labor exploitation, since Guatemalan women, being mostly indigenous, present physical features that are not much demanded in the sex market (Betanzos 2014), because of the Western beauty ideals and stereotypes that dominate it.

278 *María Amelia Viteri and Iréri Ceja*

According to the International Labor Organization, human trafficking for sexual and labor exploitation yields profits of $12 billion dollars in Latin America and the Caribbean (ILO 2014), which is why it has become safer and almost as profitable as drug trafficking for criminal groups. Human trafficking in the region could triple in the next few years according to the United Nations Office on Drugs and Crime (Guillén 2015).

Human trafficking, smuggling, and sex work are phenomena that must be considered beyond discussions of security. It is necessary to incorporate perspectives of gender and intersectionality, health, migration, labor, and "fundamentally, the clients and the sexual demand, which are the ones that move the cogs of this business and make it possible" (Patti and Gutiérrez 2008, 146).

This section has sought to discuss some of the characteristics and statistics of the phenomenon of human trafficking in Mexico and Central America from a gender perspective. In the following section, we will deepen this approach and its intersectionality by looking at South America.

Human Trafficking in Ecuador

In August 2014, through Executive Decree 1981, the Ecuadorian state declared a war against human trafficking, illegal smuggling of migrants, sexual and labor exploitation, child pornography, corruption of minors and other forms of exploitation and prostitution of women, children, and adolescents as a policy priority. Yet, there have been many difficulties in implementing a permanent and effective public policy against the crime of human trafficking in Ecuador. Among the problems that have arisen is the lack of a fixed and clear stewardship to combat trafficking. Various ministries, each one lacking a consistent position on the matter, have taken turns in leading the fight (Montenegro and Santacruz 2014).

Through the Inter-Institutional Committee against Human Trafficking, the Ministry of the Interior handles the issue, dividing its work into committees (*mesas de trabajo*): the committee on prevention, the committee on protection, and the committee on research and sanctions. Various decentralized autonomous governments have also decided to take the issue of human trafficking into account in their agendas; these include Cotacachi, Otavalo, Lago Agrio, Colta, and Guamote (Montenegro and Santacruz 2014).

Research carried out in Otavalo and Cotacachi found that in those localities there were not only the known forms of national and international trafficking for the exploitation of labor and the mendicity of children and adolescents from indigenous communities, but also parishes (third level administrative units) where trafficking is linked to Colombian irregular armed groups. According to the districts' authorities, adolescents from indigenous communities were especially used for the transport of arms and the manufacture of uniforms for these groups. The recruiters in the cantons of Otavalo and Cotacachi were mostly people close to and even relatives of the victims. This might explain why they obtained permission from the victims' parents to leave the country. The profile of these traffickers was that of urban indigenous people with a privileged economic status (Montenegro and Santacruz 2014).

In the districts of Colta and Guamote, there was evidence of trafficking for labor exploitation, domestic servitude, and forced mendicity. Exploitation is linked to the socio-economic conditions of the population, but is also closely related to internal and international migration flows in that region that date back to the 1970s. Responding to the demand for cheap labor, people from Colta and Guamote migrated to Colombia and Venezuela during the years of the oil boom (Coloma 2012).

In Lago Agrio we found evidence of human trafficking for sexual purposes, servitude, and recruitment into criminal enterprises. Trafficking for sexual exploitation is the most visible in official records. The victims are mostly mixed-race women, adults, or adolescents. By contrast, the victims of trafficking for the purpose of servitude are children and adolescents of rural origin, who are used for domestic work in exploitative conditions. Adolescents and young adults are recruited into irregular armed groups in Colombia that are linked to drug trafficking, or into local criminal gangs that traffic in narcotics and fuel (Coloma 2012). Forced recruitment of children by illegal armed groups and criminal organizations remains a significant concern, and impunity in cases of forced child recruitment remains a challenge as authorities have not convicted any member of an armed group for child recruitment since 2017. This is despite the ongoing concern that Colombian illegal armed groups continue to strengthen their operations using children in Colombia and nearby Venezuela (USA Department of State 2020).

It should be added that border crossings and their adjacent spaces are often – especially in Latin America – remote places where the state does not exercise (or is not interested in exercising) full sovereignty. These areas constitute what some authors designate as "gray zones," "lawless areas," or "empty spaces" – depending on the circumstances (Bartolomé 2003; Cirino and Elizondo 2003; Garay 2004). Examples include the triple border in the Amazon region between Colombia, Brazil, and Peru – especially the axis connecting Leticia (Colombia), Tabatinga (Brazil), and Lago Agrio (Ecuador) near the Colombian border; and Maicao (Colombia) on the Venezuelan border. These and other similar spaces are fertile lands in which, due to the scant presence or concomitance of the state, various illicit commercial ventures thrive (Arellano 2013).

Official records account for less than a half of the current cases, many of which are never even discovered or reported (Montenegro and Santacruz 2014). As an analytical category, gender allows us to examine

280 *María Amelia Viteri and Iréri Ceja*

how state actions in these territories – which include actions to regulate border crossings and/or through which people who cross the borders can overflow or reconfigure them – are materialized in the body (Camacho 2014, 26).

Human Trafficking in Colombia

In Colombia, human trafficking is criminalized in the framework of the protection of the legal right to individual freedom. The lack of control over the flow of capital from the illegal trafficking of persons in that country was one of the factors that led to the broadening of the definition of the conduct that is now considered human trafficking (Abadía 2012).

The punitive judicial reality and how it relates to the cases that are dealt with can be analyzed in depth from a historical perspective of the structural production of gender inequalities. According to Abadía (2012), the legal entitlement to personal freedom and autonomy can be (mis)interpreted as not being violated if a woman who engages in prostitution makes an adequate and reasonably proportionate profit. This interpretation means that many accused persons are not prosecuted in Colombia, even though the law states that they should be. According to the same author, in 60% of the cases of female sex trafficking in Colombia, the purported victims were not interested in going to trial. In 2010, out of 62,378 crimes brought to justice in Colombia, only five resulted in convictions within the framework of human trafficking (Abadía 2012).

Organ Trafficking

Transplant tourism and organ trafficking are assets in the medical economies of poor and abandoned countries. Thus, the "global cities" (cf. Sassen 2007) of this market are not cities like New York or London, but Lima, Manila, and Bombay, among others. For example, "the circulation of kidneys follows the established routes of capital from South to North, [...] from blacks and mulattos to whites, and from women to men [...]. Women from anywhere in the world are rarely the recipients of these purchased or stolen organs" (Scheper-Hughes 2005, 201). Historical examples cited by the same author are the case of Argentina during the Dirty War in the 1970s and Brazil during the military dictatorship, periods in which, following government orders, doctors had to meet quotas for organs and human tissue from forcibly "disappeared" persons, the mentally ill and prisoners to serve the military regime.

Scheper-Hughes (2005) explains how the organ trade takes place in a transnational space, where surgeons, patients, donors, organ hunters, and sellers circulate. They travel along the routes of capital and technology, where capitalism, in its neoliberal phase, has disrupted the

A Gender Perspective   281

relations between capital and the body, and has modified the original conceptions of life, death, and sacrifice, offering bodies and lives to the highest bidder.

According to Mexico's National Registry of Missing Persons (RNPED[8]), 56,008 people ages 0–17 went missing or were not located between 2007 and 2020 (CNB 2020). According to the same registry, there are 3,000 documented cases of children stolen in the last year and a half, and 45,000 that are considered missing; although there is no precise data on how many of them have been trafficked for their organs or for sexual exploitation (Rosagel 2014). The same organization points out that kidnapping gangs operate in the northern and southern border areas of the country and in large cities such as the capital, as well as in Estado de México, Veracruz, Tijuana, Monterrey, and Guadalajara. Furthermore, Matesanz (cited in Sevillano 2014) states that in Latin America, the illegal purchase of organs has moved from the Andean region to Mexico and Central American countries.

A perspective from gender anthropology highlights who benefits as recipient of the organs and who is sacrificed in this transaction. The fact that the organ trajectory goes from women to men is not isolated, but rather part of structural gender-based violence, where the bodies of women, whose organs are trafficked, become, once again, vulnerable and are violated by gender-based inequalities.

Localized Violence: Drug Trafficking

Illegal drug markets must be understood beyond the simplistic logic of capital flows and exchanges of services and substances for money. In order to appreciate the role that drug trafficking and its actors play in neighborhoods and communities, it is important to analyze them as commodities, symbols, and tools (Curtis and Wendel 2002).

The accelerated increase in drug crimes is explained – and is also beginning to be observed – by a specific profile of women who engage in drug trafficking, as couriers or mules. Thus, some particular gender characteristics are mentioned; for example, physical beauty or marital status, such as that of single mothers, combined with economic factors (Torres 2008):

> [...] in the crimes committed by women, those of drug trafficking stand out [...] since women are used by large-scale dealers, mainly as "couriers" or transporters of drugs from the border area with Peru in the Province of Loja and in the border area with Colombia in the East, in Putumayo and Lago Agrio. The general characteristics of the women used in the commission of these crimes are those of being people with acute economic and social problems; that is to say, unemployed, underemployed, from disintegrated homes, single

282 *María Amelia Viteri and Iréri Ceja*

mothers who have belonged to large and poor households, national or foreign migrants, many of whom possess physical features of notable beauty [...].

(Vega Uquillas et al., 1987, 107)

Carmen Antony (2004) notes that one of the "advantages" of small-scale drug trafficking is that it allows women to continue to perform household tasks. In a context where women's opportunities are severely limited, it is not surprising that trafficking is presented as an option that also allows them to fulfill their productive and reproductive roles simultaneously (Torres 2008). In this regard, Rodríguez (2004) states that

[...] drug trafficking is an activity that often allows women to continue to play the culturally assigned roles of mother, wife, and housewife, and which provides income that is impossible to obtain through other means, whether in formal or informal jobs [...] It is they who move the drugs, and since they represent the most visible part of the chain, they run the greatest risk of being arrested [...].

(Rodríguez 2004, 10)

Rodríguez (2004) emphasizes that the option of drug trafficking allows women to exercise their traditional roles of mothers and caretakers in parallel with the new role of family provider that has emerged as a result of the impoverishment of Latin American households. Yet Rodríguez also seems to indicate that, because of the demands of these roles, women enter trafficking from certain positions and not others. It is not clear whether the author is suggesting that this subordinate insertion is due to the dynamics of trafficking itself (mostly dominated by men) or to women's needs: that women cannot become full-time traffickers, that their mobility is limited by the reproductive roles they must play, or a combination of these elements. However, it is clear from Rodríguez's proposal (2004) that trafficking allows women to continue to exercise, in a sort of acrobatic game, the multiple roles that are socially and culturally assigned to them, in a context of crisis and exacerbation of women's "poverty of time" (Torres 2008).

In this regard, Hopenhayn and Arriagada (2000, 18) states that, at the local level, there is a growing participation of low-income women and minors in micro-trafficking, something that generates unprecedented judicial and criminal problems. In areas where the state has scant presence or control, micro-trafficking easily becomes a survival strategy adopted by women who are heads of household, and even by elderly people with limited resources. Many low-income people end up abandoning their previous occupations since illegal drug trafficking provides them with substantially higher incomes. Latin American mules are mostly heads of households; they come from marginal sectors

A Gender Perspective   283

and their lives are marked by various forms of violence, including sexual abuse (Amaya and Cosecha Roja 2014).

Arriagada and Hopenhayn (2000) highlight the fact that it is not only women but also other "vulnerable" groups (children and the elderly) who are increasingly being trafficked, signaling the "usefulness" these groups represent to those who run trafficking networks. In the end, they are considered expendable, and (as noted above) are to some extent presumed to be more "invisible" to mechanisms of control, given that trafficking is traditionally thought of as being carried out by young men (Torres 2008).

Maher and Daly (1996) argue that, since the 1980s, women have been taking a more active role in illegal economies because of the introduction of crack cocaine. Similarly, market expansion has allowed some women to transcend subordinate roles; however, in the study carried out by the authors on 200 women in the New York area over three years, it was found that none of them owned the business. Thus, one can speak of an institutionalized sexism, whereby women adopt male and violent qualities to reach certain roles within the drug markets.

In turn, Campbell (2008) speaks of a feminization of drug contraband that has complex and contradictory impacts on women's lives. Among these effects is the violence caused by drugs, the traffickers' coercion, and manipulation of women to get them to act as mules, and frequent threats to collect on the drug-related debts of their partners. Furthermore, the adoption of *capo* (kingpin) roles verifies forms of male domination and control that do not transform the patriarchal cultural economy, but rather reinforce macho symbolism (Campbell 2008, 236–237). Such is the case of the "Queen of the Pacific," remembered as the first twenty-first century female leader of Mexican drug trafficking who shatters the image of women as only trophies (Santamaría 2012). It therefore becomes imperative to analyze gender hegemonic constructions in *narco*-culture and its manifestations. In the Mexican context, becoming involved in drug trafficking becomes a "viable option in an environment marked by discrimination and labor segregation by sex" (Jiménez 2014, 116). Thus, women are more defenseless as they face arrest and prosecution, since they lack economic resources and social standing.

Conclusions

In this paper, we set out to broaden the view on the dynamics and processes of Latin America's global border system and illicit markets by incorporating a perspective and analytical framework from gender studies and anthropology. In this context, we highlighted the importance of understanding gender in its applied dimension and, therefore, its intersectionality with the categories of illegality. To this end, we problematized concepts such as borders, the body, illegal markets,

284 *María Amelia Viteri and Iréri Ceja*

and violence in relation to a gender perspective and discussed some of the illegal markets and categories of violence such as trafficking and smuggling, feminicide, organ trafficking, and drug trafficking based on known Latin American cases.

Considering the foregoing analysis, we conclude that it is essential to make the category of gender legible in all areas of the global border system. Elucidating both the definition and diversification of criminal offenses as well as the roles of the actors in illicit markets is a task that concerns academia, non-governmental organizations and, ultimately, states, the governing bodies responsible for eradicating this violence.

We emphasize that it is a challenge for academia to establish the role of gender as a more visible differential category in border, asymmetric, and globally connected spaces, by analyzing the sexually constructed character of institutions and processes (Herrera 2012, 37). Recognizing gender as a differential category allows us to consider the diverse fields that overlap in the same body, in the same fact.

Violence is a response to the structural frameworks within gender differentiation and to the very origin of illicit markets. In this sense, gender as a differential category cannot be separated from the understanding of these phenomena. Furthermore, the rational use of violence as a means of systematically operatizing bodies and their relationship to social and symbolic capital, along with their corresponding economic flows in a global capitalist context, should also be understood along these lines.

Notes

1. This English translation does not account for the COVID pandemic's impact on the study of Latin American Border Systems.
2. In this regard, see the work of Lina Camacho (2014), who discusses the border trajectories of transgender women in the Amazon basin's triple border region (Colombia, Brazil, and Peru). Camacho analyzes the situated context, which involves relating the order of gender and race with the territorial order at borders.
3. This concept refers to all the "ideas, practices, identities, and social capital that are transmitted through a migratory circuit" (Levitt 1996, 6–5).
4. Violent murders include femicide, murder, homicide, and women killed by organized crime.
5. For more details on this case, see Viteri (2013).
6. Feminicide holds responsible not only the male perpetrators, but also the state and judicial structures that normalize hatred against women. State responsibility for these murders takes many faces: commission of the actual killing, toleration of the perpetrators' violent acts, or the state's failure to assume responsibility for ensuring the safety of its female citizens.
7. Data obtained in an interview with personnel from the Attorney General's Office, Quito, February 2, 2015.
8. This acronym refers to the institution's name in Spanish: "Registro Nacional de Datos de Personas Extraviadas o Desaparecidas."

References

Abadía, Gloria. 2012. "Usos y abusos del sistema penal. Su uso como forma de emancipación femenina: un estudio de caso del delito de trata de personas en Colombia, Bogotá." *Revista de Estudios Sociales*, 4, 104–117.

Adler-Lomnitz, Larissa. 1994. *Redes sociales, cultura y poder: ensayos de antropología latinoamericana*. Mexico: FLACSO.

Álvarez Velasco, Soledad. 2015. *Frontera sur chiapaneca: el muro humano de la violencia*. Mexico: Universidad Iberoamericana de México y CIESAS.

Amaya, Sol and Cosecha Roja. 2014. "Informe sobre mulas: el eslabón más débil del narcotráfico." *Cosecha Roja, Red de Periodistas Judiciales de Latinoamérica*. http://cosecharoja.org/informe-sobre-mulas-el-eslabon-mas-debil-del-narcotrafico/. Accessed 8 April 2014.

Anderson, Benedict. 1993. *Comunidades imaginadas*. Mexico: Fondo de Cultura Económica.

Ángeles Cruz, Hugo and Martha Luz Rojas Wiesner. 2000. "Migración femenina internacional en la frontera sur de México." *Papeles de Población*, 6 (23), 127–151.

Antony, Carmen. 2004. "Panorama de la situación de las mujeres privadas de libertad en América Latina desde una perspectiva de género." In *Violencia contra las mujeres privadas de libertad en América Latina*, 75–90. Mexico: Fundación para el Debido Proceso Legal.

Anzaldúa, Gloria. 2012. *Borderlands/La frontera: the new mestiza*. Fourth edition. San Francisco: Aunte Lute Books.

Arellano, Daniel. 2013. "La Triple Frontera como polo de atracción de actividades ilícitas: Condiciones endógenas institucionales e ilegalidad." *Aternea (Concepción,)*, 508, 101–120.

Arriagada, Irma and Martín Hopenhayn. 2000. "Producción, tráfico y consumo de drogas en América Latina". *Serie Políticas Sociales*. 41. Santiago de Chile: CEPAL.

Bales, Kevin. 2009. *The Slave Next Door: Human Trafficking and Slavery in America Today*. Berkeley and Los Angeles: University of California Press.

——— 2012. *Disposable People: New Slavery in the Global Economy*. Berkeley and Los Angeles: University of California Press.

Balibar, Étienne. 2005. "Fronteras del mundo, fronteras de la política." *Alteridades* (July-December): 87–96.

Bartolomé, Mariano. 2003. "¿Áreas sin ley o zonas grises? Análisis de tres casos en la zona noroeste de América del Sur." VI Encuentro Nacional de Estudios Estratégicos, Buenos Aires, November 2003. http://www1.hedn.gov.ar/dependencias/Ieeri/ennee/vi/Tema%202/PonenciaBartolome-Tema2.doc. Accessed October 2014.

Bernstein, Elizabeth. 2014. "¿Las políticas carcelarias representan la justicia de género?" *Debate Feminista*, 50 (25), 280–320.

Betanzos Núñez, Mireya. 2014. "Trata de mujeres, instituciones estatales y seguridad nacional en México." Master's thesis, FLACSO-Sede Ecuador.

Bourgois, Philippe. 2010. *En busca de respeto: Vendiendo crack en Harlem*. Buenos Aires: Siglo XXI Editores.

Butler, Judith. 2004. *Undoing Gender*. New York: Routledge.

——— 2006. *Gender Trouble: Feminism and the Subversion of Identity*. London: Routledge.

286 *María Amelia Viteri and Iréri Ceja*

Camacho, Lina. 2014. "Trayectorias fronterizas de mujeres transgénero: identidad, cuerpo y territorio." Master's dissertation, FLACSO-Sede Ecuador.

Campbell, Howard. 2008. "Female Drug Smugglers on the U-S.-Mexico Border: Gender, Crime, and Empowerment." *Anthropological Quarterly*, 81, 233–267.

Carcero, Ana. 2011. *Femicidio en Ecuador*. Quito: Comisión de transición hacia el Consejo de las mujeres y la igualdad de género.

Carrigan, Tim, Bob Connell, and John Lee. 1985. "Toward a New Sociology of Masculinity." *Theory and Society*, 14 (5), 551–604.

Carrión, Fernando, Diana Mejía and Johanna Espín. 2013. *Aproximaciones a la frontera*. Quito: FLACSO-Ecuador.

Casper, Monica and Lisa Jean Moore. 2009. *Missing Bodies: The Politics of Visibility*. New York and London: New York University Press.

Cerbino, Mauro and Anahi Macaroff. 2010. "Un diálogo con José Manuel Valenzuela. Heridas abiertas en la frontera México-Estados Unidos: migración, feminicidio y narco-cultura." *Íconos. Revista de Ciencias Sociales*, 39, 169–178.

Coloma, Soledad. 2012. *Diagnóstico sobre la trata de personas en el cantón Lago Agrio, provincia de Sucumbíos*. Quito: USAID, FLACSO, OIM.

Comisión Nacional de Búsqueda. 2020. "Proyecto de Protocolo Adicional para la Búsqueda de Niñas, Niños y Adolescentes Versión borrador para consulta pública." México. https://www.gob.mx/cms/uploads/attachment/file/599897/141220_Proyecto_PABNNA.pdf. Accessed 17 January 2021.

Connell, Raewyn and James Messerschmidt. 2005. "Hegemonic Masculinity: Rethinking the Concept." *Gender and Society*, 19 (6), 829–859. http://gas.sagepub.com/ content/19/6/829.short. Accessed 2 October 2014.

Curtis, Ric and Travis Wendel. 2002. "Toward the Development of a Typology of Illegal Drug Markets." *Crime Prevention Studies*, 11, 121–152.

De Beauvoir, Simone. 2005. *El segundo sexo*. Spain: Cátedra.

De Genova, Nicholas. 2002. "Migrant 'Illegality' and Deportability in Everyday Life." *Annual Review of Anthropology*, 31 (1), 419–447. https://www.annualreviews.org/doi/pdf/10.1146/annurev.anthro.31.040402.085432. Accessed 13 September 2014.

De Sousa, Rosinaldo Silva and Isabel Anaya Ferreira. 2004. "Narcotráfico y economía ilícita: las redes del crimen organizado en Río de Janeiro." *Revista Mexicana de Sociología*, 66 (1), 141–192.

Denich, Dette. 1995. "Of Arms, Men and Ethic War in (Former) Yugoslavia." In *Feminism, Nationalism and Militarism*, edited by Constance R. Sutton, 32–45. Arlington: American Anthropological Association.

Doezema, Jo. 2002. "Who Gets to Choose? Coercion, Consent, and the UN Trafficking Protocol." *Gender and Development*, 19 (1), 20–27.

Domenech, Eduardo. 2013. "Las migraciones son como el agua: Hacia la instauración de políticas de 'control con rostro humano.' La gobernabilidad migratoria en la Argentina." *Revista Latinoamericana*, 13 (35), 119–142.

Elizondo, Silvana and Julio Cirino. 2003. "La corrupción dentro del concepto de Estados fallidos." *Revista Enfoques: Ciencia Política y Administración Pública*, 1, 169–180.

Eveline, Joan and Carol Bacchi. 2005. "What are We Mainstreaming When We Mainstream Gender?" *International Feminist Journal of Politics*, 7 (4), 496–512.

A Gender Perspective 287

Faret, Laurent. 1997. "La frontera y el Estado-nación en la perspectiva de los migrantes internacionales." In *Las fronteras del Istmo. Fronteras y sociedades entre el sur de México y América Central, edited by Philippe Bovin*, 39–43. Mexico: Centro Francés de Estudios Mexicanos y Centroamericanos.

Farmer, Paul. 1996. "On Suffering and Structural Violence: A View from Below." *Social Suffering*, 125 (1), 261–283.

Fawcett, Charles Bungay. 1918. *Frontiers. A Study in Political Geography*. Oxford: Oxford University Press.

Feldman-Bianco, Bela. 2018. "O Brasil frente ao regime global de controle das migrações: Direitos humanos, securitização e violências." *Travessia, Revista do Migrante* 83, 11–36. https://www.corteidh.or.cr/tablas/r38868.pdf. Accessed 21 September 2019.

Fernández, Raúl. 1980. *La frontera México-Estados Unidos: Un estudio socioeconómico*. Mexico City: Terra Nova.

Fiscalía General del Estado. 2019. *Boletín Criminológico y de Estadística Delictual; Femicidio*. Ecuador. https://www.fiscalia.gob.ec/pdf/politica-criminal/Boletin-Criminologico-de-Estadistica-Delictual-Femicidio.pdf. Accessed 8 August 2014.

Garay, Cristián. 2004. "Estados débiles y espacios vacíos. El caso chileno." *Security and Defense Studies Review*, 4 (2), 91–113.

Garduño, Everardo. 2003. "Antropología de la frontera, la migración y los procesos transnacionales." *Frontera Norte*, 15 (30), 65–89.

Ghezzi, Simone and Enzo Mingione. 2003. "Beyond the Informal Economy: New Trends in Post-Fordist Transition." In *Globalization the State and Violence*, 87–106. Walnut Creek, CA: Alta Mira Press.

Guillén, Juan Luis. 2015. "La trata de personas compite con el narcotráfico en América Latina." http://www.solidaridad.net/noticia/8621/la-trata-de-personas-compite-con-el-narcotrafico-en-america-latina. Accessed 7 January 2015.

Guizardi, Menara. 2020. "Movilidades, violencias y Agencias." *Las Mujeres y las Regiones Fronterizas Latinomericanas*, 289, 70–80.

Hernández Castillo, Aida. 2006. "Violencia de Estado, violencia de género en Atenco." http://www.voltairenet.org/article139314.html. Accessed 7 September 2014.

Herrera, Gioconda. 2012. "Género y migración internacional en la experiencia latinoamericana. De la visibilización del campo a una presencia selectiva." *Política y Sociedad*, 49 (1), 35–46.

Hopenhayn, Martin and Irma Arriagada. 2000. *Producción, tráfico y consumo de drogas en América Latina*. Santiago: Cepal.

International Labour Organization (ILO). 2014. "El trabajo forzoso genera ganancias por 12.000 millones de dólares en América latina y el Caribe." http://www.ilo.org/americas/sala-de-prensa/WCMS_244396/lang–es/index.htm. Accessed 13 December 2014.

Jiménez Valdez, Elsa. 2014. "Mujeres, narco y violencia: resultados de una guerra fallida." *Región y Sociedad*, special number 4, 101–128.

Lagarde, Marcela. 2006. *Violencia feminicida en el Estado de México*. Mexico: Congreso de la Unión, Cámara de Diputados, LIX Legislatura.

Levitt, Peggy. 1996. "Social Remittances: Migration Driven Local-Level Forms of Cultural Diffusion." *International Migration Review*, 32 (4), 926–948.

288 *María Amelia Viteri and Iréri Ceja*

Maher, Lisa and Kathleen Daly. 1996. "Women in the Street Level Drug Economy: Continuity or Change?" *Criminology*, 34 (4), 465–492.

Mansur, Ghilerme. 2015. "Dilemas acerca de la centralización de la trata de personas en los debates sobre las políticas de migración en Brasil". Unpublished paper.

Moi, Toril. 1999. *What is a Woman? And Other Essays*. New York: Oxford University Press.

Montañez, Gustavo and Ovidio Delgado. 1998. "Espacio, territorio y región: conceptos básicos para un proyecto nacional." *Cuadernos de Geografía. Revista del Departamento de Geografía de la Universidad Nacional de Colombia*, 7(1-2), 120–134.

Montenegro, Adriana and Argentina Santacruz. 2014. "Haciendo camino al andar: la construcción local de política pública contra la trata de personas en Ecuador." *URVIO-Revista Latinoamericana de Estudios de Seguridad*, 14, 79–92.

Patti, Mariaconcetta and Marina Gutiérrez. 2008. "Trata, tráfico y prostitución: aproximaciones conceptuales al debate." *Mora*, 14 (2). http://www.scielo.org. ar/pdf/ mora/v14n2/v14n2a07.pdf. Accessed 12 October 2014.

Radford, Jill and Diana Russell. 1992. *Femicide: The Politics of Woman Killing*. Oxford: Twayne Publishers.

Ratzel, Friedrich. 1987. *La géographie politique: les concepts fondamentaux*. Paris: Fayard.

Redfield, Robert. 1941. *The folk culture of Yucatan*. Chicago: University of Chicago Press.

Red Latinoamericana de Análisis de Seguridad y Delincuencia Organizada (RELASEDOR). 2015. http://relasedor.org/. Accessed 4 February 2015.

Revelo, Patricia. 2005. "La costumbre de matar: Proliferación de la violencia en Ciudad Juárez, Chihuahua, México." *Nueva Antropología*, 65, 149–166.

Rodríguez, María Noel. 2004. "Mujer y cárcel en América Latina." In *Violencia contra las mujeres privadas de libertad en América Latina*, 57–74. Mexico City: Comisión de Derechos Humanos del Distrito Federal y Fundación para el Debido Proceso Legal.

Rosagel, Shalia. 2014. "México tiene 45 mil niños desaparecidos y su fin es explotación sexual o tráfico de órganos, alerta fundación." *Sin Embargo.mx* http://www.sinembargo.mx/28-06-2014/1039967. Accessed 16 September 2014.

Ruiz, Martha Cecilia. 2015. *Bodies, Borders and Boundaries: Erotic Transactions and Intra-Regional Migrations in Ecuador*. PhD diss., Vrije Universiteit Amsterdam.

Sansó-Rubert, Daniel. 2010. "Criminalidad organizada y género. ¿Hacia una redefinición del papel de la mujer en el seno de las organizaciones criminales?" *Revista de l'Institut Universitari d'Investigació en Criminologia i Ciències Penals de la UV*, No. 3 (March): 3–21. http://www.uv.es/iccp/recrim/recrim10/ recrim10a01.pdf. Accessed 27 November 2014.

Santamaría, Arturo. 2012. *Las jefas del narco: El ascenso de las mujeres en el crimen organizado*. Mexico: Grijalbo.

Sassen, Saskia. 2007. "La ciudad global: emplazamiento estratégico, nueva frontera." In *Barcelona 1978-1997*, edited by Manolo Laguillo, 36–44. Barcelona: Macba.

Scheper-Hughes, Nancy. 2005. "El comercio infame: capitalismo milenarista, valores humanos y justicia global en el tráfico de órganos." *Revista de Antropología Social*. http://revistas.ucm.es/index.php/RASO/article/view/RASO0505110195A. Accessed 15 September 2014.

A Gender Perspective 289

Segato, Rita. 2004. "Territorio, soberanía y crímenes de segundo Estado: la escritura en el cuerpo de las mujeres asesinadadsen Ciudad Juárez". *Série Antropologia.* http://repositorio.ciem.ucr.ac.cr/jspui/bitstream/123456789/19/2/RCIEM010.pdf. Accessed 19 December 2021.

Segato, Rita. 2012. "Femigenocidio y feminicidio: una propuesta de tipificación." *Revista herramienta,* No. 49. https://biblat.unam.mx/hevila/HerramientaBuenos Aires/2012/no49/10.pdf. Accessed 17 September 2014.

—— 2013. "Territorios, soberanía y crímenes de segundo Estado: la escritura en el cuerpo de las mujeres asesinadas en Ciudad Juárez." Buenos Aires: Tinta Limón. https://www.feministas.org/IMG/pdf/rita_segato_.pdf. Accessed 15 October 2014.

Sevillano, Elena G. 2014. "Uno de cada diez trasplantes en el mundo procede del tráfico ilegal." *El País Online.* http://sociedad.elpais.com/sociedad/2014/03/12/actualidad/1394658467_751231.html. Accessed 3 December 2014.

Tilly, Charles. 1985. "War Making and State Making as Organized Crime." In *Bringing the State Back In,* edited by Peter Evans, Dietrich Rueschemeyer, and Theda Skocpol, 169–191. Cambridge: Cambridge University Press.

Torres, Andreina. 2008. "Drogas, cárcel y género en Ecuador: La experiencia de mujeres 'mulas.'" Master's thesis, FLACSO-Sede Ecuador.

United Nations Office on Drugs and Crime (UNODC). 2014. "Tráfico de Pessoas e Contrabando de Migrantes." http://www.unodc.org/lpo-brazil/es/trafico-de-pessoas/index.html. Accessed 10 October 2014.

USA Department of State. 2020. *Trafficking in Persons Report 20th Edition.* https://www.state.gov/wp-content/uploads/2020/06/2020-TIP-Report-Complete-062420-FINAL.pdf. Accessed 11 February 2021.

Varela Huerta, Amarela. 2017. "La trinidad perversa de la que huyen las fugitivas centroamericanas: violencia feminicida, violencia de estado y violencia de mercado." Mexico City: Universidad Autónoma de la Ciudad de México.

Vega Uquillas, Víctor, Manuel González Miño and Silvana Rivadeneira. 1987. "Tendencias de la criminalidad en el Ecuador." In *Archivos de criminología Neuropsiquiatría y Disciplinas Conexas.* Quito: Facultad de Jurisprudencia, Ciencias Políticas y Sociales de la Universidad Central del Ecuador.

Viteri, María Amelia. 2014. *Desbordes: Translating Racial, Ethnic, Sexual and Gender Identities across the Americas.* New York: SUNY Press.

—— 2013. "Gender Violence Across the Americas: Two Cities, one Problem." *Al Jazeera,* 25 March 2013. http://www.aljazeera.com/indepth/opinion/2013/03/201332581531397978.html. Accessed 4 January 2014.

Viteri, María Amelia, Iréri Ceja and Cristina Yépez. 2017. *Corpografías: género y fronteras en América Latina.* Quito: FLACSO, IDRC.

Weber, Max. 2001. *Ensayos sobre metodología sociológica.* Buenos Aires: Amorrortu Editores.

—— "Annual total number of homicides of women, aged 15 years over, killed by gender violence." CEPALSTAT. https://oig.cepal.org/en/indicators/femicide-or-feminicide. Accessed 11 February 2020.

Index

Note: Page numbers in **bold** denote tables, page numbers in *italics* denote figures. Page numbers of the form XnY denote footnote Y on page X.

Abadía, Gloria 280
Acajutla, port of 132
Acapulco 161
Acre 197, 198, 203, 204; war 40
Adler-Lomnitz, Larissa 271
Adriatic Coast 183
Agapóris River 206
agro-industry 48, 53, 54
Agua Caliente 131
Agua Prieta 153
Aguas Blancas 54, 98
Ahuachapán, department of 130
air routes: in Bolivia 56; in Peru 29
aircrafts: in Bolivia 53, 56; in Guatemala 133
airstrips 133, 134, 163; *see also* runways
Albania 182, 183
Alenquer 209
Almeirim 209
Alonso, William 149
Alps, the 173
Al-Qaeda 146
Alto Adige/South Tryrol 175, 178
Alto Alegre 207
Alto Cenepa 67; war 84
Alto Huallaga Valley 27
Alto Paraguay 54
Alto Paraná 203
Alvarado Galindo, Arturo 122
Álvarez Velasco, Soledad 270, 277
Amajari 207
Amapá 197, 198, 209, 210
Amatique Bay 130
Amazon: basin 65, 203, 284; forest 198; region 19, 66, 204, 205, 279; river 66, 204, 209

Amazonas: border 204; department of 32, 205, 207; state 197, 198, 205, 206
Ancel, Jacques 212
Andean Community 17
Andean Pact on Borders 17
Andreas, Peter 144, 146, 151, 156, 157
Angostura 69, 86n7, 227
anti-drug policy 233, 237, 240; in Peru 27
Antony, Carmen 282
Apa River 201
Apulia; coast 183; region 183
Apurimac 27, **32**
Araguari River 211
Aramburú, Carlos 19
Arellano, Diana 102
Arellano Félix Cartel 159
Arequipa 25, 28, 30, 31, 32
Argentina 41, 42, 44, 77; border studies 99–107; borders 89–99; borders with Bolivia 41, 42, 44, 53, 54, 56; borders with Brazil 96, 109, 110; borders with Chile 92, 96, 101, 109; borders with Paraguay 94, 96, 101–105; borders with Uruguay 109
Argentine Geographic Institute 96
Arica 21, 55, 253
Arizona 152, 153
armed conflict 148; in Colombia 65, 68–70; Ecuador-Peru 66; in Guatemala 7, 118, 121, 133, 136
Armijo Canto, Natalia 121, 155
arms trafficking 70, 76, 99, 108, 224, 245; in Bolivia 56; in bordering cities 255; in Brazil 213, 216; in Guatemala 122; in Italy 180, 183; in Mexico 151, 156, 162

Index   291

Arriagada, Camilo 252
Arriagada, Irma 282, 283
Arriola, Aura Marina 120
Arriola, Luis Alfredo 120, 121, 124
Arroyo, Bárbara 122
Arroyo San Miguel Convention 200
Artigas, department of 200
Ashby, Paul 151, 159
Asia 28, 42, 49, 55, 78, 259; migration in 65
Asia-Pacific Basin 236, 239
Astorga, Luis 145, 152, 156
ATF *see* Bureau of Alcohol, Tobacco, Firearms, and Explosives
Atlantic Ocean 67, 96, 127, 130, 204, 209
Ayacucho 27, 28, 32
Aycinena-Wyke Treaty 126, 129
Aziz Nassif, Alberto 151
Azul River 154

bagayeros 46, 54
Bagley, Bruce 75, 86, 156–159
Bahia Negra 201
Baja California 152, 153, 165
Bales, Kevin 276
Balkans 173, 183
balloon effect 64, 74, 77, 237, 238
Barcelos 207
Barvinsk, Georgina María 105
Basail, Alain 121
Beagle Channel 92
Belaúnde Terry, Fernando 67
Belgium 124
Belize 118, 121, 125–127, 129, 130, 135–137, 154
Belize River 126
Belem, port of 259
Beltrán Leyva: brothers 240; cartel 159
Benedetti, Alejandro 99, 102, 110
Beni 41, 55, 56
Bennett & Meany 125
Berbice, region of 209
Bermejo 54, 97
Bernardo de Irigoyen, province of 98
Bernstein, Elizabeth 276
Bethel-Frontera Corozal 129
Binational Association of Municipalities of Southern Ecuador and Northern Peru 254
binational bridge, Brazil-French Guiana 198, 201, 211
binational pairs, Mexico-US 153
birth control 277

black money 50, 180; *see also* money laundering
Boa Vista 198, 207, 208
Bogotá 206, 242, 263
Boko Haram 147
Bolívar, department of 80, 207
Bolivia 104, 144, 157, 196; borders with Argentina 40–44, 47, 53, 54; borders with Brazil 41, 42, 44, 52–54; borders with Chile 40, 47, 48, 51, 55, 58; borders with Paraguay 40, 53–56, 58; borders with Peru 49, 53, 55, 59; territory loss 43
Bolivian Institute of Foreign Trade 42
Bolognesi-Drosdoff, María Cecilia 18
Bolpebra 19, 55
Bombay 280
Bonfim 208
Boquerón 54
border: asymmetries 40, 94; conceptualization 148; definition 3, 19; and globalization 2, 65, 72, 76, 100, 144, 145, 150; symbolic 100, 196; and urban growth 261
border cities 8, 241, 250, 251, 254, 259, 262, 263; in Argentina 95, 96, 101, 102; in Bolivia 54; in Ecuador 72; in Mexico 145, 151, 153, 156, 160, 164, 258; in Peru 20, 31
border crossings: in Argentina 110n13; in Bolivia 48, *52*, 56; in Brazil 199; in Guatemala 129, 131; in Latin America 279; in Mexico *154*, 156, 163; *see also* border posts
border dynamics 171, 185, 189; in Brazil 200; in Ecuador 68, 78, 79, 83; and gender 271, 272; in Guatemala 124, 132, 135; in Latin America 187; in Mexico 155, in Peru 17, 20, 22, 34
Border Integration Zones 17
border municipalities: in Bolivia 46, 51, 57; in Brazil 207; in Guatemala 127, 134, 136
border posts 180; in Bolivia 46, 48, 55; in Guatemala 129, 131; *see also* border crossings
border strip: in Bolivia 59; Brazil 195–200, 208–211, 216, 255
border studies: in Argentina 89, 94, 99, 101, 107; and geopolitics 268; in Peru 25
border system 41, 49, 145, 186, 244; in Argentina 101; in Bolivia 43, 47; in Brazil 206, 216; in Ecuador 77; and

292   Index

gender 266; in Guatemala 118, 122, 125; in Italy 172, 173, 179; in Latin America 108, 172, 283; in Mexico 156; and migration 25; in Peru 16, 22, 28, 30, 33
Borja, Rodrigo 67
brasiguayos 202; see also *Braziguayans*
Brasilia 67, 73
Brasilia Act 17
Braziguayans 202, 203
Brazil: 1851 Convention 204; 1867 Treaty 203; 1927 Complementary Treaty 201; borders with Argentina 196, 198–200; borders with Bolivia 203, 204; borders with Colombia 205, 206; borders with French Guiana 210, 211; borders with Guyana 208, 209; borders with Paraguay 201–203; borders with Perú 204, 205; borders with Suriname 209, 210; borders with Uruguay 200, 201; borders with Venezuela 206–208; dictatorship 280; empire 109, 211
Brazil-Bolivia Mixed Demarcation Commission 203, 204
Brazil-Bolivia-Paraguay Tripartite Point 204
Brazilian Boundary Demarcation Commission 210, 213
Brenner, Neil 146–150
Brewer, Stephanie 151
Brigden, Noelle K. 121
British Honduras 155
British Guiana 209, 211
Brownsville 153
Buenaventura, port of 78
Buenos Aires 42, 53, 104, 105
Bunker, Robert J. 151
Bureau of Alcohol, Tobacco, Firearms, and Explosives 162

Caballococha 205
Cabezas Carcache, Horacio 133
Cajamarca 21, 32
Calçoene 210
Calexico 153
Cali Cartel 75, 156, 159, 239
California 152, 153, 159
Callao 28–30, 32
Camacho, Lina 284
cambistas 200
camellos 103
Campbell, Howard 283

Campeche 123, 129, 133, 154
Canada 26, 55, 164, 239, 240, 269
Cañar 80, 84
Canindeyú 203
cannabis: plantations 133, 183; production 234; seizures 104, 183; trafficking 180, 182, 183; *see also* marijuana
Cantá 208
capital accumulation 4, 150, 238
capitalism 8, 146, 147, 268, 269, 272, 280
Caquetá River 206
Caracaraí 208
Carchi 79, 80, 83, 84
Caribbean 156, 158, 231, 252
Carlos Lehder Cartel 75
Carmen Xhan 129, 154
Caroebe 208
Carrillo Fuentes Cartel 159; *see also* Tijuana Cartel
Carrión, Fernando 6, 9, 67, 72, 268
Carrión, Francisco 67
Casillas, Rodolfo 151
Caste War 153
Castells, Manuel 44, 146, 150, 225
Castilla C., Óscar 49
Castillo, Manuel Ángel 119, 120, 124, 136, 154
Castillo, Rodolfo 18
Central American Integration System *see* SICA
centralism 45
CEPAL 251, 274
Cepeda, Alice 151
Cerro Largo 200
Chaco War 40, 43, 44, 54
Champerico, port of 132
Charaña 55
Chavarochette, Carine 120
Chavarría, Cindy 21
Chiapas 120, 129, 133, 134, 154; economy 155; history 123
Chiarella, Roberto 18–20
Chicago 160
Chiclayo 30, 31
Chihuahua 145, 153, 156, 263
child trafficking: in Argentina 106, 213; in Ecuador 278–279
Chile 6, 9, 17; border with Argentina 96, 109n5; border with Bolivia 47, 55; border with Peru 18, 22, **23**, **24**; cocaine use in 234; contraband 21; and dirty money 49; and

Index   293

Guarantors 86n3; human trafficking 106; and illegal markets 231; immigration 26; informality 21; money laundering 247n25; relations with Argentina 92; relations with Bolivia 44; and War of the Pacific 40
Chimborazo 80, 84
Chiquimula 125, 130, 131, 135
Chiriboga, Manuel 68
chiveros 200
Chixoy River 123
Chone 81
Choneros, los 81
Christaller, William 149
chulco 74
chulquero 75
Chuquisaca 54
chuto cars 49, 55
Cicero-Domínguez, Salvador 151
CILA 129
circular migration 120
Cisplatin War 200
cities: binational 25; binational pairs 153; binuclear 253, 255, 256; cross-border 96, 254, 259; cross-border metropolitan 258; cross-border trinuclear 257; dynamics 18, 102, 136; global 146, 252, 280; mirror 94, 252, 255; twin 53, 54, 94, 153, 200, 202, 206, 209
citizen security 5, 71, 255, 262; cooperation in 53; and corruption 58; demand for 244, 261; and development 227, 261; in Ecuador 82; and violence 57
Ciudad Acuña 153
Ciudad Cuauhtémoc 129
Ciudad del Este 53; and cocaine trafficking 55, conurbation 97, International Friendship Bridge 202; Triple Frontier 213, 241, 253, 255, 257
Ciudad Hidalgo 129, 154, 277
Ciudad Juárez 153, 263; and El Paso 241, 252, 258; feminicide 269; twin city 153; and US security policies 164; violence 145, 161, 258, 269
Clot, Jean 120
Coahuila 152, 123
Coalition Against Trafficking in Women 276
Cobija/Brasileaia 53

coca cultivation *see* coca leaf production
coca leaf producers 55, 144
coca leaf production 6, 27; in Bolivia 45, 48, 157; in Colombia 157; in Guatemala 133; in Peru 27, 28, 157
cocaine 4–8, 232; in Africa 160, 105; in Andean region 104; in Argentina 104, 105; in Asia 160; in Bolivia 48–50, 53–56, 59; in Brazil 205, 237, 241; in Colombia 231, 247; distribution network 160; in Ecuador 65, 68, 69, 74–81, 86; extraction 48; in Guatemala 133; in Italy 179, 180, 182; in Mexico 156–163, 231; in Panama 231; paste 28, 48, 50, 157; in Peru 27–29, 260; processing 163, 238, 238, 239; routes 161; seizures 28, 29, 48, 82, 104, *158*, 234, 235; in the United States 231, 234
Cochabamba 41, 50, 51
cockroach effect 74
coffee production; in Bolivia 55, in Chiapas and Guatemala 134, 155
Cold War 91
Coloma, Soledad 279
Colombia: armed conflict 63, 73; balloon effect 77, 238; border with Brazil 198, 205–207; border with Ecuador 74–76; border with Peru 17, 18, 21–26; coca leaf production 6, 104, 157; cocaine production 5, 104; cocaine trafficking 133, 157, 158, 172; conflict with Ecuador 64, 65, 68–71; emigration from 26; feminicide **274, 275**; forced displacement 237; and global border system 4; gold 56; human trafficking 279; illegal markets 231; integrated urban systems 259; homicide rate 243; paramilitary 85; twin cities 256
Colombian-Peruvian war 21
colonization 19, 67, 81; endogenous 90
Colta 278, 279
COMAR 155
Comisión Mexicana de Ayuda a los Refugiados *see* COMAR
Comisión Económica para América Latina *see* CEPAL
Comisión Internacional de Límites y Aguas *see* CILA

294 *Index*

Como 180
complementary asymmetries 3, 9, 42, 259–262; and borders 72, 240; and cross-border cooperation 57; and illegal economies 253; and integration 245; Mexico 151; Mexico-US 144, 156, 258; and national policies 260
Concordia 97
Congress of Vienna 211
contraband 6, 72, 224, 232, 257; in Argentina 54, 101–103; in Bolivia 39, 43, 45–47, 49, 50, 55–56, 58; in Brazil 212, 213, 216; in Ecuador 69, 83, 256; in Guatemala 120, 122, 124, 126; of gold 49; in Mexico 144, 152, 155; in Peru 21, 29–31; transformation of 251; *see also* smuggling
contract killing 75, 81, 224, 243, 244; see also *sicariato*
Cook, Philip J. 151
Cooper, Stephen 151
Copán, department of 130
Corona Vázquez, Rodolfo 120
Corozal 129, 154, 155
Correa, Rafael 70, 71, 82, 86
Corrientes, province of 96–98, 105, 202
corruption: in Bolivia 50, 58; in Brazil 213; definition 271; and illegal markets 45, 46, 69, 148, 224, 232, 233, 243; in Italy 182; in Mexico 156, 160; and violence 271
Cortés, department of 130
Cortes Torrez, J. J. 53
Cotacachi 278, 279
Côte d'Azur 181
counterfeit products 181
couriers 281
COVID-19 pandemic 177
coyotes 134, 277
criminal economy 51
criminal organizations 8, 9; capacities 84; and child trafficking 279; and cocaine trafficking 76; and globalization 229–230, 239, 240; in Italy 182, 183, 187n1; in Mexico 151, 156, 159, 163; and migrant smuggling 185; and Plan Colombia 75; and sovereignty 147; *see also* drug cartels; organized crime
critical theory 146, 149, 15
cross-border subsystem 8, 160, 163
cross-border trade 6, 42, 53, 134, 152

cross-border urban system 153, 259
Cúcuta 256, 257
Cuenca 78
Cuernavaca 161
culebras 30
Cusco 25, 27, 30, 32

Dalmatia 178, 187
Dardón, Jacobo 119
DCSA 172, 173, 179, 180, 181, 182, 183
De Gasperi-Gruber Agreement 175
De León-Escribano, Carmen Rosa 119, 122
De Vos, Jan 119, 120, 123, 124
decentralization 261, 262, 263; in Bolivia 43, 45, 57; in Ecuador 73
Del Pozo, Karina 273
Demarest, Arthur A. 122
Demerara Region 209
Depetris, Jorge 103
Desaguadero 55
deterritorialization 148
Direzione Centrale per i Servizi Antidroga *see* DCSA
Direzione Investigativa Antimafia 179
dirty money 230; in Bolivia 49, 58
Dirty War, in Argentina 64
Doezema, Jo 276
Donoso, Claudia 68
drug cartels 7, 144, 147, 235; in Central America 122; in Colombia 77; in Ecuador 69; in Mexico 145, 150, 159, 161–162, 247n24
drug laboratories 157, 163, 238; in Ecuador 74, 77, 78, *79*, 247n33; in Guatemala 133
drug seizures 45, 82; *see also* cannabis, seizures; cocaine, seizures
drug trafficking 27, 186, 207, 215, 227, 228, 231; and gender-based violence 277, 281; and labor exploitation 61; and security 218; and women 282, 283; in Argentina 137–41, 103; in Bolivia 39, 43, 45, 48–51, 53, 54, 58; in Brazil 205, 326; in Colombia 74, 172, 256; in Ecuador 75, 76, 77, 80, 82; in Guatemala 133, 134; in Italy 265, 266, 269; in Mexico 150, 151, 156, 158, 159, 161, 162; in Peru 260, 309
drug-trafficking routes 8, 26, 237–239, 246n18; in Bolivia 49, 56, 58–59n10; Caribbean 156; in Central America 156; in Ecuador 65, 75, 83; global

260; in Guatemala 121, 126, 133; in Italy 184; in Mexico 157–161; in Peru 28, 19
Dube, Arindrajit 151
Dudley, Stephen 122, 150
Durango 156
Dutch Guiana 209
Dutch West India Company 209

Eastern Coast of Central America Commercial and Agricultural Company 125
Economic Commission for Latin America and the Caribbean see CEPAL
economic growth: in Bolivia 46; in Brazil 203; and complementary asymmetries 253; and dollarization 76; in Guatemala 126
economic policy 77, 226, 245, 257, 260
ecstasy 104
Ecuador: 2008 Constitution 65, 82; 911 system 82; borders with Colombia 94; borders with Peru 86, 101; Código Orgánico Integral Penal/Comprehensive Organic Criminal Code 273, conflict with Colombia 69–71, 74; conflict with Peru 65–67, 73, 74; dollarization 74, 76, 82; independence 64; Organic Code of Criminal Procedure 82; trade with Peru 85
Ejército de Liberación Nacional see ELN
Ejército Popular de Liberación see EPN
El Abra 51
El Carmen-Talismán International Bridge 129
El Ceibo 19, 154
El Chapare 50
El Chapo see Guzmán Loera, Joaquín
El Oro 80, 81, 83, 84
El Paso 152, 223, 241, 258
El Salvador 121, 125, 130
Electrical Bond and Share Company 173
ELN 73
EMCDDA 181, 182, 183
England 124
Ensenada 152
Entre Ríos 96, 97, 98
ephedrine 104, 105
episteme, definition 145

EPN 73
Escobar, Pablo 75, 77, 85, 236, 243
Escuintla 131, 132, 135
Esequibo, region of 207, 209
Esmeraldas 78, 79, 80, 81, 83
Espach, Ralph 122
Espinoza, Roque 69, 70, 71, 85
Esquipulas 260
Estado de México 281
Eurojust 180
European Commission 179, 180
European Economic Community 175
European integration 174, 179
European Monitoring Centre for Drugs and Drug Addiction see EMCDDA
European Parliament 179
European Union 160, 174, 176, 185
Europol 180, 181, 182, 183

Fábregas Puig, Andrés 119
Falklands see Malvinas
Familia Michoacana 159
Farah, Douglas 122
FARC 56, 68, 70, 73, 206
Faro 208
Fausto, Boris 202
favelas 213
Federal Administration of Public Revenues 104
Federal Republic of Central America 125
feminicide 267, 269, 271–273; in Ciudad Juárez 269; definition 267; in Ecuador 273; in Latin America 274
Fenner, Justus 123
Fernández Ordóñez, Rodrigo 122
Fernández Saavedra, Gustavo 44
Ferragut, Sergio 151
Ferreira Gomes 210, 271
Finklea, Kristin 151
First World War 173
foibe 178
forced labor 267, 270
forcibly disappeared people 276, 280
foreign policy, in Bolivia 43, 44
forestry, in Bolivia 53
Formosa 97, 98
fortress Europe 177, 185
Foz do Iguaçu 199, 202, 213, 214, 253, 255, 257; Declaration of 93
Fraternity Bridge, Argentina-Brazil 199

296 *Index*

free trade zone 55, 152, 202
freedom of movement 155
Friendship Bridge, Brazil-Paraguay
  199, 202
Frontera Corozal 129, 154
Fuentes Carrera, Julieta 121
Fuerzas Armadas Revolucionarias de
  Colombia *see* FARC

Gadsden Purchase *see* Treaty of La
  Mesilla
Galapagos Islands 78
Galemba, Rebecca 120, 122
García Aguilar, María del Carmen
  121
García García, Antonio 121
Garza, Rocío 151
Garzón Nieto, Julio 206
gas 40, 48, 56, 256
gasoline 30, 56, 256, 257
gender: crimes 272; definition 266,
  267; inequalities 280, 281; studies
  267; violence 267, 271, 272, 273, 281
Genoa 183
Georgia 160
Germany 26, 239
Gioia Tauro, port of 182, 183
globalization: in Bolivia 39, 40, 42, 44;
  definition 72; in Ecuador 65, 72, 75,
  76; scales 148; and sovereignty 147
Goes, Sydesio Sampaio Filho 208,
  210, 211
gold: contraband in Bolivia 46, 48,
  49, 55, 56; deposits 211; in Peru 29,
  30, 31
González Ponciano, Ramón 119
González-Izás, Matilde 119, 121, 125,
  133
Good, Beverly 151
Goodman, Colby 151
Goubaud, Emilio 122
Gran Colombia 205, 207
Great Chaco 54
Great Depression 40
Grimson, Alejandro 100, 101, 212, 214
Grisales, Germán 18, 21
Guadalajara 281
Gualán 122
Guamote 278, 279
Guarantors 82
Guatemala: adjacency line with
  Belize; 129; Binational Boundary
  Commission 124, 129; border
  with El Salvador 131; border with

Honduras 130; border with Mexico
  119; boundary dispute with Belize
  126; independence from Spain 123;
  maritime border 132; population
  127; territory 127
Guatemalan and Mexican Mahogany
  and Export Company 124
Guatemalan Human Rights
  Ombudsman 122
Guayamerín/Guajara-mirim 53
Guayaquil 78, 80, 84, 242
Guayas 78, 80, 81, 83, 84
Guerrero 156, 157
guerrilla 133
Gulf Cartel 159, 238, 240, 248n38
Gulf of Mexico 152, 156, 157
gum extraction 124
Gutiérrez, Edgar 122, 278
Guyana 196, 198, 205, 206, 207, 208
Guzmán Loera, Joaquín 159, 239

Harvey, David 149
Heredia Zubieta Carlos 121
heroin: in Argentina 104; in Italy 180,
  182, 183; in Mexico 144, 156, 234
Herrera-Mariscal Treaty 123, 124
Hocquenghem, Anne Marie 17,
  18, 19
Hollifield, Frank 147
homicide rates: in Argentina 98; and
  borders 224, 251; in Ecuador 79–81,
  84; in Guatemala 135; and illegal
  markets 253; in Latin America 243,
  248n35; in Mexico 145, 161, 241; in
  Peru 32, 33
Hondo River 126, 154
Honduras 118, 121, 123; border with
  Guatemala 125, 130, 131, 133;
  border with Nicaragua 163; illicit
  flows 132, 133, 144; routes 156, 158,
  159, Trifinio 260; violence 135, 243
Hopenhayn, Martin 282, 283
housing, in Peru 20, 24, 25
Huancavelica 27, **32**
Huánuco 27, 28, **32**
Huaquillas 18, 25, 260
Human Development Index 25; in
  Peru 57
human trafficking 42, 76, 149, 156, 235;
  in Argentina 99, 105–107; in Bolivia
  50, 54; in Colombia 280; conceptualization 275; in Ecuador 83,
  278–280; feminist approaches 276;
  in Guatemala 122, 134; in Italy 183;

Index 297

in Latin America 278; in Mexico 151, 155; networks 26, 107

Iauaretê 205
Ica 32
Iguaçu River 201
IIRSA 18, 45
Iguazú 241; port of 213, 253, 255, 257; *see also* Puerto Iguazú
Ilo, port of 30, 31
illegal economy 9, 156, 228; in Bolivia 49; conceptualization 224; in Ecuador 77–79, 83; in Guatemala 118; in Peru 21
illegal flows 2, 4, 148; in Bolivia 56; and borders 8; in Guatemala 122, 132–135; in Italy 173, 182
Imbabura **80**, 83
Immigration Pastoral of the Prelature of Humahuaca 106
import substitution 42
Inambari-Tambopata 27, 29
Iñapari 19, 25
Indiana 160
Initiative for the Integration of Regional Infrastructure in South America *see* IIRSA
InSight Crime 122
Institute of Comparative Studies in Criminal and Social Sciences 106
Inter-Institutional Committee against Human Trafficking 278
International Court of Justice 44, 127
International Labor Organization 278
International Organization for Migration *see* IOM
International Railroad of Central America 125
intersectionality 268, 278, 283
IOM 17, 106
Ipiales 253, 254, **256**
Ipiranga 205
Iquique 55; free zone 30, 47, 48
Iquitos **30**, 31, 78, 241, 254, 259
Iracema, municipality of 207, 208
Iraq 147, 227
iron deposits: in Bolivia 45; in Latin America 53
ISIS 147
island of peace 6, 64, 73, 85
Istria 178
Itaipu Dam 257; hydroelectric power plant 202
Italian peninsula 172, 177

Italy: borders with Austria 180; borders with France 180, 181; borders with Switzerland 180; borders with Yugoslavia/Slovenia 180, 181; Kingdom of 173; Mediterranean border 173, 182, 184–186
Itamaraty: agreement 73; palace 67
Ivirgarzama 51

Japurá River 206
Joint Commission of Limits and Characterization of the Brazil-Paraguay Border 201
Joint Commission on the Limits of the Brazil-Uruguay Border 201
Jorge Chávez Airport 49, 56
Juárez Cartel 156, 159, 161
Jujuy 97, 98, 105
Junín 27, **32**
Jutiapa 125, 130, 131, 132

Kai Miller, Benjamin 151
Kauffer Michel, Edith 121
Kentucky 160
kidnapping 224, 243; in Bolivia 51; in Colombia 236; in Ecuador 75, 81; in Mexico 282; and Plan Colombia 236
King Victor Emanuel III 208
Kopel, David 151
Krakau, Philipp 151
Kuhn, David 151
Kuhn, Thomas 146

La Convención-Lares 27
La Paz 50, 51
La Pedrera 205
La Quiaca 54, 98
La Unión 155
labor exploitation 275, 277–279
Lacandon Jungle 124; and Herrera-Mariscal Treaty 123
Lacantún River 123
Lagarde, Marcela 271, 272
Lago Agrio 78, 278, 279, 281
Laguna Merín 200
Lambayeque 21, 28, **32**
Laranjal do Jari 209, 210
laranjas 200
Laredo 153
Latin American and Caribbean Economic System *see* SELA
Laurín, Alicia 92, 93, 100, 101
Lefebvre, Henri 149
Legambiente 181

298 Index

Lehtem 208
Leticia 78, 198, 205, 241, 254, 259, 279
Levitt, Peggy 270
Liguria 175, 181
Lima 17, 25, 28, 29, **30**, **32**, 242, 280
Linares, María Dolores 100
Lisboa, Miguel María 205
Livorno 183
logging: in Guatemala 124, 127; in
  Peru 21, 29, **30**, 31, 33
Loja 80, 281
London 164n3, 208, 280;
  Memorandum 174
Lopes de Araújo, Francisco Xavier
  207
López, Julie 7, 122
Lorenzana, Waldemar 133
Loreto, department of **32**, 204
Los Ríos 80, 81, 83
Lösch, August 149
Lucatello, Simone 151, 161–163
Luna Tobar, Alfredo 65
lynching, in Bolivia 50, 51

M-19 73
Maastricht Treaty 175
Macapá 210
Machado, Lia 197
MacLeod, Murdo 121
Madre de Dios **32**, 33, 204
mafia 229, 232, 233, 238
Magnoli, Demétrio 212
Maicao 279
Malacatán 122
Malvinas 92
Manabí 78, **80**, 81, 83
Manaus 78, 198, 241, 254, 259
Manila 280
Manta 81, 86n6, 241, 259
Manta-Manaus axis 241, 259
maquila industry 144, 270
maquiladora 259, 276
Marginal Jungle Road 67
marijuana 76, 85, 144, 232, 234, 258;
  in Argentina 103, 104, 105; in Italy
  180, 183; in Mexico 156, 159; in
  Paraguay 55; in Uruguay 240; *see
  also* cannabis
Marizco, Michel 151
Marseille 181
Martínez Velasco, Germán 120, 121
Martins, Enéas 199
Mataje 64
Matamoros 145, 153

Mato Grosso do Sul **198**, 201, 202
Maturacá River 207
Mayan civilization 122
Mazzitelli, Antonio 151, 158, 161
McAllen 153
McDougal, Topher 151
Medel, Mónica 151
Medellín Cartel 75, 85, 239, 243
Mediterranean Sea 172, 177, 179,
  180, 184
Mejía Ochoa, William 26
Memachi River 207
Menck, José Theodoro Mascarenhas
  208
Mendoza, Haroldo 133
Mercosur 93, 102, 111 n21, 200,
  216n2
Mérida Initiative 162; *see also* Plan
  Mérida
Messina Conference 175
Metapan 260
methamphetamines 104, 159
Mexicali 153
Mexican Commission for Refugees
  see COMAR
Mexico: border with Belize 155; bor-
  der with Guatemala 120, 123, 124,
  129, 159, 164, 224; border with the
  United States 152, 241, 252; Federal
  Criminal Code 272; National
  Registry of Missing Persons 281;
  southern border 119, 282
Meyer Maureen 151
Michigan 160
micro-trafficking 75, 239, 282
Middle East 177, 182
migrant smuggling: in Bolivia 42,
  50, 54; conceptualization 275; in
  Ecuador 83; in Guatemala 127, 134;
  in Italy 172, 173, 178, 183, 184–186;
  in Mexico 151; networks 159; in
  Peru 26
migration: African 186; in Argentina
  93; in Bolivia 40, 42; in Brazil
  203; in Ecuador 65, 68, 80, 81; in
  Guatemala 120, 121; in Italy 9, 178,
  183, 184; management 185; and
  maquiladoras 270; in Mexico 155;
  in Peru 19, 20, 22, 25–26; routes 25,
  42, 134, 184; and sex work 277; and
  urbanization 252; and violence 267,
  270, 276
Minnesota 160
Misiones Region 97, 98, 199

Index 299

money laundering 224, 228, 229, 230–232, 235; in Argentina 108; in Bolivia 46, 49, 50; in Brazil 213; in Ecuador 74–77, 89; in Guatemala 122; in Italy 180; in Mexico 150, 151
Montana, Salvador 151
Montecristo Massif 260
Monterrey 281
Montevideo 53
Monzón, Ana Silvia 121
Morona 80
Motagua 125, 130
Mount Wamuriaktawa 208
Mount Yakontipu 208
Movimiento 19 de abril *see* M-19
MRTA 73
Mucajái 208
mulas 103; *see also* mules
mules 102, 103, 213, 277, 281, 282, 283
multinational companies 268
multinational corporations 146

NAFTA 164, 269
Nájera Aguirre, Jessica 120
Naples, port of 182
Napo 80
Nascentes de Azambuja, Joaquim Maria 206
National Liberation Army *see* ENL
nationalism 2, 44
nation-state 2, 3, 31, 46, 147; in Argentina 7, 89, 90, 100, 102; in Bolivia 143; and border dynamics 195, 214; and border societies 212; and cities 253; and criminal organizations 163; and globalization 147, 149
Navia, Roberto 51
Netherlands, Kingdom of the 209
New Mexico 152
New York 75, 161, 164, 231, 280, 283
Nigeria 83
Nogales 145, 153, 161
North American Free Trade Agreement *see* NAFTA
Northern Triangle 132, 133
Novoa, Zaniel 19, 21
Nowotny, Kathryn 151
Nueva Loja 254
Nuevo Laredo 145, 153, 161
Nuevo León 152
Nuevo Orizaba 154

OAS 240, 127, 234
Oaxaca 157
Óbidos 209
Ocós, port of 132
Ocotepeque 260, 130
Ohio 160
Oiapoque River 198, 211
oil 3, 83, 132, 260, 279
Oil War 40
Ojinaga 153
Oliveira, Samara Mineiro 208
Olson, Erick 122, 150, 151, 162
Omoa, port of 132
Operation Fast and Furious 162
Operation Sealing 155
Orange Walk 155, 130
Ordóñez Morales, César Eduardo 120
Orellana 78, 80
organ trafficking 275, 280–281, 284
Organization of American States *see* OAS
organized crime 150, 241, 262, 270; in Argentina 45, 105; in Bolivia 50, 57; definition 247; in Ecuador 76, 83; and globalization 150; in Guatemala 118, 122; in Italy 177, 179, 181, 184; in Mexico 145, 151, 158, 160–163; and violence 269, 270; *see also* criminal organizations
Orinoco 67
Oriximiná 208, 209
Oruro 55
Otavalo 278, 279
Othón P. Blanco 155
outsourcing 229, 235, 243; in Italy 185

Pacific Ocean 65, 78, 121, 131, 152, 156, 159
Palcazú-Pichis-Pachitea River 27, 28
Palermo Convention 247, 275
Palmasola 51
Pando 41, 55
Pantanal 56
Paracaima 209
Paraguay 41; border with Argentina 96, 97, 101, 102, 103, 109n5; border with Bolivia 54–55; border with Brazil **198**, 201–202; cannabis 104; conflict with Bolivia 40; drug-trafficking 53, 56; human trafficking 106, 107; marijuana 105;

300 *Index*

trade with Bolivia 58n9; Treaty of Asunción 93; Tripartite Point 204; Triple Frontier 9, 101, 106, 199, 213, 253, 255, 257
paramilitary forces 68, 85, 237
Paraná; river 41, 241, 91, 197, 198; state 199, 201
Pasco 28, 32
paseras 102
Pasión River 123
Paz River 130
Pedra Branca do Amapari 210
Pennsylvania 160
People's Liberation Army *see* EPN
Pereira Gamba, Próspero 206
Pérez Concha, Jorge 65, 66, 67
Peru: borders with Brazil 204; borders with Colombia 205; borders with Ecuador 17, 64, 65; borders with Bolivia 19, 49, 55; relations with Chile 21
Peruvian National Police 31
Petén 123, 124, 129, 130, 135, 154, 157; and Herrera-Mariscal Treaty 123
Pichincha 81, 83
Piedmont 175, 181
Piedra de Cucuhy 206
Piedras Negras 153
Pirara River 208
Pisiga 55
Piura 21, 28, **32**, 33
Plan Colombia 7; and democratic security 69, 70; effects in Central America 159; effects in Ecuador 64, 65, 69, 74; effects in Mexico 159; and reorganization of drug-trafficking 75, 77, 236, 238–239
Plan Ecuador 69, 70, 84, 284
Plan Mérida 237; *see also* Mérida Initiative
Pocitos 54
Popenoe de Hatch, Marion 122
Porto Velho 198
Portugal 104, 211
Posadas 98, 102, 106
Potosí 54, 106
Pracuúba 210
Prado, Francisco 30
Profesor Salvador Mazza 54, 98; *see also* Salvador Mazza
prostitution *see* sex work
Protocol of Instructions 201, 209, 210
Protocols of 1905 207
Puerto Aguirre 41, 53

Puerto Asís 254
Puerto Barrios 131, 132
Puerto Caballos 132
Puerto Evo 53
Puerto Iguazú 98, 213, 241, 255; *see also* Iguazú, port of
Puerto Maldonado 255, **30**
Puerto Quetzal 132, 134
Puerto Quijarro 41, 53, 56
Puerto Suárez 41, 53, 56
Puno 21, 28, **30**, **32**, 33
Putumayo River 27, 259
Puyango-Tumbes River Basins 18

Quaraí River 199
Queen María Cristina 207
Queen of the Pacific 283
Questão de Palmas 199
Quiché 129, 135, 154
Quintana Roo 155
Quintín Lame 73
Quito 71, **80**, 84
Quito Protocol 17

Radford, Jill 271
railroads 41, 152
Ramón Castilla 205
Ramón Lista 97
Ramos, José María 151, 159
Ramos Rojas, Diego Noel 120
Ratzel, Friedrich 268
Real Audiencia of Quito 66
Realuyo, Celina 151
Renoldi, Brígida 101, 103
Retalhuleu 131, 132
reterritorialization 148
Revelo, Patricia 271
Revolutionary Armed Forces of Colombia *see* FARC
Reynosa 145, 153
Riberalta 56
Richardson, Harry 149
Rio Branco 198, 204, 206
Río Bravo 8, 152
Rio de Janeiro 204, 206, 207, 242
Rio de Janeiro Protocol 65–69, 86n3, 86n5; and the US 69
Río de la Plata 67, 90, 96, 109
Rio Grande do Sul 197, **198**, 199–202
Río Negro 206, 207
Rio Protocol *see* Rio de Janeiro Protocol
Rivera 200, 255
Roboré 203

Rocha 200
Rodríguez, Daniel 151
Rodríguez, María Noel 282
Rodríguez Castillo, Luis 120
Rodríguez Gacha brothers 77
Rojas Wiesner, Martha 120
Roraima 197, **198**, 207, 208
Rorainópolis 208
Rückert, Aldomar 210
runways 53, 56; *see also* airstrips
Russell, Diana 271

sacoleiros 200, 213
Saint-Georges-de-l'Oyapock 197, 210
Salento 183
Salta 97, 98, 105
Salvador, María Isabel 67
Salvador Mazza 54, 98; *see also*
    Profesor Salvador Mazza
San Antonio 98, 256
San Diego 152, 153
San Gabriel de Cachoeira 207
San José, port of 125, 132, 134
San José de Pocitos 54
San Marcos 129, 131, 132, 134, 135, 137
San Marino 173
San Martín 27, **32**
Sansó-Rubert, Daniel 270
Santa Anna, Antonio López de 123
Santa Bárbara 130
Santa Catarina 197, **198**, 199
Santa Cruz 41, 51, 54
Santa Elena **80**, 81
Santa Isabel del Rio Negro 207
Santa Rosa 26, 131, 132, 198, 205
Sant'Ana do Livramento 198
Santiago 55
Santo Domingo de los Tsáchilas
    80, 81
Santo Tomás de Castilla, port of 125,
    132, 134
Santos, port of 41
São João da Baliza 208
São Luiz 208
Sao Paulo 42, 164n3, 242, 255
Sarstoon River 129, 130
Sassen, Saskia 147, 164n3, 233
Sayaxché 122
Schengen: agreement 174, 176; area
    176–179; convention 174, 176, 185
Scheper-Hughes, Nancy 280
Schulmeister, Gastón H. 104
Second World War 156, 173–175, 177,
    178, 187n6

security 3, 5, 72, 226; in Argentina 90,
    91, 92, 98, 110n9, 110n10; in Bolivia
    43, 51, 53, 57, 58; border 7, 17; and
    border populations 72; in Brazil
    207, 2013, 2014; citizen 71, 72, 227,
    244, 255, 262; comprehensive 69,
    71; democratic 69, 70, 71, 84; in
    Ecuador 64, 66, 82, 84, 85, 86n10;
    in Guatemala 118, 121; human 70;
    international 70, 178; in Mexico 145,
    150, 151, 155, 156, 161; and migra-
    tion 178, 276; national 39, 72, 262;
    policies 226, 227, 251, 261, 262, 275;
    private 246n8, 249n9, 249n10; pub-
    lic 72; social 224; system 235; US
    policies 163, 164, 246n17; women's
    272
Segato, Rita 169, 272, 273
SELA 19
Sepúlveda, César 119
Serra do Navio 210
Serrano, Javier 120
sex work 105, 270, 276, 278; and
    migration 277
sexism 283
sexual abuse 270, 277, 283
sexual exploitation 105–107, 275, 277,
    279, 281
sexual violence 33; in Ecuador 273
Shining Path 56, 73
Shirk, David 151
SICA 260
sicariato see contract killing
Sierra de Tumucumaque 209
Sifaneck, Stephen 151
Siles Salinas, Jorge 44
Silveira, Ada Cristina M. 213
Sinaloa Cartel 83, 158–161, 164n1, 235,
    236, 238, 239
Single European Act 175
smuggling 4, 8; in Argentina 108; in
    Bolivia 50, 53, 56, 58; in Ecuador
    76; in Guatemala 124, 126, 127, 133,
    134; in Italy 181; in Mexico 144,
    150, 151, in Peru 29–31; in Triple
    Frontier 241; *see also* contraband
social remittances 270
Soconusco 120, 123, 124, 134,
    153, 155
Soja, Edward 149
Sonora 152, 153
South Pacific corridor 157
Southern Common Market *see*
    Mercosur

302   *Index*

sovereignty: Bolivia 42; and border
  policies 72; and borders 3, 85n1, 147,
  268, 279; Brazil 255; and democratic
  security 70–71; Ecuador 6, 64, 73;
  and globalization 147–148; new
  threats 57; Peru 16
Spain: and Belize 126; cocaine
  seizures from Argentina 104; and
  criminal associations 182; Gran
  Colombia independence from 207;
  Guatemala independence from
  123, 124; investments in Guatemala
  124; Kingdom of 207; and Medellín
  Cartel 243; as migration destination
  26, 42; and Sinaloa Cartel 239
Spencer-Mariscal Treaty 155
State Department's Bureau of
  International Narcotics 104
Steiman, Rebeca 209
Stein, Eduardo 122
Subteniente López 155
Suchiate River 124, 129, 155
Suchitepéquez 131, 132
Sucumbíos 79, **80**, 81, 83, 241, 254, 259
Suriname 196; border with Brazil **198**,
  209–210
Swyngedouw, Erik 147, 148
synthetic drugs 180, 182
Syria 147

Tabasco 123, 129, 133, 154
Tabatinga 25, 198, 205, 279
Tacna 21, 26, 30–33, 253; duty free
  zone 52, 68
Tacutu River 208
Talismán 129, 154
Tamaulipas 152, 153, 159
Tamayo Pérez, Luz María 120, 124
Tambo Quemado 55
Tapachula 120
Tarapacá 205
Tarducci, Mónica 106
Tarija 54, 58
Tecún Umán-Ciudad Hidalgo
  International Bridge 129
territoriality, definition 147
Territorio Esequibo 207
Texas 152, 153, 159, 263
Theodore, Nik 148
Tijuana 145, 152, 153, 159, 161, 281
Tijuana Cartel 156, 159; *see also*
  Carrillo Fuentes Cartel
Tilly, Charles 271
Tinto River 125

Titicaca Lake 55, 56
Tobar Donoso, Julio 65, 85
Tomo River 207
Toussaint, Mónica 119, 121, 126
transgender people 277, 284
transplant tourism 280
Treaties of Laguna Merín 200
Treaty of 1872 (Brazil-Paraguay) 201
Treaty of 1904 40, 44
Treaty of Asunción 93
Treaty of Badajoz 211
Treaty of Guadalupe-Hidalgo 151
Treaty of La Mesilla 151
Treaty of Limits: Argentina-Brazil
  199; Brazil-Colombia 206;
  Brazil-Great Britain 208;
  Brazil-Paraguay 201; Brazil-Peru
  204; Brazil-Uruguay 200;
  Brazil-Venezuela 206, 207
Treaty of Limits and River
  Navigation 206; Brazil-Venezuela-
  Colombia 207
Treaty of Montevideo 199, 200
Treaty of Osimo 174
Treaty of Paris 175, 211
Treaty of Petrópolis 40, 203
Treaty of Rome 175
Treaty of San Ildefonso 209
Treaty of Utrecht 211
Trejo Peña, Alma 120
Trifinio 130, 131, 254, 260
Tri-National Border Development
  Plan 255
Triple Alliance (Argentina, Brazil,
  Uruguay) 109, 202
triple border: Argentina, Brazil,
  Paraguay 199, 143, 213, 257;
  Argentina, Brazil, Uruguay 199;
  Bolivia, Argentina, Paraguay
  27; Bolivia, Brazil, Paraguay 54;
  Colombia, Peru, Brazil 279, 284;
  Leticia, Tabatinga, Santa Rosa 198,
  205; Peru, Brazil, Bolivia 19; Peru,
  Brazil, Colombia 25, 78, 198; *see
  also* Triple Frontier
Triple Frontier: Argentina, Paraguay,
  Bolivia 134; Argentina, Paraguay,
  Brazil 9, 101, 103, 213, 241, 255; *see
  also* triple border
Tulcán 254, 256
Tumbes 21, 30–33
Tupac Amaru Revolutionary
  Movement *see* MRTA
Twin Towers, attack 161

Ucayali 27, **32**, 204
Ugarte, Marisa B. 151
Uiramutã 207, 208
Ullman, Edward L. 21
UNASUR *see* Union of South American Nations
UNDP 70
UNICEF 122
unilateralism 260, 261
Unión Juárez 154
Union of South American Nations, constitutive treaty 93
United Fruit Company 125
United Kingdom 208, 209
United Nations, and punitive drug laws 227
United Nations Convention against Transnational Organized Crime 275; *see also* Palermo Convention
United Nations Development Program *see* UNDP
United Nations Protocol to Prevent, Suppress and Punish Trafficking in Persons, Especially Women and Children 275
United Nations Verification Mission in Guatemala 51
United States: arbitration by 199; arms trafficking 162; border security 161; border security policies 7; border with Mexico 4; cocaine consumption in 78, 144, 156, 160, 235; cocaine distribution in 160; cocaine seizures in 7, 82; drug interdiction policies 155, 157; drug trafficking to 65, 75, 76, 79, 104, 156, 157; firearms market 151; gold exports to 56; investments in Guatemala 124; marijuana production in 234; migrant smuggling to 151; as migration attraction pole 8, 42, 65; migration from Central America 120, 134, 277; and NAFTA 164n6, 269; and N'drangheta 240; Operation Fast and Furious 162; and Plan Colombia 69; prohibition 152; and Rio Protocol 69; State Department 82, 83; and Sinaloa Cartel 239; security policies 163; stolen airplanes 56; trade with Ecuador 68; Treaty of Guadalupe-Hidalgo 151
unsatisfied basic needs (UBN) 252
urban complexes 251–255

urban growth rates 252
urban systems 57, 241, 253, 254, 259
urbanization 2, 5, 20, 126, 251; in Latin America 252
USAID 27
Usumacinta River 123, 129, 154
uti possidetis principle 205, 207

Valcuende del Río, José María 21
Valdez, Avelardo 151
Valley of the Rivers Apurimac, Ene and Mantaro *see* VRAEM
Vargas, Arnoldo 133
Vatican City 173
Vaupés 205
Vázquez Cobo, Alfredo 206
Vázquez Cobo-Martins Treaty 206
Vázquez Olivera, Mario 119
Vela, Lindon 30
Venezuela: border with Brazil **198**, 206–207; border with Colombia 256; child forced recruitment 279; cocaine production in 238, 247n33; drug from 133, 157; gasoline subsidy in 257; Gran Colombia 205; oil boom 279
Veracruz 157, 281
Vila Bitencourt 205
Villafuerte Solís, Daniel 121
Villazón 54
violence: and anti-narcotics policies 234; in Argentina 108; in Bolivia 39, 45, 50–51, 55, 57; in border cities 262, 263; in border regions 2, 4; in Brazil 213, 216, in Ecuador 65, 72, 77, 79–81; and gender *see* gender, violence; in Guatemala 118, 121, 133, 135, 136; and illegal markets 225, 243, 244; lack of information on 2; in Latin America 224, 226; in Mexico 145, 151, 160–163, 164; and Plan Colombia 236; in Peru 33, 34; urban 224, 251–253, 261
violence against women *see* gender, violence
VRAEM 27, 28

Wagner, Regina 122
Wallman, Joel 151
War of the Pacific 17, 40, 44
Weber, Max 271
Westphalia, Peace of 147
Woglom, William 149

304 *Index*

Yacuiba 54
Yaguarón River 201
Yauarete 205
Yavarí 205
Young, Stewart M. 151
Yucatán 162
Yucatan Peninsula 154, 157
Yunguyo 55

Zacapa 125, 130, 131, 135
Zamora 80, 81
Zepeda, Beatriz 119
Zetas Cartel 83, 158, 159, 240, 248n38
Zsögön, María Cecilia 106